CW01239201

Baltic

Baltic

The Future of Europe

OLIVER MOODY

JOHN MURRAY

First published in Great Britain in 2025 by John Murray (Publishers)

Copyright © Oliver Moody 2025

The right of Oliver Moody to be identified as the Author of the Work has been asserted by him in accordance with the Copyright, Designs and Patents Act 1988.

Map drawn by Barking Dog Art

All rights reserved. No part of this publication may be reproduced, stored in a retrieval system, or transmitted, in any form or by any means without the prior written permission of the publisher, nor be otherwise circulated in any form of binding or cover other than that in which it is published and without a similar condition being imposed on the subsequent purchaser.

A CIP catalogue record for this title is available from the British Library

Hardback ISBN 978-1-399-81427-0
Trade Paperback ISBN 978-1-399-81428-7
ebook ISBN 978-1-399-81430-0

Typeset in Bembo by Hewer Text UK Ltd, Edinburgh
Printed and bound in Great Britain by Clays Ltd, Elcograf S.p.A.

John Murray policy is to use papers that are natural, renewable and recyclable products and made from wood grown in sustainable forests. The logging and manufacturing processes are expected to conform to the environmental regulations of the country of origin.

Carmelite House
50 Victoria Embankment
London EC4Y 0DZ

www.johnmurraypress.co.uk

John Murray Press, part of Hodder & Stoughton Limited
An Hachette UK company

The authorised representative in the EEA is Hachette Ireland, 8 Castlecourt Centre, Dublin 15, D15 XTP3, Ireland (email: info@hbgi.ie)

For Pippa, Walter and Arthur

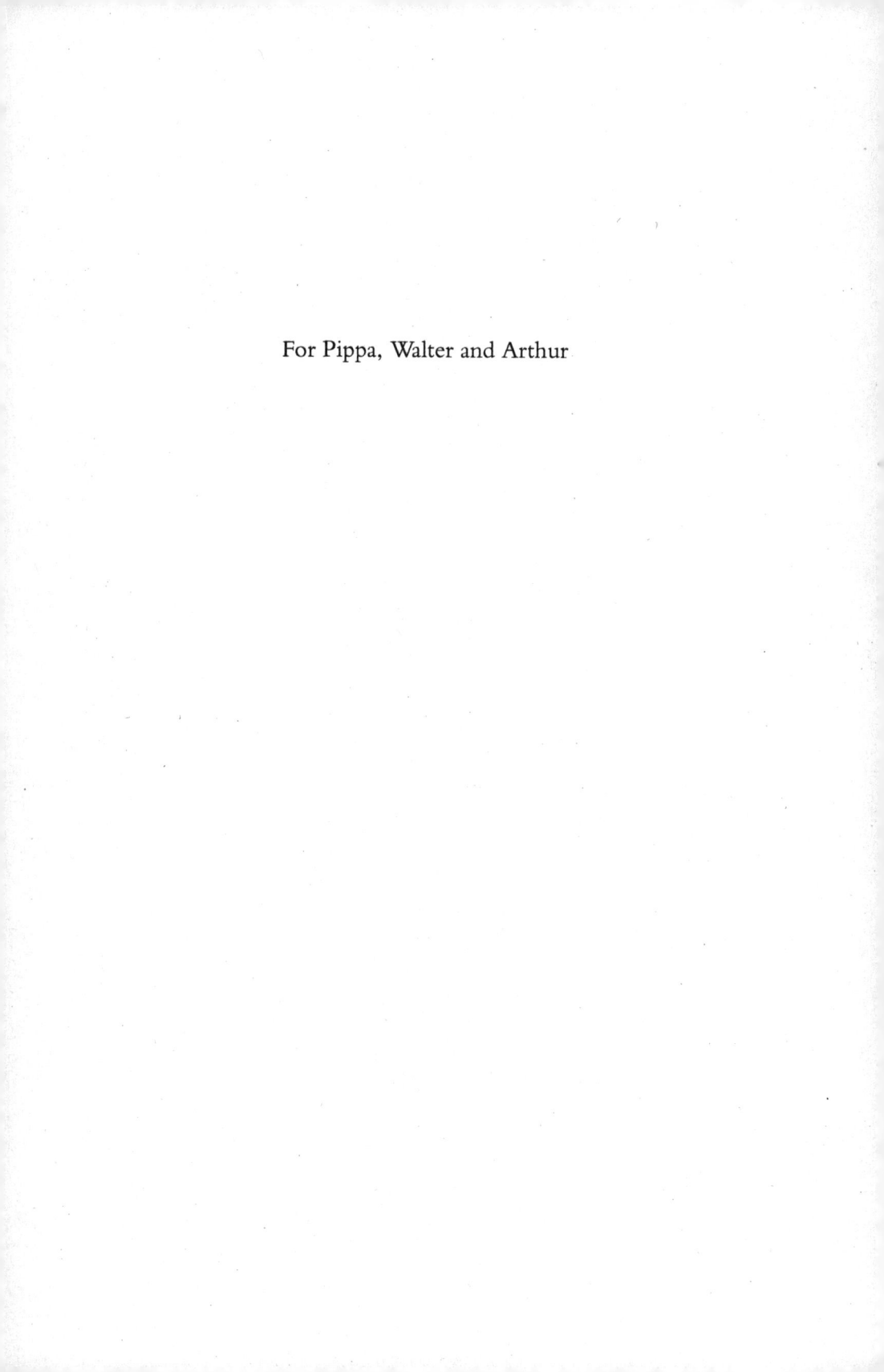

Contents

Author's Note	ix
Map	x
Introduction	1

PART I: Resilience

1. Tiger Leap: Lessons from Estonia on How to Confront Existential Threats — 15
2. Total Defence: How Finland is Building for the Future — 46
3. The Witch and the Sage: Latvia Rebuilds a Divided Nation — 75
4. Poison Lake: The Danish Approach to Environmental Collapse and Energy Warfare — 105

PART II: Resistance

5. To Europe, Yes, But With Our Dead: What to Expect from Poland, Europe's Mercurial Rising Star — 129
6. Turning Time: The German Identity Crisis at the Heart of the Continent — 150
7. The Hobbits: Lithuania and the Strength of Small States — 180

PART III: Survival

8. Imperium of Hopelessness: What the Kremlin is Doing to Us and Why — 207
9. Peace Through Superior Firepower: Europe's Struggle to Defend Itself — 237

CONTENTS

10. The Battle for the Baltic: How to Win a War
    With Russia   256

    Epilogue   279

    Acknowledgements   291
    Notes   295
    Index   355

Author's Note

All quotations not explicitly attributed to a source are taken from on-the-record interviews that I conducted.

Many of those interviewed have changed jobs since I spoke to them. In these cases I have, as a rule, referred to the interviewee with the job title they held at the time of our conversation, and then set out their subsequent role in an endnote. Excerpts from some of the interviews have previously been published in *The Times* and the *Sunday Times*: the references to these articles can also be found in the endnotes.

I have used local spellings of place names unless their English form is ubiquitous (for example Warsaw, St Petersburg or Copenhagen).

Russian names are transliterated directly except where the individual is widely known under a different spelling, such as Viktor Erofeyev or Tatjana Ždanoka.

All translations from the German are my own unless otherwise indicated.

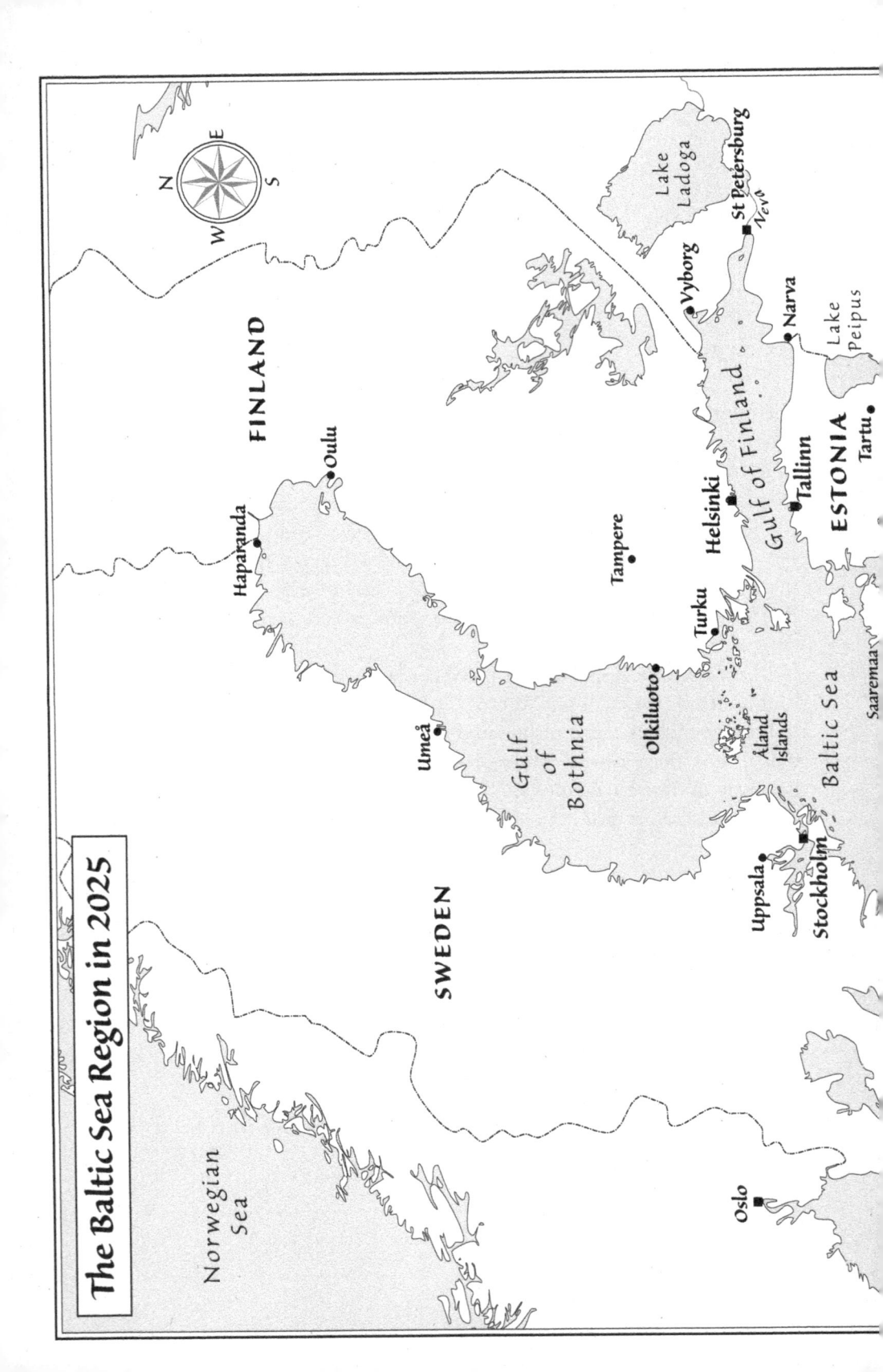

The Baltic Sea Region in 2025

LATVIA
RUSSIA
Riga
Gotland
Kattegat Strait
Liepāja
Daugava
Daugavpils
Copenhagen
Kaliningrad Oblast
(RUSSIA)
Klaipėda
Baltiysk
LITHUANIA
Kaunas
Vilnius
Bornholm
Kaliningrad
Gdańsk
Kiel
Lubmin
Rostock
Kołobrzeg
Suwałki Gap
Minsk
Greifswald
Hamburg
Szczecin
Świnoujście
Nemunas
BELARUS
Vistula
Poznań
Berlin
POLAND
Warsaw
Łódź
Oder
Dresden
Lublin
Wrocław
GERMANY
Prague
Kyiv
Kraków
CZECH REPUBLIC
L'viv
UKRAINE
Capital cities
Towns
0
100
200 miles
0
100
200 km

Introduction

The Swedish island of Fårö is primordial, scarcely bearing the imprint of the past eight centuries. The drystone huts for livestock are built on a medieval design, with steeply sloped roofs of reed thatch. Every half a century or so, each roof is repaired in a collective effort by the islanders, who pass the ancient skills on to the next generation and then get roaring drunk to celebrate. Some of the small farms are still fenced with jagged lines of crossed wooden stakes, as though to repel a cavalry assault. Along the shorelines the *raukar*, large lumps of limestone coastline slowly eaten away by the waves of the Baltic sea, are warped into strange facsimiles of dogs, triumphal arches or human heads.

When the Swedish film director Ingmar Bergman first went to Fårö in 1967, he found a 'stony shore facing infinity'. It became his sanctuary.[1] During those same years Olof Palme, Sweden's Social Democratic prime minister, also sought refuge on the island every summer, renting a cottage near the hamlet of Sudersand, with no television or telephone line. Sometimes he would bring along his closest aides or friendly world leaders to conduct discreet machinations far from the scrutiny of Stockholm. Mostly, though, he would simply clear his mind.

The tiny island, blessed with mild winters and situated closer to the centre of the Baltic than any other piece of dry land, has a very particular place in modern Sweden's national mythology. It stands for remoteness, nostalgia, safety, calm and an unbroken connection to the country's ancient past.

But this sense of security and timelessness is an illusion. Fårö and the larger adjacent island of Gotland occupy a strategic position in the middle of the shipping lanes that are the Baltic's commercial and

INTRODUCTION

military lifeblood. Modern weaponry has put them in easy striking distance of the western half of the Baltic states and Kaliningrad, a Russian exclave bristling with hypersonic missiles, jet fighters, warships and – at least in the view of some neighbouring governments – nuclear warheads.[2]

Fårö and Gotland are caught up in a war that stretches around the globe from California to Kamchatka, with the Baltic sea as its geographical and geopolitical midpoint. For now, it is Ukrainians and Russians who are doing the fighting, but the broader conflict is shaping the lives and endangering the safety and wellbeing of every person in the West, even if many of us are still oblivious to the gravity of the situation.

The first blows of the physical war have already struck the Baltic. In September 2022 a series of underwater explosions east of the Danish island of Bornholm knocked out Russia's Nord Stream 1 and 2 natural gas pipelines.[3] A year and a half later, Kyiv claimed that its special forces had set fire to the *Serpukhov*, a Buyan-M class missile corvette from the Russian Baltic fleet, at a location that may have been scarcely a hundred miles to the south of Gotland. It was the first known attack on a Russian military target in the region since 1945.[4]

It is easy to shrug these incidents off as mere collateral damage from a localised proxy war unfolding almost a thousand miles away. But that would be dangerously complacent. They are part of something much bigger: a generational contest between Russia and the West at almost every conceivable level below direct military confrontation, from energy and economics to parliaments and social networks. This contest has two fulcrums. One is Ukraine. The other is the Baltic.

Moscow has spelt this out quite explicitly. In December 2021, as Russia built up its forces near the Ukrainian frontier in preparation for the full-scale invasion that followed three months later, Vladimir Putin's negotiators in Washington issued a demand so fantastically extravagant that the American diplomats could scarcely believe what they were hearing. Moscow sought a legally binding undertaking from NATO that it would cease all military activity to the east of its 1997 borders.[5]

This would effectively turn Europe's geopolitical clock back by a quarter of a century, requiring the alliance to withdraw its forces from

INTRODUCTION

Poland and the Baltic states and leaving the latter excruciatingly vulnerable to Russian interference. At the time Sam Greene, a British Russia scholar, said the ultimatum amounted to Putin 'drawing a line around the post-Soviet space and planting a "keep out" sign'. It's not meant to be a treaty,' he added. 'It's a declaration.'[6] 'I think the Russians have been fairly transparent about what they're seeking,' says Jeffrey Mankoff, an expert on Russian foreign policy at the US National Defense University. 'They want to renegotiate the settlement from the end of the Cold War.'

Putin is evidently not going to achieve this goal through diplomacy. But might he try to do it by force? For the Europeans, that is the most important question of the 2020s.

You Can Stick Your Strategy Up Your Arse

This is a book about the return of the ancient struggle with Russia for mastery of the Baltic, how the West can win it and how its outcome will be decisive for the future of Europe and the wider West. The struggle has been going on for more than 800 years, since two Russian principalities began extracting tribute from several Estonian statelets. Before the First World War Russia controlled Finland, the Baltic states and a significant portion of Poland. Until 1989 the Soviet Union's sphere of influence extended across the sea's southern coast to the mouth of the German river Trave.

At times Putin has indicated that he would like to restore as much of it as he can, through violence if necessary. As early as September 2014, reports suggested he had 'privately' boasted that his armed forces could take the capitals of Poland and the Baltic states within 48 hours.[7] In May 2024, after numerous European states said Ukraine could use the armaments they had donated to strike targets on Russian soil, he said: 'Representatives of NATO countries, especially Europeans and especially representatives of small countries, should remember what they are playing with. They should remember that their countries are small and densely populated. Let them keep this in mind before they talk about attacks deep into Russia.'[8]

INTRODUCTION

His propaganda attack dogs are less coy. In 2008 Dmitry Rogozin, the Russian ambassador to NATO and future head of the country's space agency, named the Baltic countries alongside Crimea and other parts of Ukraine as 'traditional territory of the Russian nation'.[9] Dmitry Medvedev, the former president who was once seen by the US as a potentially reliable partner but who now spends much of his time firing off erratic social media posts, has repeatedly claimed that the Baltic states are stray provinces of Russia.[10] For the most part, western analysts are not inclined to take these outbursts too seriously, but the regime clearly means for them to sustain at least the impression that an attack on NATO's Baltic flank is possible.

It is quite likely that Putin himself does not yet know what he is going to do. Witold Jurasz, a Polish foreign policy commentator who previously served as a diplomat in Moscow, recalls a conversation he had some years ago with a Russian minister. 'I asked him: "So why are you Russians basically dealing with the tactical level and you don't seem to care about the strategic one?"' And his answer was:

> Well, you know, you think you have this grand strategy, but then we have ten little tactical wins, and you can stick your strategy up your arse. And it was exactly so until the invasion of Ukraine. Putin is sometimes called this grand strategist. He's not. He's a grand tactician. He has achieved numerous tactical wins but he's an absolute strategic loser.

That is why western governments spend much more time making projections about Russia's capacity for an attack than attempting to second-guess its specific designs.[11] Putin himself has quoted an apocryphal line from Bismarck on this point: 'It is not intentions that are important, but capabilities.'[12]

In early 2023 the Estonian foreign intelligence service said it believed the Russians still retained enough military resources to 'exert credible military pressure in our region' and could reconstitute the units on its western borders within four years.[13] This prompted a glut of further forecasts for a possible Russian attack, with a timescale ranging from three to eight years. 'We have to think about the future and how things will be in the next four, five, six or seven years,' says one senior western intelligence source.

> The Baltic states are probably somewhere in the middle of the Russians' thinking. They're not Ukraine, which [Putin believes] must be brought back home, but they're not western Europe either. The Russians still think of these countries as part of the USSR. When the war ends, the Russian military will start to reconsolidate themselves . . . At the end, when the Russians assess the situation, they will make a comparison of forces and try to understand NATO's planning. They will try to assess the combat power and make a decision based on that.

What is beyond dispute is that Russia has been steadily intensifying a campaign of sub-military harassment not just against the Baltic sea region but against Europe as a whole. It takes many forms: sabotage, assassinations, cyber incidents, disinformation, electronic jamming and spoofing, the suborning of politicians, and, increasingly, border provocations. It is essentially the ancient playbook of political warfare, waged with twenty-first-century tools on a scale that was previously impossible.[14] The Estonian internal security service says Moscow can now 'be expected to use any measures that stop short of triggering NATO's collective defence clause'.[15] The Pentagon says Russia has launched a 'hybrid war' against Finland since the Nordic state joined the alliance.[16] NATO has expressed 'deep concern' about 'malign activities' against seven of its members: Poland, the Baltic states, Britain, Germany and Czechia.[17]

The Easter Attack

In April 2021 Russia massed up to 120,000 soldiers next to the Ukrainian border.[18] Weeks later Moscow began squeezing Europe's gas supplies, leaving Germany's largest storage facility almost empty.[19] Belarus, a Russian satellite state, started flying in tens of thousands of would-be asylum seekers and trying to drive them across the borders of Poland, Latvia and Lithuania. What had seemed an intermittent

INTRODUCTION

background threat came to feel urgent and deeply ominous. This had been obvious to Europe's frontline states all along. The situation that is only now gradually dawning on western Europeans has been part of their reality for decades, if not centuries, and in many ways they have adapted to it far better than we have. By virtue of their history and their geography they are, in a sense, already living in the future.

I had spent three years covering Germany for *The Times* and had not given the Baltic a great deal of thought, but now I started travelling all over the Baltic sea and learning everything I could. I visited capitals, islands, ports, factories, power stations, NATO wargames, winter training camps, sink estates, gas terminals, offshore wind farms, decrepit mansions, a giant diving bell and a collection of mysterious Viking carvings. I spoke to heads of state and government, ministers, intelligence officers, generals, diplomats, businesses, historians, scientists, security analysts, a poet-cum-rock star and a man who dresses up as a recycling superhero. I realised that it would take a book to convey the whole picture with its proper context.

I am not the only person for whom this has been a process of delayed awakening. During the Cold War Sweden had defended Gotland, the most obvious target for a Soviet beachhead on its territory, with a 25,000-strong force, dozens of Stridsvagn 102R tanks, howitzers, Viggen warplanes, anti-aircraft guns, coastal batteries and anti-ship missiles.[20] But in the early 2000s it entirely abandoned its military presence on the island. The barracks were sold off to the local council in Visby. Much of the kit, along with an entire brigade's worth of Swedish military equipment, was donated to the newly refounded armies of the Baltic states.

Shortly after midnight on 29 March 2013, however, Gotland's brief holiday from history came to an abrupt end. Swedish radars detected four Russian Su-27 Flanker fighter jets and two nuclear-capable Tu-22M3 Backfire bombers approaching at speed from St Petersburg.[21] Instead of veering south towards Kaliningrad as usual, they held their westbound course towards Gotland, skirting its airspace at about 2 a.m. It was a simulated nuclear attack.[22] The probable targets were identified as an army base in Småland county on the Swedish mainland, and the national electronic surveillance headquarters on the edge of Stockholm, barely a mile away from the royal family's principal residence at Drottningholm palace.[23]

This was alarming, but not entirely abnormal: Soviet jets had paid plenty of similar 'visits' to Sweden during the Cold War. The shocking element was the Swedish response. The air force was supposed to maintain a minimum of two JAS-39 Gripen fighters on 'quick reaction alert' at all times for precisely this kind of scenario. But it was Good Friday and all the pilots were on leave with their families.[24] The Russian bombers were left wholly unchallenged. Had it been a real nuclear strike, Sweden would have been helpless.

'The Russian Easter attack, as we call it in Sweden, was absolutely a wake-up call,' says Magnus Frykvall, a colonel in the Swedish army. At the time, the supreme commander of the armed forces estimated that the country could only hold out for 'about a week' if it were to be invaded.[25] Gotland's regiment was reconstituted in 2018, with Frykvall as its commander, although Sweden's military capacity had become so degraded that it could spare only a couple of hundred soldiers and a handful of Leopard 2 battle tanks.[26]

Since then Sweden has begun reviving its old Cold War-era templates for crisis preparedness.[27] Its 'total defence' exercises, intended to test both the public and private sectors' ability to counter sub-military 'grey-zone' attacks, are being studied across the West.[28] It has provided households with a leaflet titled 'If Crisis or War Comes'. It appointed its first minister for civil defence since the 1940s. Micael Bydén, the commander-in-chief of the armed forces, appeared on a popular children's television programme to answer viewers' questions about what would happen in a conflict.[29] Even Crown Princess Victoria, the first in line to the throne, is being put through officer training at the national defence university.[30]

Ulf Kristersson, Sweden's prime minister, suggested in March 2024 that Gotland could be fortified.[31] Allied forces including British and American marines have practised storming the island and the Stockholm archipelago with drones, warships, armoured vehicles and paratroopers in the country's largest and most realistically detailed wargame for more than a quarter of a century.[32] Residents of Visby, the island's capital, have complained about the unfamiliar sound of sonic booms from the Gripen fighter jets flying over their heads.[33]

INTRODUCTION

Magnus Frykvall is steeling his troops for just about every conceivable kind of attack, including an amphibious special forces invasion staged with a civilian vessel such as an oil tanker. 'We need to keep the Baltic sea lines of communication open at all times,' he says. 'If we lose Gotland and if the enemy have gotten in, they can make it very hard for Sweden, Finland and the Baltic states to defend themselves.'

A Very Tectonic Place

Many of us do not think of the Baltic sea as a region, if we think of it at all. It is bordered by nine countries, each with its own language, fiercely distinct identity and particular historical trajectory. In various periods Germany, Russia, Denmark, Sweden have had their day as empires, while Finland and the three Baltic states have had to scrap just to establish and preserve their existence. Poland and Lithuania have experienced both extremes of fortune. For much of its history the Baltic perimeter has been a theatre of conflict between regional powers. After the Second World War its nations were riven by the Iron Curtain and their different sensitivities and geopolitical orientations: NATO, the Warsaw Pact, non-alignment; and the various competing interests and values within those blocs. Even today there is little evidence of a shared feeling of 'Balticness' strong enough to compete with the sense of belonging to a particular country or group such as the Nordics, the Baltic states or the European Union.

Over many years the Baltic faded away to the periphery of the wider West's imagination. Yet it sits quite literally at the heart of Europe; by a number of plausible estimates the centre of the continental land mass is somewhere in the hinterland of its southern shores.[34] This is not just a geographical truism. The focus of geopolitics is shifting steadily eastwards. The Baltic sea is becoming the nexus of a wider great game played out across Eurasia.

The countries around it, apart from Russia, are also more intensely connected to one another than almost any other region on the planet. They have been bound together by maritime trade since as far back as the Bronze Age. On an organisational level the region is the most extensively networked in the world, with a jumble of acronymous multilateral fora covering everything from jazz to high politics.[35] This is born of necessity. After all, the most obvious thing the countries share is the sea itself. They have had to learn to collectively steward a heavily polluted and ecologically fragile body of water, laced with daisy chains of gas pipelines, electricity and data cables, and above all the shipping routes on which most of their imports and exports depend.

Most glaringly, they have been thrust together by Vladimir Putin and his war on Ukraine. Five of them share land borders with Russia. They know what could happen because it has happened before. 'We feel we are living in a very tectonic place, in amongst all these tremors,' says a senior minister from one of the Baltic states.

> In all the Russian invasion plans the most predictable scenario is to attack in a western direction. Of course their first step will be to take over the Baltics because we are a small peninsula of NATO. They will also immediately occupy Finland: that's in their plans . . . We're under no illusions. A large-scale war is not excluded. It would mean the annihilation of our state and the extinction of our nation.

As a result it has never been more important to understand the Baltic, with all its dangers, possibilities and complexities, and to develop a feeling for the historic forces that have shaped its present. This is not just because it is vulnerable. The region is far more than just the hinge of an intercontinental confrontation that only a few miscalculations could ignite into a nuclear ekpyrosis. For a Europe that often seems tired and conscious of its own relative decline, plagued by low growth and identity crises, the Baltic is also a source of ideas and optimism.

This book is an attempt to bring those ideas to a wider audience. Its first section will look at the various ways in which the Baltic countries have developed resilience across a broad spectrum: through inventive nation-building in Estonia; grand strategy and 'comprehensive' security in Finland; the contest over social cohesion and the Russian-speaking minority in Latvia; and the efforts to stave off ecological disaster and climate change around the Danish island of

Bornholm. None of these examples is flawless and in some cases the lessons are negative rather than positive. It is just as instructive to examine mistakes as to admire successes.

Most of all, I am interested in what the countries of the Baltic can teach the rest of the West about how to muster collective willpower and hold societies together in the face of danger and uncertainty. We are being asked to make substantial sacrifices and commitments: defence budgets exceeding 3 per cent of national GDP, at least temporarily higher energy prices, the reorientation of our supply chains and trade networks, tension and even confrontation with states that some of our countries had once regarded as trustworthy or lucrative partners. Public consent for these measures cannot simply be assumed; it must be earned.

The second part of the book will examine how the balance of power in Europe is shifting to the north and the east and how the continent is being reconfigured around the Baltic. It includes chapters on the *Zeitenwende*, or 'turning point' in German policy; the rise of Poland; and the role of Lithuania and other frontline states in dragging the rest of Europe forward. At the centre of these chapters is a series of fundamental questions that the Baltic countries – especially the five that share land borders with Russia – have been grappling with for many years: what is it all for? What are our core values and goals as societies? What collectively animates us as citizens beyond our own individual interests?

The third and final section will look at how the conflict with Russia in and beyond the Baltic might evolve in the years ahead. It will explore how Putin and his regime view their western neighbourhood, the nature and purpose of their rapidly escalating 'hybrid' campaign against Europe, and the circumstances under which they might launch a military attack. The last two chapters assess NATO's preparations to defend the Baltic, with or without the US; what could happen in the event of a Russian invasion; and above all how to deter Moscow from gambling on one.

Since it is orientated towards the future, the book will cover a fair bit of the Baltic's modern history. There are three reasons for this. First, the history is interesting and worthwhile in its own right. These countries are some of our most steadfast friends and allies, and yet

INTRODUCTION

most of us know little about them. Second, the elites of all nine states are in their various ways obsessed with the past and its relevance to the present. They constantly use it to inform or justify their decisions, which cannot be understood without it. Third, events are moving with overwhelming speed and uncertainty. This book was completed in the autumn of 2024, under the shadow of the US presidential election a few weeks later, the German Bundestag election the following year, and the unpredictable situation on the killing fields of Ukraine. Making forecasts solely on the basis of this treacherous present is like trying to build a skyscraper from wet sand. The only way to move ahead is to analyse the deeper trends and extrapolate from what has come before, in some cases over a timespan of centuries.

Short memories and tunnel vision are luxuries that we cannot afford. Instead the starting position ought to be: how would a historian looking back on our age from 2040 or 2050 judge the decisions we take today?

PART I
Resilience

I
Tiger Leap

*Lessons from Estonia on How to
Confront Existential Threats*

Sometimes in the mornings, I –
chump that I am – am worried
by whether there's still a republic
a republic of Estonia

I ask my kid
whether she has Estonian lessons today
she does
then it's alright
then there seems to be a republic

Jürgen Rooste,
'Who Guards the Republic'[1]

When Kaja Kallas was a little girl and too ill to go to school, her grandmother would watch her while her parents went out to work. The old woman used to enchant the child with her memories of Estonia's brief window of independence before the Second World War. In her youth, she would say, a Finnish sea captain had taken her on a voyage to Hull, an industrial and fishing port on the east coast of Britain. To a small girl in Estonia after forty years of Soviet occupation, doubly severed from the West by the Iron Curtain and the barbed-wire borders of the USSR, the idea of visiting East Yorkshire was inconceivably exotic. 'I would say to her: "Don't tell me these fairy tales",' Kallas says.

The stories from the other side of the family seemed less fanciful. In 1949, her mother and her maternal grandmother had been dragged out of their house during a sudden wave of deportations known as Operation Priboi (Tidal Wave). In the space of two days, Soviet soldiers and security forces took 20,480 Estonians from their homes and piled them into nineteen rickety trains to Siberia. More than three-quarters of the deportees were women and children; Kallas's mother was a six-month-old baby at the time. About one in twenty of them died in captivity. 'Soon it will be night,' the Estonian women would sing in the Siberian camps, 'all is quiet and dark / but I don't find peace.' One of the deported mothers, Else, wrote in her diary that she did not know whether the eleven-month-old son she had left in Estonia was still alive. She was not released for another fifteen years and did not see her boy again until 1969, when he was twenty-eight.[2]

'I am of the lucky generation that didn't have freedom and obtained its freedom, so we understand the value of it,' Kallas says. 'My grandparents' generation was exactly the opposite: they had everything. They had freedom; they had prosperity. They had everything, and everything was taken from them.'

By the time I visited Kallas at the start of 2024, she was the prime minister of the most successful small European country in my lifetime (a few months later she would be appointed as the European Union's most senior diplomat).[3] Since it restored its independence in 1991, Estonia has raised its nominal GDP per capita by 2,500 per cent within not much more than a generation, overtaking Greece, Portugal and even Poland.[4] It has built up the best schools on the continent, at least according to their pupils' performance in core subjects.[5] Its childcare system is routinely held up as a model in Britain.[6] The United Nations' human development report, based on factors such as life expectancy, income and education, places it almost on a par with France.[7] Despite the entrenched legacy of graft and wheeler-dealing across the former eastern bloc, it has risen to the same level as Canada in Transparency International's global corruption perceptions index.[8]

Its technology sector is the envy of much larger countries. Relative to its population of 1.3 million, it has more unicorns – start-ups valued at more than $1 billion before they go public, such as Bolt, Skype and Wise – than any other European nation.[9] It was the first to introduce a universal electronic ID system and the first to bring in digital voting. Its influence in the European Union and NATO grows with each passing year and it was the driving force behind the EU's ammunition procurement programme, a country the size of San Diego stamping its ambition on a bloc of 450 million people.

As of the summer of 2024, it has been Ukraine's most generous bilateral donor by far in proportion to the size of its economy, from a consignment of Javelin anti-tank missiles dispatched on the eve of the full-scale Russian invasion to deliveries of howitzers, Mistral air defence systems and amphibious vehicles.[10] In 2024, on the twentieth anniversary of the Baltic states' accession to the EU, the European Commission president Ursula von der Leyen held up Estonia as an example to the bloc's other members, praising its 'outstanding and impressive' moral courage towards Russia and its 'phenomenal . . . digital leadership'.[11]

If there is something a little worthy or monotonous about the triumphal credit roll of achievements that Estonia's leaders can rattle off at the drop of a hat, that is entirely intentional. It would like nothing more than to be just another 'boring Nordic country', as Toomas Hendrik Ilves, its foreign minister and later president, put it in the 1990s.[12] But that is not quite the whole story. What separates Estonia from the Nordic states is a restless yearning for solidity, a twitchiness concerning not only its security but its identity, its future and its existence.

This twitchiness is a source of great strength and adaptability. The world of the 2020s, with all the upheaval and danger to which most other western countries are still struggling to adjust, has been Estonia's reality, *mutatis mutandis*, for more than a century, following – as many Estonians see it – 700 years of subjugation to foreign powers: to the Danes, to the Germans, to the Swedes, and time and again to the Russians.

As a result it has a good deal to teach the rest of us, if we are willing to listen. This is not just a matter of sending fact-finding missions to coo over its kindergartens and digital wheezes, only for the ensuing policy papers to gather dust in ministerial archives. It is a matter of learning from the underlying mindset: the strategically calculated embrace of risk, the intense attachment to liberty, and above all the idea that a society's defences must be much broader than bunkers and bombs.

First Hunger, Then Misery

The Czech writer Milan Kundera once defined a small nation as 'one whose very existence may be put in question at any moment'.[13] This precariousness is central to understanding the country today. The

Estonians know what the stakes are. Right from its birth in 1918, Estonia's independence was considered such a fragile anomaly by the great powers that British diplomats warned they could no longer intervene on its behalf from the early 1920s. In August 1939 a secret clause of the Molotov–Ribbentrop pact between Nazi Germany and the USSR assigned Estonia and Latvia to the Soviet sphere of influence, along with Finland and portions of Romania and Poland. Weeks later, as Poland fell to Hitler and Stalin, the Estonian government accepted a Soviet ultimatum granting the Red Army access to its territory.

Over the course of the Second World War, Estonia was invaded three times: first by the Soviets in 1940, then by the Germans the following year, and then again by the Soviets in 1944. The initial Soviet occupation lasted only eleven months but the scars it left behind were profound. The country was annexed to the USSR after rigged parliamentary elections. The national flag and other emblems of Estonian identity were abolished.

On 14 June 1941, a few days before the German invasion of the USSR, the Soviets deported at least 10,000 people in a single day in an attempt to decapitate and cow Estonian society. The other 'counter-revolutionaries' included clergy, police officers, Esperanto speakers and even stamp collectors.[14] About 10 per cent of teachers were deported or executed.[15]

The German occupiers' overriding objective was the war effort and their policy was torn between the competing agendas of the military, Himmler's SS, Göring's economic plans and the ministry for the East – so inept it was nicknamed the *Chaosministerium* – under Alfred Rosenberg, a Tallinn-born Baltic German ideologue.[16] The SS Einsatzgruppe A captured and murdered about a thousand of the 4,000 or so Jews who had remained in the country, abetted by parts of the reconstituted Estonian home guard. The occupying regime also killed at least another 6,000 ethnic Estonians and several thousand Russians, Roma and Soviet prisoners of war.[17]

Reconquering Estonia in 1944, Stalin picked up more or less where he had left off. An Estonian maxim captures the spirit of the era: First hunger, then misery.[18] The farms were collectivised. We do not really know how many Estonians were deported in total but

Rein Taagepera, an eminent political scientist, has suggested it may have been 124,000 out of a post-war population of about 1.1 million.[19] The teaching of Estonian history and geography in schools was submerged into the history and geography of the wider Soviet Union and revised according to Marxist-Leninist principles. According to one estimate, 30 million books were destroyed during the first two decades of the occupation, or about twenty-two for every person left in the country.[20]

Monuments to Estonia's past, including statues of Martin Luther, the German father of the Reformation, and Gustav II Adolf, the Swedish warrior-king who had founded Tartu university, were torn down. As many as 4,000 crosses marking the graves of German and Estonian soldiers in the Maarjamäe district of Tallinn were ploughed into the soil. The cemetery site was then used for growing potatoes.

The publication of Estonian literature dried up to a handful of volumes a year. The birth rate dropped and the abortion rate rose, in large part because of an acute shortage of living space and the sheer uncertainty of life in general.[21] In an effort to rapidly industrialise the war-ravaged and largely agrarian economy, the Soviet regime brought in so many foreign workers from Russia and other parts of the USSR that Russian speakers (including those from other Soviet republics such as Ukraine and Belarus) came to make up more than 50 per cent of the population of Tallinn and over 90 per cent of the eastern cities of Narva and Sillamäe.

Aldis Purs, a Latvian historian, points out that although the overall proportion of 'Russians' was higher in Latvia, Estonia went through a more dramatic demographic lurch. In 1935, ethnic Estonians had made up 88 per cent of the population. By 1989, it was only 61 per cent.[22] Some have argued that the intent behind this colonisation was effectively genocidal: to erase the Estonian people and their traditions. There is not a great deal of documentary evidence to support the notion. However, the historian Peeter Kaasik notes that the gradual dissolution of the USSR's 'minor' peoples was accepted in propaganda as a price worth paying for the formation of a 'Soviet' nation. By his calculations, had the trends continued the ethnic Estonians would have been a minority in their own country by the year 2000.[23]

It may not have been primarily planned or executed as a conventional genocide, but that was its slow-burning effect.

Resistance has been just as important a part of modern Estonia's story as oppression and endurance. It was always there, even when things seemed most hopeless. As in the other Baltic states, it began with a network of armed partisan groups collectively known as the *Metsavennad*, or Forest Brothers. Drawing on the core of the interwar Kaitseliit or defence league and the home guard, they probably numbered about 15,000 in total over the years from 1945 to 1953. They scored a number of initial successes, and stories of their defiance sustained Estonian morale for decades after the movement died out, sapped by merciless Soviet tactics and running out of supplies.

Non-violent dissent continued, particularly during the 'Khrushchev thaw' that followed Stalin's death in 1953. There were riots after the Soviet suppressions of the Hungarian uprising in 1956 and of the Prague Spring in 1968. The blue, black and white national colours would appear 'by accident' on cake decorations. The Estonian flag would materialise in public places overnight. Slogans such as 'Russians go home' would turn up on walls in the cities.[24] When the building where the 1918 declaration of independence had been drafted was condemned to be pulled down, dissidents quietly removed the door and hid it at a secret location in the countryside for the rest of the Cold War.[25]

Mart Laar, a historian who served two terms as Estonia's prime minister, says this sort of thing was by no means unusual. By his estimate, more than 60 per cent of the monuments to the nation's war dead were either wholly or partially saved and concealed from the Soviets until the restoration of independence. 'Estonia was entering Orwell's 1984 and everything that recalled free Estonia had to be wiped away,' Laar says.

> But the memory was still there and we protected it against the Soviets when they tried to take it from us. It was really a little bit absurd. Under foreign occupation it seems understandable that people could hide gold, weapons, even books, but risking everything to hide huge stone or bronze monuments appears absolutely implausible. But that is exactly what Estonians did.

Artists, musicians and writers also played their part as the censorship and persecution gradually eased. Their criticisms of the regime were encrypted to varying degrees in wordplay, allusion and allegory, audible to those who had ears to hear. The all-Estonian song festivals, which had been a focal point of the first national awakening in the second half of the nineteenth century, were permitted to resume. Under the Stalinist principle 'nationalist in form, socialist in content', composers were encouraged to add to the canon of songs praising Lenin and collective farms. Yet there was still scope for subversion. Roughly a hundred thousand people, or more than a tenth of the ethnic Estonian population, attended the first revival of the tradition in 1947. At the end Gustav Ernesaks, the conductor, led a mass choir performing a new arrangement of Lydia Koidula's poem 'My Fatherland is My Love', which had been sung at the inaugural festival in 1869 and became a kind of ersatz national anthem. Three years later the authorities were sufficiently rattled to arrest three of the five main conductors and denounce them as 'enemies of the people'.[26]

Tell the Balts to Stop This Nonsense

By the late 1970s a serious head of frustration was building up below the surface. The residents of northern Estonia were able to illicitly tune into Finnish television broadcasts and see a world beyond Soviet propaganda. Many grew angry at the environmental degradation wreaked on their land by heavy industry and the increasingly overbearing Russification of all walks of life. Russian was imposed everywhere, from the creches to the courts. Laar, who was born in 1960, recalls that the first words of Russian he was taught in his kindergarten were: 'I love Lenin and I love peace.'

From the middle of the 1980s, Gorbachev's perestroika and glasnost reforms served only to reinvigorate the national movement. In 1987 there was a tremendous outcry against proposals to expand the phosphorite mines around the northern villages of Kabala and Toolse, where the landscape had already been reduced to a moon-like desolation of spoil heaps and bare earth. The piles of radioactive ash were so big that locals likened them to 'skyscrapers'. There were stories of children in the surrounding villages losing their hair.[27] Scientists estimated that the industry would leech uranium and other contaminants into as much as 40 per cent of the national water supply.[28]

At the time Kersti Kaljulaid, a future president of Estonia, had just finished secondary school. 'We reacted with spontaneous children's and students' protests,' she says. 'By 1988, our [national] flags were out. They had been so strictly forbidden that you could go to jail just for wearing blue, black and white clothes. But we all felt that something was going to happen now.'

The momentum became inexorable over the following months. Over five nights in June 1988, about a hundred thousand Estonians spontaneously assembled in the song festival grounds and belted out hymns of protest from dusk until dawn, leading the pro-independence activist Heinz Valk to coin the term 'singing revolution'.[29] That October Marju Lauristin and Edgar Savisaar founded the Popular Front, the moderate engine of the national movement. Six weeks later, the Estonian supreme Soviet, the republic's parliament, issued a declaration of 'sovereignty', unilaterally seeking autonomy within what delegates hoped would be a looser federation led by Moscow. At the bolder end of the spectrum, activists from the Estonian Heritage Society such as Trivimi Velliste were already making the case for full independence from the USSR.

For perhaps the first time in the history of the Baltic states, the emerging generation of leaders began to work together in a meaningful way. They swiftly realised that they were on their own and had to determine their future for themselves. The West, in thrall to 'Gorbymania', rejected anything that might undermine Gorbachev's position in the Kremlin. In those years Toomas Hendrik Ilves, who had grown up in New Jersey, was head of the Baltic desk for the American government-funded broadcaster Radio Free Europe (RFE). One day, as the Baltic independence movements began to gather steam, Ilves got a visit at his office in Munich from an officer in West Germany's foreign intelligence service, the BND. Ilves invited him into the building for lunch. 'Then he started slamming the table, in the middle of this big canteen, saying: "Tell those Balts and the Estonians to stop this nonsense about independence,"' Ilves says. 'I mean, it was a fairly resonant table. It was echoing through this huge room that had 800 people eating lunch in the middle of the day.'

On 23 August 1989, fired up by the recent protests in Tiananmen Square, the first halfway-free elections in Poland for half a century and the impending demise of the communist regime in Hungary, this new spirit of intra-Baltic comity arrived at its culmination in one of the defining images of the end of the Cold War. On the fiftieth anniversary of the conclusion of the Molotov–Ribbentrop pact, two million people formed an almost unbroken human chain across Estonia, Latvia and Lithuania. The achievement was all the more remarkable given that barely half of the households in the Baltic republics had access to a landline, let alone an independent mass media.[30] Kaja Kallas was twelve years old at the time. 'I was at my grandparents' house, so we went to this place close to Viljandi [a town in southern Estonia] to hold hands,' she says. 'I didn't really understand it at the time. But afterwards, when you saw that there really was a chain of people from Lithuania to Estonia, all the way, holding hands, no breaks: that was very strong.'

For the first time, the 'Baltic Way' demonstration prompted Gorbachev to issue a seriously aggressive warning against 'nationalist excesses' in the three Baltic republics. 'The state of the Baltic peoples is in serious danger,' he said in a televised address.[31] But by this point no one – not Gorbachev, not Margaret Thatcher, not Helmut Kohl and not even George H. W. Bush – could turn the tide. In March 1990 the Estonian supreme Soviet voted to embark on a 'transition period' towards independence.

In January 1991 Soviet troops and tanks moved into Tallinn and tried to seize the television tower, the chief means of mass communication, which was initially guarded by only two young Estonian border police officers and, later, by a crowd of unarmed civilians. The Soviet commander ordered the tanks to train their main guns on the tower and threatened to destroy it. 'Go ahead,' a policeman said. The bluff was called.[32]

Seven months later there was another coup, this time staged by hardline Soviet reactionaries across the USSR who wanted to eject Gorbachev from power. 'Knowing the history, I was so, so afraid [during the coup] that my parents would be killed and I would never see them again,' says Kallas. 'When the [Soviet] occupation started, all the political elite, the cultural elite, the economic elite was wiped away; they were either killed or died in captivity or were sent to Siberia. I was really afraid that it was going to happen again.' But this coup also failed. Days later, Estonia formally declared its independence from the USSR.

The singing revolution had repercussions far beyond the borders of the Baltic states. While the causes of the USSR's unravelling at the start of the 1990s were legion and complex, the three popular movements spawned imitators not only in Ukraine, Moldova and Belarus but also in Russia itself.

They did not just lead by example: they actively supported similar organisations in the other Soviet republics. The Estonians printed newspapers and election leaflets for their allies in Leningrad (St Petersburg). Sajūdis, the Lithuanian counterpart to the Latvian and Estonian popular fronts, published a Russian-language news sheet called *Soglasie* (Harmony) with a circulation of up to 40,000 and a readership that stretched from Moscow and Kyiv to Yerevan and Tbilisi. Various Ukrainian dissident groups such as Rukh consciously modelled themselves on the Baltic templates, to the point of staging a human chain on 17 September 1989, the fiftieth anniversary of the Soviet occupation of western Ukraine. The Moldovans followed suit in June 1990.[33]

The Factory of the Future

When I began the research for this book, one of the first things I did was to buy a mildly foxed second-hand copy of Lennart Meri's speeches. I have come back to it time and again. It is not so much that Meri was a preternaturally gifted orator, although he (or his speechwriters) certainly had a knack for turning phrases that even from a distance of three decades can make you feel as though the world is young again. It is more that rhetoric of this calibre can only be a reflection of serious and effortful thought.

In a time when laws of politics that had prevailed for two generations were being shredded, Meri described the shapeless chaos around him with more lucidity and foresight than almost any other

European leader of his era. He expressed the hope that even a state as minute as Estonia, which might once have been written off as an entity with the life expectancy of a wheel of cheese, might one day play a part in bringing order to that chaos. 'The past becomes the present, and history becomes politics,' he said in his first speech to the NATO Council in 1992, 'and politics is, in our modern age, a factory which produces the future. And the Baltic states are the experimental workshop and research laboratory of this factory.'[34]

The Estonian workshop was quite a messy one for some years. It was full of broken and inefficient tools, bedevilled with financial gremlins, occupied by thugs left over from the previous management, and adjacent to a much larger rival firm with scores to settle. There were 132,000 Soviet troops left in Estonia, scattered across 500 military installations.[35] The country's own assorted armed forces were riddled with division. The apparatus of government had to be smashed up and rebuilt again. In the Soviet era the Estonian foreign ministry had been a powerless rump with a minimal number of officials maintained largely for the sake of keeping up appearances. When Meri took it over a year before the restoration of independence, he fired all the staff and found the library contained sixty-four books on Lenin and nothing else. The radio and TV aerials he needed to follow western news had to be brought in from Sweden, packaged as skis so that they would pass through Soviet customs.[36]

The economy was a basket case. As prices were adjusted to market rates from 1990 and trade with post-Soviet Russia broke down, inflation reached wild proportions. Salaries rose at the same time but did not come close to filling the gap. Unemployment, an almost alien concept under Soviet rule, rose from 900 to 75,000 in the space of ten months.[37] From 1991 to 1993 the average Estonian's purchasing power – what they could actually buy with their earnings – fell by two-thirds.[38] Money lost so much value that the city of Tartu ran out of rubles in 1992 and started printing its own money on old Soviet ration cards.[39]

As Moscow cut supplies of energy at the start of 1992, unheated schools had to be shut down because of the cold and most households could only use warm water at weekends. A contingency plan to evacuate most of the population of Tallinn to the countryside was only averted through humanitarian assistance from the West.[40]

Meri had not been overstating the case when he told the nation in August 1991 that its struggles were only just beginning: 'Fifty years of hard times have brought us to the situation where we must admit: time is working against us. The destructive processes are intensifying and turning those processes around will take immense efforts.'[41]

Goodbye Lenin and Just Do It

All these ructions were standard symptoms of the de-programming of oppression, dependency and inverted economic logic in post-communist societies, like the high fever that sweeps over a patient as the body wrestles with a virus. In other states they unleashed back-sliding, massive corruption, virulent populist movements, border wars and dictatorships. Estonia got off very lightly indeed. From the beginning there was an extraordinary degree of consensus among its elites about what needed to be done if the country was to 'return to normality': a rapid and stringent liberalisation of the economy; an equally swift modernisation of the administrative machinery; the strategic construction of future industries; the negotiated withdrawal of Russian forces; and more than anything a strenuous effort to wrench the country away from Moscow and towards the West so that it would hit escape velocity from the Kremlin's orbit.

While Estonian governments rose and fell with dizzying regularity over the 1990s and early 2000s, more or less all of them faithfully pursued this course to a degree that is unparalleled across the former USSR. There are plenty of reasons for this exceptionalism. For one thing, the old Soviet *nomenklatura* were largely excluded from the governing class. Many of the central players were startlingly young and full of the brio of outsiders: Mart Laar, for example, was thirty-two when he was first appointed prime minister.[42] Estonia's ties to Finland and Scandinavia also helped, partly as a source of investment and advice, but partly too as a motivation to catch up and resume what it felt was its rightful place in the Nordic ambit.

At the end of the 1930s, average incomes and life expectancy had been almost the same in Finland and Estonia. By the end of the 1980s, the average Finn lived four years longer and earned more than eight times as much as the average Estonian. It was almost as though some mad deity had set up a natural experiment to test the impact of Soviet communism. '[In the 1990s] we looked at Finland and its wealth, and we looked at ourselves, when we were actually below the World Bank's official level of poverty,' says Kersti Kaljulaid, who was the chief economic advisor to Laar during his second premiership in 1999 to 2002. 'We want to get there and everybody's in this situation where nobody knows how far our capabilities will take us, but everybody is agreed that we will all get there.'

There was also a remarkable willingness in the population at large to make short-term sacrifices in the expectation of a better future. As Meri put it: 'If you have to chop the dog's tail off, there's no point in doing it bit by bit.'[43] Estonia's capacity for tolerating financial pain became something like a source of national pride. When the kroon, its interwar currency, was revived in 1992, its low valuation – eight to the deutschmark – was held up as a symbol of Estonian resolve.

Laar came to power in 1992 with a simple pitch to the electorate: 'Goodbye Lenin and just do it.' The historian-turned-politician was a fervent disciple of Margaret Thatcher, with whom he established a close friendship. 'She had a strong influence on me and called me her political grandson,' he says. Laar's intended course of economic shock therapy was so radical that when he told Thatcher what he was planning, he described how she looked at him and said: 'You are one brave young man.'[44] He brought in Europe's first entirely flat rate of income tax. Import tariffs were set so low that Estonia had to raise them in order to join the World Trade Organisation several years later.

The bitter medicine worked. Economic growth returned to 4 per cent in 1995. Inflation was down to a manageable 8 per cent by 1998. Tens of thousands of low-skilled industrial workers were retrained and channelled into the services sector. Estonia has at times stuck by its fiscal puritanism with even more rigour than Germany and Finland. Over the years of brisk growth in the 2000s it amassed a rainy-day contingency fund worth 9 per cent of GDP, which allowed it to cushion the blow of the ensuing eurozone crisis more effectively than its neighbours. Even today the country has the lowest debt-to-GDP ratio in the EU.[45]

The New Molotov and His Ribbentrop

The second pillar of Estonia's strategy was and is what Ilves tartly calls a *Drang nach Westen* (Drive to the West), punning on the *Drang nach Osten*, a term for the successive waves of medieval Germanic colonisation to the east. This time Estonia would not allow itself to fall into the geopolitical trap of isolation that had doomed it in the 1930s. It needed to get rid of the Russian troops on its soil and bind itself as tightly to the West as it could. That meant pursuing membership of NATO, for the American nuclear umbrella, and of the EU, for economic and diplomatic integration.

The approach in the 1990s was essentially threefold. First, reform the country to the most exacting western standards as quickly as possible. Second, join every club in the US-led multilateral constellation, however small or irrelevant. Third, get yourself noticed. Estonia has been anything but a meek supplicant in this process. Lennart Meri had a natural flair for attracting international attention. In 1992, while he was technically only the ambassador to Finland, he burst in on a summit between George H. W. Bush and the leaders of the three Baltic states. Addressing the American president as 'George', Meri breezily told him that Washington had neither a Russia policy nor a Baltic policy. 'Before that, Bush hardly remembered that the Balts existed,' a US diplomat remarked afterwards. 'Now, thanks to Meri, he is furious with them.'[46]

Speaking to the Bundestag in 1995, in words that seem disconcertingly prescient, Meri lectured the German MPs on their country's 'fear of power', 'intellectual self-contempt' and 'disrespectful' habit of going easy on Russia to compensate for the sins of the Third Reich. 'The new Molotov is already there,' he said. 'He is waiting for the new Ribbentrop.'[47] A year earlier, at a dinner in Hamburg, he had delivered a jeremiad against Russia that prompted the deputy mayor of St Petersburg, one Vladimir V. Putin, to storm out of the room.[48]

Meri's tradition of unabashed directness has been continued by figures such as Ilves and Kallas. 'We are all students of Lennart,' says Kersti Kaljulaid.

Frankly speaking, you journalists only talk to us because we are so blunt . . . We sometimes don't understand the niceties and beating about the bush of other nations. It's not only a survival instinct; it's also cultural. But I believe it serves us really well.

There has also been a long and not yet wholly successful campaign to dispel the persistent idea that Estonia is a 'post-Soviet', 'eastern European' or 'former communist' country. While these terms can be relevant for comparisons with other parts of what used to be the eastern bloc, there are good reasons why the three Baltic states tend to bristle at their use. One is simply that they are freighted with stereotypes of backwardness and misrule. Another is that they are not technically accurate. With the notable exception of Sweden (and, briefly, Australia), most western governments refused to recognise the 1940 annexations in law, even if they accepted them in practice.[49] This was crucial for sustaining the Baltic peoples' sense of national identity: it implied that the forty-eight years of Soviet occupation were the anomaly rather than the twenty-two years of pre-war independence. A third and related point is that the idea of a post-Soviet space plays into Russia's hands. Moscow has always insisted that Stalin's absorption of the Baltic states was not only legal but supported by the overwhelming majority of their populations. This fiction helps the Kremlin to construct spurious justifications for meddling in their affairs today.

Almost every big decision Estonia has taken since the end of the 1980s has been judged by whether it serves to drag the country further out of Russia's clutches. Since it joined NATO and the EU in 2004, at the same time as Latvia and Lithuania, the three Baltic states have amassed an influence that far exceeds their economic weight, particularly on geopolitical issues. Along with Poland, they were instrumental in winning the European Commission's support for Ukrainian EU accession in 2023. Earlier that year, Kaja Kallas drove through a plan for the bloc jointly to procure a million artillery shells and send them to Ukraine within twelve months, although it ultimately fell short of the target.[50] With support from its neighbours, it is also leading a diplomatic initiative to get NATO's defence spending target raised from 2 per cent of GDP to 2.5 per cent or even 3 per cent in 2025.[51]

Rethinking the Whole of History

The third element of Estonia's vision for the future since the restoration of its independence has been human capital. Over nearly half a century of occupation, its education system had been thoroughly Sovietised. 'The teachers had to completely reinvent their subjects,' says Kristina Kallas, the education minister (and no relation of the prime minister). 'Our history teacher had the biggest challenge. Basically the Soviet history textbooks were just thrown away. What we did was sit in school and take notes instead, because the teacher was using every possible new source he could get to teach history.' Even the most basic facts had to be revised. Up to that point there had been no such thing as the 'Second World War' in Estonian history classes. There was only the 'Great Patriotic War', which had supposedly begun out of nowhere with the German invasion of the USSR in 1941. 'Everything that had happened between 1939 and 1941 was hidden from you for [ideological] reasons, because there was the Soviet annexation, there were the deportations, the [Soviet] invasion of Poland, the Molotov–Ribbentrop pact – things that had to be hidden and not told,' Kristina Kallas says:

> My mother, who had graduated from a Russian school because she was Russian, says her experience was that at the age of fifty she suddenly had to rethink the whole of history, the way it was told to you and what is actually true. I mean, that's a big change for human consciousness, because it turns out that everything you had been told was a lie.

As in many other areas, the Estonians charged with rebuilding the education sector from scratch looked to Finland as their chief model. The guiding principle was autonomy: give pupils and teachers the motivation and the resources to work things out for themselves, and they would learn much more effectively than if the matter were simply drilled into them from on high. This process begins in the nurseries. Estonian children do not start school until the age of seven. Instead they typically attend a crèche until they are three, and then enter pre-school, where they are placed in the care of teachers with bachelor degrees in early years education. 'We focus on the children's skills of self-management,' says Kristina Kallas.

> Basically every Estonian child needs to know how to walk to school, what time it is, how to get dressed, how to be as self-guiding and independent as possible. We need to design children in early childhood so that they can be self-guided learners later in school. It's not about whether they know maths or reading.

Once school begins, there is no segregation according to academic potential. Standardised testing is kept to a minimum, with only two rounds of national exams at the ends of the lower and upper secondary phases. The curricula tend to be fairly skeletal, prescribing 'competencies', such as the ability to parse and discuss written sources, rather than textbooks or specific areas. Strangest of all, at least to a British observer, is the schools inspection system, which barely exists. The whole thing is devolved and runs largely on trust, with the two standardised exams as a corrective. 'We don't have school inspectors because we don't inspect schools,' says Kallas. 'That's only for the cases where there are some serious complaints. We only have fourteen people working in the inspectorate section [of the ministry], for the whole national system. And we have 520 schools in Estonia.'

This approach has been handsomely vindicated. The Organisation for Economic Co-operation and Development's most recent Programme for International Student Assessment (PISA) report, which measured fifteen-year-old pupils' maths, science and reading abilities across eighty-one countries in 2022, gave Estonia the highest ranking in Europe. Because of the disruption to teaching during the pandemic, its scores in all three subjects had in fact fallen slightly since the previous edition two years earlier, but they held up better than those in other European nations.[52] That is largely down to another of Estonia's distinctive strengths: digital technology.

The Magical Servant

In Estonian myth, the *kratt* is a fickle creation. First you assemble a rough body shape out of whatever spare objects you have in your home, such as broken tools or even a few strands of straw. Then you bring it to life by dedicating three drops of your blood to the Devil. The *kratt* will carry out any tasks it is given, with a particular knack for petty theft. But there is a catch: you cannot leave it idle, even for an instant. 'Otherwise it will go crazy. It will kill you and then your soul will be damned forever,' says Carmen Raal, an advisor to e-Estonia, the national digital society.

The only way to rid yourself of a rogue *kratt* is to give it an impossible job so that it will ultimately self-destruct out of frustration. The analogy with artificial intelligence is hard to miss. In 2019 Estonia introduced a '*kratt* strategy' for the adoption of AI in an attempt to domesticate the technology into a useful creature bound by safeguards. It is already being used to produce economic forecasts, to match the unemployed with suitable job postings (supposedly it can predict with 98 per cent accuracy how likely they are to find a post within a hundred days), and to dispatch police to control bottlenecks in the flow of traffic.[53] It also provides the basis for a voice-based chatbot called Bürokratt that guides Estonians through applying for a passport, registering a marriage or borrowing a book from a library.

The digital revolution was born of necessity. It is not strictly truthful to call Estonia a small country: it covers roughly the same area as the Netherlands but has less than a tenth of the population size, which makes providing universal public services an expensive business. In 1991 it had barely any natural resources and relatively little heavy industry. Trust in the institutions of the state was low. What it did have was a fairly strong technical education system, one of the few useful legacies of communist rule. The Soviets had preserved the pre-war Tallinn University of Technology (TalTech) and equipped it with a cybernetics institute. The starlight sensors that guided the USSR's satellites and the enriched uranium that went into its first nuclear warheads were both produced in Estonia.[54]

The government decided that the logical solution to its problems was to embrace IT and the fledgling internet. 'We got very lucky with Lennart Meri as our president, because he really was a visionary,' says Jaanika Merilo, a Ukrainian-Estonian who has advised both countries' governments on digitisation.

> He had this kind of Finnish-Nokia vision that technology should drive the country because it was way too small to have a bureaucracy – that we shouldn't hire thousands of civil servants and then digitalise [the administration], but we should digitalise it from day one.

In effect this was a choice to bypass the analogue stage of modernity: to go straight from cash to credit cards, skipping the cheque book; to use mobile phones and modems rather than landlines. A budget amounting to 1 per cent of GDP was ringfenced for IT investment. The first digital privacy regulations were drawn up as early as 1994. But the pivotal element was an initiative known as the *Tiigrihüpe* (Tiger Leap), proposed by Toomas Hendrik Ilves.

One day in 1971, when Ilves was a geeky teenager at high school in New Jersey, his maths teacher brought in a teletype machine, effectively a keyboard with a printer that could be hooked up with a telephone modem to a mainframe computer 30 miles away. 'Twelve of us learned to code,' he says. 'All the other ones are tech millionaires now, except for me.' In the 1990s, when Ilves was ambassador to Washington and obsessing over how Estonia might catch up with Finland, a friend sent him a magazine clipping about a new system called a 'web browser', which you could install on your computer with a set of floppy disks. 'I uploaded them, and then I saw the web,' Ilves says.

> I looked at it and said: 'This is where we are on a level playing field.' And so I put all of it together – the problem of catching up, the level playing field problem, my own history of learning to code – and I said that what we need to do is digitalise and computerise all the schools.

Within two years, every school in the country was connected to the internet and there was at least one public web-browsing facility in each municipality. Four years after that, each Estonian was given an electronic identity that they could use for banking as well as paying taxes and accessing public services. The tax declaration forms are 'pre-populated' with answers, meaning Estonians only have to tweak them once a year to ensure they are up to date. In 2005 Estonia began experimenting with online voting. At the 2019 general election, 51.1 per cent of voters cast their ballots digitally.[55]

The entire edifice is founded on an ingenious distributed digital architecture known as the X-Road. This was created in response to a data leak in 1996, when a hacker gained access to a colossal trove of personal information, including the credit history of the prime minister, Tiit Vähi.[56] 'X-Road allows our data to travel across the public internet, which makes it very simple, but it's always end-to-end encrypted, which also makes it safe,' says Carmen Raal.

> Essentially what we've done is we've eliminated data silos in Estonia . . . Let's say I want to change my home address. I only have to change it once at the e-population register if I move house, and everybody else who needs this information will get it via the X-Road.

The technology has now been adopted by twenty other countries, including Ukraine, Colombia and, to the great satisfaction of Estonians, Finland.

Then Raal displays another website called Rahvaalgatus, or the Citizens' Initiative portal.[57] Most western countries have some kind of system for members of the public to submit online petitions that will be debated in parliament if they secure enough support. The distinctive thing about the Estonian version is that it is married to the legally binding electronic ID cards, meaning that officials can identify more or less exactly how much genuine traction each initiative is getting. If a petition reaches a thousand signatures it must be discussed in Estonia's parliament, the Riigikogu. Raal says social media debates tend towards extremes in a way that often makes the loudest voices seem the most dominant, even when they do not represent a significant current of public opinion in the real world.

Plus you have the problem of fake accounts and so on. So this is what we created in order to have a fair online discussion . . . It's also a great way to fight against populism, because if you listen to how populist politicians talk, it's often in a magnifying way as though this is something all Estonians want. If you go to their Facebook post, you might see it has a couple of thousand likes, so that's quite a lot. But if this problem reaches Rahvaalgatus and you can see that only fifty people have signed for the initiative, it's obviously not something that the entire society in Estonia cares about.[58]

All Estonians' medical records were moved online in 2008, which allows any doctor, nurse or pharmacy to call up a patient's history with only a few keystrokes. More impressively, about 200,000 Estonians, or a sixth of the population, have handed over samples of their DNA to a central biobank. That has two benefits: researchers and pharmaceutical companies can freely access the data in anonymised and aggregated form to help them develop drugs; and, as the technology improves, AI-assisted genomic screening will permit doctors to issue personalised diagnoses and treatments.

The private sector went digital with similar alacrity. In 1991 Jaanika Merilo's husband Jaak Ennuste, who is now a technology angel investor, had just graduated with an engineering degree from TalTech. He immediately founded his first IT company, importing computer parts from Finnish wholesalers. It was a wild time. His clients would put down advance payments only for inflation to wipe out their finances by the time the rest of the bill became due. 'We were young. We were just pushing forward and we didn't care,' Ennuste says.

The banks, fed up with the expense of servicing customers across a thinly populated country, seized on digitisation as an opportunity to close up to 80 per cent of their branches. Then, in 2003, came Skype, a video communication platform that was overseen by entrepreneurs from Sweden and Denmark but coded by four Estonian programmers. It became the first significant global success for the country's technology sector and was sold to eBay for $2.8 billion. 'These young guys, they didn't move to Nice or buy houses in Italy,' says Ennuste. 'They stayed in Estonia and started a cluster of new companies. That really kicked off the start-up scene.' Since then, nine other Estonian technology firms have crossed the $1 billion valuation threshold. One foreign diplomat says, not unkindly, that Estonia's real strength is taking concepts created in the US – video calling, day trading, ride sharing, identity verification – and making them more reliable and user-friendly: 'Bolt, for example, is the better and nicer Uber.'

Increasingly the country is also producing sophisticated hardware. By now Starship's six-wheeled and orange-flagged delivery robots, kitted out with special tyres to negotiate the snowy streets in winter, are a familiar sight across northern European cities. ÄIO, which is named after the ancient Estonian god of dreams, uses fermentation to 'upcycle' waste materials such as sawdust into cosmetics and substitutes for butter and palm oil.

GScan builds machines that use cosmic rays to produce 3D scans of the contents of large objects such as vehicles and buildings. The scanners can identify hidden structural flaws in a bridge, meaning that the British motorway agency was one of the firm's first foreign clients. But they can also survey the damage done to tanks or bunkers after a battle, which has caught the attention of NATO's military innovation unit. Andi Hektor, GScan's co-founder, who introduces himself as a 'typically critical and grouchy Estonian', starts by listing the problems with his homeland: a tiny domestic market, a limited number of skilled workers, a shortage of venture capital, poor flight connections. 'But throughout our history we have had a strange ability to turn our restrictions into advantages,' Hektor says. 'The super-tiny local market: our start-ups are forced to think about the global market from day one. The limited talent pool: we had a lot of distance-working already before the Covid times.'

Gazpacho and Air Strikes

Childcare, schools, start-ups, digital governance: it is easy for foreigners to gawp at Estonia's badges of Nordic honour. Ministers say the country receives hundreds of delegations from other countries each year. They come, they tour, and they go home with pithy policy proposals that are seldom put into action. This is because many of Estonia's partners have yet to grasp the imperative that makes the whole thing tick: the need for security. In the Estonian version of Maslow's pyramid, the struggle to preserve the nation is at the apex. It permeates almost every sphere of public policy.

The Estonians have to think about defence in the broadest possible terms because that is precisely what the enemy does. Military conflict is only one of nine different domains listed in Russia's 2015 national security strategy, ranging from technology and finance to ecology and the interpretation of history. Moscow's military doctrine includes an explicit provision to mobilise the entire nation's 'economic and spiritual resources' in the event of a large-scale war.[59]

The sense of threat in Estonia is a surprisingly hard thing to pin down. On one level, the language can be bleak. When I ask Kaja Kallas what it would take for her to feel safe, she replies: 'The point where I would feel comfortable is where there is an international tribunal and Russia is held accountable for starting this war [in Ukraine].'

In other settings, though, and especially in front of a domestic audience, they do their best to project a sense of calm. 'Everyone's tranquil here,' says one former minister. Kersti Kaljulaid, the former president, says she has enough faith in NATO's deterrence for the risk of natural disasters to bother her more than the prospect of a Russian invasion. The ordinary Estonians I have spoken to about this vary quite a bit in their responses. Some are unperturbed. Many scoff at foreign media reports about the danger of a Russian offensive on Narva or suggestions that their compatriots were getting ready to leave the country en masse when Donald Trump was first elected US president in 2016.[60]

Others, however, say they have made plans to move their loved ones to safety if Russia does attack. 'I do feel some anxiety when I think about it,' says one volunteer in the Estonian defence league. 'I don't worry for my own life but I do worry for my friends and family.' There is not much good data on this question, although one 2017 poll found 45 per cent of Estonians were afraid of the prospect of war with Russia.[61]

If the rhetoric appears to veer all over the place, that is probably because it is torn between contradictory objectives. Estonia's leaders have a clear interest in driving home to their allies the need to raise defence spending across NATO and to secure its eastern flank. At the same time they have no reason to sow panic in their own population. They also worry about frightening away foreign investors, who may conclude that the risk of their stake being obliterated by a stray Grad rocket is not worth the candle. 'So somehow the rhetoric has to be balanced [so that] it's enough to wake up western policymakers, but not enough to scare off investors,' says the historian Andres Kasekamp.

> As for the population: well, people obviously believe Russia is a threat. It's a memory of what the Russians do, and it's all been reawakened by what they're doing in Ukraine. It all rings familiar. Whenever people in the West look at the latest Russian atrocity and ask 'How could they be doing this to them?' people in Estonia think: that's the way it is. That's what the Russians have historically done. We've experienced it since Ivan the Terrible.

This helps to explain Estonia's unstinting support for Ukraine. 'The only thinkable solution of the Ukrainian war is Ukraine coming out as the winner: meaning the territorial integrity and sovereignty of this nation need to be restored,' says Kusti Salm, permanent secretary at the Estonian defence ministry. When his country's leaders say the Ukrainians are dying for Europe, it is not a platitude. They mean it in a very literal sense. There is a strong feeling of kinship and shared struggle but there is also a hard, calculated interest in helping Kyiv to victory. The more equipment and personnel Russia loses, the graver its strategic defeat, the less likely it is to consider taking on NATO in the future. The operative word in that last sentence is 'NATO': a Russian attack on the Baltic states would not be a local war but a continental conflagration. Estonian politicians often say they wish their counterparts further to the west would realise that what is happening in Ukraine has direct consequences for the safety of tens of millions of people far beyond the alliance's eastern flank. From this perspective, a few hundred billion euros of military assistance to the Ukrainians looks like a remarkably cheap price to pay.

One of the most formative moments for modern Estonia was the 'Bronze Night' at the end of April 2007. A large statue of a Red Army soldier was to be removed from a Soviet memorial park in central

Tallinn and taken to a slightly more peripheral war cemetery a couple of miles away.[62] A majority of ethnic Estonians saw the sculpture as an emblem of the Soviet occupation. Many ethnic Russians in Estonia – and, crucially, the Putin regime – saw it as an emblem of the Red Army's victory over Nazism in the Second World War, making it a kind of cult artefact in a secular religion.

The Russian-sponsored skirmishes quickly blew up into two nights of riots and looting. Activists from Nashi, the youth wing of the Russian ruling party, travelled over to stir up trouble.[63] Others camped out in front of what they termed the 'eSStonian' embassy in Moscow, some wearing replica Red Army uniforms. There was a big wave of cyberattacks on Estonia's government, parliament, media and banking system, later attributed to Russia and characterised by the Estonian defence minister as the 'first act of World War Three'.[64] The country's press cast it in equally existential terms, likening Russia's actions to an attempted Bolshevik coup that had shaken the republic in 1924.

It was a moment that irrevocably drove home the extent to which Moscow still saw Estonia as an uppity part of its own back yard, and the lengths to which it was prepared to go in order to secure what it regarded as its sphere of influence. Looking back on the Bronze Night a couple of years later, one group of Estonian academics said it had been 'more important than joining NATO or the European Union. Before April 2007 we lived in one country and now we are getting used to living in another one.'[65]

The most obvious legacy of those days of tumult is an intense focus on cybersecurity. A year later NATO founded its Cooperative Cyber Defence Centre of Excellence in Tallinn. The volume of Russian attempts to take down Estonian websites has actually increased quite substantially since 2007, reaching a peak in March 2024.[66] Most of the incidents, though, are primitive distributed denial-of-service attacks, where hackers harness large numbers of compromised computers into 'botnets' and use them to try and overwhelm the systems with spurious traffic. These are comparatively easy to bat away. 'The Baltic states are the usual playground for Russian troops, both criminals and others. And that has made the Baltic cyber-defenders stronger. That's the major effect,' says Heli Tiirmaa-Klaar, director of the Digital Society Institute at the European School of Management and

Technology Berlin and a former head of the Estonian foreign ministry's 'cyber diplomacy' department. Since 2022 Estonia has lent this expertise to other Russian targets, including Ukraine and Moldova.[67]

In 2015 the country established the world's first 'data embassy' in Luxembourg. It is, in effect, a digital clone of the core functions of the Estonian state, intended to allow it to keep going if the main servers come under digital or physical attack. The model has since been adopted by other small countries such as Monaco and Bahrain. Estonia's spy agencies also have an outstanding reputation among their western partners. The foreign intelligence service is regularly consulted about Russia by its counterparts, and its annual 'International Security and Estonia' reports are widely read in foreign capitals. KAPO, the main domestic security agency, excels at counter-intelligence, having secured more espionage convictions since 2010 than any other European country.[68]

Another consequence of the Bronze Night has been a concerted drive to harden society against the blandishments of Russian disinformation. In 2024 Estonia became the first of the Baltic states to oblige schools to teach courses in 'media and influencing' at upper secondary level. The national library has prepared classes on how to identify AI-generated material and a 'fake news' card game called 'Smarter Than the Trolls'.[69] Estonia now ranks fourth in the Open Society Institute Sofia's European media literacy index, behind only Finland, Denmark and Norway.[70]

There is also a touchingly lo-fi guide to spotting misinformation on 'Ole valmis!' (Be Prepared!), a civil resilience app developed by the Naiskodukaitse, or women's voluntary defence league. It seems to be on every other Estonian's phone. The contents are unexpectedly soothing. There are recipes for cooking in a power cut, including gazpacho and 'pearl barley orzotto with coconut milk, pickled mushrooms and seared moose meat (canned)'. There are instructions for how to walk on frozen lakes, where to find the nearest bomb shelter, how to deal with bears and wolves, how to seek cover in the midst of an air strike, how to shield your windows against explosions, and an entire section on conducting non-violent resistance against an occupying power.

Dear Person Interested in National Defence

The backbone of the country's security is the Estonian defence forces, which have a peacetime strength of 4,200 active personnel alongside 3,500 conscripts. In a war their numbers can at least in theory be rapidly expanded to 43,700.[71] The regular forces have come a long way since the early 1990s, when they were kitted out with 15,000 semi-automatic Makarov pistols that were confiscated en route to a British arms dealer and a batch of anti-tank rockets that were supposed to go to Nagorno-Karabakh.[72]

In 2007 Estonia's defence spending rose to above 2 per cent of GDP, seven years before this became the NATO standard. It has remained over the threshold ever since and was projected to reach 3.2 per cent in 2024. The head of the military, General Martin Herem, has argued that this needs to be doubled.[73] More than 50 per cent of the budget is spent on procurement, including American HIMARS multiple rocket launchers, self-propelled artillery and ship-killer missiles.

Unlike Germany and other western European states that have been slow to replenish their badly depleted ammunition inventories, Estonia put in a batch of orders within months of the full-scale Russian attack on Ukraine, not least to signal to manufacturers that they needed urgently and dramatically to expand production. Kusti Salm says the way some allies have allowed their stocks of shells, rockets and other munitions to run down is

> unfortunate, and clearly in the Estonian view – [in] that what we are facing is much more of a conventional threat – we would also call it irresponsible. But now is not really the time to play the blame game. Now is the time to find solutions, and one clear solution is increasing the manufacturing capacity so that the simpler stuff – artillery ammunition, mortar ammunition, rocket launcher ammunition – is manufactured faster.

The set-up is territorial defence, on the Finnish model. That means regional commands, each with an instruction to slow down and harry the enemy advance. There are also plans to set up a 'crisis reserve' of trained volunteers.[74] There will be no repeat of the capitulation of 1940. Aleksander Eiseln, the first commander of the re-established Estonian defence forces after 1991, instructed the troops to keep fighting in the event of an invasion until they receive a direct order from the president to desist.[75] 'Flexibility is the key thing. This has already been proven in our history,' says Andrus Merilo, an army colonel (later promoted to commander of the defence forces). 'We will defend ourselves in any case. It doesn't matter how strong the enemy might be.'

Since 2017 the UK has led a NATO multinational battlegroup based at Tapa in central Estonia. It is integrated into the Estonian command structure. While the equivalent German-led presence in Lithuania and the battlegroup under Canadian leadership in Latvia are being upgraded to brigades (with respective target strengths of roughly 5,000 and 3,000 soldiers), the British presence is due to continue hovering at only a thousand, with the 'balance of a brigade' held in readiness in the UK.[76] Sources on both sides say Britain's cash-strapped armed forces simply cannot spare any more troops.

In a crisis Estonia can also call on various auxiliary organisations, the strongest of which is the Kaitseliit. First formed in 1918 out of the remnants of the home guard and reconstituted in 1990, it is now based in the old Soviet radio intelligence centre. It has an annual budget of about €300 million and about 18,000 unpaid members who give up their evenings and weekends for military training. Alar Karis, the president, has described them as 'thorns' and 'spines . . . prepared to sting the enemy, and painfully so'.[77] The induction into securitised thinking starts early in Estonia: as of the 2023/4 school year, defence education is now a compulsory school subject for all sixteen-year-olds, with 35 hours of teaching spread out over two months.[78]

Security is so tightly interwoven with modern Estonia's understanding of itself that it is hard to see where defence education ends and nation-building begins. The school textbook, recently revised to take account of developments on the front line in Ukraine, does not mince its words. 'Dear person interested in national defence!' it begins.

> The Republic of Estonia has not always been independent. We have had dark times in our history, when the repressions and deportations of the occupying regime touched every family. We will never be able to forget this painful moment in Estonian history. Let it be a harsh reminder to us of why each generation is needed to stand up for independence and their country.

The pupils are taken through the principles of territorial and 'psychological' defence, hybrid warfare, survival skills, civil crises, the military theories of Clausewitz and Machiavelli, the weapons systems of the Estonian defence forces, and reams of Estonian military history, including the tactics of the Forest Brothers.[79]

One winter morning, as the temperature wobbled around a balmy −2°C after a week of extreme cold, I visited a school defence camp on a Kaitseliit shooting range at Männiku, on the southern outskirts of Tallinn.[80] The forty or so sixteen- and seventeen-year-olds, who had just put on fatigues for the first time, were all volunteers. They camp out in low, round ten-man tents, warmed only by a wood-burning stove that must be tended to throughout the night by a sentry.

Some of the pupils are square-bashing, others learning basic battlefield medicine, how to rig up a bivouac or how to strip down and reassemble an assault rifle. But the emphasis is very much on survival. In a wooded area a couple of hundred yards away, eight of them are dressed in pixellated winter camo and learning how to hide and track. While the hunters turn their backs, the hunted hide in hollows and behind tree stumps, melting away under dirty-white sheets. They are all but invisible until you are right on top of them. 'They go into the forest and learn how to move under fire,' says Jürgen Paat, the camp's director.

> Hopefully, even if they don't get called up, then at least they know how to survive in the forest: how to find shelter if something happens, in case of some kind of aggression, some kind of crisis . . . The way it looks now, with everything in the newspapers, the more they talk, the more you can see what's going to happen.

Shooting in a Personal Capacity

Pretty much everything in the preceding pages corresponds to the narrative Estonia's elites weave around their country: a future-facing pioneer state that spent the past thirty-five years pursuing its grand strategy with great determination and resourcefulness. In a sense, this narrative is one of their strongest defences. NATO's Article 5 clause is only as meaningful as other members' willingness to fight for an ally in need. The more Estonia is recognised and valued in Washington, Paris or London, the likelier it is to receive that support. I have adopted the narrative in this book because I think it is not only instructive but also largely true. As with any other country, though, the more closely you look, the more you become aware of its shadow side.

Many voters remain quite deeply dissatisfied. It is not hard to see why. For a while I kept a list of the scandals involving senior Estonian politicians, only to give up when it became unmanageably long. Within a few days in March 2024, the justice minister was obliged to resign after he was accused of pressuring the prosecutor general and improperly channelling his official housing allowance into the pockets of his stepson (he denied wrongdoing); the opposition Centre party was fined €1 million for peddling influence to a donor with a chain of supermarkets in Russia; the Centre party mayor of Tallinn was forced out of office for his own alleged involvement in the intrigue; and support for Kaja Kallas's Reform party fell to its lowest level in five years, following reports that her husband had profited from a stake in a firm that had continued to operate in Russia after the full-scale invasion of Ukraine (they have denied wrongdoing).[81]

None of this, however, quite beats the occasion in 2001 when Mart Laar had to apologise for shooting at a picture of his main political rival with a shotgun, explaining that he had pulled the trigger 'in a personal capacity' rather than in his role as prime minister.[82]

There is also a fair amount of alienation, especially among the ethnic Russians who make up 22.5 per cent of the population at large and 73 per cent in the north-eastern region around the cities of Narva and Sillimäe.

Both the economy and the tech sector in particular have their weak spots. Estonia's GDP took a battering after the European inflation surge of 2022 and is weighed down by the weakness of its main export markets, especially Germany, Sweden and Finland. The ICT trade may soak up most of the international attention but it accounts for only 7 per cent of economic output.

In April 2024 it emerged that nearly half the adult population had been affected by hackers who breached the defences of a company handling medical products. They stole a database containing 400,000 email addresses and the records of 43 million transactions in pharmacies.[83] Nor is public-sector IT always everything it is cracked up to be. Two days after the pharmacy data leak, a pilot project where 4,000 teenagers were supposed to move from paper-based to digital exams had to be suspended after the system went into meltdown.[84] 'Our e-state has been built on sand,' one Estonian columnist lamented.[85]

But the restless ambition that underpins both the successes and the failures remains integral to the Estonian national project. The historian Kaarel Piirimäe has written about the 'existential politics' of the return to independence, framed above all as a conflict between two different senses of time.[86] On the one hand was the recursive torpor of Marxism-Leninism, a boot stamping on a human face, forever. On the other was a golden moment to break free, demanding every milligram of national resolve. 'For Estonia,' Lennart Meri said in 1989, 'time threatens to become a scarce resource. We must count the weeks and months . . . The greatest danger is hidden, as ever, in people's hearts. The danger is the illusion that Estonia might already be done.'[87] More than a generation has passed since then but that same urgency still surfaces time and again in the rhetoric of Estonian leaders. They are a nation in a hurry. In some ways, it feels as though the wider West is in a comparable situation today. It is now clear that history did not end in the 1990s but our sense of it did. If we are to seize this brief opportunity to forge a safer and better future, the best thing we can learn from Estonia is to think of time and security as interrelated and existential questions for all of us.

2

Total Defence

How Finland is Building for the Future

You live the devil knows where . . . You live in bogs and forests. In spite of this you have built a state. You have fought for your state doggedly.
        Stalin to Finnish negotiators in Moscow, October 1945[1]

In Finland's entrancingly strange national epic, the *Kalevala*, the smith Ilmarinen forges a magical artefact known as the Sampo, a source of great wealth. 'On one side,' the poem says, 'there's a corn mill / on the second a salt mill / a money mill on the third.' The Sampo churns away, its 'bright lid' rocking with activity, and draws the attention of Louhi, the malign witch of the North. She steals the device and hides it inside the rocky hill of the Northland, 'inside the slope of copper / and behind nine locks'. Then she binds the chamber to the ground with roots sunk to a depth of nine fathoms (or about 16.5 m).[2]

I cannot help but think of this myth as I approach Finland's modern-day gateway to the underworld. A couple of miles away, on the south side of this island, three street-sized, uranium-powered turbines are whirring around 1,500 times every second, generating almost a third of the country's electricity. To walk through the cavernous halls that house the newest of these machines, Olkiluoto-3, is to experience something of the awe that medieval Christians must have felt as they stepped into the largest cathedrals. The chamber that contains Europe's most powerful nuclear reactor has roughly the same volume as the nave of Notre-Dame de Paris.[3] Its walls are theoretically strong enough to withstand a direct hit from a passenger jet. The complex's cooling systems, which suck water in and out of the Baltic sea at a rate comparable to a small river, discharge so much heat that they kill as much as half a million tonnes of fish each year.[4]

But the tunnel that stretches away into the darkness in front of us is something else altogether. Its sides, blasted out of the rock with dynamite, have a primitive roughness. The road, tall and wide enough to accommodate a lorry, slopes gently down, snaking back and forth for nearly 3 miles. Then, at a depth 1,380 feet below the floor of the Baltic, we reach a 50-mile labyrinth of tombs. In each of these a set of holes are being bored into the floor for copper-sheathed canisters of radioactive waste. Once the last pit has been filled, the site will be sealed off for a hundred thousand years. At some point the builders will put up a warning to generations of the human race who will live so far away in the future that they may not understand our languages or even the concept of an alphabet.

The culture of resilience is no less pervasive in Finland than it is in Estonia. But if Estonia is a country with an acute sense that time is running out, Finland is distinguished by its view of the *longue durée*: an ability to plan and execute grand strategy over periods that extend into the geological. This ranges from foreign policy and military security to education, energy and critical resources. 'The Finnish people are very pragmatic,' says Elina Valtonen, the foreign minister.

> We are in a completely different situation from our neighbours and dear friends to the west because of geography. We have always been the country to fight the wars against Russia and take care of ourselves ... We have a sort of comprehensive security model, which is very tightly linked to our history. We have a process by which our entire society can be switched into a different mode: the private sector, households, the public. It's not only an ability to defend ourselves, but also the willingness of the people to do whatever it takes.

These days there is an odd disjuncture between how the world looks at Finland and how the Finns look at themselves. Among foreign observers it is acquiring a reputation as a model country, burnished by its ostensibly abrupt conversion to NATO membership and its capacity to mobilise up to a fifth of the population for territorial defence. Sauli Niinistö, the president who took Finland into the alliance, has been tasked by the president of the European

Commission with drawing up a 'crisis resilience' strategy for the EU as a whole.[5] Others have written admiringly about how it was named the world's 'happiest' country for seven years on the trot, how it is closer to reaching net zero than any other industrialised nation and how its schools were the strongest in the western world, until it was overtaken by Estonia.[6]

Most of the Finns I know are justifiably proud of their country's achievements and international image. For some years, though, there has also been a great deal of negativity within Finland about its prospects. The economy has in effect gone sideways since 2007, when the eurozone crisis coincided with the implosion of Nokia, a telecoms company that accounted for a quarter of national GDP growth at its peak, and whose interests and governance structures had become deeply interwoven with those of the country as a whole.[7] By the end of 2022, Finnish GDP per capita was no higher than it had been in 2011.[8] There is little consolation to be drawn from official forecasts for the years ahead. The Bank of Finland expects growth to remain 'muted' and public debt to continue rising well into the second half of the decade.[9] One economist has estimated that this is the most subdued period of growth Finland has experienced since the First World War.[10]

The press is also full of angst about long-term demographic trends. Finland already has the second highest ratio of over-sixty-fives to working-age people in the EU after Italy. This figure has been rising faster than anywhere else in Europe.[11] The fertility rate, at 1.37 births per woman, is among the lowest in the West.[12] It is dropping at such a pace that some statisticians project the number of people with Finnish descent may fall below a million at the start of the next century, from more than 5 million today.[13] Nor is the previously formidable state education system the source of smugness it once was. Even before Finland lost the PISA crown to Estonia in 2023, there were frequent complaints about excessive class sizes, a lack of support for brighter students and an inadequate focus on innovation, creativity, debating and social skills.[14] Some of its rural schools are so short of pupils that they are importing 1,500 children a year from countries such as Myanmar and Tanzania for a free Finnish education.[15]

The Virtue of Pessimism

These problems are real. But they are also the symptoms of success. In the space of a century Finland has transformed itself from a largely impoverished and agrarian country, riven with internal divisions, into one of the most robust and modern states in the West. It is precisely the tendency towards dissatisfaction and gloom-mongering that is one of the nation's principal strengths. 'Perhaps,' the Finnish writer Anu Partanen has suggested, 'Finns have built a great society because of their pessimism, not in spite of it.'[16] There is much that the rest of us could learn from the country's trajectory over the past hundred years: its adaptability, its toughness, its orientation towards the future and the underlying sober assessment of long-term challenges.

The nuclear complex on Olkiluoto island is a case in point. For more than fifty years states with atomic power have been unable to work out what to do with their spent radioactive fuel, which can remain hazardous to humans and ecosystems for many thousands of years. At present most of the world's power plant-grade nuclear waste is in a kind of limbo, either buried in transitory storage facilities or stashed away in swimming pool-like baths of water. This cannot last forever: who can predict what will happen in a hundred years' time, or a thousand? But finding a more permanent answer has been exceedingly difficult.

The least extravagant and expensive solution is the deep geological repository: a network of catacombs beneath a rock formation sufficiently stable, remote and impermeable that the radioactive isotopes will be locked safely away. While the practicalities might sound straightforward enough, the politics are usually fraught. However compelling the scientific arguments may be, locals tend to be uncomfortable with the prospect of living on top of a toxic grave. The Americans have been arguing about whether to put a repository under Yucca mountain, Nevada, since the late 1970s. The Germans have spent even longer trying to find a suitable site.

In Finland, however, two municipalities – Loviisa and Eurajoki – competed for the right to host one. In 2001 the authorities chose the island of Olkiluoto in Eurajoki. The excavation of the Onkalo (Little

Cave) facility began in 2004 and was more or less finished by the time I visited in 2023. The plan was that from 2025 no human being would ever have to set foot in its tunnels again: the waste capsules would be lowered down from the surface in a lift and then buried by robots. The real marvel of Onkalo is not so much the engineering as the political architecture behind it: the trust, patience and calm deliberation that made the project possible.

The People and the Trees

There is a gyroscopic quality to public life in Finland. Often its rhythms can be quite hard for outsiders to read. There are long periods of equilibrium when elite consensus settles on positions calibrated with an almost theological delicacy, only to be entirely re-orientated in a matter of days or weeks as external circumstances change. Even individually popular prime ministers are routinely turfed out by the voters at the end of each four-year electoral cycle, as Sanna Marin was in 2023.

An eminently sensible and collegiate tone of political discourse coexists with a pronounced maverick streak: heroic drinking bouts, wildly colourful verbal outbursts, and a raucous and fairly successful right-wing populist outfit, the Finns party. When Alexander Stubb narrowly won the run-off vote for the presidency in 2024, after a campaign marked by almost cloying courtesy and agreement on both sides, his first act was to visit his defeated rival and lard him with praise at a joint press conference.[17] It was a handsome advertisement for Finnish democracy. But it was no less characteristically Finnish when Kari Kairamo, the chief executive of Nokia, resolved an industrial dispute at a paper factory by challenging the union leader to a naked foot-race through the snow around his mansion.[18]

Underneath the churn the basic principles of Finnish strategy have remained remarkably constant. Like Estonia, it has always been a country with a small population on the geographic periphery of Europe, trapped between the competing ambitions of great powers and with few natural advantages beyond its extensive forests and the willpower and ingenuity of its population. As Kari Kairamo once laconically put it: 'Finland has quite a few resources. Briefly put, there are two of them: the people and the trees.'[19]

Today there is a great vogue across NATO for talk of 'whole-of-society' and 'whole-of-government' resilience. These have been traditions in Finland for decades. They were forged above all by two historical factors that are worth exploring in a little detail: the intense hardship that confronted most of the population until well into the twentieth century and the gruelling struggle to keep the country from being absorbed into the Soviet Union.

It can be difficult for people in the 2020s to imagine how tough life used to be in Finland. It is a country of long, harsh winters and brief, mercurial summers, where eking out a living from farming or forestry was for many centuries almost an act of defiance against nature, especially in the north.

A hundred thousand people, or about a third of the population, died in a series of famines during the 'little ice age' of the 1690s.[20] A group of French travellers who visited the territory at the time found peasants making bread from ground fish bones and the bark of the silver birch. The bark-bread, known as *pettuleipä*, remained an occasional staple as late as the grain shortages that followed the declaration of independence in 1917, despite efforts by the authorities to encourage Finns to bake with lichen dust instead.[21] Then at least another hundred thousand Finns died of starvation and disease during the very cold summers of the late 1860s, when the frosts began in August and the frozen Baltic sea delayed vital shipments of grain.[22]

This long battle against the entropy of the north had three lingering effects on modern Finland. The first and most obvious is the national cult of *sisu*, a characteristic that means something like 'grit' or 'relentless determination'. The Finnish author Anu Partanen explains it in an anecdote: as a ten-year-old girl, she had to walk a mile to school each morning. One day she found herself battling through deep drifts of snow. 'With every step I had sunk into the snow all the way up to my hips,' she wrote. 'But I'd discovered that if I crawled on all fours I wouldn't fall through. After that the going was easy.'[23]

The second legacy has been an eager tendency to adopt any new technologies that might make life a little easier. On occasion this magpie-like technophilia can shade into outright intellectual property theft. In 1863 the Finnish mining engineer Fredrik Idestam made an illicit tour of a state-of-the-art wood pulp-processing plant at Mägdesprung, a village in the Harz mountains of central Germany. Before he was turfed out by the owner he saw enough of the machinery to build a copy near the southern Finnish town of Nokia. It was the beginning of the eponymous manufacturing conglomerate, which became the apex predator of corporate Finland a century later.[24]

The third and final lesson has been a sharp awareness of dependency on resources and precarious supply chains. In the past, whenever the harvests failed, Finland relied on grain brought in by sea from the southern Baltic littoral. From the earliest days of independence, successive governments tried in vain to establish agricultural self-sufficiency. During the Second World War, however, the continuing need for fuel and grain shipments from Nazi Germany was a significant factor behind Finland's decision to enter a *de facto* military alliance with Berlin against the Soviet Union.[25]

This situation still shapes the Finnish approach to geoeconomics today. The country has been far ahead of most of its European neighbours in attempting to ease reliance on China for the strategic metals and their derivatives that will determine the course of the green transition. It has also been a pioneer in efforts to protect critical infrastructure, particularly at sea. 'Over 90 per cent of our imports come through the Baltic sea, so we're kind of an island,' says Major General Sami Nurmi, the deputy chief of staff in the Finnish defence forces in charge of strategy.

Bad Neighbours

The other seriously formative influence on Finnish history has been the shadow of Moscow. The Finns sometimes talk about the Russians as though they were Voldemort: they-who-must-not-be-named. For generations their military exercises simply referred to 'the enemy' or 'the yellow state'. Even today Finnish politicians often euphemistically allude to 'the neighbour'.

Since the foundation of St Petersburg on the easternmost shores of the Baltic in 1703, the Russian empire and its successors have regarded Finland and the gulf to its south as a buffer against attacks from the west. Tsar Alexander I took the territory from Sweden in 1809 and incorporated it into Russia as a semi-autonomous 'grand duchy'. Finland ultimately seized on the Bolshevik revolution and declared its independence in 1917, only to slip into a vicious civil war between the socialist Reds, who were backed by Moscow, and the broadly conservative Whites. After a decisive intervention by the Germans, the Whites won within three and a half months, but at considerable cost. More than 8,000 Red soldiers, as well as 58 women and 364 children, were killed. Another 11,000 died in prisoner-of-war camps, usually as a result of being denied medicines, adequate amounts of food or clean water.[26] The result was a profound and bitter cleavage in the new country's society.

Another hard lesson followed two decades later, when a Soviet invasion exposed Finland's lamentably ill-equipped armed forces. On the eve of war in 1939, they had a single tank company, thirty-six field guns and howitzers, 118 working aircraft and precious few anti-aircraft guns. Watching a unit of reservists, many without uniforms, conducting training exercises that August, the prime minister Aimo Cajander boasted:

> We are proud of the fact that we do not have a lot of weapons and rifles rusting away in warehouses, or a lot of uniforms gathering mildew in store – but we do have a high standard of living and an education system of which we may be justly proud.

Carl Gustaf Mannerheim, the veteran general who had commanded the Whites in the civil war and led his country's forces throughout the Second World War, estimated that the army had less than a month's worth of artillery shells, and barely enough fuel and rifle bullets for two months. When he lobbied the governor of the Bank of Finland for more funds, the official replied: 'What's the use of spending so much money on the armed services when there won't be a war?'[27] Finland was about to learn the cost of this complacency.

Stalin struck on 30 November 1939. The 9th Soviet army, under General Mikhail Dukhanov, headed towards Oulu and Tornio with a cargo of parade uniforms and brass instruments, ready to celebrate the impending triumph. Instead it strolled into a disaster. Highly mobile Finnish units in winter camouflage used their knowledge of the terrain to carve up and surround the Red Army units. Two whole divisions were all but wiped out.

In the south, however, the Soviets poured such overwhelming force into Karelia that Mannerheim decided the defence could no longer be sustained after only a few weeks of fighting. Eventually he prevailed upon the government to sue for peace. Finland was forced to cede the Baltic port of Viipuri (now Vyborg in Russia), about half of the surrounding Karelia region and other, smaller patches of border territory to the north, leading to an influx of more than 400,000 refugees. The defeat came as a shock to the Finnish public. In moral terms, though, it was a victory. The Soviets lost about 150,000 soldiers killed and another 200,000 wounded or incapacitated through illness, while the Finnish casualties were roughly a fifth of those totals. More importantly, Finland had achieved something that eluded every other European state that fought in the Second World War, with the exceptions of Britain and the USSR: it had preserved its independence.

The Winter War was a foundational moment for modern Finland. In 2022 and 2023, at a whole lifetime's remove from the conflict, at least 700 Finns gave more than €140,000 to a company that allowed them to write messages on artillery shells that would be donated to Ukraine. Some chose words to the effect that this was payback for what Stalin had done to their country.[28] Virtually every family was scarred by the war. 'That was the key,' says the historian Henrik Meinander.

> During the war it was clearly a larger proportion of the population that was mobilised in Finland than in most other European countries. And that meant people would say 'My uncle was killed in the war' or 'My father took part in the war.' It was a way to bond and to express the continuation of that tradition.

The stories of individual heroism in the face of improbably adverse odds are legion. 'We are so few, and they are so many,' one Finnish soldier famously said. 'Where will we find room to bury them all?'[29]

Desperately short of anti-tank weaponry, the troops would fill 'burn-bottles' with petrol or spirits, light a rag wick and then toss them in through the vehicle's vents. The improvised firebombs were nicknamed 'Molotov cocktails', after the Soviet foreign minister who had claimed that the air raids on Helsinki were dropping food parcels rather than explosives.[30] Others paralysed the tanks by sticking tree branches in the spokes of their wheels, or simply stood in front of them and fired bullets through the slits in their armour. Simo Häyhä, a sniper immortalised by Finnish propagandists as the 'White Death', was said to have killed more than 500 of the enemy, at a rate of about five a day. Jorma Sarvanto, a lieutenant in Finland's tiny air force, shot down six Soviet warplanes within four minutes.[31]

The Finno-British War

The Winter War was Finland's version of the Battle of Britain, a cauldron of national myth-making. In many ways, though, the years that came afterwards were every bit as important in making the country what it is today. Over the course of the 'Continuation War' with the USSR from 1941 to 1944 and the awkward settlement with Moscow that followed, a different set of subtler, less obviously charismatic virtues came into play: endurance, compromise, forethought and cold-blooded geopolitical calculation.

No sooner had the fighting ceased than Risto Ryti, the new prime minister (and previously the Bank of Finland governor who had been so dismissive of Mannerheim's warnings), promised that the nation would be rebuilt 'with sword in one hand and trowel in the other'.[32] While Finland had not been entirely abandoned by the West, the help it received had been meagre and late. Britain had played a particularly duplicitous game. At the same time as encouraging the Finns to fight, Winston Churchill had reassured the Soviets that their demands on Finland's territory were 'historically normal' and 'fully natural and legitimate' compensation for the losses the Russian empire had incurred during the First World War.[33]

Finland drew the painful but logical conclusion: it was on its own. Caught between Nazi Germany and the Soviet Union, it risked annihilation unless it could cautiously align itself with one of the two totalitarian powers in its neighbourhood.

Initially it chose Germany. Hitler, Göring and other leaders in the Nazi regime had been assiduously courting Helsinki's support for Operation Barbarossa, their impending assault on the USSR. Berlin offered fuel, weapons and food. The result was a tricky balancing act. Mannerheim, the Finnish commander-in-chief, agreed to install a German liaison officer in his headquarters and allow German troops passage across Finland, but there would be no formal alliance. Officially, the two countries just happened to be fighting parallel wars against the same enemy. Churchill, however, was undeceived. 'It would be most painful to the many friends of your country in England if Finland found herself in the dock with the guilty and defeated Nazis,' he wrote to Mannerheim in November 1941. In the end he felt obliged to declare war on Finland, although it was a very token effort that involved little more than the RAF dropping a few bombs off the coast of Turku.[34]

At first the Continuation War went precisely according to plan. The Finns declared war on 25 June 1941, three days after Germany had begun its invasion and the Soviets had mounted bombing raids on several Finnish cities, ports and airfields. They made rapid advances through Karelia and around the shores of Lake Ladoga. By the end of August they had won back all the ground they had lost in the Winter War. They pressed on towards Leningrad (St Petersburg), halting several miles from its outskirts while the Germans piled in for a siege that would last nearly two and a half years.

If the Winter War was the point where the social divisions that had been wrenched open by the civil war meaningfully began to heal, the Continuation War was the fire in which a new sense of national unity was hardened, especially as the tide turned and the exhausted Finnish soldiers were driven back into their own territory. 'Their previous slackness had given way to vigour and a will to fight. The men spoke of nothing except that now it was time to start fighting for real,' Väinö Linna wrote in his war novel *Unknown Soldiers*. '"National defence" just seemed like a self-evident duty as soon as the surface of their own land appeared.'[35]

That summer Finland gingerly extricated itself from its deal with Germany and made peace with the Soviets. Stalin exacted a hefty price. Helsinki had to give up more than a tenth of its pre-war territory, including most of Karelia and the important nickel mines at Petsamo. It was forced to hand Moscow $300 million worth of mostly industrial goods by way of reparations, although the total value was much higher in practice as the Soviets insisted on applying pre-war valuations. The White civil guard, a nationalist paramilitary force, was abolished. The Finnish Communist Party was restored. There was a very real concern that Finland would now become a satellite state of the USSR. Britain was so convinced of an imminent communist takeover that it refused to sell the Finns warplanes, partly for fear that the technology might fall into Soviet hands.[36]

Mannerheim warned the government that he believed the country could not survive the decades ahead as an independent entity. If that was the case, the prime minister Juho Kusti Paasikivi sarcastically replied, then he and his cabinet should simply walk out into the forest and shoot themselves.[37] Speaking to an American journalist in April 1945, Paasikivi struck a positively Churchillian pose:

> We will shoot from behind every stone and tree. We will go on shooting for fifty years. We are not Czechs. We are not Dutchmen. We will fight tooth and nail, behind every rock and over the ice of every lake. I am old, but others will carry on.[38]

A Free Country, But One Must Not Offend Russia

The belligerent rhetoric was pure bluster. What actually emerged was a survival strategy of realpolitik that established the fundamental dynamics of Finnish politics to the present day. The historian Henrik Meinander has argued that the chief lesson the country drew from the Winter War was that

> no western power was prepared to bleed for Finland if the conflict was about something as insignificant as the Finns' independence and continued national existence. Consequently, the country's national security policy has ever since been guided by a level-headed aim to ally itself or at least keep on good terms with the great powers of the Baltic sea region.[39]

Today that means NATO. For the half-century after 1944, however, it meant the Soviet Union.

Led by Paasikivi and Urho Kekkonen, a hard-drinking hunting companion of Brezhnev who became the dominant figure in postwar Finland, the country's elite decided that the only viable course was to persuade Moscow that their country could never again pose a security threat. Instead it would become a self-imposed geopolitical twilight zone between the eastern and western blocs.

In practice this entailed a raft of uncomfortable concessions: a solemn and quite Soviet-flavoured declaration of neutrality; an abstention from the US-funded Marshall Plan for the reconstruction of western Europe; and a purge of 'anti-democratic' officials directed by the communists. Crucially, though, Finland managed to preserve a degree of room for manoeuvre. The thoroughly unpopular Finnish Communist Party was eventually locked out of power. Soviet overtures to station troops in Finland under the pretext of 'mutual defence' were politely but effectively fended off with a spot of cunning sauna diplomacy. Over the following decades, the country was able to tentatively integrate itself into the new global order and even to strike trade deals with its western neighbours, including the forerunner of the EU.

The awkward accommodation pervaded almost every level of Finnish life. Each official of any significance was assigned a 'house Russian', a KGB officer to whom they had to deliver regular intelligence briefings. The press often pulled its punches on criticism of the USSR. Publishers and film distributors frequently avoided works that might upset Moscow, such as Solzhenitsyn's *The Gulag Archipelago* and the cinema adaptation of his novella *One Day in the Life of Ivan Denisovich*.[40]

Households had to record every visitor in a 'housebook' that was to be submitted to the nearest police station once a year. As usual, Nokia was a bellwether of the national mood. The conglomerate benefitted handsomely from these arrangements, building telecoms links for Soviet natural gas pipelines and the scoreboard at the Lenin stadium in Moscow. In the 1980s it may even have broken Ronald Reagan's embargo on electronics exports to the Soviet Union. 'Finland is a free country,' the Nokia chief executive Björn Westerlund said in the 1970s, 'but one must not offend Russia.'[41]

Critics in the West derided this process as 'Finlandisation'. The implication was that the Finns had unnecessarily bent over backwards to please the Soviets, to the point of abject subjugation. It is understandable that Finnish commentators have tended until quite recently to reject this line of reasoning, arguing that it strips their country of agency and its positions of nuance. Today, though, it is increasingly clear that Finland's leaders did take things further than they needed to, and that this often suited them quite nicely.

This is more than just a purely historical debate. Pekka Virkki, the author of a book called *Jälkisuomettumisen ruumiinavaus* (The Autopsy of Post-Finlandisation), makes the case that something of this excessively deferential approach to Moscow – and the shady mutual back-scratching that went on beneath it – lingered on long after the break-up of the USSR in 1991 and Finland's entry into the EU in 1995.

'Keeping these connections to Soviet intelligence and [communist] East German intelligence was part of the Finnish state identity,' Virkki says.

> Our new allies in NATO have a right to know what happened, because it still affects us . . . It became more or less an instrument of domestic corruption and certain domestic power structures that kept Finland in a somewhat liminal position geopolitically, but also mentally. We weren't ready to identify as a western country in a full sense until now.

Alpo Rusi, a veteran diplomat who has led the campaign for a historical reckoning with the 'Finlandisation' period, says he has documentary evidence that the KGB asked Mauno Koivisto, Finland's president, to put 'bumps in the road' to the Baltic states' independence in 1989. 'They have tried to keep the files closed but now, when the situation has changed and Finland is a member of NATO, our duty is to open the files in order to understand the depth of Finlandisation,' Rusi says. 'It was not a joke.'

Since then Finland's leaders have often taken a notably conciliatory line towards their Russian counterparts, including Vladimir Putin. For more than thirty years the prevailing idea was to cast Helsinki as a diplomatic bridge to Moscow, while remaining on good neighbourly terms with a country that was still Finland's biggest trade partner. This was a 'doubletalk' strategy based on circumspection rather than trust. It could also be quite a lucrative business. Esko Aho, Finland's prime minister from 1991 to 1995, later took a position on the board of Russia's largest bank, which is mostly owned by the state.[42] Paavo Lipponen, Aho's successor from 1995 to 2003, subsequently became a highly paid advisor to the Russian-backed Nord Stream 1 and 2 gas pipeline projects.[43] It was not until after the full-scale Russian invasion of Ukraine in 2022 that Aho resigned his position at the bank and Lipponen's consultancy stopped working with Nord Stream.[44]

A more intriguing figure is Tarja Halonen, the hugely popular president from 2000 to 2012. Halonen prided herself on maintaining 'excellent' relations with Putin, whom she met in person up to four times a year.[45] In the process she frequently upset the Baltic states. In 2001 she pointedly declined to endorse their accession into NATO, arguing that Europe had to take account of Russian security interests. 'We know Russia better than anyone else [in the West] does,' she said, 'from numerous wars and political conflicts, but also from the longest phase of peaceful coexistence and close cooperation in our history.'[46] Rather than financial gain, Halonen appears to have been motivated by sincere conviction and the clearly justified belief that it was what most Finnish voters wanted.[47]

'I personally think that we had a certain kind of hubris here in Finland that was not dissimilar to Germany's, in a sense, although it was based on different premises,' says Minna Ålander, a research fellow at the Finnish institute of international affairs. 'We thought we had found the best way to deal with Russia. And I have to say: for the longest time it did kind of work for Finland.'

A certain measure of this ambivalence lingered on right up to the full-scale Russian invasion of Ukraine. I first visited Helsinki at the end of November 2021, when an opportunity came up to interview Sanna Marin, the prime minister, alongside two other British journalists. Russia had already massed 100,000 troops along the Ukrainian border and was establishing military bases inside the Arctic Circle, while Belarus was driving migrants across its frontiers.

Marin welcomed us into Kesäranta, the attractive wooden villa by the shore of the Baltic that serves as the premier's official residence. She was animated enough when she talked about her country's successes in women's rights, education, welfare and the environment. On the security situation, however, she was stonily guarded. There was not a trace of her imminent self-reinvention as the hawkish champion of Russia's western neighbours. No, she said, there was no sign of trouble on the Finnish-Russian border (her government would later start fencing large portions of it off). No, there was currently no case for Finland to join NATO. The key thing, she said, was to talk 'proactively' to the Russians.

Sauli Niinistö, the president, was more interesting. In a sense, he said, the times were becoming more dangerous than they had been during the Cold War, and the world needed a revival of the 'spirit of Helsinki', the Finland-brokered deal that stabilised the West's relations with the Soviet Union in the middle of the 1970s.[48] Niinistö was evidently wary of Russia and more open to the prospect of NATO membership than Marin.

I was particularly curious to hear what he had learned from meeting the Russian president at least a dozen times, including at a Putin–Trump summit that he had hosted in Helsinki in 2018. By way of response, Niinistö trotted out an old Finnish proverb that later became his catchphrase on the subject: 'A Cossack takes everything which is loose.' 'You have to be firm with your position,' he said. 'If you make clear in a very straightforward way that this is what we keep in honour . . . it becomes easier, because the line is recognised by both of you.'

When I asked him how vulnerable he felt his country was to a Russian attack, however, Niinistö laughed. Finland, he pointed out, could field a force of 280,000 soldiers if it called up its trained reserves. It had more artillery than any other EU country and nearly as many tanks as the biggest armed forces in the bloc. It was in the middle of buying sixty-four F-35A jet fighters from the US. 'With our own resources we can build a threshold so that anybody trying to come here [and invade] will realise that it will become expensive,' he said.

The Red Carpet

That is the other side of the 'Finlandisation' era. At the same time as modernising its economy and building the apparatus of the welfare state, post-war Finland was also preparing a formidable array of defences. The government set about reconstituting the armed forces, officially in readiness for a potential NATO attack via Norway or Sweden. By early 1949 there was a proposal to create a 174,000-strong rapid deployment force and another 229,000 reservists who could be called up in wartime.[49] The Finns resorted to subterfuge, drawing up a secret territorial defence plan under the codename *Polttoainehankinta* (Fuel Procurement). The country was to be divided into four geographical areas, each with its own brigade structures and separate corps headquarters for the north and south.[50] Later in the 1950s the high command began explicitly but very quietly considering how these arrangements could be adapted to repel an invasion from the east.[51]

The basic idea, with various tweaks, still exists today. As Niinistö said, the point is not to make Finland impregnable, but to raise the cost of an invasion until it outweighs any possible benefit to the aggressor. The motto was: 'Even the biggest bear will not eat a porcupine.' Ultimately the country was split up into seven defence zones, each theoretically capable of independently resisting an attacker in depth. The regular brigades would provide the backbone, with mobile reserve forces belabouring the invader's flanks and lines of supply and reinforcement.[52]

'We call it the red carpet,' says Pekka Toveri, MP for the National Coalition party and a former general and head of Finnish military intelligence. 'The whole of Finland is covered with forces and if anyone is stupid enough to attack Finland, the deeper they go, the more trouble they are in.' The idea, Toveri continues, is that there is plenty of empty space in the border zones, 'so when the enemy comes, you delay, delay, causing him losses. And then, when he is far enough from his bases, when he has suffered enough losses, well-coordinated counter-attacks destroy him.'

What has changed is that Finland now has long-range weapons that can strike deep into Russia. Soon it will acquire a batch of

American JASSM-ER cruise missiles with a reach of more than 600 miles. 'The main reason why the tactic used to be to let them come into our territory was to let them come within reach of our weapon systems, and the artillery and all that had a maximum range of 30 km,' says Toveri. 'Now we don't need to let the enemy come into our territory. We can start hitting his key systems nodes and vulnerabilities, and create losses before they reach the Finnish border.'

Finland has consistently stuck to these doctrines for decades, even when other states tended to regard them as myopically old-fashioned after the end of the Cold War. While the core strength of the Finnish defence forces consists of only 8,500 regulars and 13,000 conscripts, it can be bolstered by another 250,000 reservists in wartime.[53] A further 900,000 or so trained civilians can be summoned for refresher courses at short notice. 'In Finland it's part of society,' says a retired general. 'Every family has a connection to defence, because their sons and daughters have done the service.'

By one admittedly woolly estimate, the proportion of Finland's population with military training is comparable to that of ancient Sparta.[54] The national service system remains the most comprehensive in mainland Europe, training about 22,000 conscripts, or roughly 70 per cent of each cohort of young men, and another 18,000 reservists a year.[55] The 'Soldier's Mind' programme for conscripts emphasises individual initiative, resilience and self-reliance.[56] 'What we have found out,' the defence minister Jyri Häkämies said in 2007, 'is that the Playstation and Nokia generation of young men and women make excellent soldiers when given proper training and equipment.'[57]

Yanking Out the Syringe

As early as the 1960s Finland began laying down further layers of security throughout its society. Under the presidency of Urho Kekkonen, it set out a list of priorities that included buttressing national resolve, planning for a war economy and ensuring that it had sufficient reserves to continue functioning even if the country were completely cut off from the outside world, with Switzerland as a model.

It set up a planning board for psychological defence, drawing on British Second World War-era thinking about how to inoculate the population against propaganda. In 1960 the National Defence Council also instructed the War College in Helsinki to start providing three-and-a-half-week courses on the rudiments of national defence to people in public life such as politicians, journalists, civil servants and business leaders.[58] Today these include detailed role-playing games where the participants take the places of Finland's leaders and attempt to pilot the nation through a crisis. 'There's a two-year waiting list if you want to take part,' says one figure who used to organise the courses. 'If you get there, it's the highest status. Everyone wants to have the symbol to pin on their lapel.'

There are detailed and constantly revised plans to evacuate residents from Lappeenranta and other towns and cities near the Russian border in an emergency.[59] Under a programme that was introduced in the 1950s, Finland has 50,500 bomb shelters with enough space for 4.8 million people.[60] More recently the country has been testing its preparations for a 'war economy' through measures such as ordering textile factories to switch to producing bulletproof jackets or establishing a national facility for manufacturing explosives, which are scarce across Europe.[61] 'Now every country should send the defence industry a crystal-clear message that we are returning to the Cold War *modus operandi* in a certain sense,' said Antti Häkkänen, the defence minister. 'It's about a permanent increase in the threat level.'[62]

Since the end of the Cold War the focus has also broadened to preparedness for other kinds of crisis, such as natural disasters, pandemics, grid outages or mass influxes of immigration. The 2017 'security strategy for society' defines a clear division of labour for government, businesses, NGOs and individual citizens to contribute to keeping the show on the road in an emergency.[63] 'This is the concept of total security. It's not just focusing on the army or the military: you want to make sure that society is resilient to all kinds of shocks,' says Niku Määttänen, professor of macroeconomics at Helsinki University. 'We have all sorts of key resources stored here across the country, so that we can sustain our economy or [to] help us overcome a very difficult winter or something like that . . . We also have legislation that in times of crisis allows the state to interfere very strongly in the private sector.'

This philosophy extends to the education system. Finland was the first country in Europe to introduce compulsory media literacy classes in schools, building on decades of experience. 'It starts from kindergarten, and then it's part of the official curriculum, first of all to learn how to use media and how to differentiate advertising from other media content,' says Anneli Ahonen, a Finnish expert on information warfare. 'Then in recent years concepts like fake news and disinformation were added there as well. I had it as a kid – I was born in 1981 – and now my kids have had it too, right from first grade.'

Jyri Raitasalo, a security policy lecturer at the Finnish National Defence University, has argued that a combination of strong education, a society with high levels of trust and cohesion, and an ingrained scepticism of Russian narratives mean that the Kremlin's disinformation campaigns have had 'practically zero effect' in Finland.[64]

There is another scenario that exercises the minds of Finland's policymakers. The country takes the green transition very seriously. It aims to hit net zero by 2035, earlier than any other industrialised nation. But it also requires vast amounts of electricity relative to the size of its population, largely because of the cold climate. In 2023 the average Finn used 14.8 megawatt-hours of power, twice as much as the average person in France or Germany and even a little more than the average American.[65] Most of the sources of this electricity are comparatively clean: hydropower, nuclear, biomass, a rapidly expanding wind sector, and imports from Sweden (although, curiously, Finland still burns more peat than any other EU member state).[66] The country aims to generate significantly more electricity than it consumes by the end of the decade. On the face of it, then, Finland does not have much of an energy security problem.

On closer examination, though, it is by no means as insulated from geopolitics as it might appear. Before February 2022, it relied on Russian imports for about 40 per cent of its total energy consumption, a higher proportion than Germany or Latvia. This included 32 per cent of its coal, 38 per cent of its enriched uranium, 91 per cent of its oil and petroleum products, and 100 per cent of its natural gas.[67]

It had even signed a contract with Rosatom, the Russian state-owned nuclear energy conglomerate, to build a new atomic reactor at Hanhikivi, near the apex of the gulf of Bothnia.[68] Since the full-scale invasion it has quietly but almost entirely yanked out the 'hypodermic syringe' of energy dependency on Moscow. The Rosatom deal has been scrapped. Kai Mykkänen, the environment and climate minister, says Finland has very nearly finished securing alternative sources of nuclear fuel. 'I must say we were surprised ourselves by how easily we could in the end actually replace Russian energy with other sources,' he says.

But the shock was a cautionary one. The shift towards electrification and green energy involves a whole new set of potential strategic chokeholds. From aluminium to yttrium, the minerals Europe requires are overwhelmingly mined and processed elsewhere in the world. China already controls 94 per cent of the global market for gallium, 91 per cent for magnesium and 77 per cent for silicon, as well as 87 per cent of the planet's rare-earth refining capacity. It also increasingly dominates green manufacturing, from photovoltaic cells and wind turbine components to lithium-ion batteries and cheap electric vehicles. Experts worry about the emergence of a Beijing-led 'organisation of mineral-exporting countries' (OMEC) with enough leverage to paralyse western economies every bit as effectively as the Saudi-led OPEC alliance did in the 1973 oil crisis.[69]

Finland was alive to the threat much earlier than most of its European peers. 'We have to see that the world is changing, and not in a good way. We are seeing that with the United States, China, Russia, there are more geopolitical tensions there,' Sanna Marin told me in late 2021. 'So we should have our own capacity to produce the necessities that we will need in the future, and for our societies today ... If you are dependent, then you are fragile.' As a result, the country has embarked on a drive to establish a grip of its own over critical raw materials and especially over the essential ingredients for batteries, such as copper, nickel, lithium, cobalt and vanadium. It has poured billions of euros into its mines and set up dozens of facilities for refining, processing and recycling battery chemicals.[70]

Finland is also beginning to move into the production of rare-earth metals. In 2023 prospectors discovered the world's largest deposit of carbonatite, a kind of rock that tends to be rich in strategic minerals, at the Sokli mining reserve in Lapland.[71] Months later, the country became the first in the EU to resume the extraction of its own uranium, which had previously been discarded as an unwanted by-product at the giant Talvivaara nickel mine in central Finland.[72] 'We are ourselves producing many of the minerals we need,' says Mykkänen. 'We would be able to actually supply a large share of our own nuclear production if needed. So I would be very surprised if the green transition would be stopped because of some mineral trade war.'

If You Hit Helsinki, We Can Hit Moscow

Finland's leap into NATO in 2022, prompted by the Russian attack on Ukraine, was both a revolution and an incremental step. In purely political terms, it was an extraordinary volte-face. The country had formally kept open a 'NATO option' to join the alliance since 2004. But most Finnish voters had no desire to see it exercised. The majority of politicians worried about getting their country on the hook for a potential conflict with Russia over the Baltic states.

Even in the months before the full-scale invasion, barely 25 per cent of the electorate were in favour of NATO accession.[73] In 2017 one survey found that 45 per cent of Finns believed NATO membership would actually harm their country's security.[74] 'They didn't want to be obliged to come and defend the Baltic countries,' says one former senior figure in the Finnish military. 'I burned my fingers so many times on NATO topics in Finland that I can't even count them.'

The situation changed drastically in the days after the first Russian missiles fell on Kyiv. 'Finland is a relatively small country, albeit it has one of the largest militaries in Europe. So any time there's a security threat, it's potentially existential,' says Alexander Stubb (we spoke before the former prime minister was elected president).

> That threat is close to home, basically an hour and a half's flight from Helsinki to Kyiv, and people reacted. I think for Finland, foreign policy has never been ideological in the same way that it has been for Sweden. Swedish neutrality was ideological for 200

years. We were never neutral out of ideology. It was out of necessity. So basically we've been able to switch tack or change direction at every hinge of history that has been significant for us.

The striking thing was not just that a clear majority of Finns suddenly wanted to get into NATO: it was that even more were prepared to change their minds if the government came out and told them it was a good idea.[75] It was a stirring case study in how public and elite opinion can reinforce each other. The voters wanted leadership and they got it. 'The Finns are a very security-oriented people. They're not afraid of the neighbour, but of course if some major changes are happening in Russia, people follow those very carefully,' says Pekka Haavisto, who oversaw the NATO accession process as foreign minister.

> I have to say it was a unique political situation in spring '22 when I . . . went to the parliament and discussed the situation with the parliamentary groups . . . At the beginning of the meetings, people had one opinion and by the end of the meeting they had another.

Finland applied for membership in May 2022 and was admitted to the club in April 2023. Minna Ålander recalls:

> My mother used to be this kind of typical left-wing sceptic of the EU and she was definitely not pro-NATO until December 2021. But when Putin said that we can't join NATO, that was the red line for many people, and it was so funny: my mum was there drinking champagne on April 4 [the accession date]. I asked her: 'Mother, since when are you such an ardent supporter of NATO?' And she said: 'Since Putin said we can't join, of course.'

What the German chancellor Olaf Scholz called the *Zeitenwende*, the shift with the changing times, really did happen in Finland. The country sent significant quantities of armaments into Ukraine, the first time it had dispatched weapons into an active warzone. It closed the border with Russia indefinitely after an increase in migrant crossings over the winter of 2023/4. Unlike in many other European countries, the government and the defence industry invested €120 million in doubling production of artillery shells.[76] Finland announced a plan to open another 300 shooting ranges to encourage more people to train with firearms.[77]

But the headlines about a lurch away from neutrality were a touch overdone. In reality, Finland had been working with NATO since the mid-1990s, stepping up its programme of joint exercises after the Russian occupation of Crimea in 2014. In the short term the biggest differences were of scope rather than kind: a fuller calendar of joint wargames, NATO reconnaissance flights through Finnish airspace, and real-time intelligence sharing, especially over the eastern Baltic.[78]

In the longer run, though, NATO accession will be a stiff adjustment, comparable to the period when Finland joined the EU in 1995. It is one thing to plan for a re-run of the Winter War in defence of your own country; it is quite another to be a fulcrum of the strongest military alliance in history. 'We are geopolitically one of the most important frontline states in Europe,' Alexander Stubb said on the presidential campaign trail in late 2023. 'Our feet are in the Baltic and our head is in the Arctic.'[79]

To the south, Finland will be a logistical hub and source of air and naval defence for the Baltic states, where it is likely to station a few hundred soldiers on rotation. It will also merge its anti-ship missile batteries with Estonia's, turning the Gulf of Finland into a potentially impassable gauntlet for the Russian Baltic fleet.[80]

To the east, its 830-mile land border with Russia is more of an asset than a liability for NATO. The single stretch of railway linking St Petersburg to the far north-western Russian military bases in Murmansk and the Kola peninsula suddenly looks very vulnerable to a missile strike.[81] And to the north, Finland will be a buffer against any attempt to attack the Norwegian ports the alliance needs to secure its Atlantic sea lanes in the event of a large-scale war. 'Today,' as a pair of Finnish security researchers put it, 'the defence of the north Atlantic starts from northern Finland.'[82] 'It's a huge change,' says Kai Sauer, a senior foreign ministry official.

> The map of the Baltic sea will be redrawn with the accession of Finland and Sweden, and of course it puts NATO in a better

position to defend itself . . . Our goal has been and will be to maintain stability in our region. We want to be a security provider instead of a security consumer.

That is only the beginning. There are more fundamental questions of identity to be answered, from autonomy of command to what it means to 'win' a war when you are no longer solely focused on grinding down the enemy within your own territory. Finland is now bound up in the alliance's entire spectrum of geopolitical anxieties, from China and Moldova to central Africa and the Red sea.

For the first time, its establishment is even having to think seriously about nuclear weapons and whether they might one day be stationed on Finnish soil. 'NATO has the capabilities that if you harm Finland, we can harm you directly and we can do similar things in response: if you hit Helsinki, then we can hit Moscow,' says Pekka Haavisto. 'It's a big threat, of course, in this situation. And this of course changes our thinking. Maybe not everybody has understood it yet. But this definitely changes with our NATO membership.'[83]

Roosevelt Was an Amateur

One of the reasons Finland gets such glowing coverage in the international press is that it polishes its image with great assiduity. The government and the corporate lobby frequently invite foreign journalists to tour state-of-the-art factories, interview political and business leaders, and spend their evenings chewing elk steaks and stewing in saunas. By the standards of spin, it is all fairly harmless: they ask for nothing more than a fair hearing. But cumulatively it does impart a certain roseate tint to the spectacles.

In the hope of getting a more rounded impression of modern Finland, I decided to visit Oulu, a city near the northernmost tip of the Baltic. As the plane dropped below the clouds, I was momentarily confused by a flat expanse of glaring and almost featureless white, punctuated only by slashes of gunmetal-grey and the occasional house or wind turbine. It took me a few seconds to realise that this was the sea, locked beneath a layer of ice for the past six months. It was late

March but in Oulu, barely 60 miles south of the Arctic circle, the snow still lay thick on the gridded streets. A few days before the 2023 parliamentary election, the political parties had set up little wooden cabins in one of the central squares. The prevailing mood was mildly mutinous. Oulu is a traditionally right-of-centre city where Sanna Marin and her Social Democratic party tend to get short shrift.

This is quite a different version of Finland to the sparkly modernity of the south. Not much more than a century ago, peasants would still float logs and barrels of tar down the rivers of the Ostrobothnian interior to the sawmills and warehouses of Oulu, sometimes from regions so remote that the journey took as long as two years.[84] At the end of the eighteenth century this 'Stockholm' tar became an indispensable resource for the British Royal Navy, which repaid the favour by burning down much of the port in 1854 during the Crimean War. There has always been a streak of wildness to this part of the country, which was once famed for its gangs of knife-wielding and heavy-drinking bandits, known as *Puukkojunkkarit*.

The local political scene is still fairly volatile. The Finns party is strong here, in part because of its robust response to a 2018 scandal where it transpired that a group of asylum seekers and refugees had been grooming and sexually abusing young girls in Oulu. A few months after the 2023 election, the party sacked one of its city councillors because she had written a post on Facebook about threatening to run over antisocial men from 'underdeveloped' nations.[85] It is a reminder that despite Finland's reputation as a social democratic utopia, large parts of its society remain quite strikingly small-C conservative, there is a sizeable minority of outright reactionaries and right-wing extremism is not uncommon.

In June 2024 two people of 'foreign background' were stabbed in separate and apparently racist attacks at one of Oulu's main shopping centres.[86] In 2018 an EU report found 63 per cent of black people in the country had experienced racial harassment, triple the level in the UK and the highest proportion in any of the twelve countries surveyed.[87] A rowdy digital message board called Ylilauta, which functions as a kind of Finnish-language version of 4chan and is estimated to account for 96 per cent of the country's online hate speech, claims to have 2.5 million regular active users.[88] Shortly before the final round of the 2024 presidential election, another poll suggested that a third of voters were reluctant to support Pekka Haavisto because he was in a civil partnership with a man from Ecuador.[89]

Traditionally Oulu's great strength was high-tech telecoms. The city's main university has one of the best electronic engineering faculties in the Nordic region, generously lubricated with private funding. In its heyday, Nokia built some of its biggest facilities here, forming the core of an ecosystem that sustained 15,000 IT jobs in a boom known as the 'Oulu miracle'. The first phone call on the GSM system, the original digital backbone of the mobile phone, happened here in 1991, at a time when Finns still referred to the handsets as 'gorbas' because Gorbachev had showcased the initial prototype.[90]

When Nokia stumbled in 2009, however, it took 2,000 of those technology jobs with it.[91] The local unemployment rate hit 16 per cent, twice the national average. Jussi Leponiemi, head of ICT at Business Oulu, a state agency that notionally cheerleads for the private sector, is downbeat. Skilled workers and capital are in short supply, he says. Start-ups are struggling to expand. A number of entrepreneurs have simply moved away, grumbling that the generous welfare system makes it too hard to fill vacancies. 'I think that we are on the edge of our social security system being maybe even too good,' Leponiemi says.

This makes Oulu's economic resilience all the more striking. A leading centre for research on 6G, the next generation of internet infrastructure, it is home to a cluster of more than 600 medical technology companies. The local Nokia 5G base station manufacturing plant, where knee-high robots trundle around the aisles, has been singled out by the World Economic Forum as a paradigm of the 'factory of the future'.[92] Increasingly Oulu is also a focal point for military and dual-use technology. In 2024 NATO's DIANA innovation agency struck a deal to use Oulu as a test bed for the battlefield communications of the future.[93]

One of the most promising firms in this field is Bittium, which began life as a start-up in a garage, building computer mice for the early incarnations of the internet. These days it makes all kinds of networked gadgets, from wireless electrocardiogram machines and sleep apnoea diagnosis kits to battlefield comms links and the Tough

Mobile 2, an ultra-secure handset backed by encrypted servers and data connections. The executives are too discreet to say anything about who buys the smartphones but the clients are thought to include world leaders, intelligence agencies and armed forces. 'It's kind of a James Bond device that destroys its contents if someone tries to mechanically open it,' says Karoliina Malmi, Bittium's vice-president for communications. 'Nowadays it's very, very clear that there's demand for these kinds of European manufactured products with European heritage, where you can be sure that you have full control of the product from the development phase to the final assembly and beyond, and there's no dependencies on Asia and so forth.'

Over the past couple of years, Finland's geopolitical reawakening has brought about something that almost resembles a delayed closure of intergenerational trauma. This phenomenon is especially noticeable among my fellow millennials, who came of age in a fundamentally secure environment where their older relatives' war stories once seemed quaint and passé. The security researcher Minna Ålander says she and her friends used to laugh at older Finns' fixation on the Winter War and how *Helsingin Sanomat* would publish an entire supplement about it every month. 'It seemed so excessive and a bit silly. But then last year [2022], the experience for my generation was very powerful, like "Oh my God, all of this had a point to it. Our parents were on to something,"' she says.

> I'm only just realising myself how much we are conditioned in Finland in the spirit of the Winter War . . . I think it really messed up the Finnish relationship with Russia big time that we were invaded twice and at the end of it we had to cede territory and pay reparations, and we were forced into this friendship treaty [with the Soviet Union]. People didn't even get any time to grieve. We were immediately forced into this really twisted and weird relationship with the Soviet Union, where everyone was actually still really sore from the war experience.

What strikes me most of all in Oulu is that these old instincts – the drive for self-reliance, the flexibility in moments of crisis, the stoical ability to ride out periods of hardship, the will to squeeze the most out of limited resources, the anticipation of dangers that larger, more complacent countries either cannot or will not take seriously – are now coming back to the fore. They are also turning out to be some of the cardinal virtues of the 2020s. Finland is equipped with a hereditary toolkit for times like these. Juho Kusti Paasikivi, who as prime minister and president guided the country out of the Second World War, once said it was far harder to keep a small state alive than to keep a big one ticking over. 'What kind of people [the great powers] have had by way of world politics . . . Baldwin, Chamberlain, Roosevelt, Attlee, Bevin: ignorant, naive, easily cheated,' he said. 'Do they know history? No. Do they know geography? Do they know foreign languages? No . . . If our fates as small nations would be directed by such amateurs, we would have perished long ago.'[94]

3

The Witch and the Sage

Latvia Rebuilds a Divided Nation

Having come home, the Man of the World takes off his grey great coat, takes off his boots caked with blood and mud, washes his hands and face, looks at himself, winces, and suddenly becomes aware of a horrifying question: Who am I?

Pēteris Ķikuts, 1930[1]

In a park near the left bank of the Daugava river, a pair of track-mounted hydraulic drills are nibbling away at a mess of concrete whose twisted steel reinforcing rods poke out like the rib cage of a stricken leviathan. Half a dozen police cars are stationed at the corners of the surrounding fence, keeping watch for any signs of protest.

Until 25 August 2022, this part of western Riga's skyline was dominated by a 259-foot Soviet victory column, erected in the mid-1980s to honour the Red Army soldiers who had driven Nazi Germany's forces out of Latvia towards the end of the Second World War. It loomed over half the city, drawing up to 200,000 of its Russian-speaking residents each 9 May to commemorate the triumph of the Soviet Union. To many ethnic Latvians, though, it was simply the 'rapists'' or the 'occupiers'' monument, an inescapable reminder of the oppression their people had suffered under nearly fifty years of communist rule.[2]

I have been mesmerised by the videos of its demolition: a moment of stillness before the base starts to crack, then a tilt that begins achingly slowly and abruptly gathers speed as the column crumbles and falls, throwing up two vast clouds of dust. Now it is just a blank space.

Plenty of memorials have been dismantled in the former Soviet sphere since 1989, but this one is different, and not only because of its scale and the suddenness of its demise. For one thing, it is part of a systematic campaign by the Latvian state to erase almost every visible trace of communist oppression from its landscape. Since 2022 more than 300 Soviet plaques and memorials have been taken down across the country. Pushkin's statue has been removed from another park in the capital. A bust of Mstislav Keldysh, the Riga-born Russian engineer who worked on the USSR's first cruise missiles and spacecraft, has been dismantled and stored in a warehouse. Streets named after other classic Russian writers such as Lomonosov, Turgenev and even Gogol – a proud Ukrainian and a jagged critic of nineteenth-century Russian society – have been rebranded.[3]

The chief reason why the fall of the victory monument in Riga matters, though, is its totemic significance for the ethnic Russians who make up 24.5 per cent of Latvia's population, and the wider pool of native Russian speakers, who account for 35 per cent of the country's residents, including ethnic Ukrainians and Belarusians.[4] This large but disparate community has been in a state of turmoil since the second Russian invasion of Ukraine in February 2022, which turbocharged a programme of assimilation that had already been going for more than thirty years.

Most Russian state-sponsored television channels have been banned.[5] A new law was passed that punishes the declaration of support for the war with the revocation of residency permits and strips Latvian citizenship from Putin supporters with dual nationality.[6] The local Orthodox church, which had been part of the Moscow patriarchate for nearly two centuries, was ordered by the Saeima, the Latvian parliament, to break away because of Patriarch Kirill's virulently pro-Kremlin rhetoric.[7] The deadline for eradicating school classes taught in the Russian language was brought forward to 2025, prompting a rebuke from the United Nations.[8] About 20,000 Russian citizens must pass a Latvian language exam or have their residency permits withdrawn.[9]

But it was the erasure of the Soviet victory column that hurt the most. Mārtiņš Kaprāns, a communication scientist at the University of Latvia who has spent a decade studying the country's Russian minority, said the demolition of this 'centrepiece of Russophone identity' had been felt as an act of 'symbolic violence'.[10] That is, if anything, putting it mildly. A survey found 76 per cent of Russian speakers in Latvia opposed the demolition.[11]

THE WITCH AND THE SAGE

Ever since Latvia declared its independence from the USSR in 1990, the Russians who stayed behind have been depicted as fifth columnists-in-waiting, saturated with Kremlin propaganda and ready to rise up in revolt the moment Moscow gives the word. These anxieties have intensified since Latvia joined NATO in 2004 and the Putin regime invaded Georgia in 2008, prompting speculation that these ethnic tensions could act as the spark for an intercontinental nuclear war.

In 2016 the BBC imagined precisely this scenario in a documentary called *World War Three: Inside the War Room*. It simulated an uprising of the majority Russian-speaking population of Daugavpils, the country's second city, which led to a successful Russian military intervention and ultimately to the disintegration of NATO.[12] Two years after that ARTE, a Franco-German broadcaster, aired a lurid programme with the title *Kulturkampf in Lettland* (Culture War in Latvia), in which members of the Russian minority accused the Latvian state and various right-wing Latvian groups of oppressing them in line with the 'mad ideas of the Nazis'. Its factual errors and inflammatory content were denounced by the Latvian embassy in Berlin.[13]

These two caricatures go hand in hand: a radicalised and largely Kremlin-supporting minority of Russian speakers whose identity is being ruthlessly crushed by the ethnonationalist Latvian majority. Both have been staples of Russian propaganda since the 1990s and have been widely and uncritically adopted by people in the West. This chapter will argue that neither is accurate. The reality is less garish but more interesting. The war in Ukraine is catalysing a process of nation-building that stretches back 150 years, accelerating it at such a speed that you can almost watch it unfold in real time. The results are often messy. But Latvia is rapidly cohering in a way that challenges outsiders' assumptions about how integration works, how a country can live with a divided society, and the place of nationalism in twenty-first-century Europe. 'Younger Russian people already learn Latvian,' says Evika Siliņa, the Latvian prime minister.

> They are going to Latvian schools and they are integrating very well into our labour market . . . I believe we already have the fruits

of success with integration, because the younger generation can choose: either they want to be with the Russians, or they want to be part of Europe. And they mostly want to be part of Europe.

Two numbers are crucial for grasping the ethnolinguistic divide at the centre of Latvia's politics: twenty-two and fifty-two. Twenty-two is the number of years for which Latvia had been an independent state before it was forcibly subsumed into the Soviet Union: barely a generation. Fifty-two is the percentage of the population who spoke Latvian as their first language by the final census of the Soviet era, in 1989. The Latvians were on the brink of becoming a minority within their own country.

All three of the Baltic states have required great reserves of tenacity, ingenuity and willpower to cement their independence and anchor themselves in the West since 1990. But Latvia, with the largest number of Russian speakers both in absolute terms and relative to its population, has faced arguably the greatest obstacles. To its north, Estonia could draw on enduring cultural and linguistic ties to neighbouring Finland; to the south, Lithuania had a more fraught but similarly close relationship with Poland. Latvia had no comparable patron apart from Sweden, which functioned in the 1990s as an absent-minded and periodically selfish fairy godmother. It also had the deepest historical connection to Moscow, having furnished the early Communist Party of the Soviet Union with some of its leading political figures and the Red Army with some of its most formidable units.

Latvia can only be properly understood through the nationality question, but the reverse is also true. The question has deep roots in the history of the Latvian nation itself, together with its cherished cultural traditions and the literature and song in which they are embedded. It is not for nothing that the path to independence is known as the 'singing revolution': poetry and politics are inextricably linked in Latvia. This is at its heart a story of myths, in all their subtle power.

The Hero With the Furry Ears

One of Latvia's most enduringly powerful myths is the epic poem *Lāčplēsis* (The Bear-Slayer), which was published in 1888, as the national awakening began to gather serious momentum. At this point the Latvian people had been under Russian imperial rule since 1710 and dominated by a Baltic German landowning class since the thirteenth century. Just as Finland had the *Kalevala* and Estonia had *Kalevipoeg*, Andrejs Pumpurs, an ardent Latvian nationalist and former officer in the Russian army, wanted to give his compatriots a single work of literature that would synthesise their spirit, traditions and folklore. The result was a strange but engaging chimaera of paganism and Christianity, in which the old gods lay claim to the true message of Christ against a lively backdrop of witches feasting on little children's limbs, demons wearing caps of human fingernails, and a store of lost ancient knowledge that must be recovered from a castle beneath a lake.

Lāčplēsis, the poem's eponymous hero, is a bear–human hybrid who earned his name by tearing a bear apart in hand-to-paw combat. His bear ears are a source of freakish strength.[14] He is charged by the gods with fending off an invasion of German crusaders, 'the bearers of the faith, whom all think pure', who are in thrall to a warped version of Christianity but convinced of their righteous cause – a metaphor that Latvians would apply to the Baltic Germans, the Russian empire and the Soviet occupiers alike. Lāčplēsis is, the narrator repeatedly stresses from the beginning of the poem, doomed to fail, but in his failure he will one day inspire his compatriots to rise up and win their liberty:

> Do not grieve, oh countrymen, but know,
> remembering the deeds of men of yore,
> as ages pass the people's strength will grow,
> and battles won will free our race once more.[15]

On his quest Lāčplēsis encounters two particularly memorable adversaries. Spīdola, a witch, initially seduces him with a love potion and tries to drown him in a pit full of man-eating fiends, but ultimately repents and reneges on her deal with the Devil. Kangars, a duplicitous Latvian shaman, conspires with the Germans and ultimately reveals to them that Lāčplēsis can be defeated if his magical bear-ears are lopped off, rendering him as powerless as Samson without his hair. Like the twisted faith of the German knights, both figures have become timeless fixtures in Latvia's national mythology.

The epic reaches its climax with a duel between Lāčplēsis and the Germans' champion fighter, the Black Knight, who duly slices off the hero's ears. In one final display of courage, however, Lāčplēsis rugby-tackles the Black Knight off the Staburags cliff and into the waters of the Daugava, where they both drown. 'But still,' the poem concludes,

> the day will come, is sure,
> when he the Black Knight will cast down:
> in Staburags' raging maw,
> his deadly foe alone will drown.
> Then for the folk new times will dawn;
> At last their freedom will be born.[16]

(The literal meaning of the last line is: 'The battle continues and will not end'.)

After the 1917 Russian revolution, Pumpurs posthumously got his wish. The Latvians seized their independence in the chaos at the end of the First World War through a battle royal that sucked in White Russians, German paramilitary Freikorps and Landeswehr units, Poles, Britons, Estonians and the fledgling armed forces of independent Latvia. It was not until early 1920 that the last of the Germans and the Soviets – by now a motley force – were cleared out with support from Estonia, the Royal Navy and Poland. For the first time since 1200, Latvia was fully free.

From then on 11 November became Lāčplēsis Day, marking the anniversary of the Latvian army's reconquest of Riga. A writer suggested that the fallen soldiers had demonstrated the fearless spirit of the Bear-Slayer, and the name stuck.

Bloodlands of the North

The nineteen brief years of the First Republic began in a ruined and empty country. By 1920 Latvia's population had fallen by more than a third, from 2.5 million to just shy of 1.6 million, even after it was bolstered by returning refugees.[17] The polity was fractured: alongside the nationalists were Bolshevik sympathisers, roughly 150,000 Russians, and a rump of disempowered and disaffected Baltic Germans. In 1922 Latvia acquired its first constitution, with a strong parliament, the Saeima, modelled loosely on the Reichstag of the Weimar Republic, and a clause recognising the Latvian nation as one of several nations in the state.

In 1934, however, Kārlis Ulmanis, a former leader of the independence movement, seized power in a bloodless coup, dispensing with parliamentary democracy and curbing dissent through a political police force in concert with the army and the national guard. Five years later, as the USSR fired up its war machine, Ulmanis sought sanctuary in neutrality, hoping to balance Nazi Germany against the Soviet Union and presenting itself as a threat to no one and a prize scarcely worth the bother of conquest. Little help was to be expected from the West. The US was preoccupied with domestic policy, France was concentrating on its own defences and Britain, which had stepped in to protect Latvia during the war of independence, effectively handed the Baltic sea over to Hitler with the Anglo-German naval agreement of 1935.

Like Estonia and Lithuania, Latvia was backed into signing a 'pact of defence and mutual assistance' with Moscow in October 1939, two months into the Second World War. Latvia recognised that this would be tantamount to an annexation and protested. As Moscow massed troops on the borders, however, it gave in. Ulmanis consoled himself with the hope that he could safeguard the structures of the Latvian state long enough for the Germans to show up.[18]

This was a delusion. The Kremlin engineered a supposedly spontaneous 'socialist revolution' and shipped in administrators. After a flagrantly rigged election in July 1940 a hastily convened puppet legislature voted to join the USSR. Ulmanis was deported to Stavropol and died from dysentery two years later at a prison in what is now Turkmenistan. His body has never been found.

So began the 'horrible year', eleven months of terror that have left a deeper and more enduring scar in Latvia's memory than several far bloodier eras of occupation and violence. The banks, the big industrial firms and any large private houses were confiscated. The armed forces were purged and melded into the Red Army. As in Estonia, as the Wehrmacht advanced from the west in the summer of 1941, the Soviet security forces (NKVD) moved in before dawn on 14 June. Its soldiers dragged 15,000 Latvians from their homes and bundled them on to trains running off to gulags in the Siberian wilderness, where many of them died. In strictly numerical terms it was by no means the gravest blow the Soviets inflicted on Latvia, but it decapitated the country's society. The NKVD took away politicians, priests, civil servants, army and police officers, as well as their wives and 3,000 children, some of whom were separated from their parents.

Eight days later the Germans arrived. Latvia fell within a fortnight. At first the new conquerors were widely greeted as liberators. Contrasting Nazi against Soviet rule, some Latvians still recount mitigating details such as German soldiers paying for food or conducting themselves with a modicum of politeness. There were a few small mercies: Latvians were permitted to display their national symbols again and the Germans made a show of resurrecting several institutions from the First Republic. In reality, though, this occupation was nearly as vicious as the one that had preceded it, and incomparably worse for Latvia's once thriving Jewish population. Virtually all of the country's 70,000 remaining Jews were killed, with help from local collaborators. Viktors Arājs, a Latvian policeman, was put in charge of a unit of roughly a thousand 'patriotic' volunteers, who murdered some 26,000 Jews in Latvia and Belarus. As Operation Barbarossa gave way to Operation Bagration and the Red Army rolled towards Germany in 1944, about 110,000 Latvians were mobilised for the battle of the Baltic.

Once again, Britain and the US stood by, having quietly agreed to give Stalin a free hand in the Baltic states at the Tehran conference in late 1943. In September and October 1944 the Soviets blasted their way towards Riga through the vastly outnumbered German-Latvian defenders, who were forced back into the Courland peninsula, where they held out until the end of the war. More than 100,000 Latvian refugees fled west to Germany, while about 4,000 more escaped across the Baltic to Sweden. By the end of the war, Latvia had once again lost roughly 30 per cent of its population. This time, though, the future held only indefinite darkness.

To Vote For Stalin Will Be Our Fun

As in the other Baltic states, the second Soviet occupation of Latvia left an imprint that shapes the country to this day. There were 14,072 political arrests in 1945 alone. By 1950 at least 140,000 Latvians were incarcerated in Soviet labour camps and prisons.[19] The administration was largely staffed by Soviet apparatchiks who spoke no Latvian. Needing manpower to implement a programme of hasty re-industrialisation, and faced with a badly depleted workforce, they began bringing in workers from Russia, Belarus and Ukraine. Russian was made the official language of the business and public spheres. Riga was turned into a Soviet garrison city.

The agricultural smallholdings that had been the focal point of national pride during the First Republic were gradually ground down through heavy taxes, adverse regulations and propaganda attacks painting the independent farmers as kulaks, but, even so, collectivisation across the Baltic states was progressing too slowly for Moscow's liking. In the early hours of 25 March 1949, the NKVD took 42,000 rural Latvians from their homes and deported them to the gulags. Three-quarters of them were women and children. Over the next nine months 93 per cent of Latvia's farms were merged into collectivised kolkhozes.[20]

One of the few avenues through which Latvians could still express themselves with even a small degree of liberty was poetry, albeit in the form of cryptic verses published under the beady eye of the censor. Print runs, which often amounted to tens of thousands of copies, sometimes sold out within hours of appearing in bookshops.[21] But many stars of Latvia's literary firmament felt obliged to grovel before the authorities in order to preserve their careers and their freedom.

Collectors of Latvia's dainas, a vast corpus of folk poems said in some cases to have been preserved through oral tradition since the Bronze Age, were ordered to shape the material in accordance with Soviet ideology, delivering hymns to life on the kolkhoz or paeans of praise to Stalin.[22]

No figure illustrates this enforced debasement of moral and artistic values better than Aleksandrs Čaks, who in the interwar period had been one of the country's most iconoclastic and influential poets. After 1945, he tried to avoid deportation to the gulag by churning out studiously sycophantic dross about the glories of Soviet heavy industry and the marvels of Riga's recently repaired water distribution network. 'Our happiness will rise with the sun,' he wrote in one poem, 'to vote for Stalin will be our fun.' In the end Čaks managed only five more years of this humiliation before dying of a heart attack in 1950. There is a possibly apocryphal anecdote about a young fan of his poetry confronting him about the supine verses he churned out under Soviet rule. 'Don't you worry, little girl,' he is said to have replied, 'when the times change, so will the poems.'[23]

By the 1970s Latvia was stabler but stagnating. Corruption was rife, basic goods frequently ran out, and a vigorous black market whooshed into the spaces vacated by its official counterpart. The birth rate plunged and levels of crime, abortion, divorce and suicide surged. So did alcoholism, to which a third of the deaths among men between the ages of twenty and fifty were attributed.

The Russification intensified. Street names were changed. The history textbooks were rewritten to imply that the Soviets had moved in at the spontaneous behest of the Latvian people. Midsummer's eve and other folk festivals were prohibited. In order to force the pace of industrialisation, staggering numbers of workers were imported from other parts of the USSR. In the decade from 1945 to 1955 there had been 535,000 arrivals and by 1948 nearly half of the industrial workforce was non-Latvian.[24] Another 1.47 million came between 1961 and 1989, with 330,000 of them settling down permanently. Latvians had made up 80 per cent of the population in 1945. In 1959 the figure was 62 per cent; in 1989 it was 52 per cent, the lowest percentage of native residents in the Baltic states. By 1985 fewer than half of the new books printed in the republic were being published in Latvian.[25]

The Russians were portrayed as the 'older brother' bringing enlightenment to their backwards Latvian siblings and forming an intelligentsia and nomenklatura class. Most led insular lives, segregated in their own communities and military bases. The 1989 census found that only 21 per cent could speak Latvian.[26] The contempt was mutual. Latvians spread stories about Russian officers' wives going to the opera in their nightgowns or washing their hair in toilet bowls.[27]

The Bear-Slayer Returns

On the evening of 23 August 1988, a capacity crowd packed into Riga's main sports arena to await the first chords of a new rock opera. For the hundredth anniversary of the publication of *Lāčplēsis*, the epic had been set to music with a libretto by Māra Zālīte, a writer who had been born in the Krasnoyarsk gulag weeks after the 1941 deportations. To Zālīte, it felt like a moment of existential importance. 'Latvians are presently on the threshold of extinction,' she had told a summit of the national writers' union a few months earlier. 'We are the last generation of intellectuals of a disappearing nation.'[28]

The atmosphere was charged with solemnity and an edge of tension. As the opera's composer Zigmars Liepiņš wrote in the booklet accompanying the premiere, *Lāčplēsis* was 'our seriousness, our history, and our legend. It is our tragedy. It is our hope.'[29] As the hero's final battle with the Black Knight approached, the character of Lielvārdis, Lāčplēsis's foster father, launched into a solo: 'The land of Latvians stands open. It is like a vein, ripped open.' The last lines were sung by the dying Lāčplēsis himself: 'Call me louder, children! I still hear. I still have my language and words. Call me, children! Call me louder!'[30]

They did. In the 1960s the Soviets had built a giant hydroelectric dam at Pļaviņas on the Daugava, flooding the gorge and drowning the Staburags cliff, from which Lāčplēsis and the Black Knight supposedly fell to their deaths, in 20 metres of water. But the epic's nexus of nationalism and poetry was not so easily submerged. As the rock group Dienu Virpulī sang in 1960, squeezing their lyrics into the straitjacket of the daina: 'Leaders speak, and leaders fall. Song is not crushed. The sun rises and the sun sets. Song goes on.'[31]

The story of the 'singing revolution' in the Baltic republics has already been told in chapter one and does not need to be rehearsed in detail. Latvia's trajectory closely shadowed Estonia's. After Mikhail Gorbachev took charge of the USSR in 1985 and introduced the perestroika reforms, Latvians began testing the boundaries to see what they could get away with.

This started with the 1985 all-Latvian song festival in Riga. The Soviet authorities had instructed the censors to strike from the programme a *Lāčplēsis*-based song called *Castle of Light*, about the hidden fortress raised from the depths of a lake by the Bear-Slayer. But the massed ranks of the choir and the audience demanded that it be performed anyway, and it was, with minimal repercussions. As in Estonia, some of the strongest early protests crystallised around environmental issues, primarily the occupying regime's plan to build another vast hydroelectric plant on the Daugava.

In June 1988, after a year of calendar marches marking the anniversaries of the Molotov–Ribbentrop pact and the 1941 mass deportation, another poet, Jānis Peters, pushed for the foundation of a popular front on the Estonian model. Notably, the fledgling movement attracted a fair number of Russians, who shared the Latvians' concerns about the economy, the rule of law and the environment. It has been estimated that by 1990, when the campaign's goals had shifted from greater autonomy within the USSR to full-blown independence, about 40 per cent of 'non-Latvians' had swung behind the cause.[32] Ethnolinguistic differences were largely set aside as the leading activists led the Russians to believe they would enjoy much the same rights as under Soviet rule, including a 'zero option' by which all residents of Latvia would unconditionally receive citizenship.

But not all Russians were so enthusiastic. A number of them joined a pro-Soviet organisation called Interfront under the aegis of Tatjana Ždanoka, an ardent communist who is today one of the most infamous pro-Kremlin leaders of Latvia's Russian community.

The hardliners on the other side, however, proved to be a far more potent force. In 1989 a circle led by Eduards Berklavs, who had been deposed from a high-ranking post in the communist administration for resisting Russification, founded a radical nationalist wing of the pro-autonomy movement, the LNNK. It soon successfully bounced the moderates into pushing for independence and the restoration of the First Republic's constitution. This became one of the decisive dynamics of modern Latvia's politics, with the LNNK and its contemporary descendant, the right-wing National Alliance party, driving an ever-tougher agenda towards the Russian minority from the heart of successive coalition governments.

The Latvian supreme Soviet, the closest thing the republic had to a parliament, formally voted for independence on 4 May 1990, subject to an indefinite transition period. Given Gorbachev's struggles against reactionaries in Moscow and the presence of a sprawling Soviet security apparatus in Latvia, however, this was more of an aspiration than a reality, and de jure independence was suspended. In early January 1991 OMON, the USSR national guard's armed police wing, seized the central newspaper printworks, the interior ministry and the domestic telephone exchange in Riga, attempting to establish a grip over the republic's communications. This prompted the Popular Front to assemble a 700,000-strong rally and oversee the erection of impromptu barricades throughout the city. OMON killed six Latvians and launched aimless attacks on infrastructure before eventually backing down.

On 3 March, the same day as Estonia's independence referendum, 74.9 per cent of the republic's population voted to break away from the USSR. Just as in the other Baltic states, the final impetus was provided by the botched coup against Gorbachev that August. The supreme Soviet brought the transition period to an end on 21 August. Recognition followed from the US on 2 September, and from the Soviet Union itself four days later.

Dangerously Alien

As in 1918, the reborn state was confronted with a formidable array of problems, both practical and existential. But the most fundamental of them all was a new one: who belonged to Latvia? Almost half the population were not ethnic Latvians. There were roughly 900,000 Russians and nearly 200,000 largely Russian-speaking Ukrainians and Belarusians in the country. Some had ancestral roots in Latvia stretching as far back as the seventeenth century; but two-thirds of them had arrived after 1945. In the heady days of 1990 it had seemed plausible, even probable, that they would all be made citizens. After all, the supreme Soviet vote for independence would not have been possible without the support of their deputies.

Under pressure from the LNNK and other staunch Latvian nationalist groups in parliament, however, this option was swiftly discarded. In 1993 Latvia, uniquely among the countries of the former USSR, revived its pre-war constitution. Only those non-Latvians whose families had been living in the country before 1939 were automatically to receive citizenship. The remainder – some 730,000 people, two-thirds of them ethnic Russians – were reduced overnight to *nepilsoņi*: 'non-citizens'.

The LNNK regarded them as Soviet 'colonists' who ought to be grateful that they were not shipped out of the country under the terms of the Geneva convention.[33] The official justification for the policy was, as the Latvian political scientist and liberal MEP Ivars Ijabs has put it, that 'a sudden demographic expansion of Latvia by a great number of people, whose cultural and historical links to Latvia are extremely superficial, would not be permissible'.[34] 'It was a very drastic decision,' says Una Bergmane, a Latvian historian at the University of Helsinki. 'But to some extent it was inevitable, because how [else] do you avoid turning Latvia into some sort of Russian satellite?'

Some human rights groups have claimed that this condition, which also exists in Estonia, amounts to statelessness.[35] Nils Muižnieks, a Latvian-American political scientist who previously served as the Council of Europe's commissioner for human rights, has described the Baltic non-citizens as 'legal ghosts'.[36] The status certainly brings disadvantages. Latvia's non-citizens cannot vote. They are barred from taking many public-sector jobs.

At the same time, though, they also have rights that are not afforded to the stateless, not least the ability to travel across both Russia and the Schengen zone without a visa. Those who wished to acquire citizenship were forced to jump through demanding hurdles, including a Latvian language test and a catalogue of questions on the country's history and politics, which require examinees to acknowledge that it was occupied by the Soviet Union.[37]

A great many Russian speakers in Latvia felt that the promises of 1990 had been betrayed.[38] Their political leaders, and indeed Boris Yeltsin, the president of the Russian federation, characterised the citizenship criteria as discriminatory or worse. Commentators both inside and outside Latvia issued warnings that the nationality question was a bomb waiting to go off, and that the resulting conflagration could draw NATO into war with Russia. That perception still exists in some quarters today.

It is a curious feature of Latvian nationalism that its positions and policies have hardened even as the threat of demographic extinction has receded. The proportion of ethnic Latvians in the country has risen by ten percentage points since independence, while the proportion of ethnic Russians has fallen by a similar margin. As of early 2022 the number of non-citizens had also fallen to 195,159, less than a third of what it was in 1991.[39]

In the late 1990s, seeking membership of the EU and NATO, the Latvian government initially moderated its approach. The 1994 regime for the naturalisation of non-citizens, the strictest in the Baltic states, was watered down in 1998, although even this compromise was blocked by nationalist MPs in the Saeima and only passed through a subsequent referendum, where it scraped 53 per cent of the vote. The Organisation for Security and Co-operation in Europe (OSCE), a human rights watchdog, also forced the country to stop requiring knowledge of Latvian as a precondition for elected office. Satisfied, the OSCE ended its Riga mission in 2001, signalling that Latvia was ready for NATO and EU accession.

But the ink had barely dried on the treaties before the Latvian state went back on the offensive. The Latvian language had already been enshrined as the country's sole lingua franca and made mandatory for public university tuition in 1992. Six years later a law designated Russian and all other minority tongues in Latvia as 'foreign languages', not to be routinely used in public life. In 2004 the curriculum was reformed, forcing Russian-language schools to teach at least 60 per cent of their classes in Latvian. This prompted the largest ethnic Russian protests in the country's history.

In 2014 the Saeima added a preamble to the constitution, with a host of clauses stipulating that the Latvian state existed to 'ensure the existence of the Latvian nation through the centuries, preservation and development of the Latvian language and culture'. It also emphasised the role the 'Latvian ethno-cultural *dzīvesziņa*' (wisdom of life, or outlook on the world) had played in shaping the nation, while stressing that it 'recognises and protects fundamental human rights and respects national minorities'.[40]

The full-scale Russian invasion of Ukraine in 2022 has dramatically sped things up. About 13,000 Russian nationals living in Latvia must now pass intermediate-level Latvian language exams in order to retain their right to stay in the country, with an exemption for the over-seventy-fives. By the end of 2023, only half of them had demonstrated enough knowledge of Latvian to meet the criteria. A little over a thousand were stripped of their residency permits: 200 left of their own accord but only four were facing imminent deportation.[41]

That is hardly a mass expulsion, but it does have a certain exemplary effect as the centrepiece of a broader campaign of Latvianisation. From 2025, nursery schools will only be permitted to use Latvian, with schools expected to follow suit in due course.[42] While nearly half of Latvian schools still teach Russian as a second foreign language after English, in some cases because they do not have enough teachers to do otherwise, it will be phased out and replaced with other EU languages such as German or French from the autumn of 2026. Pupils already have a right to refuse to learn it.[43] Political parties are now banned from using Russian in their election campaigns.[44]

Get Behind Us or Get Out

Artis Pabriks is one of the more intriguing politicians in Latvia. The former defence and foreign minister joined the independence movement as a young student, then moved to Denmark and obtained a doctorate in political science, submitting a thesis on the Latvian nationality question. Early in the 2000s, while he was still a full-time academic, Pabriks put his finger on the nub of Latvia's dilemma: 'Latvian nationalism, as an indivisible ideological shadow of any nation-state building process, had to be associated and intertwined with the basic principles of human rights and freedoms.'[45] Pabriks was bothered by the thought that these two commitments might have become irreconcilable. It was not that the Russians' human rights had been infringed; more that the arc of Latvia's cultural policy was constraining their freedoms.

The war in Ukraine, oddly enough, has presented the Latvian state with a way out of the conundrum. It has simply reached into a different part of the liberal toolbox. Its support for Kyiv has been enthusiastic, lavish and virtually unimpeachable. The Ukrainian flag flutters from almost every street in central Riga. Latvia has a friendly competition with Estonia over which country has donated a higher percentage of its GDP to the Ukrainians; at the time of writing both contributions are well above 1 per cent. Ukraine's struggle for freedom and territorial integrity mirrors Latvia's own. It is cast as a moment of unavoidable decision for the country's population: side with liberal democracy and the rules-based international order, or side with the very worst species of imperialistic dictatorship. 'There is overwhelming public support for [Ukraine],' Pabriks says.

> Seeing what the Ukrainians experience with Bucha [the site of Russian atrocities against Ukrainian civilians early in the war], with the torture, the rapes, et cetera. This is what our countries and societies have been experiencing from the Soviet and Russian regimes ourselves. People know what we are dealing with.

In the context of the war, Latvia has in some ways established impeccable liberal democratic credentials, better than those of most other western countries. It is standing up for the Ukrainians' freedoms because it regards them as an extension of its own. There is no doubt that the ruling parties do so out of conviction that it is the right and necessary thing to do. But it does also deliver at least two secondary benefits on the home front. First, it is a highly effective wedge issue, splitting opinion in the Russian community and weakening its mainstream political representatives.

Second, and more importantly, the black-and-white moral certainty of this moment has provided Latvia's leaders with an opportunity to try and solve the nationality question once and for all. Russian speakers now have a choice between subscribing to the ethnic Latvian vision of the state's values, its history and its place in the world, or finding themselves in the outer darkness. Against this backdrop, the demolition of the Soviet victory monument in Riga became simultaneously an act of history politics and a symbol of resistance to Russian imperialism in the present.

'Probably the fall of the Third Reich upset many Germans too, didn't it?' says Pabriks when I ask about the Russians' sorrow at the demolition of the column.

> For many Russians, this war will, let's say, bring them into a political dilemma. This is understandable, but it's better if they understand the truth early, before it isn't too late. This is Latvia. This is a free, liberal democratic country. There is no place for totalitarian views in the public sphere. And there is no way we would ever again give up our freedom. Very simple. This monument is against the values of a free democratic country. That's the point. And if somebody's upset by our freedom, by our language, our democracy – well, maybe they should choose a different place to live, right?

Egils Levits, the president at the time, took a similar line, even bristling a little when I pressed him on the issue.* 'The majority of the Russian-speaking population understands that an emotional connection to a regime of terror has no place in a democratic state,' he says. 'A minority still haven't recognised this, because they are still tied to Russia through their cultural connections. But if you live here, in a democratic state, you must adopt a democratic attitude.' This position boils down to an ultimatum to Russian speakers in Latvia: get behind us, or get out.

The Whole World Around Us Is Against Us

The slew of curbs imposed on Latvia's Russians since February 2022 have demoralised a group that already had a higher than average unemployment rate and low representation in public institutions. The

---

* Levits subsequently stood down at the end of his first term in 2023.

fall of the Riga victory monument was only the most visible and painful of these steps.

While there is a great degree of heterogeneity in the Russian-speaking minority, the majority of its members are patently saddened and disaffected, caught in an identity crisis between two worlds. Asked in a 2010 survey if they had felt better under Soviet rule than under Latvian independence, 80.6 per cent said they had. In the same poll 30.5 per cent described the Red Army's victory in the Second World War as the greatest event in Latvia's twentieth-century history.[46]

It is hard to know how they really feel about Putin and the war. Four months into the full-scale conflict, a survey found 40 per cent of Russophones in Latvia condemned the invasion, 12 per cent endorsed it, 28 per cent said they were neutral and 19 per cent declined to answer.[47] A year after that, only 16 per cent said they supported Putin's policies, while 50 per cent said they liked Russia but rejected what its regime was doing. Putin's net approval rating among Latvian Russian speakers had fallen to minus twenty-five points.[48]

Both Latvian and Russian politicians take these numbers with a pinch of salt, suggesting that support for the 'special military operation' was probably higher and some of the Russians surveyed did not disclose their true opinion to the pollsters. 'I think that some of these Russians in Latvia do not answer honestly,' says Edgars Rinkēvičs, the long-serving foreign minister.* 'I'm not naive, or I don't want to lie [to you] that everyone is behind the government, although the solid majority are.'

At the other end of the political spectrum, Miroslav Mitrofanov, the joint leader of the Latvian Russian Union (LKS) party alongside the Interfront veteran Tatjana Ždanoka, agrees. 'It's very difficult to analyse these figures, because I do not trust them,' he says. 'What I feel [is that] the support for Russia is rather high; that is, not the majority, but it's higher than according to the results of this social investigation. But the majority do not support the Russian nation or the western reply.' Mitrofanov is unmitigatedly pessimistic about the future of Latvia's Russians. Soviet rule, he says, resulted in the

---

* Rinkēvičs replaced Egils Levits as president in 2023, a few months after our interview.

'complete atomisation' of society. 'Nobody trusts each other, and everybody cares only about his or her own interests,' he says.

> We tell our voters that the only way to survive is to save our identity and culture in these conditions. The whole world around us is against us . . . [The Latvian authorities take] a very simple position: 'You are the foreigners, you must be silent, and in these conditions we will allow you to live in this country.' If they will not change this behaviour, it will lead to open violence. Open violence and murder.

Not all Russian speakers in Latvia feel this way. Despite their alienation, or perhaps because of it, large numbers have indicated support for reconciliation. In the 2010s they voted in their droves for Saskaņa (Harmony), a centre-left party that was notionally cross-ethnic but in practice drew about three-quarters of its support from Russian speakers and was for much of the decade the strongest force in the Saeima. Nils Ušakovs, one of its leaders, even became Riga's first post-independence mayor of Russian descent. But the party found itself frozen out of national government in perpetuity.

Boris Tsilevitch, one of Saskaņa's founding members, embodies the lost middle ground. He comes from an ethnic Russian family that has lived in the Latvian city of Daugavpils for four generations. When he went to university in Soviet-occupied Riga, he says, he could barely speak a word of Latvian and had to learn it by chatting to his dormmates. It was the late 1980s and Tsilevitch saw no future in the USSR, so he joined the Popular Front. He has been thoroughly disillusioned by the past thirty years. 'Some of the parties who declare themselves liberal, they speak about dialogue, but their understanding of dialogue is quite peculiar,' he says.

> The dialogue is just one way: 'You must listen to what we say and you must obey' . . . [The Latvian nationalists] say we are not welcome here because there are too many Russians, and this is absolutely destructive from the point of view of integration.

On the eve of the October 2022 parliamentary election, a poll found that only 23 per cent of Russian speakers in Latvia said they could express political opinions without fear of the consequences, and 55 per cent said they felt resentment against the Latvian state. The emotions they most frequently cited were fear, outrage and pessimism.[49] On polling day the Russian vote splintered like never before. Saskaņa and LKS were wiped out. The chief beneficiary of their losses was an obscure Russian party called Stabilitātei (For Stability), an upstart postmodern jumble of Russian nationalism, euroscepticism, anti-vaxxer conspiracy theories and homemade TikTok videos.

At the extreme end of the spectrum are pro-Kremlin agitators and a number of alleged Russian intelligence assets. Tatjana Ždanoka allegedly answered to two handlers at the Russian FSB security agency from 2005 to 2017, asking them for money to fund a rally commemorating the Red Army's victories.[50] Ždanoka maintained her innocence but was fined for misconduct by the European parliament.[51]

Glorija Grevcova, a populist TikToker who used to be a Stabilitātei MP, was charged with justifying crimes against humanity after she published a video describing the national museum of occupation as a 'propaganda' outlet that peddled a 'parallel, fictional history'.[52] The case was due to come to trial in the second half of 2024. Grevcova has pleaded not guilty. An arson attack on the museum in February 2024 was allegedly ordered from a cell in Daugavpils prison by a Russophone convict.[53] Another Russian speaker in Riga was arrested on suspicion of helping to smuggle American aviation technology into Russia.[54] 'You have to understand', says Evika Siliņa, Latvia's prime minister,

> that Russia has put billions in funding into propaganda to capture people's minds, not just in the Baltics but in Europe, everywhere, to convince them that Russia is a very good thing and that these countries – it could be any of us, [each] with our own historical issues – are the ones who are doing something wrong, or something different ... That's why there are always politicians and people who want to try their luck.

The political fragmentation of the community makes Latvia's Russian speakers an increasingly tricky proposition for Moscow. It is hardly possible to rally or control a population that is so fissiparous, sharing little more than a language, a few objects of nostalgia, and a strong sense of precariousness.

In any case, many Russian speakers may not be anything like as fractious as they are made out to be. Indra Ekmanis, a Latvian-American who grew up in the US, spent two years carrying out anthropological fieldwork in Latgale, Latvia's easternmost region. The area has historically been closer to Russia than any other part of the country and still has the densest population of Russian speakers, as well as the highest rate of unemployment, at twice the national average.[55] Its main city, Daugavpils – nicknamed Little Russia – is 54 per cent ethnic Russian and 80 per cent of its residents speak Russian at home. The street signs may be in Latin script, but the cinemas screen almost exclusively Russian films.[56] As in the melodramatic BBC2 documentary about the outbreak of the Third World War, Daugavpils is often portrayed as the likeliest lightning rod for a Russian rebellion in Latvia.

Instead of an ethnic powder keg, however, Ekmanis found what she calls a 'hum of banal integration' in Latgale. Russian and Latvian speakers alike were far more likely to identify with Latvia than with Russia. Russian children took part in Latvian song and dance festivals nearly as often as their Latvian classmates did.[57]

Ekmanis believes this is a truer picture of the nationality question in Latvia than the strident accounts of rival nationalisms. 'In Riga and those other places where multilingualism is quite common, you really do have that kind of banal integration, where it's happening on a very regular basis,' she says. 'And it's not something that's pointed out because [people don't think] it's anything to be pointed out.' In other words, while plenty of Russian speakers may cherish grudges against the Latvian state, they tend not to hold them against their neighbours. In fact, insofar as it is possible to tell, many 'Russians' in Latvia appear to be sincerely wary of Putin and irritated by suggestions that he might try and step in on the pretext of 'protecting' them against oppression.[58]

There is little sign of enthusiasm for Moscow's sporadic and half-hearted efforts to 'repatriate' them.[59] After all, the adjacent regions of Russia, some of the poorest in the country, are hardly a persuasive advert for incorporation into the Russkiy Mir (Russian World). As the Estonian historian Andres Kasekamp has put it: 'Rather than asking Russian-speaking residents of Narva or Daugavpils their opinion about Crimea or Putin, it would be more insightful to ask whether they would prefer rubles to euros, or the Russian healthcare system to the Estonian or Latvian one.'[60]

The Theory of Lies

There is, in fact, reason to believe that Moscow has more or less given up on trying to foment genuine ethnic unrest in Latvia. It certainly had every opportunity to do so in the past: analysis by the Latvian political scientist Andis Kudors shows that the country's Russian speakers effectively lived in a parallel media world before the war. TV channels from the Russian federation such as PBK (privately owned, but often accused of spreading Kremlin propaganda[61]), NTV Mir Baltic and RTR Planeta Baltija (both Russian state broadcasters) drew more viewers than LTV7, the flagship Russian-language service from Latvia's public broadcast network. With scarce funds for programming in Russian, Kudors argues, Latvian public broadcasters such as LSM Rus or Latvian Radio 4 cannot compete with the lavish resources available to their rivals from Russia.[62] A 2024 study of 179 countries found that Latvia faced one of the highest levels of foreign state-sponsored disinformation in the world and by far the biggest disparity between false information from foreign governments (very high) and from the domestic authorities (very low).[63]

There are about two dozen independent Russian media outlets and at least 380 journalists that have moved to Latvia, including some fairly prominent platforms such as Meduza, the *Novaya Gazeta* and elements of the *Moscow Times*.[64] In December 2022, however, the Latvian authorities shut down TV Dozhd/TV Rain, one of the widest-reaching Russian opposition broadcasters, which had labelled Crimea on a map as Russian territory and referred to the Russian forces in Ukraine as 'our' troops.[65] This appears to have spooked a number of other Russian journalists in Riga.[66]

The pro-Kremlin channels, along with more familiar outlets such as Sputnik and RT (previously known as Russia Today), have all been banned in Latvia since February 2022. But the ban was a little like using a sledgehammer to crack a bouncy castle. While plenty of older

Russian speakers in Latvia still rely on television, technology has long moved on for the rest of the country. Seventy-seven per cent of Latvia's population are now active on at least one social media platform and 47 per cent are exposed to Facebook adverts.[67] Nearly 80 per cent of teenagers and young adults use YouTube every day.[68] Russian disinformation is increasingly shifting to networks such as TikTok and Telegram. Mysterious websites with opaque ownership structures pop up, disseminate a spray of falsehoods and then migrate elsewhere if the authorities notice. Experts say the tactics are shifting, with less blatant fake news and more sardonic satire, less full-spectrum broadcasting and more algorithm-driven microtargeting. One poetically described the experience of trying to keep track of this protean whirl of half-truths as 'not seeing a flower, but smelling it'.[69]

For a country on the front line of an information war, Latvia's defences against this sort of thing were for many years quite poor. The country has no formal counter-disinformation strategy. There was little qualitative audience research. Media literacy is low, albeit improving. Fifty-four per cent of fifteen- to twenty-four-year-olds say they think social media is generally trustworthy, and 40 per cent admit to reposting content without attempting to verify it.[70]

The task of monitoring and rebutting this barrage of nonsense has fallen mainly to independent media platforms such as the excellent Re:Baltica; academics such as Mārtiņš Kaprāns; and civil society activists such as the Facebook-based 'elves unit' set up to battle Russian trolls, an analogue to movements in other central and eastern European countries. TV3, a commercial TV channel, has broadcast a regular programme called *Melu teorija* (Theory of Lies), in which experts expose and dissect Russian propaganda.[71] Radio Free Europe/Radio Liberty also opened a Riga bureau in January 2023, with a daily Russian-language news programme specifically designed to combat misinformation in the Baltic countries.[72]

A Certain Fundamental Set of Values

There is a kernel of truth in the Russian propagandists' claims that Latvia is slowly emptying out, though. Since 1991 its population has fallen from 2.6 million to 1.9 million primarily as a result of net outward migration, although the decline has slowed in recent years. The effects of the 'great departure' are especially visible in the countryside. In some areas the fabric of rural life has frayed as the young depart for Britain, Germany and other countries to the west, having had their fill of unemployment, debt, low pay and a state that is widely felt to have abandoned them. The number of people in Latvia has been dropping by between 11,000 and 18,800 a year for the past decade, with the exception of an influx of Ukrainian and Russian citizens in 2022.[73]

When the anthropologist Dace Dzenovska conducted fieldwork across some of these districts in 2010, her interviewees complained that 'social life had broken down, because so many people had left.' Foreign agribusinesses, predominantly from Denmark and flush with generously termed loans, were buying up farms from Latvians, who often ended up renting their holdings back. For a people whose national awakening had been inextricably tied to winning ownership of their farmland, this was a severe blow to their sense of sovereignty and identity. Dzenovska heard one continual refrain, repeated so often that it almost acquired the character of a proverb: 'What the Russians did not do to us, we will do to ourselves.'[74]

On top of this, the prevailing sense of despair among Latvia's Russian speakers has worsened the depopulation of the country in a literal way: in a typical year they account for about 30 per cent of emigrants.[75] Less obviously, though, it is a symptom and quite possibly a contributing cause of a widespread sense that social cohesion and the social contract itself have been broken. Latvia is consistently ranked as one of the unhappiest countries in the EU.[76] Its population as a whole is mistrustful of just about every conceivable public institution. Only 41 per cent trust the legal system, 30 per cent trust the national government, 22 per cent trust the parliament and 6 per cent trust the political parties.[77] They even look askance at one another. A 2020 survey found that a mere 32 per cent of Latvians believed other people could be trusted.[78] Another poll before the 2022 election suggested 53 per cent believed their country's future was in danger.[79]

Almost all the researchers I spoke to said economics had been a big factor. Like the other Baltic states, in the 1990s Latvia zealously adopted the 'shock-therapy' reforms thrust upon the post-Soviet sphere by the IMF and other western financial institutions, smashing up its state-owned enterprises and accepting recession and upheaval as the price of competitiveness and foreign investment.

The plan was, in the words of one early central bank governor, to turn Latvia into the 'Switzerland of the Baltic'.[80] Instead it became the region's Cyprus. Chaotic privatisation and lax regulation led to the emergence of politically influential oligarchs, a controversial 'golden visa' scheme for super-rich Russians and an offshore financing sector involved in so many dodgy deals that the US government has described it as a danger to the West's security.[81] Even the Liberian warlord Charles Taylor got in on the act, buying dozens of luxury flats in Riga.[82] Corruption and speculation were and remain rampant. The GDP figures whipsawed with every tremor in the global economy, collapsing by nearly a quarter when Latvia's real estate bubble popped in 2007/8. The welfare state is weak. After social transfers have been taken into account, Latvia has the second highest level of income inequality in the EU, after Bulgaria.[83]

But there is also evidence of an emotional fragmentation. Many Latvians mourn the demise of the 'spirit of the barricades' that galvanised the people to defend their institutions against the Soviet assault in 1991, irrespective of language and ethnicity. 'The desire to escape the Soviet empire was boundless. We have never been so united again,' Viesturs Kairišs, the director of a film about the January events in Riga, said shortly after its release in 2023.[84] As Dace Dzenovska puts it, the front line in the battle of identity is no longer between the Latvian people and a foreign occupier, but a cleft through the middle of the polity. She suggests Latvian politics has become so fixated on the nationality question that it has neglected the state's other duties.[85]

It might seem as though Latvia has little to teach the wider West about how to run a country. But this haste to judge is precisely the problem. The currently dominant brand of western liberalism in some of its broad and demotic senses – social, cultural, economic – has put Latvian society under intense strain, and then condemned it for the consequences. Like the German crusaders in *Lāčplēsis*, 'the bearers of the faith, whom all think pure', liberalism has arrived in Latvia on a civilising mission, with the implicit aim of turning the country into an inferior copy of itself. It can seem as though this variety of liberalism is not much more than a slightly amorphous stick that bigger countries use to assert their dominance over smaller ones.

Seen through western European liberal eyes, the country is a curate's egg. The worst fears of the early 1990s have proven misplaced. Latvia has bound itself firmly into the institutions and geopolitical architecture of the West. Despite the dizzying churn of coalitions and parties over the first twenty-five years of its modern state, there has been a fair degree of underlying cohesion and stability in its governance, and the political power of the oligarchs has dwindled. The country's social policies are rapidly converging with western European norms: in 2024 it ratified the Istanbul convention on violence against women and recognised civil partnerships between gay and lesbian couples.

By far the most disorientating issue from a western liberal perspective is the Russian minority question. It is a junction of conflict between two strands of liberal thought: decolonisation, as Latvia wrestles with its long history of subjection to foreign empires, and multiculturalism, as it seeks to assimilate its Russian speakers. The rest of Europe is struggling with similar problems: the politics of naturalisation, migration and integration are fiercely disputed even in self-proclaimed bastions of liberal democracy such as Germany and Britain. But in Latvia the underlying power dynamics are uniquely scrambled. Unlike the UK, France or Germany, it has no colonial guilt to atone for; quite the opposite.[86] Its predicament does not fit into any straightforward moral calculus.

Latvia only exists today because of a peaceful ethnonationalist movement. This has given its leaders a lodestar around which to orientate the state and to develop their own form of social resilience. They are intensely alive to the tug of war between competing spheres of influence, and have a strong sense of the world as a cultural and political battleground in which great powers have tended to show little respect for national borders, particularly those of smaller countries. And they are in no mood to be lectured at. Egils Levits, the Latvian president, became almost dyspeptic when I persisted in asking him about his country's language reforms. 'I stress once again, we are a democratic state under the rule of law,' he said. 'We have this consciousness of the values of a democratic state under the rule of law, perhaps more deeply than some western European countries do, because of our historical experiences.'

Artis Pabriks, the former defence and foreign minister, argues that the state's treatment of the Russian minority sits squarely in the tradition of European liberalism. He conjures up the spirit of John Locke, the English Enlightenment philosopher whose 1689 *Letter Concerning Toleration* made the case for the coexistence of different religions, but only if they themselves preached religious tolerance. 'If, after thirty years of independence, they're still hating democracy and Latvians, maybe we simply have to accept that some of them won't integrate,' Pabriks says.

> But then, I mean, do we need to integrate them? They simply have to respect the place where they live, because apart from integration there are also other ways to live along[side other groups]. And there are certain things where compromise is not possible. I think it touches upon fundamental values as far as democracy, liberty, individual rights, human rights are concerned. There must be a certain fundamental set of values which simply are there and if you do not follow up those rules, well, sorry, it's your problem. There are limits for tolerance, starting with John Locke.

He might just as well have cited the nineteenth-century liberal thinker John Stuart Mill, who argued that a democratic polity could only be sustained if it were 'possible for one nationality to merge and be absorbed in another', at least in civic and political terms. It would be better for a Breton or a Basque, Mill argued, to become a fully engaged French citizen than 'to sulk on his own rocks, the half-savage relic of past times, revolving in his own little mental orbit, without participation or interest in the general movement of the world'.[87]

I am not making a case here for abandoning liberal values but rather for a more pluralistic understanding of what western liberalism is. A society with strong rule of law, easy-going tolerance of ethnic, linguistic and religious minorities, and equal rights for all of its members regardless of their sex, gender or sexual orientation seems to me like the most humane and sustainable way of organising a state. But these beliefs can and often do also harden into a kind of unreflecting missionary heterodoxy that is deaf to nuance and seeks to stamp its faith on the world. We have to be careful of ending up like the Baltic German pastors who preached down from the pulpit to their Latvian congregations and then went home to ridicule the Latvian people's 'nonsensical beliefs' in a language the Latvians could not read.[88]

The Frames Left Empty

After I interviewed Levits, one of his aides took me on a tour of Riga castle, the presidential residence. First built by the Germans in 1330, it has repeatedly been reconstructed and restored, leaving an incongruous patchwork of the Gothic, the baroque, the neo-classical, art deco and a number of Latvian folk designs added during a kind of arts and crafts revival in the 1930s.

Since 1988 the residents of Riga have gathered around its walls every 11 November, reviving the tradition of marking Lāčplēsis Day by laying tens of thousands of candles, surrounding the castle with a moat of light. The president appears and makes a short speech honouring the soldiers who died to secure or preserve Latvia's independence, with the occasional allusion to the trials of the present. 'Our army had to fight the war of independence in very harsh and even hopeless conditions at times,' Levits said in his 2020 Lāčplēsis Day address, during the worst of the coronavirus pandemic. 'Latvia was devastated, ravaged by outbreaks of diseases, and hunger. But the dream of free Latvia had been fulfilled. We, too, must remain strong, take care of each other and face the current challenges together in a united front.'[89]

It is unclear what place the Russian minority has in this united front. Lāčplēsis and the Black Knight are long dead. Eight hundred years of foreign tyranny and false faith have been cast off. Two antagonists from the epic survive in Latvia's mythology: Spīdola the witch, who betrayed her nation but repented and obtained a measure of absolution, and Kangars the scheming sage, who was beyond redemption. The Russians have in effect been confronted with precisely this choice: to recant and find their way back into society like Spīdola, or to turn their faces against it and face ostracism like Kangars.

This blunt approach is not pretty, but ultimately it may well work. On its own, though, it will not establish a cogent national identity that goes beyond ethnicity and language, nor repair the gaping rent between the public and the institutions of the state. In a perceptive essay on *Lāčplēsis*, the communication scientist Sergejs Kruks noted the strangely unending and passive quality of the national trauma in the poem. 'Whenever Latvians read *Lāčplēsis* or see it performed or otherwise indexed, they are reminded that the hero perished without hope of fulfilling his duty,' he wrote.

> They are asked to wait for his return instead of concerning themselves with figuring out ways to assume responsibility and undertake redressive action themselves. Perhaps *Lāčplēsis* once provided relief for a nation subjugated to foreign power . . . Today, civic society requires a cultural frame that supports the imagination of an active, confident community.[90]

Will it get one? In the festival hall on the top floor of Riga castle, where the president receives foreign heads of state and governments, the ceiling is decorated with murals depicting episodes from Latvia's history. Some date from 1938, depicting events in the romanticised and half-imagined middle ages. Others are from the Soviet era. The newest ones, added in 2021, show the founding of the First Republic in 1918 and a huge crowd of pro-independence protesters waving the red-and-white national flag by the banks of the Daugava in 1988. At either end of the hall, several frames have been left empty, waiting for the next chapters. As the last line of *Lāčplēsis* has it: the battle continues and will not end.

4

Poison Lake

*The Danish Approach to Environmental
Collapse and Energy Warfare*

> It's the sea. Who will exhaust it?
> Clytaemnestra in Aeschylus' *Agamemnon*[1]

Tejn, a fishing village on the Danish island of Bornholm, was once so impoverished that an official who visited the island in the early nineteenth century recorded that its inhabitants had earlier had a reputation as the 'scum of the human race'. The bad name was wholly unwarranted. Over a dozen generations, Tejn hauled itself out of destitution by dint of sheer industriousness. When the sea froze over in the winter, the men would lug giant rocks out on to the ice so that when it melted in the spring they would sink and form a breakwater. In the summer they would toil through the Baltic's frequent storms and range as far afield as the Åland islands, 400 miles to the northeast, to bring in salmon, cod and herring. Eventually they amassed enough capital to acquire the island's first motorised fishing boat, its first filleting plant and an ice-making hall that churned out 200 tonnes of ice a day so the catch would keep fresh on the long voyage to the markets in Copenhagen.[2]

Now, though, that factory, the symbol of so much thrift and hard labour, is echoing with the scream of an angle grinder as builders convert it into a cafe and environmental education space. There is not much call for ice these days. The fish stocks of the southern Baltic have been so hammered by the chemical degradation of the sea that the quotas have been hacked back to almost zero. 'I think in general the sea is forgotten,' says Marie Helene 'Miller' Birk, a local marine biologist and co-founder of the ecological education NGO Ivandet ('In the Water'). 'For everybody else except people like us who work with the sea, it's just this mirror, a blank surface, and you don't really see the nature down below. You don't really see the catastrophe down there.'

On some level, it is hard to shake off the feeling that the sea is an infinite and invulnerable resource. But the Baltic is a shattering illustration of how wrong this feeling is. Western military analysts sometimes talk about turning the sea into a 'poison lake' for Russia, bristling with so many deterrents that the Kremlin would not dare to take any offensive naval action. Yet it is already a poison lake in a very literal sense. It is one of the most polluted bodies of water on the planet, tormented by climate change, an unsettling casualty of north-eastern Europe's path to prosperity.

It is also a conflict zone in which war is already a reality since the 2022 bombing of the Nord Stream gas pipelines off Bornholm and the Ukrainian attack on a Russian corvette in 2024. Subsequent incidents of damage to an underwater gas pipeline between Finland and Estonia, as well as a number of submarine telecoms cables in the eastern Baltic, have only exacerbated worries about the fragility of the dense cobweb of maritime links on which so much of the region's security and economic activity depends.[3]

But the Baltic sea is a case study in hope as much as in anxiety. The lessons learned from hardening its infrastructure against attack are being applied across the north Atlantic and beyond. The NATO member states around its shores are rapidly disentangling themselves from reliance on Russian energy and developing their own clean sources of power. And the fightback against the environmental collapse of the sea is already well under way.

Life on the Edge

Bornholm is one of the uncanniest places I have visited on the Baltic. While it has been under Danish suzerainty for most of the past millennium, the kingdom's easternmost territory is closer to Sweden, Germany and even Poland. It exists in a state of itchy semi-detachment from Copenhagen. On Danish maps it often appears in a separate box to the mainland. The Bornholmers once responded with a map of their own that put the island at the centre and the rest of their country as a 'Denmark-remainder' squashed up in a tiny space at the side.[4]

The deep and semi-mythical past, a world of intense violence and long-forgotten micro-civilisations, feels close to the surface here. The residents have kept alive a number of traditions with medieval origins, such as the myth of Krølle-Bølle (the 'Curly-Headed Thug') and his fellow bulbous-nosed gnomes. Local legend has it that the true Garden of Eden was located on Bornholm and that these 'little folk' were the first children of Adam and Eve.[5] Equipped with three-legged horses and tiny cannon that fire thunderbolts, they are reputed to have turned up in the island's hours of need and helped to drive away the many invasions it has suffered over the centuries.[6]

Bornholm is also a place where you cannot help but notice the startling strangeness of the sea. The waters of the Baltic swirl with phenomena including waterspouts, inexplicably foul stenches, gleaming yellow slicks of tree pollen, lurid blue-green spirals of algae so big they can be seen from space, and *fata morgana* mirages on the horizon.[7] Sometimes they spew up mysterious, moss-like globes, or thousands of almost perfectly rounded spheres of ice the size of grapefruits, or chunks of raw amber bigger than an adult's fist.[8]

But the nature of the Baltic's magic is changing. Those almost luminous streaks of algae, dozens of miles across, are a sign of how the forces that ruined Bornholm's fishing industry are steadily choking the sea to death. Back in Tejn, in the former ice factory, Miller Birk explains that the ecosystems were already delicate enough to begin with. This is because the Baltic is a very peculiar sea. Formed only 12,000 years ago at the end of the last ice age, it was originally a lake of meltwater. Since about 6,000 BC, however, it has had a slender connection to the North sea through a sieve of straits and islands between Sweden and the Danish mainland. At intervals large volumes of ocean water sluice in from the west. Mostly, though, the Baltic is fed by rivers from a catchment area covering about 20 per cent of the European landmass, including the north-western borderlands of Ukraine.

That makes it a brackish mixture of saltwater and freshwater. The concentration of salt varies from about 20 grams per kilogram in the Danish straits to less than a tenth of that level in the sea's northern and eastern extremities.[9] When you go swimming off a Baltic beach in Finland or Lithuania, for example, the water tastes more or less just as it would in an inland lake. In the sea baths of Copenhagen, on the other hand, it is more like the water you get when you have been cooking pasta. At a depth of between 40 and 80 metres there is a kind of physical barrier known as the halocline, where the salinity increases so abruptly that it vertically divides the sea into parallel worlds. As a result the Baltic is fragmented into fragile micro-habitats, each finely adapted to the particular conditions of the local waters. Because the water circulates so slowly, with each cycle of replacement taking as long as forty years, the contaminants that leak into the sea linger and build up over decades. With the prodigious population growth and fertiliser-heavy agricultural methods of the twentieth century, enormous amounts of nitrogen and phosphorus-based nutrients have accumulated across almost the entire span of the Baltic.[10] Those who remember their biology classes from school will know what this means: eutrophication, where micro-organisms such as algae and cyanobacteria frenziedly multiply and upset the food chain from the bottom up. In doing so, they foster the growth of other microbes that deplete the oxygen from the water, especially at lower depths below the halocline. This leads to the emergence of anoxic 'dead zones'. The largest of them, which starts off the coast of Estonia and envelops the Swedish island of Gotland like the jaws of a snake, is bigger than the landmass of Lithuania.[11]

The Cascade

That is by no means the only problem. At the end of the Second World War the Allies dumped about 40,000 tonnes of mustard-gas shells and other chemical weapons into the Baltic, mostly off the coasts of Bornholm and Gotland. Unofficially, the practice continued into the 1980s.[12] There are also about 160,000 mines and possibly another 200,000 tonnes of bombs, torpedoes and conventional artillery shells. Studies suggest the casing of about half of these munitions has by now rotted away, allowing their contents to leach into the surrounding sea.[13] Some of the chemicals have started turning up in fish, prawns and lobsters. The risk to human health has yet to be fully assessed, as has the cost–benefit balance of going to the astronomical expense of retrieving what is by now essentially a slurry of corroded metal and sediment from depths of more than 80 metres.[14] The munitions may grab the attention but purely in terms of scale they are dwarfed by the vast array of other contaminants that more than a century of shipping, heavy industry, metropolitan sewage and littering have strewn over the Baltic. After the Nord Stream pipeline bombings scientists modelled the 'toxic plume' of dangerous substances the blasts might have stirred from the seabed. There were twenty-eight on the list and only half of them were chemical weapons. In fact, the researchers concluded, the chemical munitions had probably accounted for only 0.1 per cent or so of the toxicity. By far the biggest contributor was TBT, a family of pesticidal compounds that used to be painted on to the hulls of ships but were banned in 2008, followed by lead, copper and caesium-137, a radioactive isotope largely deposited in the aftermath of the Chernobyl disaster.[15]

The pollutants sometimes interact with one another in invidious ways. One example is the Baltic's unexpectedly high concentration of thallium, an intensely poisonous metal released as a by-product of cement manufacturing. The sea contains what one researcher recently called 'the geographically most extensive area of thallium contamination ever documented'. For the time being, much of the thallium is effectively locked away by the hypoxic dead zones, which prevent organisms from recycling it into the food chain. If these zones are reoxygenated, however, there is a risk that the thallium will come back into play.[16]

The effects are compounded by global warming. Since 1980 the Baltic has been heating up faster than any other coastal sea in the world.[17] Depending on the course of global carbon emissions, most forecasts suggest the sea temperatures will increase by 2 to 4°C by the end of the century. At Kemi, a Finnish port near the northernmost tip of the Baltic, the ice season is already eighteen days shorter than it was a hundred years ago. At Loviisa, between Helsinki and Kotka on Finland's south coast, it has declined by forty-one days.[18] The winter of 2022/3 was one of the warmest on record in the Baltic and about 1.5°C hotter than the long-term average.[19]

The upshot is what ecologists call 'regime shifts'. Some species, such as the sprat and the pikeperch, are doing nicely. The round goby, an invasive fish thought to have hitched a ride from the Black sea or the Caspian in a ship's ballast water, is spreading along the southern Baltic coast at a rate of about 20 miles a year.[20] The blue-green algae have spread tenfold since detailed records began.[21] The *Mnemiopsis leidyi* comb jelly, also known as the 'sea walnut', probably arrived from the east coast of the US in the 2000s. Naturally suited to waters with very low oxygen levels, it is quite successfully competing for food with native fish species.[22] Some infectious pathogens are thriving. One study found that the number of cases of vibriosis, an infection caused by a seaborne bacterium and frequently resulting in diarrhoea, rises around the Baltic by as much as 200 per cent in especially warm years.[23]

For other Baltic fauna, though, such as the cod and herring that have traditionally been the staples of the region's fisheries, the new balance of biological power is a disaster, aggravated by historically heavy fishing. They are suffering from a cascade effect: the bladderwrack, eelgrass and other aquatic plants that form their habitats are in stark decline, as in turn are the invertebrates and smaller fish they prey on.[24] The cod catch in the central Baltic has fallen by more than three-quarters since its peak in the early 1980s. The herring catch has dropped by about two-thirds and is due to hit zero in the mid-2020s because it is effectively banned under the EU's quota system. The mature fish that are caught are now on average barely a third of the size that they were forty years ago.[25] All this has ramifications for the larger and more charismatic species further up the food chain, such as seals, porpoises and seabirds.

The porpoise population in the Öresund and the Kattegat, around the western gateway to the Baltic, has halved since the year 2000.[26] The eider duck is on the brink of regional extinction, clinging on in a handful of breeding colonies on the Åland islands between Sweden and Finland.[27] Virtually all forms of life visible to the naked eye have been wiped out below the halocline in the deep waters next to Bornholm and Gotland.[28] The map of biodiversity metrics compiled by HELCOM, the Baltic's intergovernmental conservation group, is awash with red. Only four of the twenty-four measures for the Bornholm basin are judged to be satisfactory.[29]

It is easy to get sucked in by the apocalyptic undertow that pervades environmental commentary. The situation is bad. But that is all the more reason to concentrate on our agency and ability to turn things round.

Crushing Nappies

It takes me a while to track down 'Bofa Brian'. After a half-hour's trudge through the rain out of Rønne, the small town that passes for Bornholm's capital, I arrive at a municipal waste centre surrounded by heaps of fishing nets and piles of broken tarmac. It does not look much like the future. Eventually one of the boiler-suited workers in the incinerator points me towards an old brick water tower a couple of hundred metres away. Inside it is Brian Johansen, a cheerful man with a round face and a plate of cinnamon rolls. Johansen, from Bornholms Affaldsbehandling (Bofa), the local rubbish-processing authority, is an evangelist for Bornholm's plan to become the industrialised world's first 'zero-waste' district by 2032. The aim is to do away with the concept of waste entirely: no more landfill and no more incineration.[30]

Bornholm regards itself as a 'test island' for the green transition. This reinvention is born of necessity: with the slow death of its fisheries, it needed to find a new economic niche and source of collective purpose. 'When I first moved here twenty years ago, you still heard the old stories about the fishermen and the home-smoked herrings and all that. It was in a kind of quiet limbo, a bit of an identity crisis,' says Johansen. 'And then at that time the [local] media started a thing called the "bright green island" vision, to put the identity into something green instead.'

In 2012 Bornholm launched Europe's first experimental 'smart grid', hooking up a tenth of its 20,000 households to a system that cut power prices whenever there was a glut in electricity.[31] If you look at the satellite images of Rønne's harbour on Google Maps, you will see what looks like a giant's cigarettes laid side by side over half a mile of quayside. These are wind turbine pillars destined for one of the world's largest offshore wind farms, which will ultimately generate as much as 3GW of electricity, equivalent to three standard nuclear reactors. In theory, the power will not only meet the island's needs but also leave a big enough surplus to supply up to 4.5 million homes in north Germany and the Danish island of Zealand.[32]

The zero-waste idea is also an attempt to turn adversity into a virtue. The incinerator on Bornholm, which burns about 25 per cent of the island's waste, will reach the end of its lifespan at the start of the 2030s. Johansen explains:

> We had this window of opportunity where we said: OK, we could try to raise money for a new incinerator, we could try to make some agreements with other waste sites in Denmark, saying 'Can you take our waste?' – or we could say: Hey, nobody's supposed to be incinerating at all . . . We want to recycle and reuse all the waste.

At present Bornholm recycles about 70 per cent of its waste, which is impressive but not quite champions-league material: there are districts in Italy and Japan that have reached 80 per cent.[33] Getting hold of the remaining 30 per cent is exceedingly tricky. The plan is currently to issue every household with twelve separate waste containers for things such as cardboard, batteries and small electronic devices. Six recycling centres on the island have forty different bins for more exotic categories of rubbish.

With enough effort, Johansen says, virtually anything can be recycled. But 'enough effort' is a highly subjective concept. It is, for example, technically possible to recycle asbestos, but this involves heating the material to 1250°C until it fuses into glass. The bottles used for household cleaning products can be made from as many as seven different kinds of plastic, all of which have to be manually pulled apart and processed separately. Disposable nappies must be cleaned and then crushed under forty times the pressure of the Earth's atmosphere at a temperature of 250°C. Other substances, such as hard PVC plastic, have to be shipped off to specialist facilities in Germany at considerable expense. There are also limits to the amount of time, money and thought the average human is able to commit to recycling. Twelve bins is a lot, even in a sustainable utopia.

Yet it would be wrong to call the zero-waste endeavour quixotic. Even if Bornholm's recycling rate is quite unlikely to hit 100 per cent, it will serve as a model for the rest of Europe. It is also a question of changing ways of thinking, of giving people a sense of stewardship over nature and a conviction that the future can be better than the present. That is why Johansen spends so much of his time in the persona of Bofa Brian, proselytising the project to the public. 'We start with the kindergartens and train them to be like world champions or superheroes, and give them the mindset of why it's important,' he says.

A Sturgeon Called Maria

Hundreds of these local civil society initiatives are springing up across the Baltic. In Tejn, Miller Birk and her fellow marine biologist Magnus Heide Andreasen at the Ivandet NGO have set up experiments to grow back the island's seagrass and cultivate blue mussels, which rinse the seawater of the algae that cause so much of the eutrophication. A mile or so off Rosenort and Nienhagen on Germany's Baltic coast, researchers have cobbled together 13 acres of rocks, concrete blocks and mesh to create artificial reefs for fish to shelter and breed in.[34] Others are constructing 'fish hotels' and bladderwrack farms around the bases of offshore wind turbines.[35] Even Moomintroll and Little My have been deployed to raise €1 million for biodiversity and clean-up operations to mark the seventy-fifth anniversary of Tove Jansson's first children's book, *The Moomins and the Great Flood*.[36]

A cynic might sniff at these projects as isolated cases of hopeless do-goodery, a kind of futile displacement activity in the face of an overwhelming systemic problem. But they are the most visible and tangible end of a genuine shift. This change is also happening at the level of high politics.

Today Denmark is one of the leading countries on environmental policy, ranked top of the NGO Germanwatch's climate change performance index for the past two years in a row.[37] In June 2024 it unveiled a plan for the world's first carbon emissions tax on agriculture, at a time when most of its European peers were trying to appease their restive farming lobbies. The 'tripartite agreement', forged between representatives of the government, conservationists and the private sector, also includes a proposal to spend €5.4 billion on converting 250,000 hectares of farmland – an area the size of Dorset in the UK or the Saarland in Germany – into new woodland, partly in the hope of reducing the volume of fertiliser running off into the sea.[38]

Across the wider Baltic, similar initiatives have wrestled the level of nutrient pollution flowing into the sea back down to levels last seen in the 1960s, with each country assigned a limit to the tonnage of nitrogen and phosphorus it can dump. There is still a long way to go, and given the slow rate at which the water circulates, the measures have yet to make any discernible difference to the bonfire of eutrophication.[39] But it is at least a start.[40]

More significant progress has been made on other contaminants. The revival of Baltic trade after the end of the Cold War brought about a surge in sea traffic, with the amount of cargo shipped through the biggest harbours at the eastern end of the sea rising by 60 per cent in the space of five years.[41] At any given point in time there are about 2,000 large ships on the sea and roughly a fifth of them are oil tankers.[42] They continuously leak, flake and disgorge an extraordinary range of pollutants. Sometimes they also crash into each other, run aground, or simply dump fuel. At the turn of the millennium there were up to 700 illegal oil discharges a year and Finland alone reported an oil slick in its waters every three days.[43] At the time this was thought to be an inevitability. But through a combination of aerial surveillance, radar imaging, data analysis, tougher enforcement and banging heads together in the private sector, the Baltic sea countries brought down these numbers by more than 90 per cent. There is now a target to reduce them to zero.[44]

Increasingly the states are simply resorting to prohibition. Some harmful chemicals, such as the pesticide DDT and the carcinogenic PCB family of compounds, have been almost entirely eliminated from the Baltic through international bans.[45] Since 2023 it has been illegal for passenger ferries to discharge human sewage into the sea. A year later, Denmark became the first country in Europe to impose a blanket ban on the release of 'scrubber water', the toxic fluids left over after a ship's exhaust pipes have been rinsed with seawater.[46] There are already sporadic signs that these measures are cumulatively beginning to work, and not just in terms of the graphs of chemical concentrations. Conservationists in particular have had a few successes. The white-tailed eagle, which was practically extinct in the Baltic half a century ago, has now recovered around the Gulf of Bothnia to the point where its predations are becoming a nuisance for eider ducks and reindeer.[47] The Atlantic sturgeon, which was once wiped out in the region after a fisherman mounted the last specimen and named it 'Maria', has recently returned to Finnish waters.[48]

The forests of wind turbines sprouting off Bornholm are also the vanguard of a concerted push towards clean energy. In 2022 the leaders of the eight EU member states around the Baltic declared an ambition to install 19.6GW of offshore wind power – about seven times the current capacity – by the end of the decade.[49] Sweden alone plans to build a 5.5GW cluster of wind farms, capable of providing enough electricity for 5 million households, around the island of Gotland.[50] In the North and Baltic seas Denmark is attempting to raise its own offshore wind capacity from 6GW to 10GW, including an expansion of the Kriegers Flak II cluster off the Baltic coast of Zealand and another two new ones in the Kattegat.[51] With the fervid grandiloquence it usually reserves for energy imports, the German government has set out a vision of the southern Baltic as a 'green European power plant', with a 470-mile submarine connector cable linking its north-east coast to Estonia's offshore wind farms.[52]

You could be forgiven a little scepticism as to how many of these lofty pledges will actually be realised. Europe's wind industry is in a sorry state, ground down by cost inflation, Chinese competition and the meagre appetites of investors, and local politics have a habit of getting in the way.[53] There are worries in Copenhagen that the Bornholm 'energy island' scheme could end up becoming an inordinately costly white elephant, like a similar plan that was ultimately shelved in the North sea.[54] As with the zero-waste scheme, though, what matters is not so much the objective per se as the momentum and direction of travel. Both are pretty clear. Denmark and Estonia both plan to generate 100 per cent of their electricity through renewables by 2030, while Lithuania is aiming for 90 per cent and Germany 80 per cent.[55] A consortium of forty energy firms from eight Baltic sea region countries hopes to establish Europe's first regional green hydrogen network of any significant size, producing 100,000 tonnes of the gas a year. Sweden, Finland and Poland intend to build new nuclear power stations, and the Baltic states are beginning seriously to contemplate constructing reactors of their own.[56]

They Start Soft

There is a baleful presence looming over and in many cases driving this activity. Where the Russia tsar Peter I saw the Baltic as the 'sea of confusion' and Napoleon called it the 'waters of promise', Vladimir Putin sees a flotilla of threats.[57] And to a man with a civilisational grudge, everything looks like a weapon. That includes energy, the environment, and international dialogue itself.

After the break-up of the Soviet Union in 1991, Germany and some of its neighbours invested a great deal of hope in collaboration on cleaning up and electrifying the Baltic as a kind of pilot scheme for binding Russia into the European community. The results were modest at best. For the first three decades Russia paid lip service to marine protection initiatives and dutifully turned in the necessary strategy and policy papers. It even made the odd token effort in practice, such as a short-lived beach-cleaning drive in Kaliningrad. But it never backed up the promises with remotely adequate funding.[58]

While Russia only accounts for a small fraction of the total Baltic coastline, its ecological footprint on the sea is dire. The average Russian discards 59 kg of plastic waste a year, compared to 12.7 kg for the average Dane and 29.3 kg for the average Swede, and about 14 per cent of this rubbish winds up in the rivers. As a result the country is estimated to leak as much as 15,000 tonnes of plastic into the Baltic annually, more than any other littoral state.[59] It operates a 'ghost fleet' of at least 400 tankers to circumvent western oil sanctions that have cut off access to credit and insurance, as well as another 2,000 smaller vessels.⁶⁰ The tankers are thought to carry about half of Russia's seaborne oil exports, the economic mainstay of the country's war machine.⁶¹ Many of the ships are old, dilapidated, uninsured and staffed with crews who have little knowledge of the Baltic's treacherous maritime geography.⁶² They are, in other words, an environmental calamity waiting to happen.⁶³

They are also a serious security concern. Many of the ships are equipped with antennae and other sensors that could be used to conduct military reconnaissance and intercept communications. Senior commanders in the Swedish military have suggested they could be used in a crisis to block up a port or to land a cargo of troops and armoured vehicles on a target such as Gotland.⁶⁴

It is not just that the Russian state regards its neighbours' anxieties about the state of the Baltic with abject contempt. It is that it treats them as a tool. Leaks suggest that in January 2023 a directorate in the Kremlin drew up plans to plant intelligence agents in Baltic environmental networks and stoke fears of an ecological catastrophe through Russia's array of state propaganda outlets.⁶⁵

This was not the first attempt of its kind. Two years earlier, operatives working for the late Yevgeny Prigozhin, a mercenary warlord-cum-oligarch who subsequently launched an infamous rebellion against Putin, organised an apparently innocuous conference on Baltic environmental questions in Berlin, attended by a number of prominent politicians from the region and co-sponsored by a German business lobbying group. The ostensible harmlessness of the subject matter may be precisely the point. 'They start "soft",' Indrek Kannik, an Estonian security analyst, said at the time.

> Only when they gain some public trustworthiness and a moderately positive image [do] they take on more relevant topics for the Kremlin, such as security, criticism of the Baltic states, Russia's talking points about dialogue between Europe and Russia, not to mention everything else to do with Crimea and Ukraine.⁶⁶

The weaponisation of Russian energy has been more flagrant. When the Soviet Union disintegrated, it left behind a tentacular profusion of cables and pipelines pumping energy into the heart of

Europe. For a long time, some of the recipients were reluctant to go to the expense of disentangling themselves from what they saw as an established and reliable source of fuel. The three Baltic states, which were the most exposed to blackmail, did gradually take some steps towards cutting these links, such as Lithuania's decision to anchor a floating liquid natural gas import terminal at the port of Klaipėda in 2014. Even at the outbreak of the full-scale Russian invasion of Ukraine in 2022, however, they remained hooked up to the old Soviet 'BRELL' power grid network with Russia and Belarus. In Lithuania, for example, the company handling grid-balancing – the ironing-out of local disparities between supply and demand for power – was still a subsidiary of the Russian energy conglomerate Inter RAO.[67] They are not expected to finish severing the connection and synchronise their grids with the EU's until the start of 2025.[68]

At least the Baltic states were aware that this Soviet legacy was a problem that needed to be mitigated. Before 2022 Germany not only bought 55 per cent of its imported gas, 50 per cent of its coal and 35 per cent of its oil from Russia.[69] It also actively and enthusiastically increased its exposure, even after the Russian occupation of Crimea in 2014. A few months after the first attack on Ukraine, BASF, a giant German chemicals company with a sideline in energy, was permitted to hand over a clutch of gas storage facilities – including Rehden, the largest in the country – to Gazprom in exchange for shares in a Siberian gas field.[70]

In 2015 the German subsidiaries of Rosneft, another Russian state-owned fossil fuel conglomerate, acquired a 54 per cent controlling stake in the PCK oil refinery at Schwedt, which supplies most of the petrol consumed in Berlin and the surrounding districts. The German competition authority then approved Rosneft's plan to raise this to 91.7 per cent on 21 February 2022, three days before the Russian tank columns made their first thrusts towards Kyiv.[71] Russia's penetration of the German energy sector was so deep and intricate that new predicaments kept cropping up even long after the start of the full-scale invasion of Ukraine. In April 2024, for example, a Russian state-owned company charged with handling Germany's nuclear waste declared insolvency because of western sanctions.[72]

The Ace That Wasn't

But the gravest misstep of the lot was the Nord Stream 1 and 2 pipelines. The original Nord Stream 1 project, which came online in 2011, consisted of a pair of gas conduits running 760 miles along the Baltic seabed from Vyborg to Lubmin on the north-east German coast. It was a farewell present to Europe from Gerhard Schröder, the Social Democratic party (SPD) chancellor from 1998 to 2005, who immediately took up a €250,000-a-year job as Nord Stream's chairman after leaving office.[73] In 2017 Schröder also became the head of Rosneft's supervisory board, reportedly earning himself another €600,000 a year.[74]

Angela Merkel, his centre-right successor, could have pulled the plug on the Nord Stream fiasco after the annexation of Crimea in 2014. Instead she doubled down on it the following year, approving the construction of a second pair of pipelines with the same capacity (55 billion cubic metres a year) and largely following the same route as the first. Some of Germany's allies had warned from the very beginning that the entire scheme was a dangerous mistake. First, it would weaken Ukraine's fragile position as a channel for Russian gas exports into central Europe, which brought Kyiv not only transit fees but also geopolitical attention from the West. Second, it would increase Moscow's leverage over Germany and other neighbouring countries that bought the Nord Stream gas. In 2006 Radosław Sikorski, Poland's defence minister, had gone so far as to liken Nord Stream 1 to the Molotov–Ribbentrop pact.[75]

Delayed time and again, not least by haggling over the precise route the pipelines should take around the chemical weapons dump off the coast of Bornholm, Nord Stream 2 was ultimately finished in September 2021. Germany clung on to the hope that it would enter service until 22 February 2022, two days before the full-scale invasion of Ukraine. After Moscow declared that Ukraine's Donetsk and Luhansk oblasts were independent entities, however, the German chancellor Olaf Scholz read the writing on the wall and froze the project indefinitely.

Dmitry Medvedev, Russia's erratic former president, gleefully responded that Europe's gas prices were about to double: 'Welcome to the new world where Europeans will soon have to pay 2,000 euros per thousand cubic metres!'[76] In fact Moscow's long-awaited energy offensive had already begun, with a particular focus on the Baltic sea countries. Russia had started throttling the westbound flow of gas the previous summer, sending European spot prices – the sum energy firms must pay for short-term deliveries – to record levels.

In April 2022 Moscow cut off gas deliveries to Bulgaria and Poland altogether, citing their refusal to settle bills in rubles under the new EU sanctions regime.[77] Then, three days after Finland submitted its NATO membership application, Gazprom did the same to Helsinki.[78] That same month Moscow also stopped exporting electricity to Finland.[79] A couple of weeks later Denmark got the same treatment.[80] Germany was kept dangling a little longer. Gas shipments through Nord Stream 1 were slowly wound down, ostensibly because of technical difficulties with a turbine. Then they ceased for ten days, started again at a low level, and finally stopped for good at the end of August 2022.[81]

This Russian strategy was supposed to be a form of exquisite torture, measuring out the pain in calibrated doses to maximise its effect. In a limited sense, it was. The TTF, Europe's benchmark natural gas price index, shot up from barely €30 per MWh to €340 in the space of twelve months. But most of the countries around the Baltic sea shrugged their shoulders. They had seen this scenario coming for years and already done what they could to minimise their exposure. In Germany, which had not, there was initially a palpable sense of panic. The gloomiest forecasters predicted that the gas embargo would knock as much as 5 per cent off the country's GDP, hitting the economy even harder than the first year of the pandemic had done.[82]

In the event, however, nothing of the sort materialised. Energy officials worked around the clock on identifying alternative sources of gas and drawing up incentives for businesses and households to cut their consumption. A hastily formed central trading unit threw billions of euros at the spot markets to fill Germany's gas storage caverns for the winter ahead. It was wildly expensive, but it did the trick.

The ace up Putin's sleeve turned out to be a joker.[83] By 2024 Gazprom was in serious financial trouble,[84] with a modest increase in gas exports to China utterly failing to compensate for the loss of its European markets.[85] 'We are not talking about an energy crisis any more. We are talking about an energy realignment,' says Agnia Grigas, a Lithuanian-American security analyst at the Atlantic Council. 'That winter was in fact a great test case that demonstrated that Europe can do without Russian gas. Europe used to depend on Russia for about 40 per cent of its imports. Suddenly that number dropped to 9 per cent.'

'Deep-Sea Research'

On 26 September 2022, scarcely three weeks after the Nord Stream gas turbines had fallen silent, three bombs went off on the floor of the Baltic sea, a few nautical miles to the north-east and south-east of Bornholm. Hours later, Danish and Norwegian F-16 interceptor jets spotted several huge cauldrons of seething froth as nearly 500,000 tonnes of natural gas bubbled up to the surface. It was the largest methane leak ever recorded.[86]

As of mid-2024 the source of the attack had yet to be definitively identified, although the German investigators seemed to be increasingly convinced that it was a Ukrainian operation. In June that year the German Federal Court of Justice issued an arrest warrant for Volodymyr Zhuravlov, a Ukrainian diver based in Poland, on suspicion of having taken part in the sabotage. Zhuravlov, who denied any involvement, fled to Ukraine before he could be detained.[87] Whoever was responsible for the act of sabotage, it was a spectacular demonstration of how easily the Baltic's maritime infrastructure can be torn apart. The frailty of these gas pipelines, electricity interconnectors and data and telecoms cables has been bothering the region's security experts for decades but it took the Nord Stream explosions to thrust the issue to the forefront of public consciousness.

Only a year later these concerns were underscored by damage to the Balticconnector gas pipeline between Finland and Estonia, as well as two submarine telecoms cables linking Estonia to Sweden and Finland.[88] Initially the prime suspect was a Chinese-owned container ship called the *Newnew Polar Bear*.[89] In August 2024 the Chinese government was reported to have acknowledged that the vessel had wrenched open the pipeline by accident after losing control of its anchor.[90]

These episodes may be only a mild foretaste of what Russia could do to the other connections were it so minded. More than half a century ago the Soviet defence ministry created a 'main directorate of deep-sea research', which is usually known by its Russian acronym, GUGI. Headquartered in St Petersburg but with most of its assets based on the Kola peninsula in the country's far north-west, GUGI's purpose is notionally to map the seas and carry out sensitive underwater engineering jobs.

Under the Putin regime, however, it has been built up into something almost like an ocean-going intelligence agency in its own right, with the world's biggest fleet of covert sub-sea vessels, including up to eight nuclear stealth submarines.[91] The newest of them is the K-329 *Belgorod*, which is thought to be the longest submarine on the planet and began operations in 2022. GUGI also has several surface surveillance vessels such as the *Yantar*, which has been spotted sizing up data cables around the UK.[92] These are complemented by a number of oceanographic 'survey' ships belonging to the Russian navy and other arms of the state, some of which can launch small submersibles of their own.

What happens in the murky depths of the Baltic will matter a great deal to the wider world. Underwater data cables are effectively the nervous system of modern global communications. They have roughly doubled in number in the past decade and now carry 99 per cent of internet traffic between countries.[93] Some of them are long enough to stretch halfway around the planet. China's PEACE cable from Mombasa to Marseilles extends for 13,000 miles, including 7,500 miles of seabed and detours to Karachi, Cyprus and the Seychelles.[94] The potential for havoc is considerable.

That is why observers as far afield as Australia and California are keeping a nervous eye on events in the Baltic. As early as 2015, Russian naval vessels sailed into Lithuanian waters and harried the ships laying down an electricity cable to Sweden.[95] Since then western security officials and open-source intelligence analysts have repeatedly observed GUGI, the Russian navy and various non-military vessels lurking around offshore infrastructure in the Baltic, including the sites where the Nord Stream explosions later happened.[96] 'We have seen increased activity for quite some time now in the Baltic. And of course we are on our toes even more,' says Jimmie Adamsson, chief information officer for the Swedish navy. 'That the Russians use civilian shipping for intelligence-gathering is nothing new. We saw that in the Cold War as well.'

It is entirely possible that Moscow could use a Nord Stream-style incident to probe the boundaries of NATO's willingness to defend the Baltic allies. The alliance has previously indicated that a 'hybrid' attack on a member state's critical infrastructure could trigger the Article 5 mutual defence clause much as a conventional attack would.[97] In practice, though, it is a grey area. As we have seen with Nord Stream and the *Newnew Polar Bear*, it can be tricky to attribute acts of undersea sabotage or even to distinguish them from run-of-the mill accidents. The truth can get lost in a rampant scrum of speculation and misinformation. Nor is it clear what the 'united and determined' response promised by Jens Stoltenberg, the alliance's previous secretary general, would entail.[98] If the Americans and the Germans refuse to give Ukraine long-range cruise missiles for fear of upsetting Russia, it hardly seems likely that they would risk going to war for the sake of a severed cable off the bay of Riga.

In any case, experts unanimously agree that such attacks cannot be prevented. It is even quite difficult to detect them promptly, let alone to see them coming. The Baltic is comparatively shallow and the NATO members in the region have an elaborate and highly classified array of sensors, including radar, sonar, hydrographs, electronic intercepts, and aerial, naval and satellite surveillance. But they cannot keep watch everywhere all the time. The sea's layers of water with different temperatures and salinities are a particular nightmare for submarine tracking. NATO officials also suggest that Russia may already have planted mines on some of the infrastructure.[99] As the German interior ministry admitted in the aftermath of the bombing, although the navy is continuously monitoring both the surface and depths of the sea, there are no 'targeted' measures to protect critical sub-sea infrastructure against the 'abstract threats' it faces. 'Several thousand kilometres of cabling cannot be wholly secured against every risk,' it said.[100]

Another obstacle is that most of the infrastructure in question is in the hands of private companies, which are often secretive about their assets and reluctant to take full responsibility for them. 'Up to the present day, we have no complete overview of the underwater situation in the Baltic sea,' says Heiko Borchert, a German defence and security consultant.

> That would involve not just bringing in the armed forces, but also civilian border forces or the police, plus the civilian operators of the offshore infrastructure. That is really a big challenge, because each of these actors is of course incredibly restrained in the way they share data.

But the Nord Stream bombing has on the whole had a salutary effect on European NATO. A few months after the attack, the alliance set up a 'critical undersea infrastructure' cell at its headquarters in Brussels, followed by a dedicated security centre at the NATO Maritime Command base in Hertfordshire, south-eastern England. Its new defence plans, agreed in July 2023, are believed to assign different elements of offshore infrastructure to specific countries.[101] The British-led Joint Expeditionary Force (JEF), a sub-NATO alliance that includes most of the Baltic sea countries, has run naval drills around Finland and Estonia to practise protecting gas pipelines and data cables.[102] With its customary pugnacity, Poland has even passed a law permitting its military to sink ships or down aircraft if they are caught sabotaging critical infrastructure in the Baltic.[103] Collectively, these measures may not make much of a practical difference but they have a certain theatrical value, both for deterring aggression and reassuring the public.

The best way to ward off an attack, though, is to render it pointless. The more infrastructure there is and the stronger a country makes its energy security, the less damage a campaign of sabotage can do. 'The more you look at this maritime infrastructure, the more the question actually is: "Which bits of it are really critical?"' says Göran Swistek, a captain in the German navy and analyst at the Institute for

International and Security Affairs, who has since moved to a post at the German defence ministry. 'In the case of Nord Stream we saw that our energy supply didn't collapse. It's a similar situation with data or electricity cables. If two or three of them are cut, the internet and the energy supply won't collapse.'

In that sense, the Baltic is getting more resilient with every passing year.

PART II
Resistance

5

To Europe, Yes, But With Our Dead

What to Expect from Poland, Europe's Mercurial Rising Star

> It is possible that there is no other memory than the memory of wounds.
>
> Czesław Miłosz, 1980 Nobel lecture[1]

The scene is Vilnius, at the start of 2024. The foreign policy elite of the Baltic region have spent the day discussing the threat from Russia. The mood is sour. A lamentably outgunned Ukraine is losing ground in the east, and more than €100 billion worth of military aid from the US and the EU is being held up by political wrangling. The states of NATO's eastern flank are nervous about their own safety. By the end of the evening, according to sources, the chairs have been pushed into a circle. Spurred on by alcohol and the existential seriousness of the situation, the conversation breaks free of the usual platitudes and constraints.

At this point Radosław Sikorski, Poland's veteran foreign minister, begins to hold court. If the Ukrainian front degenerates into a full-blown rout and the Russians make a significant breakthrough, he says, Poland will not wait for them to approach its borders. 'We are going to move into the west of Ukraine and help them take back control,' he says, according to two people who were in the room. There is a brief moment of consternated silence as the other participants digest Sikorski's words. Tobias Billström, his opposite number from Sweden, is so shocked that when he reaches for the glass of wine by his feet, he knocks it over.

The story says a good deal about Poland in the 2020s. First, and most obviously, there is the sheer bombast, shading into hyperbole. Ever since February 2022, Warsaw has tested the boundaries of western support for Ukraine over and over again. In the earliest days of the war, as other European countries agonised over the armaments they could send, it pressed on and started handing over its old Soviet-era inventories of armour and other heavy weaponry. It became the West's primary conduit for munitions and led the way in supplying tanks and fighter jets. Poland also launched itself into a round of quixotically bold megaphone diplomacy, publicly proposing that NATO establish a no-fly zone or an armed peacekeeping mission in Ukraine.[2]

Then there is the calculation and the messianic undertone behind Sikorski's words. Poland is not just worried about a Russian attack on its own territory. Regardless of which constellation of parties happens to be in government, it consistently regards itself as a resurgent regional power whose interests, history and civilisational values give it a special responsibility to defend the frontiers of Europe against Moscow's designs. Each 15 August its leaders and armed forces solemnly mark the anniversary of the 'miracle on the Vistula' in 1920, one of the great military turning points of the twentieth century, when Poland hauled itself back from the brink of defeat, crushed the invading Red Army on the outskirts of Warsaw, and drove the Soviets all the way to Belarus. The increasingly extravagant parades on this day are more than merely commemoration. They are meant to be understood as a signal that the country is steeling itself to make a second epochal stand for the liberty of Europe, if it has to.

As the second part of this book turns towards how the continental balance of power is being reconfigured around the fulcrum of the Baltic, it might seem eccentric to start with Poland rather than Germany. In some ways, though, the two countries are switching their traditional roles. Poland now has much of the decisive importance for NATO and Europe that West Germany had during the Cold War: as an ideological bulwark against Russia, as the militarily strongest of the frontline states, and as an indispensable base for the projection of American force across the alliance's eastern flank. Even if it does not achieve its goal of doubling the size of its armed forces to 300,000 by the middle of the next decade, it will still be a formidable prospect, with more tanks than Germany, France and Britain put together.[3]

It began rearming several years before 2022, raising the basic army salary by more than 80 per cent and doubling its troop numbers to almost 200,000, including 148,000 professional regulars.[4] It then increased the defence budget to nearly 4 per cent of GDP, the highest level in NATO, and ordered more than a thousand tanks from the US and South Korea, as well as 468 multiple rocket launch systems and as many as 800 Korean-made howitzers. The burgeoning self-confidence is also founded on an extraordinarily lively and resilient economy. Polish analysts have often characterised the past three decades as an unparalleled 'golden age' in which purchasing power quadrupled and the country brushed off a series of financial crises that floored most other European nations.[5]

Once treated by its neighbours as a low-grade workbench and source of cheap labour, the country is now gradually moving up the value chain. Spending on research and development doubled over the last decade.[6] The share of the population educated to upper secondary level or higher is bigger than in Germany. Polish teenagers also outscore their German counterparts in exams.[7] After he came back to power in 2023, Tusk told the Polish electorate that by the end of the decade they would be richer than the average Briton, although some economists have taken issue with the underlying projections.[8]

That is not the end of its ambitions. In a speech to parliament in April 2024, Sikorski said he wanted Poland to 'return to the group of countries creating Europe'.[9]

Poland, according to one official in Warsaw, wants to become the shop steward in an arc of frontline states stretching from Norway to Romania. After Tusk returned to power in December 2023, he immediately announced a trip to visit the leaders of the Baltic states in Tallinn and then travelled to Finland, where he signed a bilateral border security deal.[10] His Finnish counterpart, Petteri Orpo, repaid the courtesy by inviting Poland to join the Nordic and Baltic countries in thrashing out common positions before EU summits.[11] 'I see this as very much the beginning of a real engagement and a turning of Poland towards the Baltic,' says Michał Baranowski, a senior research fellow at the German Marshall Fund of the United States. 'We are talking about Poland finally becoming a Baltic nation.'

At the same time, Poland hopes to join France and Germany at the top table, presenting itself as the team captain of the EU's more hawkish faction and taking advantage of the ceaseless squabbling and strategic divisions between Berlin and Paris. It was notable that when

Sikorski made his programmatic foreign policy speech he took pains to emphasise that his vision of Europe was complementary to Emmanuel Macron's. The Franco-Polish axis, an old warhorse that has been repeatedly buried by reality over the past 500 years, appears to have been exhumed and saddled up to ride again.

Does Anyone Like the Polish Government?

Those who have been following European politics for a while can be forgiven a certain sense of déjà vu. This is not the first time Poland has been talked up as the next big thing. There was a particular vogue for this line of analysis a decade ago, towards the end of Tusk and Sikorski's last stint in power, when you could scarcely open a copy of *The Economist* or *Le Monde diplomatique* without encountering some learned reference to the sixteenth-century imperial heyday of the Polish-Lithuanian commonwealth, an internally fractious superpower whose territory once stretched from the southern Baltic to Crimea and the gates of Moscow.

Then the ruling Civic Platform party came crashing down at the 2015 parliamentary election. The victorious national conservatives of the Law and Justice (PiS) party were steered by Jarosław Kaczyński, a man who spoke no foreign languages and had not taken a holiday outside Poland since a family trip to Odessa in 1967.[12] Kaczyński smashed up the diplomatic structures his predecessors had erected, casting Germany as Poland's nemesis and the European institutions as an elaborate German conspiracy to keep Warsaw down.

One PiS ideologue suggested the western side of the EU was at risk of a 'collapse' that would leave Poland and its like-minded neighbours as a kind of 'life ring' for European civilisation.[13] Another said Poles should be more afraid of the West than of Russia.[14] By the end of 2021 Poland's international relations were in such a mess that Jacek Czaputowicz, who had recently been junked as foreign minister, said: 'Does anyone abroad like the Polish government? Nobody comes to mind.'[15]

Two years later, Tusk and Sikorski ousted PiS at the head of an unwieldy electoral alliance ranging from the left to the centre right.

The election result was widely celebrated by liberals in the rest of Europe as a reversal of the populist tide. Yet Poland's 'diplomatic revolution' is a tricky business for even the friendlier of its neighbours. This is not just because of the tensions in its new governing coalition and the possibility that PiS could come back to power in 2027. It is also because Tusk himself is to some degree a prisoner of his country's peculiar political dynamics.

A foretaste of these complications came after Tusk had been back in office for barely a hundred days. Loath to hand his domestic opponents a stick to beat him with, the prime minister found himself lining up alongside Viktor Orbán, Hungary's avowedly illiberal leader, to criticise a new EU mechanism for distributing migrants across the member states.[16] He has continued his predecessor's policy of pushing for tighter import restrictions on Ukrainian grain, under pressure from the Polish farming lobby.[17] His government has made efforts to patch things up with Germany but has also stuck with PiS's demand for Second World War reparations from Berlin.[18]

Behind these contortions is a battle over Poland's identity. In many ways, the traditionally Catholic and largely small-C conservative population is becoming more liberal. While 71 per cent of Poles still identify as Catholics, the share of this group who actually go to mass on a regular basis has fallen to 28 per cent.[19] A little over 50 per cent of the population now backs the government's proposals for a thoroughgoing liberalisation of the country's abortion laws, which PiS had made some of the most restrictive in Europe.[20] A similar proportion say immigrants generally make their country a better place to live in, which is higher than in Sweden, Norway and Germany.[21] Most strikingly, 66 per cent favour the introduction of same-sex civil partnerships and 50 per cent even express support for gay marriage.[22]

But there is a hefty counterweight to these changes. Especially in the countryside and in smaller towns, PiS and other parties of the populist right can draw on a base of social conservatives who feel that their country is under siege from the West. Fifty-three per cent of PiS voters want the death penalty reinstated, 69 per cent believe there are too many immigrants in Poland and 63 per cent would like to see the country's borders closed to migration.[23] Mutual distrust has reached almost American proportions.[24] In 2023, after eight years of

PiS-dominated governments that portrayed Poland's public institutions as irredeemably corrupt and stocked with its own loyalists, 40 per cent of Poles said their country was no longer a democratic state under the rule of law.[25]

An important feature of these conflicts over Polish identity is that they are often expressed as conflicts over history and its interpretation, to a degree that can be hard for western European observers to appreciate. Modern Poland has been profoundly shaped by forces beyond its control. At the end of the eighteenth century it was entirely erased by a series of three partitions between Russia, Prussia and Austria. It flickered back into existence between the two world wars. Then it was devastated by Nazi Germany and the Soviet Union, physically shunted to the west and ethnically homogenised by Stalin, and subjected to another forty-five years of repressive communist rule. It was only after Poland had thrown off the Soviet yoke in 1989 and dashed into NATO and the EU at the turn of the millennium that a real breathing space emerged for debate about what kind of country it should be and what place in the world it should occupy.

Jarosław Kuisz, a liberal intellectual, calls this phenomenon 'post-traumatic sovereignty'.[26] The cardinal dividing line in Polish politics today is, in his view, over how best to secure the country's independence from foreign control and what purpose that independence should serve.

> The point that is often overlooked as to eastern and central Europe is that we are talking about a very basic sovereignty in the sense that these countries were basically wiped off the map . . . Their cultural codes are immensely strange, because they were like a method for surviving without your own state. So when we saw the war in Ukraine, [the sovereignty question] simply reappeared on the political agenda on a scale that is virtually unprecedented. It's the comeback of an existential threat in its most primary form.

In other words, understanding the cultural codes that determine this debate is the key to understanding the role Poland could play in the future of Europe.

War on Poland

Gdańsk, the largest Polish city on the Baltic coast, is on the face of it a bit of an odd place to look for an answer. It has always been an awkward presence on or just beyond the periphery of a nation that has tended to look inland rather than out to sea. Like most places in the southern Baltic, its history is striated with the traces of passing empires: first the early medieval Polish Piast dynasty from the tenth century, then semi-autonomy under the influence of the Hanseatic league, subjugation to the Teutonic order between the thirteenth and fifteenth centuries, then another period of quasi city-state existence under Polish rule, followed by Prussian and German hegemony, and then finally a return to Poland in 1945.

The modern city centre, which was almost completely levelled in the Second World War and then rebuilt, is an eerie simulacrum of its own past. It is not just the magnificent northern Renaissance gables of the Great Armoury and the town hall that were wholly replaced in the middle of the twentieth century. The population was, too. At the end of the war the 15,000 Germans left in the city were expelled. Their place was taken by 150,000 Poles, about two-thirds of them from the old ethnic Polish heartlands around cities such as Łódź and Lublin, and a significant minority from what had been the Lithuanian borderlands.[27]

Ever since it was detached from Germany and established as the 'free city' of Danzig under the treaty of Versailles a century ago, Gdańsk has been a place where Polish identity is contested and defined. In the interwar years the Polish press fixated on the struggle to reclaim it as the national 'duty of the future'.[28] At the beginning of the Second World War the heroic defence of the Westerplatte, a beleaguered Polish garrison that held out for six days against a vastly larger German force, became a staple of the national story of gallant resistance.

When the Poles got the city back, they cleansed it of most of the residual architectural traces of German 'barbarism', preferring to restore buildings that had either been erected or redesigned in the earlier period when it was under Polish control.[29] The new regime's propagandists insisted that Gdańsk and the other territories 'recovered' from Germany had always been quintessentially Polish.

Since then, however, it has often proved to be a source of subversive irritation to the authorities in Warsaw. In 1970 the city's shipyard joined a strike against an abrupt increase in food prices announced by the communist government. As sporadic rioting broke out, the military sent in a column of armoured vehicles and shot dead eight people. A decade later, the shipyard formed the cradle of the Solidarność (Solidarity) revolution, an alliance of workers and intellectuals that ultimately overthrew the communists and initiated the disintegration of the entire eastern bloc. Among the younger Solidarność activists were Donald Tusk, Jarosław Kaczyński and his twin brother Lech, who later became president and then died when his plane crashed at Smolensk in western Russia.

In the brief window of euphoria that followed, Tusk, a historian of the city, was part of a wave of Gdańsk residents who rediscovered the complex past that had been suppressed by the communist regime. 'Germanic' architectural details such as volutes and turrets came back into fashion. Novelists such as Stefan Chwin excavated Gdańsk's long German legacy and explored how it had become interwoven with Polishness. With its history of mingled cultures, trade networks and ambiguously layered sovereignty, the city began to be touted as a model for everything Poland and Europe supposedly aspired to be in the twenty-first century.

During the Kaczyński years from 2015 to 2023, however, it was an opposition stronghold, derided by PiS and its media outriders as a symbol of 'German' and anti-Polish disloyalty. In 2019 *Sieci*, a stridently pro-PiS weekly, launched a full-frontal attack on Tusk and his city in an editorial headlined 'Gdańsk's War on Poland'. The cultivation of a distinct 'free city' identity, it thundered, should make 'every person who knows at least a little about the history of Poland feel anxious'.[30]

That same year the ugly atmosphere culminated in the assassination of Paweł Adamowicz, the city's outspokenly liberal mayor and a favourite target of the state broadcaster, as he gave a speech on stage at a charity concert. He was stabbed with a knife by a young man with paranoid schizophrenia. It is hard to say to what extent the propaganda campaign contributed to the murder.[31]

Today Gdańsk is once again at the centre of Poland's identity politics. It is not only the home of the prime minister; it is also a kind of paradigm for the new Baltic-facing dimension of his foreign policy, according to Wojciech Duda, the editor of the Gdańsk-based political journal *Przegląd Polityczny* and an old friend of Tusk's from his Solidarność days, also his closest advisor from 2007 to 2014.

Duda argues that it is impossible to understand how Tusk thinks without understanding Gdańsk's characteristic blend of cosmopolitanism, composite identities and openness to influences from across northern Europe, in contrast to the narrower and significantly more inward-looking vision of Poland peddled by his political opponents. A cynic might add that Tusk has also inherited something of the city's tradition of protean pragmatism and alienation from the country's agrarian interior.

But there is a measure of truth to the suggestion that Gdańsk is still the main place where Poland's manifold competing neuroses come into a kind of productive contact with the wider world. A case in point is the political onslaught against the city's monumental museum of the Second World War, which had been founded under Tusk's auspices in 2008. Its permanent exhibition tried to give a balanced assessment of some Poles' complicity in the Holocaust and the mass expulsion of Germans in 1945.

This was a period in which Polish intellectuals were asking searching questions about how much substance there really was to the national myth of martyrdom and how their country should come to terms with the darker elements of its past. In 2000 the author Maria Janion published a book about the steadily accumulating body of research into the more discomfiting aspects of Poland's history, including its persistent currents of antisemitism. Its title was *Do Europy – tak, ale razem z naszymi umarłymi*: 'To Europe, Yes, But Together With Our Dead'.

To PiS and its allies, however, this sort of soul-searching was a betrayal. Jarosław Kaczyński himself made a speech in parliament describing the Second World War museum as a covert tool for Tusk and his cohorts to 'destroy Polish national identity'.[32] After he came to power in 2015, Kaczyński kicked out the museum's director, the historian Paweł Machcewicz, and the exhibition was heavily retouched to put the emphasis on Poland's innocent victimhood.[33] Among the additions was a prominent panel displaying a kind of league table of national losses with Poland far ahead in first place, at least in percentage terms.

For Our Freedom (And Yours)

Underlying all of these debates is a centuries-old argument about Poland's sacred national purpose, which still has significant implications for the future. The word 'sacred' is not out of place in that sentence. With the partitions of the late eighteenth century there emerged a strongly Catholic-tinged cult of martyrdom that looked for a higher meaning in the catastrophe. Many Poles sought consolation in the idea that their people had been branded by destiny as the 'Christ of nations', in the words of the national poet Adam Mickiewicz. They had been condemned to suffer so that others might be redeemed.[34] If they could not have their own liberty, they would wage unrelenting war across the continents for the liberty of others. The Poles not only staged uprising after uprising against the Russian occupation; they also embraced virtually every other revolutionary cause they could find. Their rallying cry was 'For our freedom, and yours'.

As the years went by, however, a vicious split opened up in the Polish nationalist cause. Some wanted the restoration of a baggy, multi-ethnic, multilingual, multi-confessional polity loosely along the lines of the old Polish-Lithuanian commonwealth. The other camp made the case for a much narrower, more homogeneous Poland built around the Catholic faith and the Polish language.

By the end of the nineteenth century, as independence finally came within reach, this rift became the central cleavage of Polish politics. The *Endecja* or National Democratic movement led by Roman Dmowski, who had grown up in the Russian part of Poland, set out a vision of a Polish state with a 'healthy national egoism' to which all 'foreign bodies' would be expected to assimilate.[35] The movement had a pronounced antisemitic streak, organising a boycott of Jewish businesses in 1911. Their rhetoric frequently inched into territory now reminiscent of Nazism: their 1919 manifesto lamented the 'many foreign and hostile elements' that were polluting the 'Polish organism'.[36]

Dmowski, who served as a member of the Duma or Russian imperial parliament from 1907 to 1909, was also entirely prepared to work with Moscow against what he saw as the greater threat from Germany. Although he was largely frozen out of power in Poland's interwar republic, serving only as foreign minister for a few weeks in 1923, his legacy has been profound. Norman Davies, the leading British historian of Poland, has described Dmowski as 'in terms of political attitudes . . . probably the single most significant figure in modern Polish politics'.[37]

Dmowski's nemesis was Józef Piłsudski, a military hero who assumed dictatorial powers in the 1920s but is still widely regarded as the father of the twentieth-century Polish revival. Born in Vilnius and raised on the poetry of Mickiewicz and other romantic nationalists, Piłsudski had a deep if sometimes patronising and aggressive sense of Poland's responsibility for its former imperial subjects to the east, including Jews, Ukrainians, Belarusians and Lithuanians. 'Poland,' he told an audience of French dignitaries in 1921, 'is aware of its peaceful and civilising mission which has fallen to it in eastern Europe and which corresponds to the mission of France in the West.'[38]

Piłsudski was a contradictory figure. A pluralist by principle, who had converted from Catholicism to Protestantism to marry his first wife, he was just as often a chauvinist in practice.[39] His government was remarkably tolerant of national minorities by the European standards of its day, asking only that they assimilate to Poland's civic values rather than its language or Catholic culture.[40]

But Piłsudski also ordered his army commanders to seize Vilnius in 1919 and refused to hand it over to the Lithuanians, even attempting to mount a coup in Kaunas, their ersatz capital. What mattered to him above all was giving Poland the strength it would need to survive. The overriding imperative was to hold back Russia and later the Soviet Union, even if this meant working with Germany. 'I want to be neither a federalist nor an imperialist,' Piłsudski said in 1919, 'until I can talk about these matters . . . with a gun in my pocket.'[41]

It is not an accident that there are statues of Dmowski and Piłsudski at opposite ends of Ujazdowskie avenue in the heart of Warsaw's government district. They have been the rival presiding deities of Polish nationalism since their deaths in the 1930s. They do not map on to today's politics in a straightforward way. The Second World War and the subsequent communist regime shattered Poland's historical lineages so irrevocably that they serve less as direct inspiration than as a storeroom of myth and metaphor whose contents can be wheeled out as circumstances dictate. PiS and its supporters are just as ready to conjure the ghost of Piłsudski as they are to depict themselves as Dmowski's heirs. The National Democrats' virulently anti-Jewish sentiments are largely alien to them.

But in other respects their guiding philosophy of majoritarian nationalism, protecting an insular and tightly defined notion of Polishness against the twin threats from the west and the east, is very much in Dmowski's spirit. Their fiery denunciations of traitors to the nation also strongly echo Dmowski's invective against the *Pół-Polacy*, the 'half-Poles' who had in his eyes 'lost their attachment to the aspirations of the nation' and had to be forced to assimilate through 'physical and moral tyranny'.[42] 'The conservative themes we see today have a lot to do with the conservative themes of the 1920s,' says Adam Michnik, one of Poland's best-known liberal intellectuals and the editor of the newspaper *Gazeta Wyborcza*.[43]

Working With the Big Ones

Donald Tusk has a more complicated relationship with these strands of the past. He and his allies spend a lot less time talking about history than PiS does. One person who knows him well says he has little truck with ideology in general and regards talk of Dmowski and Piłsudski as sentimental cant. It is certainly hard to imagine the words 'sacred mission' ever falling from his lips. Implicitly, though, his way of conducting politics and talking about Poland's place in Europe is an emphatic rejection of the Dmowski tradition.

This is above all tangible in his foreign policy. Like Józef Piłsudski, Tusk regards Russia as by far the most serious danger to his country and its neighbourhood, and treats France and Germany as potentially useful allies rather than a domineering menace. He and his fellow Polish 'Europeanists' are broadly relaxed about EU integration and see the partial cession of sovereignty as a price well worth paying for security and prosperity. It is, in the words of the liberal commentator Jarosław Kuisz, 'what guarantees the permanence of the state in a content and form adequate to the twenty-first century'.[44] In 2024, on the twentieth anniversary of Poland's accession to the EU, Tusk cast it as the zenith of the 'creative and imaginative' efforts of previous generations of Polish leaders.[45]

Unlike Piłsudski, who let his conception of Poland's national interest get in the way of proposals to assemble some kind of Balto-Scandinavian defensive military alliance in the 1920s and 1930s, Tusk aspires to make his state a pillar of NATO in the region. But finding a place in Europe is considerably harder. Sławomir Dębski, director of the Polish Institute of International Affairs, argues:

> On the one hand, Poland is the largest and the most potent country in central and eastern Europe, so one can sometimes say that it's too big for the region of small nations but actually too small in the wider context of Europe . . . The challenge is to try to consolidate the region and build it into a coalition to such an extent that Poland can represent its interests and make it much more vocal in Europe. The other strategic option is to work with the big ones, with Berlin and Paris, and present them with a coordinated position from the region. I think this is the central dilemma of our foreign policy.[46]

The auguries for Donald Tusk look substantially better than they were for his predecessors. As a former president of the European Council and a congenital pro-European and Atlanticist, he can draw on a broad reservoir of goodwill that allowed him to unlock up to €137 billion of frozen EU funds within a few weeks of returning as prime minister.[47] For most of his partners, he has the incontrovertible advantage of not being Jarosław Kaczyński. 'The main change compared to what we had before,' says Michał Baranowski, the Polish policy analyst, is that instead of having a government in Poland that basically says 'I'm allergic to everything European' . . . you have a government that says 'Hey, we know that our future is within Europe. We know that we are not where we need to be within Europe. But we are bringing a clear-eyed perception of the threat and clear resources for this.

Tusk has also been lucky in his timing. The Russian attack on Ukraine and the prospect of another 'big bang' of EU enlargement are an impetus for reform of the bloc. Yet France and Germany are at loggerheads. Given Olaf Scholz's personal frictions with Emmanuel Macron, they are likely to remain so at least until a new German chancellor takes power, in autumn 2025. The Nordic and Baltic states, which have traditionally looked to Germany to take the lead on this sort of thing, are frustrated with the lethargy in Berlin and the political chaos in Paris.

When you factor in Warsaw's growing military clout and the thorough vindication of Warsaw's warnings about Russia, Tusk holds potentially the strongest hand of cards that any Polish leader has had in the century since Piłsudski. Bartosz Wieliński, the deputy editor of the liberal *Gazeta Wyborcza* newspaper, who has been reporting on Tusk for two decades, says he believes the prime minister's time in Brussels has mentally equipped him to look beyond the often parochial confines of Polish politics. 'Living in Poland, being a Polish politician, it forces you to be a bit obsessed with history. Every city suffered during the war from the Soviets, from the Germans. You constantly need to keep the victims in mind,' Wieliński says.

> But when you enter the level of European politics, if you want to succeed, you need to think about the future. You need to be intellectually engaged in these processes that are well above the national level. And I think he's been through this transformation and he does now think about how things are going to be in ten or twenty years.

But there are also reasons to rein the optimism in. While the other smaller countries around the Baltic are well-disposed towards Tusk, it is not necessarily clear that they are ready to be led by him. Their interests may be aligned on Russia and Ukraine but they diverge in other areas, including economic policy. Witold Jurasz, a foreign policy commentator for the Onet news website, also doubts that any meaningful Franco-Polish axis will emerge. 'Moscow had to provide [economic perks] like Nord Stream to make the Germans fall in love with the Russians, whereas the French love the Russians for free,' he says.

> France always had a soft spot for Russia and it was trying for many, many years to get rid of the US from Europe. So I don't really see Poland getting closer to France. It's not an option. It never was and I don't think it's ever going to be.

Poland's high defence spending and sizeable orders of American weapon systems may not help much if Washington's appetite for fixing European security problems continues to dwindle. 'The United States won't give a flying fuck about what we think, and they're going to do what they're going to do anyway,' says one former Polish official.[48] Tusk will also be conscious of PiS breathing down his neck from the opposition benches in the Polish parliament. Any measures that can be construed as selling Poland out to Brussels or Berlin will be used mercilessly against him. 'Polish politics under Tusk will be a copy, or rather a shadow, of German politics,' says Beata Szydło, a PiS politician who was prime minister from 2015 to 2017. 'This is what it was before 2015 and we are expecting nothing new.'[49]

The Prayer of the Steel Trowel

Another snag in Poland's Baltic turn is that the country has until recently given strikingly little thought to the region. Consider the shambolic state of the Polish navy. In 2024 its principal assets were a pair of second-hand American frigates from the 1970s, two corvettes, a minehunter and a single Soviet-era Kilo-class submarine that is perennially in dry dock for repairs and used almost exclusively for training.[50] Tusk at least inherited a plan to modernise and expand the fleet. The defence ministry has ordered three new frigates and two signals intelligence ships from Saab. Another €2 billion or so has been earmarked for submarines.[51]

This programme is freighted with historic symbolism. At the start of 2024 the state-owned naval shipyard in Gdynia, founded during Poland's first push towards the sea a century ago, laid the keel for its first new ship for twenty-three years. The frigate is to be christened the *Wicher*, after the destroyer that Józef Piłsudski sent into Danzig's harbour for a display of force in 1932, prompting an international crisis that sucked in Germany, France and Britain.[52] 'I think the conviction has been that Poland is first of all a land power, and if it will face a military challenge, that will come from Belarus or Kaliningrad, not so much from the Baltic sea direction,' says Justyna Gotkowska, a defence analyst at the Warsaw Centre for Eastern Studies.

> So the priority was to invest in the land forces . . . and to have some minimal or small-scale naval capabilities. But now I think the situation has changed a bit with regard to the significance of the Baltic sea. With Poland investing more and more in its Baltic ports and its LNG [liquefied natural gas] terminal, people have realised that you need capabilities that will allow you to protect those assets.

Poland has in fact been estranged from the Baltic sea for most of its history. After the First World War, when the Allies granted the newly restored republic a 40-mile strip of coastline, it decided to turn the tiny fishing village of Gdynia, a few miles north of what was then the free city of Danzig, into a cutting-edge industrial port.* The project was portrayed as a leap into modernity, an act of collective transformation from a 'nation of peasants and farmers' into a creative, enterprising nation of 'seafarers and sailors'. Poets dutifully churned out reams of atrocious verse about the 'epos of concrete' and the 'prayer of the roar of steel trowels and hammers'.[53] Even after 1945, Eugeniusz Kwiatkowski, the economist in charge of coastal infrastructure, spoke of the Baltic's 'still hidden yet powerful strength . . . which can gradually lead us from the stale backwater of today's and yesterday's

---

* The 40-mile figure excludes the long, thin Hel peninsula north of Gdańsk.

economic and civilisational primitives, along the path of great progress to a truly modern, technical and science-based civilisation'.[54]

But there was a very basic problem: Poland had no seafaring tradition. It had precious few sailors. Its language even lacked most of the necessary vocabulary. The words had to be borrowed or calqued from other tongues: first Russian and Serbian, then French and, finally as a last resort, German or Dutch. A shipwreck, for example, is known as a *wrak*, derived from the German *Wrack*. The Polish terms for 'starboard', 'sloop', 'anchor' and 'bay' all appear to come from Dutch.[55] Nor were there any obvious maritime role models for Poland. When the authorities wanted to put up a suitably nautical statue on Gdynia's seafront, the best they could do was Joseph Conrad, who had at least been born to a Polish family but wrote in English and did all of his sailing in other nations' merchant navies. 'I would argue that this building of Polish maritime identity failed,' says Marta Grzechnik, a historian at Gdańsk university. 'I don't think it's possible [to reorient Poland towards the Baltic]. It would be like a complete turning-over of everything. I would say that the land-based identity would always prevail.'

After the Second World War, Poland acquired nearly 450 extra miles of Baltic coastline, which was more than it could initially digest. It had severe shortages of skilled dockers, shipbuilders, sailors, pilots and even fishermen. Many of these posts were filled at first by several thousand Germans, who were kept on despite the mass deportation of their compatriots. Over time, Poland developed maritime industries of its own, but in a strategic sense its general 'sea-blindness' lasted long after the fall of communism.

Now, though, Poland is slowly growing into its role as a Baltic nation. Łukasz Wyszyński, a scholar of Polish security and foreign policy at the 'Heroes of Westerplatte' Naval Academy in Gdynia, points out that the transfer of cargo from the central and eastern European interior to the sea accounts for an unprecedented share of its GDP, as trade has boomed since the collapse of the Iron Curtain. Gdańsk is now one of the ten biggest transshipment ports on the continent. The country has begun importing North sea gas via Denmark through the sub-sea Baltic Pipe, which came online the day after the Nord Stream bombings in September 2022. It also depends on the Baltic for electricity interconnectors and LNG imports, which come in through a terminal at Świnoujście near Szczecin, with a second floating terminal expected to be moored in Gdańsk by the end of the decade.[56]

All of these developments are overshadowed by the naval threat from Russia. There is increasing recognition that if Poland is called upon to help defend the Baltic against an invasion, tanks and artillery will not be enough. Wyszyński says that maintaining NATO's superiority in the region will require a 'constant ability to identify and eliminate threats in any part of the Baltic sea', from Poland's coastal waters and Gotland to the ability to bottle up the Russian Baltic fleet around St Petersburg and Kaliningrad.

The Unfinished Revolution

There is one final chapter of Poland's Baltic history that is worth briefly dwelling on. The Solidarność movement that emerged from Gdańsk was hugely formative not just for Tusk and his country but for modern Europe as a whole. Yet it has been curiously absent from Polish public life since the early 1990s, and elsewhere it has been diminished to little more than a footnote in the grand narrative of the Cold War. What distinguished the non-violent revolution against communist rule in the 1980s was not just the campaigners' bravery and the alliance across the classes. It was also the sense, inherited from the national struggles of the nineteenth century, that the Polish rebels were fighting for other people far beyond their borders. In that moment the word 'solidarity' was anything but banal; it was a powerful but subtle understanding of how any individual's freedom is contingent on the freedom of strangers with whom they might share nothing more than a common oppressor.

I keep returning to the letters written by Adam Michnik, one of the leading intellectuals of Solidarność, during his spells in Gdańsk prison and various other jails. What strikes me about them is not so much their idealism as the way it is tempered with realism and nuance. In one of these essays, titled 'Angels and Maggots', Michnik revisited the bogeymen of Polish historiography, including a number of figures that he personally found unpalatable, and reassessed the circumstances that had shaped their decisions.

Among them was Józef Piłsudski and his pluralistic vision of Poland and its neighbourhood. In words that now seem uncannily prescient, Michnik concluded,

> Today, when even the most stupid and backward government can toy at will with feelings of animosity toward neighbours (Ukrainians, Czechs, Russians, Germans); when brief press campaigns can reawaken passions, deaden mental faculties with xenophobia, or corrupt people with hatred towards those who are different – we should remember the utopia of that nobleman from the Vilna province who faced the slander and calumnies of his 'native' Polish enemies for daring to have such dreams.

The real lesson he took from Piłsudski, Michnik continued, was that Poland's battle against tyranny was inextricably linked with those of the Ukrainians, the Lithuanians and the Belarusians.[57] That sense of solidarity is no less relevant today.

It is not hard to see why Solidarność petered out so rapidly after Poland sloughed off the chains of dictatorship in 1989. Its liberal and conservative wings had already been pulling apart towards the end of the 1980s. 'For as long as the various factions of the Solidarność movement had their [communist] occupier, they could fight,' says Michnik. 'As soon as the occupation was over, the resistance movement was lost.'

The unequally distributed pain of the subsequent economic transition soon dealt the death blow to any illusions that the Poles were all in it together. As in other societies of the former eastern bloc, shock therapy and privatisation turned into a kind of centrifuge in which the sharp-elbowed and well-connected made a packet while millions of others found themselves marginalised and scarcely better off than they had been under communism. The historian Paweł Machcewicz recalls that back then, even as an assistant professor at the national academy of sciences, his salary was barely enough for him to feed his family. 'I can really sympathise with the people who felt frustrated, who became unemployed, who lost their status,' he says.

The Polish writer Dominika Kozłowska is one of many commentators who believe that Tusk, Michnik and their fellow liberals bear a significant share of responsibility for the populist ascendancy that followed. 'A few years [after the 1990s],' she wrote,

> the same Solidarność people [from Gdańsk] arrived at the conclusion that not every citizen could be trusted to recognise the seriousness of the situation and the catastrophic condition of the Polish economy, and that it was not expedient to include society as a whole in decisions about the economy and the welfare system. Nor did the Solidarność people show much understanding for how important the feeling of dignity is.[58]

By the time PiS came to power in 2015, polls found that more voters felt the political system was in need of radical change than had felt this way in 1989.[59] 'I do believe that it is to a large degree the fault of the liberals, much like it is my fault,' Michnik says.

> We should have been more sensitive to the people from the periphery, from small towns. We were talking about all these big things, like road-building, NATO and the EU. But we forgot about them. We didn't have a project for how to throw them a lifeline. PiS threw money at them, as well as the most brutal form of propaganda.

And yet Solidarność, which achieved its goal a few weeks before I was born, has shaped today's Europe as much as any other popular movement I can think of. As a demonstration that totalitarian power could be broken on its own contradictions, it marked the beginning of the end for the extended Soviet system. The former German president Joachim Gauck and other leading members of the East German pro-democracy revolution that brought down the Berlin Wall a couple of months later have said it was Solidarność that first gave them the belief they too could succeed.[60] 'We wanted to find a shared language around our liberal democratic values for this grouping of countries,' says Michnik.

There were differences between us, but of course there were similarities, too. The similarity we had was a common project of liberal democracy. At the same time, we cared about creating a common project that went beyond the nation states. Liberal democracy is the system in which people live most honourably and most comfortably.

Solidarność may have outlived its original purpose but it can also serve as a model for the present. Basil Kerski, the German-Polish director of the European Solidarity Centre at the old Lenin shipyard in Gdańsk, describes it as an 'unfinished revolution'. Especially now, he argues, at a moment when Vladimir Putin is testing the limits of European cohesion and seeking to restore Russia's old sphere of dominion in the eastern part of the continent, Solidarność should be a template of resistance: this time not through unarmed opposition, but through the insight that our freedom is defined and upheld by the suspension of small differences in the face of a greater common danger. If Poland has anything special that qualifies it to be one of Europe's foremost powers in these testing times, that is exactly it.

6

Turning Time

The German Identity Crisis at the Heart of the Continent

> I'm an ancient drayhorse
> from another age;
> was it the Pleistocene
> or last Saturday?
> The Nine-Nine-Nine,
> the Nineties are long gone by
> for me and my washboard stomach
> and for Lady Di.
> Bye, bye.
>
> Rainald Grebe,
> 'Die 90-er' (2008)

Out of the blue, a ferocious electrical storm rolls in off the southern Baltic and a fork of lightning stabs down somewhere a few miles to the north of the southern terminus of the Nord Stream 2 gas pipelines. From high up on the bridge of the *Neptune*, Stephan Knabe appears to be enjoying the pathetic fallacy. The raging tempest is a suitable backdrop: in a matter of months, the tax consultant from Potsdam and his hastily founded company have hired this hulking liquefied natural gas import ship, which is the size of an aircraft carrier, and hooked it up to the German grid at the Baltic port of Lubmin, leapfrogging a decade's worth of bureaucratic hurdles with enthusiastic support from the authorities. On 14 January 2023, the German chancellor Olaf Scholz stood on the deck in a fluorescent yellow vest and turned a wheel ceremonially to unleash the flow of gas. 'This is the new Germany-speed,' he said. 'We are making ourselves independent and strengthening security of supply by acting early and swiftly.'[1] *Geht also doch*: so it is possible, after all.

On 27 February 2022, a little less than twelve months earlier, Scholz had made the most important speech of his career. For three days Russia had been bombarding Ukraine's cities with missiles and mounting a wholesale ground offensive that had shredded the foundations of German policy. Like most of its western allies, the chancellery assumed that Kyiv would fall within days. Russian tanks and warplanes would advance into the heart of central Europe. The continent was facing its blackest hour since 1945.

Scholz understood that he needed not only a decisive response but a rhetorical vision to rally German public opinion for the necessary change: the *Zeitenwende*, literally a 'turning of the times', a watershed moment in history. 'At its heart,' he told the Bundestag that day,

> this is about the question of whether power can be allowed to break the law, of whether we allow Putin to turn the clocks back to the age of the great powers of the nineteenth century, or whether we can muster the power to set boundaries for warmongers like Putin. That requires a strength of our own.[2]

Few things matter more to the Baltic than the success or failure of the *Zeitenwende*, which has in the meantime become a shorthand for the wholesale reorientation of German policy, from diplomacy and warplanes to wind turbines and taxes. Conversely, the Baltic matters just as intensely to Germany.

Most Germans may seldom think of the sea beyond the occasional beach holiday at Rügen or Travemünde. But Germany is not just a Baltic country; it is the region's centre of gravity. Its armed forces, its bases and its infrastructure are, in tandem with the US military presence, the pivot of the eastern flank's defence. It does more trade with its Baltic neighbours (excluding Russia) than it does with China or the US.[3] Its political weight in the EU and NATO, although somewhat diminished in recent years, is still considerable. It also bears a heavy burden of historical responsibility towards the countries it invaded and devastated during the Third Reich.

Germany has been moulded by many of the same historical forces and principles as its Baltic neighbours, and above all by the same very recent struggle between totalitarianism and liberal democracy. For centuries, Danzig/Gdańsk, Königsberg/Kaliningrad, Riga, Reval/Tallinn and even St Petersburg were part of the German cultural world. For better and for worse, Germany has profoundly shaped these places and has in turn been shaped by them.

The German government is not blind to this. It has explicitly acknowledged in its defence doctrine that the safety of the frontline states is coextensive with its own safety. Olaf Scholz and his ministers have spent far more time building links with the Nordic and Baltic states than their predecessors did. They talk about moving towards a Finnish-Swedish model of comprehensive security. They have launched an IT 'innovation club' with the three Baltic states and Volker Wissing, the German digital minister, has hailed them as the 'trailblazers' of digitisation.[4] The permanent deployment of a German armoured brigade to Lithuania is a genuinely significant break with the past.

All these factors give Germany tremendous potential for both good and ill in the Baltic, whether as a supportive first among equals or as a weary old patriarch clinging to what little remains of his authority and the world he once knew. But it still has to work out what kind of strategic leadership role it wants to play in the region. 'I don't think Germany is quite clear on that yet,' says one official in Berlin.

> There's definitely more attention getting paid to the region than before. If you had asked a German three years ago where the Baltic states are, very few would have been able to say. I think that's different now. These countries tend to have a high level of trust in and a cultural affinity towards Germany. You criticise people you trust more than people you don't trust.

Foaming at the Mouth

In the moment when Scholz declared the turning of the times, and in the few weeks that followed, the change was indisputably real. Under the impression that Ukraine was about to fall, the chancellor announced a €100 billion fund to rearm Germany's dilapidated armed forces, the Bundeswehr, and a commitment to fulfil the pledge all

NATO allies had made to spend at least 2 per cent of their GDP on defence.

Berlin then tore up its post-war taboo on sending weaponry into conflict zones, supplying as much as half of the bilateral military aid that Europe has provided to Ukraine. It spent €10 billion on a fleet of F-35 combat jets to secure the future of the American nuclear bombs at the Büchel airbase, which Scholz's party (the SPD) had long wanted to remove from German soil.[5] It withstood an energy crunch, replacing the gas that it had previously imported from Russia. It vowed to become 'fit for war' and a 'leading power' in Europe and beyond.[6]

The implicit promise was that this was only the beginning. Germany would, Scholz vowed, finally become the 'guarantor of European security that our allies expect us to be', the moving force behind the revitalisation of the EU and NATO.[7] Over the following years there was further sporadic progress: in July 2024, for example, Berlin agreed to allow the US to station Tomahawk cruise missiles, with a range of up to 1,500 miles, on German territory.[8] Yet as the months went by and the war in Ukraine dragged on into a harrowing stalemate, many of Germany's partners – and not just those in the Baltic sea area – increasingly questioned whether anything had really changed.

The momentum has unmistakably flagged. Military reform, foreign policy and Ukraine have fallen a long way down the electorate's list of priorities, behind not just immigration and affordable housing but social care, inflation and schools.[9] Political discourse is currently dominated by budget cuts and the resurgence of the radical right-wing Alternative for Germany (AfD) party. While there is still unambiguously strong public support for at least a limited rearmament of the Bundeswehr, half of voters want to see more diplomatic efforts towards a peace deal with Russia and four out of five feel that the government's assistance to Ukraine is either sufficient or excessive.[10]

The AfD and a newer populist start-up movement called the Sahra Wagenknecht Alliance (BSW), both of which oppose most aspects of the *Zeitenwende* and favour reconciliation with Moscow, are gaining ground in fits and starts, particularly in Germany's eastern states. Olaf Scholz, campaigning with the election slogan 'secure peace', has sought to portray himself as a cool-headed voice for restraint in a cauldron of reckless warmongering. When a long list of western elder statespeople, including Hillary Clinton, Sanna Marin and Boris Johnson, put their names to an open letter advocating a NATO 'air defence shield' over parts of Ukraine, Scholz suggested the signatories were 'foaming at the mouth'.[11]

So far this kind of language has not done a great deal to redeem the chancellor's dismal approval ratings. But it does reflect a clear shift in the balance of public opinion. Even the Christian Democratic Union (CDU), the main centre-right opposition party that appears likely to take the chancellorship in 2025, has begun to tailor its positions accordingly. After two years of consistently pressing the government to put more life into the *Zeitenwende*, the CDU has itself begun to entertain doubts as to whether this strategy might be doing it more harm than good at the ballot box, especially in the eastern states.[12] This process is about far more than the fortunes of any particular chancellor or party. It is a matter of Germany's national identity and its position in Europe. It is intimately linked to a prevailing sense of economic and geopolitical decline, and a widespread desire for a return to 'normality'. This is a question of whether Germany can revive its fortunes in the years ahead and become the fulcrum of renewal in the West. The Baltic will be the crucial test of this process. It is the only part of the world that is actively crying out for German leadership, where Berlin has not only a binding duty to protect its neighbours but an opportunity to strengthen and learn from them.

This chapter is a health check on the *Zeitenwende*. It will examine how much progress has been made on the three central axes of reform – energy, defence and foreign policy – as well as what remains to be done and how Germany's leaders might extricate their country from its present state of aporia. Before that, though, it is important to understand the basic political conditions they are working with.

Republic of Fear

Greifswald is the embodiment of Baltic Germany. The smallish city, 10 miles west of Lubmin, is distinguished by a profusion of attractive

Hanseatic architecture, an almost Dutch-level network of cycle lanes, a state-of-the-art atomic fusion reactor, and one of the oldest universities in northern Europe, with strong ties to other research institutes in Poland, the Nordic countries and the Baltic states. It is also the centre of BioCon Valley, one of Germany's leading biotechnology clusters. In the early nineteenth century the landscape painter Caspar David Friedrich, Greifswald's most famous son, depicted the city as a shimmering mirage of spires and ships' masts, serene and modestly prosperous. If you squint hard enough from a distance, it does not look so very different today.

But the local politics are going through an upheaval. For thirty-one years this was the parliamentary seat of Angela Merkel, who was the German chancellor from 2005 to 2021 and an avatar of difference-splitting CDU centrism. The surrounding state of Mecklenburg-West Pomerania, however, was solidly SPD, under the aegis of Manuela Schwesig, one of the most powerful figures in the party and until 2022 one of its most prominent Russia sympathisers. Before the full-scale invasion, Schwesig held annual 'Russia day' festivals to promote business links and fought tooth and nail to preserve Nord Stream 2.[13] She even helped Gazprom to found a local 'climate foundation' as a way of skirting American sanctions on the project.[14]

Merkel is long gone and Schwesig is losing her grip. Ahead of the state election in 2026, the AfD is the most popular party in Mecklenburg-West Pomerania, as it is across the rest of the former German Democratic Republic (GDR).[15] At the local elections in June 2024, the party came first in the district around Greifswald, with 30 per cent of the vote. The similarly Putin-curious BSW picked up another 10 per cent.[16] Even within the city limits, where about a quarter of the 60,000 residents are students or researchers at the university, the AfD emerged as the second-biggest force on the council and won first place in the simultaneous European parliamentary election.[17]

The sense of angst and disillusionment in this part of Germany is as diffuse as it is profound. Greifswald's hinterland is poor, thinly populated and deeply marked by the mistrust and sclerosis of forty-five years of communist rule. Its unemployment rate is 11 per cent, twice the national average, and its GDP per capita is barely half that of Germany as a whole.[18]

Merkel's successor as the local MP is Anna Kassautzki, from the SPD. Born in 1993, three years after Greifswald ceased to belong to the parallel world of the GDR, and raised in the west German state of Hesse, Kassautzki first came to Greifswald for an MA in political science. Doubly an outsider, she has had to put a lot of effort into understanding what her constituents went through and why so many of them have turned away from the established parties. 'To some extent people have experienced traumas, above all in the time of reunification, with a great loss of prospects for the future, a transformation, mass unemployment,' she says.

> No one really knew where things were actually heading. So I've listened to a lot of people and time and again it was the case that these people felt it was the first time they were really being listened to. That broke my heart a little bit.

The tone of politics can be quite raw in this corner of Germany. Shortly before the 2021 Bundestag election I travelled to the nearby Baltic port of Stralsund to watch one of Angela Merkel's rare stump speeches. As the chancellor walked on to the stage in torrential rain, her words were drowned out by jeers from the crowd and chants of 'Merkel must go' and 'we are the people', an old slogan of the GDR pro-democracy movement that has been repurposed by east Germany's right-wing populists. Kassautzki says she had to stop advertising on Facebook during the campaign because she started getting death threats.

This is uncomfortable territory for the advocates of the *Zeitenwende*. The Nord Stream pipelines not only make landfall in Lubmin, 15 miles to the east of Greifswald; they were also laid by ships operating out of the port of Sassnitz on the northern end of the constituency. Geopolitics, economic hardship and a sense of long-term political neglect often seem to have fused together into an amorphous cloud of disgruntlement. When Kassautzki talks about the *Zeitenwende* in a local context, it is not foreign policy or defence that she brings up in the first instance, but welfare, infrastructure and the minimum wage.

Antonia Huhn, a social work student in Greifswald, has been helping to run a centre for Ukrainian refugees since the start of the full-scale invasion. 'I remember very clearly how I woke up that morning, read the first news reports about the Russian war of aggression,' she says. 'I thought: OK, that's almost right on my doorstep. It's crazy.' For her, it is personal: her flatmate had fled the Russian war in Donbas eight years earlier.

Yet even Huhn has reservations about how far things have gone in Germany. 'There are absolutely a lot of people here who really don't think Russia is so bad,' she says.

> A large part of the population think it's terrible that we've cut off relations [with Moscow] . . . I think people found it understandable at the beginning that we were helping [the Ukrainians] but as soon as it was a question of arms deliveries, I had the feeling that even in my friendship group there was a good deal of scepticism, which I can understand up to a point. I myself am a bit torn on the subject. But I think the people are above all afraid that Germany will get dragged into the war. That's the biggest worry.

In some ways, Greifswald is an oddity within an oddity: a comparatively comfortable university city set in an impoverished region that has living memories of communism, a widely cherished yearning for peace and a pervasive mistrust of the country's westward orientation.[19] But its anxieties, its grumbles and its political fragmentation are not atypical of the country as a whole.

The standard diagnosis is that modern Germany is what the historian Frank Biess called a 'republic of fear', more strongly shaped by angst than any other large country in Europe.[20] There certainly is a peculiar quality to German angst. Each year since 1992, the insurer R+V has published a survey called 'the fears of the Germans'. Strikingly, the fear of Germany getting sucked into a war was only fifteenth on the list in the latest edition.[21]

Instead German politicians have to contend with a very generalised set of anxieties about decline and the unravelling of the social and economic order that voters are used to. It is a country where the headline 'The internal combustion engine is safe for the next hundred years' is meant to be reassuring.[22] Two-thirds of older Germans and more than half of under-thirty-fives say they would rather live in the past than in the future.[23] Barely a quarter look forward to the months ahead with a feeling of hope, the lowest level on record since 1950.[24]

At the Rheingold Institute in Cologne, the psychologist Stephan Grünewald compiles regular reports on the national mood through a mixture of polling and in-depth qualitative interviews. He describes the most prevalent attitude as a 'retreat into the snailshell'. Respondents, he says, tend to be very gloomy about the country and its prospects, but simultaneously quite sanguine about their personal situation. Eighty-seven per cent say they are optimistic about their own prospects, while 77 per cent say they are pessimistic about politics in general. Only 39 per cent follow global news attentively, 34 per cent trust the government and 23 per cent have faith in politicians as a class.[25]

The central problem here is that the fear is not specific enough. If there is a war between Russia and NATO, the chances are that Germany will not only be expected to make a very substantial military contribution but will also become a prime target for Russian missiles, drones, sabotage and cyber-attacks. Power plants, airports, factories, road junctions, ports, stations and even hospitals would be in the firing line. 'We have to accept that the rear areas [behind the front lines of a conflict] will be severely contested,' says Alexander Sollfrank, the lieutenant general in charge of NATO's Joint Support and Enabling Command (JSEC) in the south-west German city of Ulm.

> We see this in the Ukraine war, where Russia ... has attacked civilian infrastructure but also logistics and the armament and procurement industry. That is an example of how our own strategic depth, not only the front line will most probably be contested by the aggressor. We have to accept that long-range weapon systems exist and they are intended to contest the strategic hubs, too.[26]

This is what Germany's generals are getting at when they say that the security of their eastern allies is identical with German security. A war with Russia would strike deep into the heart of the continent.

In fact, some officers privately worry that the Kremlin would single Germany out for particularly heavy punishment in the belief that Berlin is one of the alliance's weakest political links and its resolve would crumble in the face of a brief but exemplary bombardment.

The *Zeitenwende*, then, is not primarily an act of charity or moral rectification. There is nothing abstract about it. It is an urgent and overriding national interest. With the creditable exception of Boris Pistorius, the SPD defence minister, Germany's leaders have not been frank with the public about how high the stakes are. They ought to be. As you can see in Finland, Poland and the Baltic states, there is a certain sort of paradoxical liberation, a readiness to take calculated risks and face down the bluster of your adversaries, that comes with a direct sense of danger. 'We're in a wartime mentality where anything is possible,' says a diplomat from one of the eastern NATO states. 'The people in the German ministries are still in a peacetime mentality.'

The Energy Turn

The first of the three main dimensions of the *Zeitenwende* is the rewiring of Germany's energy system. Ostensibly it is here that the shift has been most swift and impressive. Before 2022, Moscow provided the lion's share of the gas that heated 49 per cent of German homes, generated 13 per cent of German electricity, powered the overwhelming majority of German blast furnaces and fed the German chemicals industry.[27] The fuel was supposed to be the national 'bridge' into the green energy transition. Then that bridge was swept away by the war.

When he became chancellor in late 2021, Scholz was alarmed to discover that the Russian energy conglomerate Gazprom had left Germany's largest gas storage caverns almost empty. He asked the energy ministry what contingency plans it had drawn up in case the Russians cut off the gas altogether. There were none, it replied. And so at the start of 2022, a few weeks before the invasion, Scholz initiated a series of top-secret energy security summits in the 'bunker', a windowless and bug-proofed room on the fourth floor of the chancellery. At one of these meetings 'Herr M', a hitherto obscure gas expert from Germany's foreign intelligence service, the BND, suggested an answer: floating storage regasification units (FSRUs), vessels that could take supercooled LNG, restore it to gaseous form and pump it into the grid at relatively short notice.[28]

This was where Stephan Knabe and his business partner Ingo Wagner came in. The pair had previously made a small fortune in the property trade and flirted with the idea of setting up a hydrogen terminal at Lubmin because of its existing gas pipelines. They decided that Wagner, a fund manager, would use his contacts in the gas industry to find an FSRU ship, moor it in Lubmin and set up Germany's first LNG terminal from scratch.[29]

At the time, the idea seemed almost hopelessly American in its build-it-and-they-will-come entrepreneurialism. 'You had a country that had made itself totally dependent on pipeline gas from Russia and so no one was interested in the costlier alternatives,' says Knabe. In early 2022, however, as the US and UK repeatedly warned of an imminent Russian attack on Ukraine, Wagner and Knabe took the initiative, founding a firm called Deutsche ReGas and spending several million euros of their own money to get it off the ground. They called in gas engineers from Norway, energy lawyers from Britain and shipbrokers from around the world. Eventually they found the *Neptune*, a Korean-built and Norwegian-owned FSRU that had previously been stationed off the Ionian coast of Turkey.[30]

Setting up a new kind of energy infrastructure in Germany entails nearly enough paperwork to fill the great library of Alexandria: a harbour extension permit, an operations permit, light and sound pollution audits, a dozen different conservation reports, including one on how any nitrogen released by the ship might affect the grass in a paddock half a mile away. For once, though, the authorities were on warp speed by German standards. The whole thing took three months.

The symbolism is unmissable, not least because the former gas pipeline terminal in Lubmin is to be converted into a green hydrogen production facility by the end of 2026.[31] Here, half a mile from the ruins of a communist-era nuclear power station and right between the spots where Nord Stream 1 and 2 reach mainland Europe, is a physical reminder of what Germany can do when it has a strong enough sense of urgency.

Those were months of fervid exigency. Robert Habeck, the Green party minister for energy and business, found himself compelled to reactivate dormant coal-fired power stations, pour tens of billions of euros into the gas market and even to postpone the closure of Germany's last three nuclear reactors by a few months to balance the grid. Further to the chagrin of the Green party base, the government approved the expansion of a huge open-cast coal mine at Lützerath. At one point a pair of whistleblowers alerted the ministry to a plot to plunge the German branch of Gazprom into bankruptcy, which would have disabled a large part of the country's gas infrastructure. Working through the night, officials drew up a plan to pre-empt the coup by putting the company under public supervision.[32] It used a similar method to seize control of the Rosneft-owned PCK refinery at Schwedt.[33]

On the face of it, energy has been the outstanding success story of the *Zeitenwende*. Despite the short-lived coal revival, over 2023 Germany derived more than 50 per cent of its electricity from renewable sources for the first time. It hit a target to install a record 9GW of new solar capacity with more than four months to spare. That year coal consumption actually dropped by a quarter, falling behind wind.[34]

Yet the country still has a long way to go if it is to meet its goal of generating 80 per cent of its power from renewables by the end of the decade. By 2024 it had installed only 40 per cent of the necessary solar panels and 48 per cent of the required wind capacity.[35] It is adding new onshore wind turbines at less than half the rate it managed in the early 2000s and mid-2010s, while its offshore wind output has actually shrunk since 2020.[36] Many of the existing turbines will have to be replaced as they become obsolete or reach the end of their operational lifespans. In the long run, a revival of nuclear power under a future administration might help to ease the strain on renewables. Thanks to the dogmatism of the successive governments that ran German nuclear power down for over a quarter of a century, however, this would involve building a new fleet of reactors at inordinate expense.

The other big thing the ministerial press releases skate over is that electricity generation overall has fallen by 13.3 per cent since the start of the Ukraine war.[37] Partly this was by design: the emergency subsidies were deliberately set up to encourage households and businesses to cut their energy consumption by 20 per cent.[38] But there is only so much fat you can burn before you start to eat into the muscle tissue. Production in the most energy-intensive areas of industry – sectors such as chemicals, metals, ceramics and paper – has dropped continuously, declining by 16.7 per cent over the first eighteen months after the full-scale invasion.[39] It is little wonder BASF, the largest chemicals company in the world, has cut jobs in Germany and moved production to places with cheaper energy, such as China.[40] Two-thirds of other German manufacturers say they have done the same.[41]

The effect of this 'creeping deindustrialisation' is a little reminiscent of the economic impact of Brexit: not the abrupt, cataclysmic shock that some had feared, but a long, slow, attritional drag. Industrial electricity prices declined from a peak of €0.54 per kWh in mid-2022 to €0.18 in early 2024, and some economists suggest they could sink as low as €0.05 by the end of the decade.[42] But even if they do, Germany will still struggle to compete with the gluts of energy and state subsidies in the US and China.

The industrial lobby argues that only a concerted programme of public energy subsidies can keep the show on the road. But some of Germany's leading economists say there is not much point in further putting off the inevitable. Parts of the country's industry are now fundamentally uncompetitive, they argue, and will ultimately have to die so that new ones can take their place. Monika Schnitzer, the government's chief economic advisor, suggests that outside certain strategically indispensable sectors it makes sense simply to let this creative destruction happen unimpeded. 'There will have to be a certain structural adjustment, especially in energy-intensive industry, and that's OK,' she says.

> Think of chemical precursors such as ammonia. Yes, we invented the processes for making ammonia in Germany. But that doesn't mean that we will have a comparative advantage in producing ammonia in the future. So you could let it be produced elsewhere and then import it back here.

The Military Turn, Part One

The second big aspect of the *Zeitenwende* is defence. The lamentable state of the Bundeswehr was so evident that on the morning the full-scale Russian invasion of Ukraine began, Lieutenant General Alfons Mais, the head of the army, publicly complained that his forces had been left 'more or less naked'.[43] The ammunition stocks were so depleted that they would run out after only two days of land warfare with the level of intensity seen in Ukraine.[44] One group of economists calculated that since the end of the Cold War Germany had piled up a 'peace dividend' of defence underinvestment that totalled €680 billion (calculated relative to an annual budget of 2 per cent of GDP). That works out at €20 billion a year, more than the GDP of Moldova.[45] Most estimates suggest it needs to spend another €300 billion to €600 billion just to catch up with its existing NATO commitments.[46]

But it is only when you look at the detail that you see what this means in the real world. In 2022, the first year of the *Zeitenwende*, the problems were eye-popping. Soldiers said the shortage of modern radios meant that during exercises they had to open the hatches of their armoured vehicles and shout at each other, or simply get out and walk over to the next tank. The defective T-10 parachutes, which cannot be properly steered in high or shifting winds, were blamed for sixty-six accidents in twelve months. Basic kit, such as helmets, gloves and head torches, was in such short supply that the troops often had to buy their own. Units in the German-led NATO battlegroup deployed to Lithuania ran out of underwear and warm socks for the harsh Baltic winter.[47]

As much as anything else, it is this accumulation of wretchedness that eats away at soldiers' morale and capacity to fight. It is hardly surprising that 26 per cent of new recruits quit in their first year of service, 17.6 per cent of military posts are vacant and the Bundeswehr's total strength is shrinking by 1,500 soldiers a year despite an official target to raise it by another 22,000.[48]

That is now supposed to change. Olaf Scholz promised to turn the Bundeswehr into a 'capable, ultra-modern, progressive' force and the largest conventional NATO army in Europe, which is a slightly odd claim given that Germany's personnel numbers are already smaller than Poland's.[49] This will be an enormous challenge that could take the greater part of a generation to resolve. The latest German defence guidelines explicitly recognise Germany's role as the logistical 'turntable' for the defence of NATO's eastern flank and as an especially likely target for Russian aggression. They pick out infrastructure, logistics, civil defence and a 'cumbersome working culture and formalistic working processes' as problems that need to be fixed. They also warn that the defence budget risks falling off a cliff edge when the €100 billion rearmament fund runs out in the late 2020s. Germany, they conclude, must become *kriegstüchtig* (fit for war).[50] At present, the ministry concedes, it could 'basically' fulfil its NATO obligations if it had to, but only with 'grave limitations' in certain domains.[51]

The clanking machine of German military bureaucracy has taken a long time to get going on the reform. Not a single cent of the €100 billion was spent in the first year. But the pistons are slowly beginning to pump. By mid-2024, Germany had committed virtually all of the money, including €10 billion for the 35 F-35 fighter jets, €7.2 billion for 60 CH-47 Chinook heavy transport helicopters, €4 billion for the Israeli-American Arrow-3 air defence system and €1.1 billion for 50 Puma infantry fighting vehicles.[52]

Yet the biggest single item on the list is the €13 billion eaten up by taxes, interest and debt repayments.[53] There are other puzzling holes in the order book. Boris Pistorius, the defence minister, says Germany needs to procure at least €20 billion worth of ammunition just to get its inventory up to the minimum NATO standard. In the first twelve months of the *Zeitenwende*, however, it bought precisely none. The year after that, it spent only €845 million.[54] It was only in June 2024 that the state agreed a deal to buy up to €8.4 billion worth of 155 mm artillery shells.[55]

The Military Turn, Part Two

Every military in the world has its problems with procurement. Germany's, however, are especially dire. Orders get interminably delayed by legal wrangling and constantly shifting specifications as officials try to obtain what one defence ministry insider calls the 'egg-laying wool-milk sow', an impossibly perfect product with an unimpeachable range of functions. Every tranche of kit worth more than €25 million, a figure fixed in the 1980s and unadjusted for inflation since then, must be approved by the Bundestag's budget committee, which leaves plenty of space for local pork-barrel politicking.

The authorities are above all terrified of getting sued or reproved if they make a mistake. 'German bureaucracy,' in the words of Carlo Masala, a professor at the Bundeswehr university in Munich, 'is more afraid of the federal court of auditors than it is of the Russian federation's armed forces.'[56]

Much of the existing equipment is broken. The defence ministry used to release annual wodges of data on the 'operational readiness' of its kit but stopped in 2021, presumably because the numbers were so embarrassing that they were felt to be undermining Germany's contribution to deterrence. The last of these reports revealed that only 77 per cent of the main weapon systems were in working order, including 63 per cent of the Bundeswehr's Leopard 2 battle tanks, 40 per cent of its helicopters and fewer than 30 per cent of its warships.[57] Even these figures may be misleadingly flattering, as they do not include the equipment that has been sent out to private contractors for repairs.[58]

The one thing NATO and especially its frontline member states are really counting on Germany for is its ability to move stuff around. If 30,000 high-readiness troops are to be rapidly funnelled into the southern Baltic in a crisis, followed in due course by another 300,000 in the worst-case scenario, most of them are going to have to be shunted along with their equipment across German motorways and railway lines. Most Germans do not realise what this truly entails. It is not just that the military will suddenly have to commandeer much of the transport capacity of sixteen separate federal states, each with their own regulations. It is that much of the underlying infrastructure is in an abysmal condition and would very probably be targeted by the Russians.

For this reason Germany is overhauling its old territorial defence plans, which were last drawn up in 1989. Back then the country had twelve 'homeland defence' brigades and fifteen regiments.[59] Today it is struggling to raise six civil defence regiments with a strength of 6,000.[60]

It remains to be seen whether the military side of the *Zeitenwende* will amount to much more than what Michael Schöllhorn, the chief executive of Airbus Defence and Space, describes as a 'short-term political straw-fire' that burns out too swiftly to be useful.[61] When Eva Högl, the Bundestag's defence commissioner, made her annual tour of the Bundeswehr in 2023, she found plenty of encouraging signs of progress. The order books were filling up as never before. Soldiers' eyes 'lit up' with pride when they showed her their new personal equipment, supplied through a €2.4 billion fund approved by the Bundestag with uncharacteristic alacrity.[62] Most of the complaints she recorded were exactly the kind of bog-standard gripes you would expect to encounter in soldiers' Facebook groups anywhere else in the rich world: 'monotonous' Polish food, long commutes, overdue medals, the obligation to build 11 km of fencing on a naval air base to protect a colony of endangered sand lizards.[63]

But the Bundeswehr was still plagued with shortages of other kit, 'from heavy equipment to spare parts', exacerbated by the military gear donated to Ukraine. Many units, including on the flagship NATO deployment in Lithuania, had no modern digital radios and were often compelled to use analogue sets left over from the Cold War. The infrastructure was in many places 'disastrous' and 'desolate'.

'I have received letters from parents whose children have just begun serving in the military, in barracks with dilapidated dorm rooms, mouldy showers and blocked toilets,' Högl wrote. 'It is to a certain extent shameful and entirely out of line with the service of our soldiers that the barracks in Germany are in such a terrible condition.'[64] It later emerged that indefinite delays to the procurement of a new standard-issue assault rifle had left the military with as few as 50,000 ageing Heckler & Koch G36s to go round more than 180,000 troops.[65]

Most importantly, the Bundeswehr as a whole was 'enormously stretched' by staffing problems. These left the troops so overworked that they were 'at the limit of what they can tolerate'.[66] This is the crux of the matter. Even if Germany manages to hit the 2 per cent target in the long run, it will not have the necessary resources to fulfil its commitments. These currently range from protecting itself and securing the seas and skies of the Baltic, as the region's 'framework nation', to freedom-of-navigation missions in the South China sea and knocking down Houthi drones off the coast of Yemen. If the US continues its gradual strategic disengagement from Europe, these duties will only proliferate further.

It is impossible to expect the Bundeswehr to perform them when it is at least 20,000 soldiers short and operating on a budget from the 1990s. Estimates circulating in the defence ministry suggest another 75,000 professional soldiers will be needed just to fulfil Germany's obligations under the NATO minimum capability requirements. In a war scenario, the total strength might have to rise to 465,000, including at least 200,000 more reservists who are yet to be trained.[67]

None of this can be achieved on 2 per cent of national GDP. Half a century ago, when West Germany stood on the faultline between the Soviet and capitalist worlds, it routinely spent more than 3 per cent on defence, not least because its leaders understood that firepower brought with it a certain degree of diplomatic leverage. The danger and the opportunity to convert military strength into geopolitical influence are no less great today.

The Diplomatic Turn, Part One

A visit to the German foreign office is a disconcerting but not unpleasant journey backwards through time. The path goes through a security check in the hyper-modern entrance next to the museum island, across an open space and into the old headquarters of the Nazi German Reichsbank, which were last fully redecorated when the ruling party of communist East Germany moved in sixty years ago. Heading up a huge flight of stairs, you step into a paternoster lift, a wooden box on a cable that runs ceaselessly up and down between the floors.

I have come for an interview with Anna Lührmann, the Europe minister. 'The expectations of us are very high, because we are clearly so capable in economic terms. I understand that. That's precisely why the chancellor said we are in a *Zeitenwende* and are radically changing our policy,' Lührmann says.

> I come from the Green party, and I grew up in the 1990s with the mindset that defence of our territory and our allies were the stuff of history. But that has really fundamentally changed since February 2022 . . . So we're going to keep doing more and pursuing a more active German foreign policy.

It is a truism that the core orthodoxies of German foreign policy died with the second Russian invasion of Ukraine in February 2022. I ought to know: I have written enough analytical obituaries on the subject in my day job to be able to trot them out in my sleep. Since then, however, I have heard so many serving and retired officials in Berlin defend the course they pursued in the past that I am beginning to wonder how much is truly different now.

For the best part of fifty years, most German policymakers cleaved doggedly to the tenets that had brought their country reunification and prosperity. The arc of history, they believed, bent towards dialogue and détente. International commerce was not simply a mutually lucrative exchange of goods and services but a civilising force that would bring about a gradual liberalisation of the partner state's values through an alchemy known as *Wandel durch Handel* (change through trade). The only way to secure a lasting peace in Eurasia was to integrate Russia and China into the US-led multilateral order, with due regard paid to their respective national interests, even at the expense of smaller neighbouring states. Germany had a particular debt towards Russia because of all the suffering it had inflicted on the Soviet Union during the Second World War. Europe would be steered through the triangulation of French and German priorities. America would take care of its security, which in any case was in no direct danger from hostile states.

To illustrate how far things have come since then, Anna Lührmann recounts a recent trip to Kyiv. At one point the sirens suddenly went off and she was rushed into an underground shelter. 'It was one of the heaviest air raids that had yet happened,' she says, 'and they all told me that in the end the only reason why the attack failed was because of the [western-supplied air defence] systems, including the German IRIS-T.' She is proud that Germany has become the second-biggest supplier of military, humanitarian and financial aid to Ukraine, after the US.

Germany's Ukraine policy has both exceeded expectations at home and disappointed them elsewhere. A desire to support the Ukrainians for 'as long as it takes' has been tempered by acute concern about scarce resources and the danger of nuclear war. Decisions are constantly pulled in both directions. So far Germany has taken in about 1.2 million war refugees, which is more than any other EU country, including Poland.[68] It has publicly pressured its European neighbours, including France, to cough up more assistance.[69] It has signed a bilateral security guarantee that promises Ukraine 'unwavering support' in its fight to 'restore its territorial integrity within its internationally recognised borders'.[70]

At the same time, though, Scholz has repeatedly refused to endorse a Ukrainian victory as his war aim, saying only that Putin cannot be allowed to win the conflict. Germany was a relatively late convert to Ukraine's candidacy for EU accession and I am told that it was also one of the biggest obstacles to an invitation for Kyiv to join NATO at the alliance's 2023 summit in Vilnius. It has often put the brakes on EU sanctions, such as oil and gas embargoes or kicking Russian banks out of the SWIFT international payments system. Sometimes allies have had to alternately wheedle and bully Berlin into delivering new categories of weapons, like parents trying to persuade a small child to eat broccoli.

Those who regard Ukraine's struggle for the right to exist as an existential issue for Europe tend to see Scholz's posture as the exact opposite of the leadership he promised. Stefanie Babst, a German security analyst who used to run NATO's strategic foresight unit, tells an anecdote about a dinner at the British ambassador's residence in Brussels. A diplomat from one of the eastern flank states turned to her and said: 'How do you tell the difference between apathy and lethargy? You look at the colour of the German ambassador's tie.' He went on: 'Gradually we're getting fed up. We have no time for niceties. This morning was the sixth session in which our German colleague repeated his tentative objections . . . You seldom hear a clear position from Germany. Only reservations.' Then a southern European diplomat sitting on the other side of Babst recounted how an American defence official had described Germany as 'a country with money and no balls'.[71]

'This government is really not good with its messaging,' says Babst.

> Everybody asks: what is our strategic objective? What is it that we want to achieve? What is our end goal? And answering this question by saying we will support Ukraine for as long as needed is not enough . . . It's a lack of mental agility. We remain on autopilot. We just carry on doing what we used to.

Yet several sources who know Scholz well argue that he has in fact exercised a brand of leadership that is carefully tailored to the situation. They say his understanding of Berlin's role is as a central pillar of western unity, holding the coalition together without frightening the German public, exposing his country to a Russian attack or yielding to what he sees as the reckless impulses of his eastern allies. 'These are the kind of people who run topless across the street into incoming traffic. It's just stupid,' Scholz once said.[72] In fact, he believes his authority is defined precisely by his will to ignore the pressure to do more and do it faster. 'It's absolutely clear that in a situation like this, someone will always turn up and say "I'd like things to go in this direction, and that's leadership,"' Scholz told an interviewer a few weeks into the war. 'But I have to say to some of these boys and girls: I'm leading because I don't do what you want.'[73]

The way the chancellor's allies depict his style of foreign policy is not so different from Angela Merkel's method of thrashing out consensus in Europe or even to Bismarck's notion of Germany as the 'honest broker' in the great-power disputes of the nineteenth century. One high-ranking official says the chancellor has taken great pains to move 'in lockstep' with the similarly cautious Biden administration. His overwhelming concern is not to give Putin any additional grounds for targeting Germany. He feels his critics ask too much of a country that is only a 'medium-sized power' in a fiscal and historical straitjacket.

He views the war as a marathon in which collective resolve and the state of German public opinion will be decisive. That means he often ends up pursuing a circumspect middle course between appeasement and resistance. 'I think the government would risk losing public support if we were to follow the example of the people criticising the chancellor from the sidelines,' the senior official says. 'We want to be able to support Ukraine until the very end. And that means we need to keep the people on board.'

That helps to account for Scholz's wooden style of communication. To him, negotiations are to be conducted under total secrecy and with a bare minimum of publicly declared red lines. He is uncomfortable about speaking openly unless he has something specific to announce. Since allied consensus moves slowly, usually he has nothing to say.

The Diplomatic Turn, Part Two

But China is where the new contours of Berlin's foreign policy start to look an awful lot like the old ones. Other countries in the Baltic region, most notably Lithuania and Sweden, have concluded that although Beijing does not pose a military threat to Europe its geo-economic ambitions, human rights abuses and 'no limits' partnership with Russia demand a stiffer response. Germany, however, has barely modified its approach.

There is a tradition that began in the early 1990s, when China was beginning to open up to western investment and the chancellor, Helmut Kohl, would visit every couple of years with a gaggle of industrial chief executives in tow. They would shake some hands, flog some Volkswagens and then fly home, congratulating themselves on having advanced the edifying cause of *doux commerce*.

Outwardly, the rituals were almost identical when Olaf Scholz stepped off his charter flight at Chongqing Jiangbei international airport in the middle of April 2024: the military guard of honour, the long wooden tables, the group photograph in front of an endless flight of red-carpeted stairs and the accompanying delegation of executives from the likes of BASF, BMW and Siemens.

On this occasion, however, two things were radically different. The first was that the balance of power had palpably tilted in the hosts' favour. The days when the German elite could afford to condescend to China about its open markets and industrial modernisation are long gone. Today China is by a narrow margin Germany's largest trading partner. It is not an equal relationship. Chinese exports to Germany exceed the goods heading in the opposite direction by €58.4 billion a year, or more than the German defence budget.[74]

Germany relies on China not only for 8 per cent of its exports but also for a strikingly high proportion of its strategically significant imports, from raw materials to precisely the kind of high-tech manufacturing that German businesses used to dominate.[75] This explains why Scholz's trip was riddled with minor humiliations. The moment the chancellor arrived, he was greeted on the tarmac not by Xi Jinping but by the lowly deputy mayor of Chongqing.[76] He left with little more than token Chinese agreements to lift bans on German beef and apples.[77]

The second big change was that only nine months earlier the chancellor had signed off on a China strategy that explicitly recognised Beijing's attempts to exploit these one-sided dependencies and committed the government to an 'urgent' shift to 'de-risking' the relationship.[78] This was supposed to be the defining proof that Germany had learned its lessons from the Russia debacle, the moment where it came of age as a 'leading power' and figurehead of a united West. And yet there Scholz was, doing what he could to help some of his country's largest industrial companies double down on their exposure to the Chinese market.

Most of the 5,000 or so German firms with branches in China are already acutely aware of the danger. One German business figure says he knows plenty of companies that are trying to shift their activity elsewhere, fed up with the lopsided market access, the abrupt and arbitrary changes in regulation, and the various geopolitical risks. Andreas Fulda, a German China scholar at Nottingham university, estimates that up to €200 billion of German corporate investments in the country could be held hostage if Berlin is sucked into a transpacific trade war or an exchange of tit-for-tat sanctions should Beijing try to seize Taiwan by force.

The Federation of German Industries has warned that Germany is now more heavily dependent on many minerals from China than it ever was on Russian gas and oil. That includes 61 per cent of its gallium imports, 87 per cent of its bismuth and 94 per cent of its rare earths.[79] More broadly, the German Economic Institute has identified 298 categories of products where Germany depends on China for more than 50 per cent of its imports, from medicines and magnets to batteries and laptops.[80]

China has also deeply penetrated Germany with spies and cyberattacks. At a Bundestag hearing in 2022, Bruno Kahl, the president of the foreign intelligence service, said his agency had spent the previous five years on largely futile endeavours to persuade the rest of the German establishment that it was 'painfully' exposed to Chinese influence. Thomas Haldenwang, his counterpart at the Office for the Protection of the Constitution (BfV), said ultimately Beijing posed a much greater threat to Germany's security than Moscow: 'Russia is the storm; China is the climate change.'[81]

The German public has got the message: 60 per cent of them believe the country should pare back its dependency on China, even if it means paying a price, 84 per cent of them see China as an economic threat, and over 60 per cent of them take a negative view of China's rising influence.[82] Yet still their government's policy appears to be under the spell of a handful of large companies that believe they have more to gain than to lose in the country. Despite all the warnings and the slowdown in the Chinese economy, German firms invested a record €11.9 billion in the country in 2023, according to a report that concluded there had been 'barely any trace of diversification'.[83] 'Quite the contrary,' Roland Busch, the chief executive of Siemens and head of the German business lobby's Asia-Pacific committee, once said. 'Without China, no diversification is possible.'[84]

Friedrich Merz, the CDU leader and apparent chancellor-in-waiting, has suggested that Germany would take a more assertive course should he win power. He has argued that Scholz 'lacks the readiness to re-evaluate the risks we are exposed to'.[85] China, Merz says, is a 'threat to our security': 'Every German business would be well advised to analyse and minimise the risks . . . In a few years' time we should not be saying with hindsight, just as we did with Russia, that we got it wrong.'[86] Yet observers with long memories will recall that Angela Merkel struck a similarly confrontational tone towards China at the start of her chancellorship in 2005, only to abandon it as the structural pressures of business interests and domestic politics came to bear on her leadership.[87] What was true then remains true for the coming years: a meaningful and lasting shift in Germany's China policy would demand considerable reserves of political capital and clear consensus across government. Both are likely to be in short supply.

Guns, Butter and Hydrogen

Germany, then, is stuck in Schrödinger's *Zeitenwende*. On any given issue, you cannot know whether it is dead or alive until you open the box. What began as a rush of good intentions, driven by those few weeks when it seemed that Ukraine and the post-war European security order were on the brink of collapse, now stumbles on in a semi-zombified daze, sustained chiefly by inertia and pressure from allies. At least in the medium term, I have a fair amount of faith that Germany will stay away from Russian energy, keep on sending money and weapons to Ukraine and hit the NATO 2 per cent defence spending target, not least because to do otherwise would be diplomatic suicide. But there is little evidence that it will move much further forward. This is not Scholz's fault alone: the fatigue is systemic and unlikely to improve substantially under the next chancellor unless there is another external shock of a similar magnitude.

Over the past two years I have asked many German MPs from across the political spectrum why they think the *Zeitenwende* is running out of steam. Almost invariably the answer comes down to money. With the export-dominated private sector in such shaky health, one MP from Scholz's coalition argues, Germany can scarcely afford to make any economically risky moves. Nor can it find the public funds it needs. The country is patently crying out for investment, from its doddery railway network to its military and fledgling green industries. As Marcel Fratzscher, the president of the German Institute for Economic Research, has pointed out, the total net value of the German state's assets has shrunk by almost half a trillion euros since 2000, in large part because it is failing to replace or upgrade infrastructure that has reached the end of its lifespan. 'The lost wealth is no longer available for future generations and is weakening our economic potential,' Fratzscher wrote. 'The losses endanger good jobs, and so our prosperity.'[88]

Yet the government's hands are tied by the 'debt brake', a constitutional clause that restricts public borrowing to 0.35 per cent of GDP a year. Past governments contrived an ingenious array of workarounds, such as off-balance 'special funds' like the €100 billion for the Bundeswehr. But some of these practices were effectively torpedoed by a constitutional court ruling towards the end of 2023.[89] The consequence was a fiscal shortfall that had widened to €30 billion by the time the coalition parties got round to starting negotiations on the 2025 budget.[90] This forces choices not just between guns and butter but between hydrogen, pensions and public transport. The political scientists Mark Copelovitch and Daniel Ziblatt have made the case that ultimately the debt brake poses a 'deep threat to democracy, not only in Germany but in Europe more broadly', because the resulting economic damage nourishes the German far right and spills over into neighbouring countries.[91]

A significant number of politicians in the ruling coalition, including several cabinet ministers, think the rule should be loosened or jettisoned altogether. Some hope that if Friedrich Merz takes power he will be able to pull off the reform without damaging his party's brand in the way that an SPD chancellor such as Scholz would.

But there are still plenty of MPs on both sides of the Bundestag who believe that would be a grave mistake. One senior politician in Scholz's coalition argues that the debt brake is not only popular with voters but a way of securing Germany for the coming decades, almost as though fiscal policy were itself a dimension of national security. It would, he acknowledges, be possible to borrow several hundred billion euros for investment, but those investments would lock in fixed costs for years to come. And once the iron girdle of fiscal discipline is relaxed, he reasons, every special interest group would start lobbying for extra funds. 'We would be taking that money away from future generations,' he says.

Pouring Neat Wine

It is possible to go round and round in circles on these questions, and that is exactly what all of Germany's parties are doing. But the basic problem is not that the money constrains the politics. It is that the politics constrains the money. Ultimately Germany will either have to increase its tax burden or accept a structural deficit, at least for a limited period of national reconstruction.

For all the complaints about the current level of taxation (48.2 per cent of GDP, a shade above the EU average but some distance behind France, Italy and the Nordic states) and national debt (63.7 per cent of GDP, which is pretty much the EU median), Germany is one of the few European countries with the economic firepower to take either option.[92] A splurge of investment would not only help the state meet its obligations; it would stimulate growth, too. Even allowing for arms imports, every euro Berlin spends on defence yields €1.23 in domestic output, according to a group of Italian economists.[93]

Whether Germany can muster the requisite political will is another question. The most significant obstacle to the *Zeitenwende* is the same fundamental problem that the populists are feeding off: a lack of faith in the future. Or, more accurately, a lack of faith that a better future could be both realistic and desirable. As a result the government finds itself interminably attempting to square the contradictions and anxieties of public opinion in the belief that boldness is not a vote-winner. This assumption is shared by the mainstream opposition.

It would be unwise to underestimate the system's capacity for muddling through. There is, as the economist Adam Smith once said of imperial Britain, a good deal of ruin in a nation. But if the art of German politics continues to be framed as the management of distributional conflicts in a zero-sum game, the consequence will be relative decline on every level. It will get harder and harder to buy off every influential special interest group and to build coalitions that are not paralysed by internal bickering. The competitive posturing of the three parties in Scholz's 'traffic light' alliance that has frustrated so many voters will become the norm for future governments. That in turn will keep chewing away at trust in public institutions. The vicious circle will keep on turning.

Norbert Röttgen, a CDU MP, former cabinet minister in the Merkel era and author of two recent books on how the Russian invasions of Ukraine have altered Germany's identity, says 'the world has become so confused and threatening that it frightens a lot of people'.[94] At the same time, he explains, people 'also see that something must and can be done about it', but that the country 'lacks political leadership'. When I ask other German politicians if they see any scope or appetite for visionary leadership, they almost always look at me as though I must have taken leave of my senses. But from Konrad Adenauer in the 1950s to Helmut Kohl in the 1980s and 1990s, German chancellors have in the past brought about radical change while pretending to do the opposite. That is where the decisive element of skill will lie: in pitching wholesale reform and modernisation as an imperative to preserve everything Germany has built since 1945.

The best basis for this leadership would be a salutary dose of honesty, or *reinen Wein einschenken* (pouring neat wine), as the German idiom has it. The world of the 2010s is not coming back, let alone those of the 1980s and 1990s, which surveys suggest are the main focal points of German nostalgia.[95] The country is in a precarious position. It may no longer be a front state in a purely geographical sense, as it was before 1990, but a buffer of a few hundred miles affords little protection against twenty-first-century warfare, from missiles and cyberspace to economics and energy. It has already come under sustained Russian attack with some of these tools. Germany is not directly at war in Ukraine but it can no longer kid itself that it is at peace, either. It will not be safe unless and until Russia suffers a sufficiently heavy defeat on the battlefield that it is forced to recalibrate its ambitions.

Nor will the economy rouse itself from stagnation unless the framework conditions change. High energy prices and chronic underinvestment are by no means the only obstacles. Economists also point to lethargic digitalisation, labour shortages and an overburdened state pension system. Nine out of ten German companies complain that significant amounts of their time and energy are wasted on excessive bureaucracy.[96] The average working week in Germany is now 30 per cent shorter than it was fifty years ago.[97]

The 'five sages', the panel of economists who advise the government, have calculated that the ceiling on productivity growth is about 0.4 per cent a year for the foreseeable future.[98] 'It's just a third of the average growth rate that we had in the year 2010 and the year after,' says Monika Schnitzer, the chief economic advisor. 'That is really low.' Parts of German industry, especially in the chemicals sector and others that process raw materials, cannot survive without substantial and long-term state subsidies. They will have to be let go and the workers and capital tied up in them will have to be directed elsewhere.

Yet a frank assessment would also include the country's strengths and its enormous potential. Germany has proven its resilience in the energy war with Russia. It can draw on a highly educated population with an outstanding research base. Its status as a safe haven for bond investors in Europe gives it plenty of latitude to borrow for investment. It has its own admirable traditions of solidarity that came to the fore during reunification and the pandemic. Beyond the narrow nationalism of the AfD, surveys attest to a reservoir of mild patriotic pride that could be a constructive resource in the hands of a responsible and forward-thinking leader.[99] And it finally has an opportunity to overcome the atrocities of the twentieth century, not by shackling itself with guilt and self-doubt, but by mobilising its considerable resources for the security and prosperity of Europe, as well as its own.

As the German philosopher Bettina Stangneth wrote in a withering jeremiad on the stagnation of the *Zeitenwende*:

What is the point of all the preoccupation with our own past, all the memorials commemorating war, crimes and lust for extermination, the battle for freedom and democracy, the prizes for civil courage, if not to strengthen ourselves for the present and to defend the future against similar crimes against humanity? . . . An admission that you are overwhelmed is not an excuse. It is a promise.[100]

7

The Hobbits

Lithuania and the Strength of Small States

The smaller peoples have a broader horizon precisely because they cannot get past the existence of the bigger ones.

                      Uku Masing, Estonian philosopher, in 1940[1]

Shortly before midnight on 2 July 1940, the newly installed Lithuanian deputy prime minister is waiting nervously in an anteroom at the Soviet foreign ministry.[2] Vincas Krėvė-Mickevičius has good reason to worry. Eight months earlier his country had been forced to sign a 'treaty of mutual assistance' with the USSR, under whose terms the Soviets had stationed 20,000 soldiers on its territory. But Moscow keeps asking for more. Juozas Urbšys, the Lithuanian foreign minister, likens his attempts to resist these demands to 'peas thrown against a wall'.[3] The Lithuanians correctly fear that they are about to be occupied by the Soviet Union, despite the fulsome promises that their sovereignty would be respected.

Eventually a door opens and Krėvė-Mickevičius is ushered in to meet Vyacheslav Molotov, Stalin's foreign minister. He is about to experience one of the moments in modern Russian history when the mask suddenly drops, all pretences of normality are set aside, and the regime's true intentions are laid unmistakably bare. It is the kind of moment that haunts the nightmares of today's Baltic leaders just as it did back then.

The Lithuanian, who is really more of a literary scholar than a politician, does his best. After a few polite but fruitless exchanges, however, Molotov's patience snaps. 'You provoke my candour, Mr Minister,' he says. 'You force me to say something which I had no wish to say at this time. Therefore we shall speak openly [and] without sentimentality, of which there is already enough.'

Molotov tells Krėvė-Mickevičius to 'take a good look at reality' and understand that 'in the future, small nations will have to disappear'. Lithuania, Estonia, Latvia and Finland will 'have to join the glorious family of the Soviet Union'. Now is the time for him to prepare his people for absorption into 'the Soviet system, which in the future shall reign everywhere, throughout all Europe'. A 'small island' like Lithuania cannot be permitted to obstruct the righteous arc of history. In a miracle of Marxist cliodynamics, Molotov predicts, the Lithuanian people will spontaneously vote to annex themselves to the USSR within four months.

The Lithuanian is stunned. Molotov pauses to order a pot of tea and then resumes his tirade. The elimination of the Baltic states is only the beginning, he says. The USSR will give Nazi Germany a bare minimum of support until the 'miserable and starving masses of the warring nations become disillusioned and rise against their leaders'. Then the Red Army will roll in to defend the insurgent working class. 'In the territory of western Europe, I believe, somewhere near the Rhine,' Molotov says, 'the final battle between the proletariat and the degenerate bourgeoisie will take place, which will decide the fate of Europe for all time.'

Molotov was far from the only twentieth-century figure to feel that the existence of the Baltic states was a kind of affront against the laws of geopolitics. From the moment the three countries seized their independence at the end of the First World War to the point where they regained it at the start of the 1990s, politicians and diplomats across the West thought they were unviable at best and dangerously provocative at worst.

Today, though, they are not only a fixture on the map but part of an emerging constellation of power. In a horseshoe that sweeps around the Baltic from Copenhagen to Helsinki to Vilnius and then down through Warsaw to Prague, a group of 'smaller' states that were traditionally on the passive periphery of Europe have become important actors in their own right, capable of tilting the policies of the EU and occasionally of NATO itself. 'I think western European leaders are starting to listen to us,' says Gitanas Nausėda, the Lithuanian president.

I think sometimes it takes a longer period of adjustment, because you have to change your mindset, and sometimes it's not so easy to do because the countries are far away from Russia or Belarus, but I think we are able to do this and that is the strength of NATO: that all alike are listening to each other, adjusting themselves to the changing situation.

All of these countries in one way or another feel directly menaced by Russia, either because it looms on their borders or bombards them with aggressions that never quite rise above the threshold for military conflict. What unites them is a perception that the core values of the West are at stake and can only be preserved by the West's standing up for them with greater conviction and commitment. If there is a way out of Europe's current crisis of confidence and purpose, these are the countries where it will begin.

Denmark has offered its entire inventory of artillery to Ukraine, joined forces with the Netherlands to set up a coalition for donating F-16 combat jets to Kyiv and set out a proposal for the creation of an EU cyber-defence 'brigade'.[4] Sweden was the first European country to shut down its Confucius institutes and 'classrooms', tools of Chinese state influence in the guise of cultural exchange.[5] Estonia initiated the ammunition procurement drive for Kyiv and publicly contemplated putting troops on the ground in Ukraine for training or air defence.[6] Latvia, which had counted Russia among its top five import and export partners before 2022, has debated whether to sever these trade ties altogether with a blanket embargo.[7] In early 2024 the presidents of Latvia and Estonia made a joint appeal to their NATO allies to consider following the example of the frontline states and bring back conscription.[8]

When Antony Blinken, the US secretary of state, told the foreign ministers of the Baltic states that they were 'leading the way' in NATO, it was more than just a condescending pat on the back. It was a recognition that they have been the activist wing of the transatlantic alliance.[9] The three countries, often acting in concert with their neighbours, have lobbied Brussels to confiscate frozen Russian assets and senators in Washington to release a $60 billion package of weapons for the Ukrainian armed forces.[10]

They have consistently urged their western allies to be bolder and more creative in resisting Russian pressure and not allow themselves to be so intimidated by Moscow's efforts at nuclear blackmail. 'We need to understand that Putin is a gambler and all the threats he makes are not because he's strong, but because he feels weak,' says Gitanas Nausėda.

> Probably this is the best deterrent: to stay strong, united and show that we cannot be intimidated by Vladimir Putin, because otherwise Putin will receive the signals of our vulnerability immediately and reach the conclusion that the western countries are again weak and unable to take decisions.

Poland's swashbuckling security leadership has already been detailed in chapter six. Czechia, although only loosely part of the Baltic world in a geographical sense, has often been an integral part of these ad hoc coalitions.[11] It was the first western country to donate main battle tanks to Ukraine. As Kyiv ran desperately low on artillery ammunition, Czechia took the initiative, identifying available stocks of 800,000 shells and pressing its larger neighbours to help pay for them.[12] 'We are the hobbits,' Tomáš Kopečný, the Czech government's special representative for Ukraine once said. 'We are small and peaceful, but in a moment of crisis we leap up and deliver results.'[13]

Constant Coercion

But the clearest case of unilateral bravery and globe-spanning ambition is Lithuania. In 2021, Taiwan, a self-governing island that Beijing regards as an irksomely errant Chinese territory and which it intends to reunify with the mainland, by force if it has to, had asked whether it could open a quasi-diplomatic 'representative office' in Vilnius under its own name, rather than the usual euphemism 'Taipei'. The Lithuanians said yes. What might sound on the face of it like a minor technicality, amounting to a single Chinese character, was an unmistakable provocation: a rare gesture of European support for Taiwan's struggle to maintain its autonomy.

China bristled. The Chinese foreign ministry, warning that Lithuania must 'bear all the ensuing consequences' for its 'mistake', said it would scale back bilateral relations.[14] It then withdrew its ambassador to Lithuania and expelled the Lithuanian ambassador from Beijing. The Lithuanian embassy in China closed a few weeks later after its last senior diplomats were kicked out.[15]

That was only the hors d'oeuvres. China decided to make an example of Lithuania by instigating a full trade war. Even before the Taiwan dispute it had been creating difficulties for Lithuanian food exporters. That December it then blocked a Lithuanian company from unloading a shipment of wood in one of its ports. It emerged that not only had Lithuania been wholly erased from the Chinese customs system, but foreign firms that had Lithuanian elements in their supply chains were also being put under pressure.[16]

Chinese goods trains bound for Europe no longer stopped in the Baltic state. Beijing instructed large European manufacturers, including the German car part makers Continental and Hella, to cut Lithuanian components out of their products or suffer the ramifications. The main German business lobby criticised China for the campaign of coercion but also indirectly denounced Lithuania for moving 'out of step' with the rest of the EU.[17]

But Vilnius rode out the storm. The government lent the private sector €130 million to help it cope with the losses. The US stepped in with a $600 million export credit fund and strong expressions of support from figures as senior as Antony Blinken, the secretary of state, and Kamala Harris, the vice-president. Taiwan provided a $200 million high-tech investment fund and $1 billion in loans. Latvia, Estonia and even Slovenia's proudly illiberal prime minister rallied round their neighbour.[18] Germany also stood by Lithuania, albeit after a certain period of humming and hawing.

The EU made a formal complaint to China, took up the case at the World Trade Organisation, and accelerated the development of a common mechanism for fighting back against similar cases of geoeconomic coercion. China lifted the embargo on Lithuania barely a week later.[19] It was an extraordinary case where a country of 2.8 million had defied a superpower of 1.4 billion people and left the wider West stronger as a result, not least by obliging its allies to show their real colours.

The Lithuanian government had various reasons for making its stand, not all of them points of principle. Margarita Šešelgytė, the director of Vilnius University's Institute of International Relations and Political Science, says part of the calculus was an appeal for America's goodwill and attention.[20] But it was largely the fruit of a long process of moral reckoning. As early as 2013 the country's formidable president Dalia Grybauskaitė, sometimes nicknamed the Steel Magnolia, had vexed Beijing by welcoming the Dalai Lama to Vilnius.[21] At the end of the decade Lithuanians demonstrated against China's heavy-handed abolition of civil liberties in Hong Kong, prompting one Chinese tourist to vandalise a protest sign on the Hill of Crosses, a venerated place of pilgrimage in northern Lithuania.[22]

The national security agency issued a public warning about Chinese intelligence activities on Lithuanian soil. The following year, a new centre-right coalition government that had pledged to 'defend those fighting for freedom around the world, from Belarus to Taiwan' fulfilled its promise. It made Lithuania the first country to pull out of the '17+1' format, a vehicle for Chinese trade with central and eastern European countries that has since been abandoned by the other two Baltic states.[23] It blocked a Chinese state-owned technology company from supplying scanners to its airports and decided to phase out Chinese-made components from its drone industry.[24]

Gabrielius Landsbergis, the Lithuanian foreign minister, has also called on the EU to prepare for the possibility of an enforced economic 'decoupling' from China should Beijing invade Taiwan.[25] He says he and many other Lithuanians instinctively bridle at China's harassment of its south-east Asian neighbours because of their own recent history. 'There are many points that we do recognise when it comes to a greater non-democratic power trying to assert dominance over its neighbourhood,' he says.

> We've seen throughout our decades of independence since 1990: there was a way Russia behaved, with economic coercion, energy coercion, diplomatic coercion . . . There's a lot of resemblance to this when it comes to the Pacific. Taiwan, that's one case, but there are others. We're seeing rather similar patterns in the Philippines and other countries in the region that are really now trying to [raise

the alarm] and saying: 'Look, we are already finding ourselves in this situation of constant coercion. We need assistance.' And that is what brings us closer together.

In 2023 Landsbergis published his country's first strategy for the Indo-Pacific, which included promises to help safeguard democracy and human rights in the region and to build ties with NATO partners such as Japan and South Korea.[26] From a less credible country of Lithuania's size, the document might have seemed comically self-important. Yet it formalised an approach that is being studied by much larger states in the West.

Lithuania has since acquired enough clout on the international stage for both Japan and the US to send senior representatives to a Vilnius conference on economic coercion in May 2024. '[This] is a testament to Lithuania's resistance and spirit, and also proof that countries can and should stand up to economic bullying,' Jose W. Fernandez, one of the Biden administration's top economic policy officials, said during the meeting.[27]

Small States Behaving Badly

No less instructive is a case where Lithuania found itself more isolated on the western side. Kaliningrad looms large over the country's security. A historical oddity, the territory originally belonged to the German province of East Prussia but was annexed by Stalin to the USSR in 1945, in large part because it provided him with an ice-free port and naval base on the Baltic. The area has been a weeping sore between Russia, Lithuania and the rest of Europe since the end of the Cold War.

The Kaliningrad question returned to Europe with a vengeance in 2022, after the full-scale Russian invasion of Ukraine. That June and July, as the EU imposed sanctions on Russian products including steel, iron, cement, coal, petrol and various luxury goods, Lithuania announced that these would be implemented on the transit trains to Kaliningrad as well.[28] According to the Russian authorities, these measures affected about 50 per cent of the territory's imports, although they could still be rerouted in limited quantities by sea or air.[29] Moscow was enraged. The Kremlin inaccurately accused Lithuania of 'blockading' its territory and threatened that the 'unprecedented' and 'hostile' step would lead to retaliation with a 'serious negative impact on the Lithuanian population'.[30] Anton Alikhanov, Kaliningrad's governor, warned that the Baltic states' logistical infrastructure would be 'destroyed' and half of the Lithuanian economy wiped out.[31]

This time, Lithuania's larger western partners did not have its back. Its most outspoken opponent in the EU was Olaf Scholz, the German chancellor, who upset the Lithuanians by publicly criticising the restriction of goods transit between 'two parts of Russia'.[32] The European Commission in Brussels issued legal guidance that the sanctions were not to be applied to the Kaliningrad trains.[33] However, two Lithuanian sources have confirmed to me that the most 'forceful' pressure on Vilnius came from Washington. Spooked by intelligence estimates suggesting that Putin was prepared to launch a low-yield nuclear strike after the Ukrainians sank the *Moskva*, the Russian Black sea fleet's flagship, a few weeks earlier, American diplomats are understood to have browbeaten Lithuania both through direct channels and indirectly by way of Berlin.

Some analysts, as well as the opposition parties and sections of the media in Lithuania itself, argued that Vilnius had 'lost' the tug-of-war and should not have risked it in the first place. The incident had shown, they said, that the West as a whole was inclined to blink first in a stand-off with Russia. That last part is certainly a tenable view. But I find it hard to see what Lithuania did lose from the dispute, apart from a bit of face in the short term.

To borrow a metaphor from Annalena Baerbock, the German foreign minister, the maintenance of western unity does not require every state to follow the same line at all times, any more than a football team benefits from having eleven defensive midfielders on the pitch. In the current situation, activist states such as Lithuania take on the role of impish wingers probing away at the flanks. Sometimes they get stranded upfield and give the ball away. Without their endeavours, though, the side as a whole would be much more pedestrian and easy to read.

'It's a funny thing that many countries, many representatives, would like to say the same things [we do],' says Gabrielius Landsbergis. 'They feel the same tensions, but they do not find themselves in a situation where they could say the same things themselves. For them . . . it's easier to support somebody rather than to say these things yourself.'

This is not how small states were classically supposed to conduct themselves. Through much of the twentieth century, international relations were largely thought to be governed by a set of doctrines known as 'realism'. This is a fairly broad church but centres on the notion that geopolitics is an essentially anarchic affair in which the more powerful entities use their strength to assert their interests. In its crudest form this has often boiled down to the motto of the cannibals in David Mitchell's novel *Cloud Atlas*: the weak are meat, the strong do eat.

Today, however, Lithuania and its neighbours have not only re-established themselves on the map of Europe, broken away from the Russian sphere of influence and battered down the doors into the EU and NATO. They have also asserted a claim to moral leadership of the West itself. To understand why they have done so, and to understand why much bigger western countries could benefit from following their example, it is useful to take at least a peremptory look at Lithuania's modern history.

Rebel Nation

On 23 October 1988, a vast crowd is gathering in the square next to Vilnius cathedral.[34] Marcelijus Martinaitis, a bearded poet with thick-rimmed spectacles and unruly grey hair, is hauled up on to an impromptu stage. For decades he has been playing a game of literary cat-and-mouse with the Soviet censors, gradually mixing Lithuanian traditions and subversive elements into the rigid social realist style prescribed by Moscow.

Now, though, Martinaitis, a founding member of the Sąjūdis national independence movement, is finally free to speak from the heart. The masses begin to chant a word that has been suppressed from the country's public spaces for almost half a century: *Lietuva*

(Lithuania). But silence falls as Martinaitis recites a poem about the joys of spring, 'when all of Lithuania returns / after a long winter's exile / to the fields'.

Then the crowd sings along en masse to an ancient folk ballad that has become the anthem of their peaceful revolution against Soviet occupation. It is about a young horseman who must blow three trumpets before he rides out to war. The first blast will make his parents weep for his impending death. The second will make the city of Vilnius rise. And when he sounds the third, the song concludes, the entire earth will tremble.

The rally, marking the founding conference of Sąjūdis and the beginning of the final leg of the journey towards the restoration of independence, encapsulates something distinctive and important about Lithuania's understanding of itself. It is saturated with imagery from the country's days as the last pagan empire in medieval Europe, when its territory extended south and east into what is now Ukraine. It is also infused with a sense that what happens in Lithuania will shape the course of world history.

Some commentators have plausibly suggested that the country has its own entrenched version of the Polish 'Christ of Nations' complex. After all, the Polish national poet Adam Mickiewicz, who coined the phrase, was born in Vilnius to a polonised Lithuanian noble family and *Pan Tadeusz*, his most famous work, began with an apostrophe to 'Lithuania, my fatherland'.[35] Žygimantas Pavilionis, the chair of the Lithuanian parliament's foreign affairs committee, says: 'From the middle ages we have had the same spirit, together with our Polish brothers and sisters: we fight for our freedom and yours.'

Lithuania's long experience of subjection to foreign powers was also in some ways quite unlike those of its Baltic neighbours. While the incipient Latvian and Estonian national awakenings of the nineteenth century had to contend with the 'double yoke' of Russian imperial rule and the Baltic German aristocracy, they were at least able to define themselves fairly clearly in geographic, linguistic and ethnic terms. Lithuania, on the other hand, was a much more nebulous concept after more than 400 years of progressively tighter and more subservient union with Poland, followed by absorption into the Russian empire in 1795.

After a rebellion in 1830, Russia did everything it could to stamp out Lithuanian nationhood. The word 'Lithuania' was banned and the province was rebranded the 'Northwest Territory'. Printers were forced to use the cyrillic alphabet, including for religious literature. Vilnius University was closed down. Russian law was imposed on the courts and the Russian language was imposed on the administration.[36]

In response Lithuania became, as the historian V. Stanley Vardys put it in the title of one of his books on the country, a 'rebel nation'. In 1863 there was a failed uprising against both the Russian and Polish overlords. Operating from the neighbouring German province of East Prussia, which included Neringa and Klaipėda, Lithuanian book smugglers snuck astonishing quantities of printed material in Roman type across the border, including nationalist newspapers, Catholic devotional texts and scholarly works on folklore. From 1891 to 1902 the Russian authorities seized 172,000 pieces of contraband literature, bound for a population of barely 2.5 million, and these were only the items that got intercepted.[37]

The twentieth century was one long, bitter and recurring lesson that for all the fine words from the western powers, ultimately only the Lithuanians could secure their own nationhood. Over and over again, they were left to their fate and had to take matters into their own hands, while Washington, London, Paris, Berlin and Moscow used them as little more than minor counters in some vast Eurasian boardgame.

Lithuania was only able to achieve its independence after the end of the First World War through a three-front conflict against the Poles, the Bolsheviks and a rogue Russo-German army freebooting through the Baltic states. Poland took Vilnius, the Lithuanian capital, but in 1923 the Lithuanians staged a lightning paramilitary operation and grabbed Klaipėda, which had been detached from Germany and put in a sort of geopolitical limbo under French administration.[38]

At the end of the 1930s Britain and France were prepared to sell Lithuania down the river to the Soviets. The French were quite happy simply to consign the Baltic states to the Kremlin's sphere of influence in exchange for an alliance with Moscow against Nazi Germany, although the British had more reservations about allowing the USSR to send troops into the countries under the thinnest of pretexts.[39]

Yet the negotiations broke down in 1939 and Stalin arrogated dominion over Lithuania through the Molotov–Ribbentrop pact with Hitler instead.[40] When the USSR unilaterally annexed the Baltic states a year later, Stafford Cripps, the British ambassador to Moscow and future post-war Labour chancellor, covertly pressed London formally to acknowledge them as Soviet territory. 'There are flaws in Soviet methods,' Cripps wrote, 'but one can be positive about the population being healthier than would be the case in any Lancastrian industrial town.'[41]

The Soviet and Nazi German occupations during the Second World War scarred Lithuania every bit as deeply as they did the other two Baltic states. But the near-total eradication of the country's ancient and sizeable Jewish minority left a particularly dark legacy. Vilnius, which the Soviets had returned to Lithuania in September 1939, had once been known as the 'Jerusalem of the north', home to at least 55,000 Jews and a distinguished tradition of Torah studies.[42] There were perhaps 200,000 Jewish people living in Lithuania as a whole, accounting for almost a tenth of the total population.[43] In per capita terms, more of them were murdered in Nazi-occupied Lithuania between 1941 and 1944 than in any other occupied country.[44]

What makes these massacres especially uncomfortable is that many of them were carried out by Lithuanians, sometimes acting on their own initiative. As the Wehrmacht drove the Red Army out of the country, Lithuanian newspapers and the provisional Lithuanian government itself began pumping out antisemitic propaganda that linked the Jews to the communist occupation. 'The greatest enemy of Lithuania and other nations was and in some places remains a Jew,' one said. 'Today we are free of the Jewish yoke ... To exterminate the Jewry and communism along with it is a primary task of the new Lithuania.'[45]

The most controversial figure in the Lithuanian Holocaust was Jonas Noreika, a ferociously anti-communist partisan nicknamed 'General Storm', who has been posthumously accused of collaborating with the Nazis and personally ordering or approving the murder of anything between 1,800 and 14,000 Jews. Until quite recently Noreika was widely remembered as a martyr of the national struggle against the Soviets. There is a school named after him in his native village, Šukioniai, and a plaque erected in Vilnius to celebrate his memory was taken down in 2019, only to be replaced a few weeks later.

This remains a heavily contested element of Lithuania's history. The country is still in the early stages of what the Germans call *Vergangenheitsaufarbeitung*, the 'working-over' of its past. This is a much more delicate and morally fraught process than the history politics of the Soviet occupation. But the inner discomfort does lend a certain edge to the Lithuanian government's stand for liberal democratic values around the world, from Ukraine to Taiwan. It is quite possible that the knowledge of how easily those values can be compromised makes the compulsion to define, display and defend them a little stronger.

The Queen of the Pancake Ball

Lithuania mounted an unusually determined resistance to the Soviet occupiers, culminating in the Sąjūdis independence movement that emerged in the late 1980s and later formed the nucleus of Gabrielius Landsbergis's Homeland Union party, the ideological motor behind the country's recent foreign policy.[46]

The Lithuanian Forest Brotherhood, which waged an underground war against the second Soviet occupation from 1944 until the mid-1950s, may have involved as many as 100,000 people in total.[47] In the early days it had at least 33,000 partisans hidden in the country's dense forests, launching raids, assassinating Soviet officials and publishing at least fifty-four different newsletters and other pamphlets. For a few years they frequently paralysed the machinery of occupation, sucking in as many as thirty Soviet security soldiers for every Lithuanian guerrilla and ultimately requiring the personal attention of Lavrentiy Beria, Stalin's secret police chief.[48]

It was a doomed and unequal battle from the very beginning, but the Lithuanians fought it with tremendous bravery and skill. In his history of the movement, Dan Kaszeta tells the story of Anelė Senkūtė, a municipal accountant in the south-western Marijampolė district and a clandestine liaison to the Forest Brothers, known as the 'queen of the pancake ball'. Senkùtė earned this nom de guerre after she held a sham engagement party with vodka and pancakes for local Soviet officials, complete with a fake fiancé, a Forest Brother called Kazimieras Pyplys. Since they could not obtain any poison to put in the food, Pyplys simply consumed a great quantity of pork fat to line his stomach, drank a copious amount of vodka with the bureaucrats, and then shot them all dead.

The resistance, which had initially styled itself as a kind of shadow government, was crushed after less than a decade through sheer brutality and force of numbers, and by its shortages of equipment. As in Estonia, though, it gave the Lithuanians something to cling on to in their darkest years. After the humiliating capitulation to Stalin in 1939/40, they had gone some way to redeeming their national honour and laid down inspiration and organisational structures for the struggle ahead.

Mantas Adomėnas, who was deputy foreign minister during the Taiwan and Kaliningrad episodes, says the idea that the state could live on through partisan fighters even after its structures were destroyed by a foreign invader has a formal place in the modern Lithuanian constitution and serves as a potential model for the future. 'The postwar military resistance against the Russians was extremely important for the current situation where a direct threat to Lithuania is not inconceivable,' Adomėnas says. 'It also informs our attitude towards NATO.'

But there is another less well-known dimension to the Lithuanian Forest Brothers that makes them relevant for today's purposes. Since the 1990s researchers have shown how the British and American intelligence services tried to harness the partisans, leading them to believe that they were to be the spearhead of a western-backed insurgency against the USSR. Yet the actual plan cooked up by MI6 was much more limited in scope and executed with a half-hearted ineptitude that recalls the botched insertion of an agent into communist East Germany in John le Carré's novel *The Looking-Glass War*.

Under the aptly named 'Operation Blunderhead', the British spies Harry Carr and Sandy McKibbin recruited a ring of agents from the

Baltic refugee community, primarily in Sweden, and trained them at various sites in the UK. They were then to be smuggled back into Lithuania and the other two Baltic republics on motorboats from German ports via Bornholm through a front organisation known as the 'British Baltic Fishery Protection Service'.[49]

But Soviet intelligence were monitoring every step of the plan through their moles in MI6. When a group of agents landed on the Lithuanian coast in May 1949, they were immediately caught in an ambush and all but one of them were captured and turned into double agents. At least five more groups were compromised in a similar fashion, allowing the Soviets to worm their way into Baltic émigré organisations in the West. The whole enterprise was a fiasco and McKibbin was ultimately forced to resign.[50] Once again, the Lithuanians had been left in the lurch by western bungling and cynicism.

The second important aspect of the occupation is how little success the Soviets subsequently had in their efforts to grind down Lithuanian identity, even in comparison to the other two Baltic states. Like Latvia and Estonia, Lithuania was subjected to a wholesale programme of social engineering. Mikhail Suslov, the communist ideologue and close ally of Stalin who oversaw the purging of Lithuanian nationalists from 1944, once said: 'Yes, there will be a Lithuania. But without Lithuanians.'[51]

About 280,000 people out of a population of 2.5 million were deported, including 18,000 in only a few days during the mass arrests in June 1941.[52]

In a strongly Catholic country, the Soviet administration set about waging Stalin's 'war against God' with great zeal. Vincentas Borisevičius, the bishop of Telšiai, was shot dead and buried in a mass grave in 1946 for allegedly supporting the partisans. A year later Mečislovas Reinys, the archbishop of Vilnius, was arrested and deported to the infamous Vladimir prison near Moscow, where he died in 1953. Seminaries were forbidden to train enough priests to cover all the parishes, clergy were banned from administering the last rites, and toddlers were to be brought up as 'real atheists' from nursery school on.[53] The Soviets predicted that the church would die out in two decades.[54]

All the repression, though, did not so much stamp out national sentiment as condense it. The severity of the measures reflected the recalcitrance with which the authorities had to contend. Mikhail Suslov's prediction of a Lithuania without Lithuanians also turned out to be entirely wrong: unlike Latvia and Estonia, it not only had a pronounced religious identity and an imperial past of its own but also received comparatively little immigration from Russia and other Soviet socialist republics (SSRs), in part because it was less urban and industrialised.

In the 1950s Antanas Sniečkus, the first secretary of the SSR's Communist Party from 1940 to 1974, infuriated Khrushchev by approving the reconstruction of the magnificent medieval castle on Trakai island, the old seat of the Lithuanian grand dukes, and preventing the dmolition of Thomas Mann's former summer house on Neringa.[55] Over the next two decades, both official newspapers and internal Communist party briefings repeatedly complained of the 'individualism' and 'nationalist tendencies' among young Lithuanians.[56]

In an echo of the nineteenth-century book smugglers, it has been estimated that Lithuania had a higher number of samizdat publications and protest rallies in per capita terms than any other SSR. By the start of the 1980s there was such a volume of underground dissent, including against the Soviet invasion of Afghanistan and the suppression of the Solidarność movement in Poland, that the Kremlin began to perceive it as a serious threat.[57]

Lithuanian writers disobeyed the regime with remarkable frequency. A great many of them were incarcerated in psychiatric institutes. This tactic allowed the authorities to dismiss them as mentally disturbed while pumping them full of mind-altering drugs. Vytautas Bložė, a poet whose pharmacist father had been deported to Siberia for giving medicines to the Forest Brothers, was also shut up in an 'asylum' for ten years. As his consciousness fractured under the influence of the pills he was forced to take, Bložė turned his broken thoughts into a metaphor for Lithuania itself in an extraordinary series of free-verse lyric poems whose manuscripts circulated from hand to hand.[58]

We Cannot Endanger Everything We Have Achieved

It is worth briefly dwelling on the manner in which Lithuania wrenched back its independence at the end of the Cold War, because it set so many of the patterns that have continued to the present day. Sąjūdis, whose name simply means 'movement' in Lithuanian, was the SSR's first opposition party, formed in June 1988 by three dozen artists, writers and public intellectuals. The most significant of them was Vytautas Landsbergis, a flamboyant academic musicologist. The Landsbergis dynasty has 150 years of rebel pedigree: his great-grandfather fought against the Russians in the 1863 uprising, his father was a minister in the short-lived anti-communist provisional government of 1941, and his grandson Gabrielius has been the architect of Lithuania's activist foreign policy.[59]

Unlike the gradualist wings of the popular fronts in Latvia and Estonia, Sąjūdis had little appetite for compromise with Gorbachev and was increasingly influenced by radical currents in Lithuanian public opinion.[60] In February 1990, less than two years after the movement was created, its candidates overwhelmingly won the elections to the ruling supreme Soviet. Four weeks later this council, now chaired by Vytautas Landsbergis, became the first in the Soviet Union to declare full independence.

Far from being pleased by this development or granting diplomatic recognition, most western governments were profoundly alarmed. Denmark issued Lithuania with a collective démarche, or formal complaint, from the states of the European Community. Almost without exception, they and the Americans had placed a big bet on cordial relations with Gorbachev and fretted that the 'Lithuanian crisis' would weaken his position against the reactionaries in Moscow. The West Germans in particular were terrified that the issue could derail the negotiations over their own country's reunification.

Western officials also tended entirely to misread the strength of national feeling in the Baltic republics and failed to anticipate the speed at which events were about to unfold. Sir David Lidington, a former British Europe minister who was a special advisor to the foreign secretary Douglas Hurd at the time, recalled that his colleagues had been 'totally taken aback' by what was happening.[61]

The archive of the German foreign office offers an even franker insight into the dismay and perplexity in Washington, Bonn and other European capitals. At first one senior West German diplomat confidently averred that the Soviets would '*de facto* ignore' Lithuania's 'rash' declaration of independence and recommended to his superiors that the West offer the Lithuanians no material encouragement whatsoever.[62] He was mistaken. That April Moscow responded with a full economic blockade, including the cessation of the fuel deliveries on which Lithuanian industry depended.

In public the main western states appealed to both sides to find a compromise solution, but in practice they applied pressure only to the Lithuanians. The American committee on US–Soviet relations dismissed Lithuania's independence as a 'parochial' matter and a poll found 61 per cent of Americans preferred to prioritise ties with Gorbachev. When Kazimira Prunskienė, the Lithuanian prime minister, visited George H. W. Bush in the White House, she was forced to go in through the tourist entrance and display her Soviet passport, lest common courtesies of state relations might be interpreted as a signal of diplomatic recognition.[63]

François Mitterrand and Helmut Kohl, the French and West German leaders, immediately wrote a joint letter to Vytautas Landsbergis. They strongly advised Landsbergis to suspend the effect of all resolutions and legislation passed by the independent Lithuanian parliament.[64] No letter was sent to Gorbachev. In fact, a few days later the Soviet ambassador to Bonn thanked Hans-Dietrich Genscher, the West German foreign minister, for the Landsbergis letter, describing it as a 'gesture of goodwill'. In turn, Genscher asked Moscow to interpret the West's reticence as a mark of how 'the Soviet Union is gaining respect in the world'.[65]

The West Germans set about badgering Prunskienė to 'unconditionally suspend' her country's independence.[66] Months later, when Gorbachev started ranting to Kohl about how 'the nationalists will realise that their time is over', the West German chancellor simply replied that 'a success for President Gorbachev was important for Germany and for Europe. For this reason it was necessary to bring together under one roof all of the nationalities that are pulling apart.'[67]

Mantas Adomėnas, the former deputy foreign minister, argues that these were the years when his country's 'habit of acting alone in extreme circumstances' was formed. 'There are circumstances where Lithuania has broken ranks,' he says.

> It was told it should have kept quiet about its independence. It was not encouraged by anybody at that point ... The Lithuanian popular movement and its political heirs had to make a decision and act on their own. This is a template for many instances later.

In the end, Prunskienė took the British-German-American advice and opened negotiations with Moscow. The blockade was lifted in July 1990 after the Lithuanian supreme Soviet agreed to suspend the laws and motions stemming from independence – but not independence itself – for a hundred days. Vytautas Landsbergis, who had vociferously opposed Prunskienė's more conciliatory approach, likened the West's policy on the issue to Neville Chamberlain and the 1938 Munich agreement. He predicted that the USSR would fall apart.[68]

Six months later, elite Soviet military units began moving into Lithuania in a final, desperate roll of the dice. On 11 January 1991, they seized several administrative buildings across the country. The local Communist Party, which was loyal to Moscow, announced the creation of a 'national salvation committee' that regarded itself as Lithuania's sole legitimate government. That night Lithuanians poured into Vilnius and formed human shields around physical centres of power: the supreme council headquarters, the main television tower and the telephone exchange.

In the early hours of 13 January a column of Soviet armoured vehicles surrounded the TV tower. The tanks started ploughing a path through the mass of Lithuanians and soldiers fired into the crowd. Fourteen civilians died. But the line held and the Soviet forces withdrew.

The 'January events' in Vilnius and Riga were an important turning point in Baltic history. The Soviet retreat from Vilnius prefigured the failure of the August 1991 coup attempt against Gorbachev that brought an end to the USSR itself. Footage of unarmed Lithuanians standing up to Soviet tanks appeared on news bulletins around the world. Vytautas Landsbergis, sublimated for a time into an international hero, assured an interviewer that he had 'no plans for personal survival'.[69] Here was proof that a fading superpower's bluff could be called through courage and resolve. The Lithuanians know that a bully can be faced down because they have already done just that.

Even then, though, the West only began to swing behind Lithuania with some reluctance.

The best many outside observers, and indeed some Lithuanian ministers, thought the country could hope for was to persuade the USSR to grant it an arrangement similar to the neutralisation of Finland after the Second World War. It would be part of the Soviet sphere of influence, with Moscow wielding substantial powers to mould not only its foreign and security policy but its internal affairs, too.[70] Even that was too much for Mitterrand. 'We cannot endanger everything we have achieved,' he told Kohl, 'just to help countries that have not had an existence of their own in 400 years.'[71]

Yet not everyone was so wary. On February 11, 1991, a month after the January events, Iceland was the first country to recognise Lithuania as an independent state. The demonstration of confidence and solidarity mattered so much to Lithuanians that streets in Vilnius, Kaunas and Klaipėda were renamed in Iceland's honour and Iceland's national day is celebrated in Lithuanian cities.[72] Mantas Adomėnas, the former Lithuanian deputy foreign minister, says it had a hugely formative effect on his country. 'This quixotic gesture by Iceland was very important,' he says. 'It was seen as a model and we were obliged by this act to follow their example: on the one hand, by supporting democratic and pro-independence movements in other countries; on the other, by affording recognition when we see a similarly unjust situation.'

The Berlin of the 2020s

The point of this excursus through Lithuania's history is not just to explain where its foreign policy is coming from but to prompt the West as a whole to reconsider its own. Too often our governments have cleaved to fossilised notions of realpolitik, to the idea that affairs of high politics ought to be left to the grown-ups who know best. In these cases they frequently lacked both any kind of positive vision and any accurate appreciation of the facts on the ground and the pace at which they were changing. They have led vulnerable and transitional states caught in the middle of superpower conflicts down the garden path through feeble reassurances, false promises and on occasion outright appeasement of Moscow.

The wider West continued to make the same mistakes with respect to the Baltic states many times after they had conclusively won the battle for their freedom in 1991. Once again, they were expected to remain immovably lodged in Russia's orbit and deemed unsuitable for EU membership, let alone NATO accession. That October a British foreign office official circulated a memorandum so pessimistic about the three countries' prospects that it might have been written in the 1920s. 'As time passes, the Baltic states will attract less attention and less western sympathy, especially if the illiberal treatment of minorities by Landsbergis's Lithuanian government becomes endemic,' he wrote. 'Collectively they muster only eight million people and few economic resources.'[73]

The parallels with Ukraine today are hard to miss. The western powers' failure to stand up for the newly formed Baltic states in the 1920s and early 1930s, while Britain, France and the US were still in a position of relative strength, was symptomatic of their broader failure to contain Hitler and Stalin.[74] Similarly, the wider West's ambivalence towards these countries from the end of the Cold War until 2022 was an expression of the blinkered and over-cautious mindset that led it to leave Ukraine in limbo after the 2004 Orange revolution.

In a 1996 speech to a Washington think-tank, the Estonian president Lennart Meri made a characteristically memorable defence of his country's aspirations to join NATO. 'People often say NATO cannot expand into the Baltic states because the Baltic states are seen as indefensible,' Meri said. 'But allow me this question: was Berlin defensible in the Cold War? . . . The Baltic states are the Berlin of the 1990s.'[75]

Those are the terms in which Lithuania and its neighbours on the eastern flank see Ukraine today. For them, it is not only a fight to roll back Russian aggression. It is a test of the West's will to uphold, assert and develop its core principles. The British philosopher of international relations Christopher Coker argued a few years ago that we had collectively redefined freedom in 'negative terms – not as the power to refashion the world on [our] terms but the right to be left alone, the right to suffer from one's mistakes rather than from the malice of others'.[76] The 'hobbit' states are making the case for a new, more positive definition of freedom.

Now they have their opportunity. France and Germany are so divided that the lowest common denominators they can agree on are very low indeed.[77] That leaves a vacuum for others to fill. The ideal is ultimately to marry the power of western Europe to Baltic, Nordic and central European activism, leading to an EU that is capable of fulfilling its geopolitical promise.[78]

This is a part of the world where the concept of the future still holds real meaning for many people. 'There is a perception among the middle class in the Baltic states that today is better than yesterday. And that is backed up by economic data,' says Una-Aleksandra Bērziņa-Čerenkova, a Latvian foreign policy analyst. In her native country, she points out, GDP per capita has doubled in dollar terms over the past twenty years.[79] 'Within my generation we have seen this growth in the purchasing capacity of the population grow so quickly, and it feels like we've gotten out of something. So the big question now is how to keep it for the next generations,' Bērziņa-Čerenkova says.

Žygimantas Pavilionis, the head of the Lithuanian parliament's foreign affairs committee, says something similar. 'Look, I remember '91 and the January events,' he says.

> I was standing in front of the TV tower. I saw a friend from my own school killed by a Russian tank. I remember my first salary in the foreign ministry was $5, I repeat, five dot zero zero dollars, a month. The last time I counted, my salary had grown 600 times. I'm rich. I'm happy. I have four kids . . . I'm in the best clubs of the world and the leaders of those clubs have started to listen to me. And I have a chance to create the Europe that all our leaders dreamed of.

Lithuania is the poster child for a very real change in Europe. 'Sometimes I think of Lithuanians like the generation after the Second World War in western Europe, in the generation of Robert Schuman [the French godfather of what eventually grew into the EU],' says Pavilionis.

> They too were romantic people trying to create a unity after the devastation of a world war. Unfortunately, Lithuania and other countries in this region had their own war that lasted until we declared independence [in 1991]. Thirty thousand Lithuanian troops died in the woods, fighting the Soviet aggressor. We have the mentality of freedom fighters. I think it should never be forgotten, even if we live for seventy-five years in freedom. You should always be ready.

The language of this movement is also beginning to spread to larger western countries. Speaking at the old royal castle in Warsaw a month after the beginning of the full-scale Russian invasion of Ukraine, Joe Biden conjured memories of Solidarność's defiance of communist power and quoted the Polish pope John Paul II's 1979 address to the free world: 'Be not afraid.' At times, Biden's rhetoric recalled John F. Kennedy's *Ich bin ein Berliner* speech from 1963. The Ukrainians' 'brave resistance', he said, was 'part of a larger fight for essential democratic principles that unite all free people: the rule of law; free and fair elections; the freedom to speak, to write, and to assemble; the freedom to worship as one chooses; freedom of the press'. The West had to steel itself for 'the long fight ahead'.

A year later, Emmanuel Macron also began to sound distinctly like a Baltic leader. First he told the central and eastern Europeans that France and the other countries of 'old' Europe had 'missed opportunities' to listen to them and that their 'voices must be all of our voices'.[80] Then he repeatedly suggested that NATO members could send troops to Ukraine, arguing that the important thing was to preserve 'strategic ambiguity' and keep Putin guessing about what the West might do.[81] Finally Macron capped off his conversion with a long speech warning that Europe was in 'mortal' danger and needed to assume responsibility for its own defence.[82]

As with Joe Biden and the British and German ministers who have talked a decent game on these subjects, Macron's actions have not yet corresponded to the stirring radicalism of his words. According to the latest international comparison, his country's bilateral military aid to Ukraine has so far been lower in absolute terms than Denmark's or Sweden's.[83] Its nominal defence spending per year is expected almost to double between 2017 and 2030 but only just squeaked above NATO's 2 per cent target in 2024.[84]

But the Baltic states tend at least to be grateful for the rhetorical reinforcement Macron has given them and the way he has brought a note of daring and unpredictability back into western Europe's posture. 'Well, there's always space for a fourth Baltic country. We'll leave [Macron] a chair at our table,' says Gabrielius Landsbergis.

Against the backdrop of history, this is an extraordinary phenomenon. A coalition of small and traditionally peripheral countries, whose destinies used to be traded between the great powers with less respect than horses, have become the ideological vanguard of the most powerful military alliance on the planet. The question is now whether the rest of us will have the humility to listen to them as equals and learn to see the world the way they see it.

Regardless of whether we do, Lithuania and its allies show no sign of backing down. As Romualdas Ozolas, an influential Sąjūdis activist and MP, said during the Soviet siege of Vilnius in January 1991:

Should we quietly suffocate? Excuse me: I did not rise to freedom for that. Independently of how events will unfold around us, I will be a person whose children will not be able to accuse me that again, like in the 1940s, not a single shot was fired.[86]

PART III
Survival

8

Imperium of Hopelessness

What the Kremlin is Doing to Us and Why

> Don't ask when the war will end. It doesn't exist at all, and it will never end, for our homeland knows no boundaries
>   Victor Erofeyev (2023), Russian novelist[1]

On a grey January afternoon, I am returning to Berlin from a NATO base in Sczczecin when the Flixbus stops at the German-Polish frontier. Three German border police officers climb aboard and rigorously examine the passengers' travel documents, baulking when a Ukrainian war refugee offers up the Diia app that has largely superseded the physical ID card in his home country.

As I reach for my residency permit, I see a security alert on my iPhone: malware is 'possibly' present on the device. My mind races back to all the accounts I have read of Russian electronic warfare: sinister messages appearing in the inboxes of Ukrainian soldiers on the front line, and NATO units on the eastern flank discovering that their phones have been infected with everything from Russian-language maps to hip-hop tracks.[2] A couple of years earlier I was one of a number of *Times* journalists whose emails were breached by hackers apparently working for Chinese intelligence, who snooped on correspondence with my wife as well as imaginatively trawling for search terms such as 'Tibet' and 'Xinjiang'.[3] The more you learn about this sort of thing, the less you believe in coincidence.

During the rest of the journey I carry out a dozen anti-virus scans, none of which works. The technicians from my network provider are supremely unbothered, suggesting that it is bound to be a false alarm. I get the phone wiped anyway.

From hacking the directors of a Finnish intelligence agency and Germany's two largest political parties to arson, the sabotage of infrastructure and a string of assassinations, Russia's security services and their associates are waging what can only be described as an industrial-grade 'shadow war' on Europe, with ever-increasing intensity. The possible hijacking of a reporter's smartphone seems trivial in comparison. But I think there is something telling about its triviality.

The overwhelming majority of these incidents – fires in shopping centres, graffiti on underpasses, patently propagandistic social media bots, the vandalism of the Estonian interior minister's car, pointlessly blunt cyber-attacks on the Latvian public broadcaster – seem to have an almost aimless quality to them, more like spam or displacement activity than elements of a systematic plot to destroy NATO from the inside.

The standard explanation for this behaviour is that it is a cheap way to try and tie up resources, to sow paranoia, to exacerbate tensions within and between societies, to intimidate voters and policy-makers, to demand attention and above all to test how the western allies respond. The unifying theory is destabilisation, keeping the West and especially the Baltic sea region jittery and off balance. None of these answers is implausible. Yet none of them is wholly satisfactory, either.[4]

It is not just that the 'grey-zone' tactics risk falling foul of the law of diminishing returns, which may help to account for the recent uptick in their volume. It is also that ultimately they are in danger of backfiring by strengthening the West's resilience and cohesion. They often feel less like a strategic tool deployed by the upper levels of the regime than a sort of opportunistic hyperactivity by the 'adhocracy' beneath them: at most, an exercise in 'putting a hedgehog in the enemy's trousers', as Nikita Khrushchev said of the 1962 Cuban missile crisis.[5] If this is a political war, we have to interrogate its aims. In the end, there is no getting round the most basic question of the lot: what does Putin actually want with us?

The Entire Force of Impotence

This chapter is an attempt to answer that question. I have put it to two dozen Russia analysts, Russian émigrés, government ministers and officials, intelligence officers, and present and former diplomats with experience of Moscow. The result was *quot homines, tot sententiae*: there are as many opinions as there are people.

The most optimistic school of thought suggests that we are in danger of putting two and two together and making seventeen. There are many experts who argue that most of the disruption is exactly as unfocused as it appears to be: the handiwork of junior Russian intelligence grunts and their affiliates in the criminal underworld, jockeying for position and trying to impress their superiors. Busyness for busyness' sake. And at the centre of it all, these observers say, Putin and his inner circle are simply out for what they can get. If there is a strategic goal, it is to weaken the West and chip away at its cohesion, not to defeat it on the battlefield.

But the more disconcerting reading is that these are the preparations for a possible invasion of the Baltic region. Much of the activity, according to this theory, has an unmistakably military character: scoping out bases, mapping the vulnerabilities of critical transport infrastructure, planting destructive software in computer systems and above all constantly testing the NATO allies' commitment to their Article 5 mutual defence clause. The pettier stuff is a form of complementary psychological warfare. Russia's armed forces may be indefinitely bogged down in Ukraine. Yet the regime consistently characterises the war as a kind of sub-plot in an epochal conflict with the West. Putin's mobilisation machinery and arms factories are running at such a scale that the Kremlin could conceivably amass the capacity for an effective strike on NATO within only a few years of an armistice with Kyiv.

In an effort to square this circle I have read countless books and academic papers on Russia. The text that has indelibly stuck in my memory is a 2023 German-language novel recommended by a retired diplomat who had spent many years in Moscow: the Russian exile Victor Erofeyev's *Der große Gopnik* (The Great Gopnik).

Since the Brezhnev era Erofeyev has been a satirical thorn lodged in the side of successive regimes. He had a distinctive place in Putin's Russia: an insider–outsider, on first-name-and-patronymic terms with many of its political elite, unattached to any particular dissident faction, marinated in Russian culture and yet intimately acquainted with the Baltic sea region and northern Europe in general. For many years he stayed on in Moscow even as his friends and colleagues left for the West. 'In Russia it was [previously] possible not to be black or white. You could be in a grey zone,' he says.[6]

A few days after the full-scale invasion of Ukraine, however, Erofeyev finally packed up his possessions, drove into Finland, took a ferry to Estonia and wound up in Berlin. It is a natural transitory home for a highly cultivated Russian dissident writer following in the footsteps of Vladimir Nabokov, Boris Pasternak, Vladimir Mayakovsky, Vladimir Sorokin and Ludmila Ulitskaya.[7] When I meet Erofeyev at a cafe near his new home in the genteel Prenzlauer Berg district, the first apple blossoms of spring are just starting to appear and both the war and the Russia he left behind feel very far away.[8] But neither is ever completely out of his thoughts. His book *The Great Gopnik* is an excoriating denunciation of Putin and Russia's wider political culture, full of scatological wrath, erotically charged dream sequences and half-encrypted recollections of Erofeyev's encounters with the Moscow elite. The gopnik of the title is a ubiquitous figure across the Slavic world, a petty hoodlum who compensates for his intellectual limitations by bullying the weak.

The main thing I want to know from Erofeyev is what he thinks is driving Russia's approach to Europe: a desire for conquest, the restoration of its former sphere of influence, the hope of pegging back NATO, a yearning for 'respect' and superpower status, or simply aggression for aggression's sake.

His answer is, crudely summarised: all of the above. The regime is pursuing an 'imperium out of hopelessness', he wrote in *The Great Gopnik*. Its 'attempt to bring these sodding Yanks to the negotiating table for a Yalta mark 2 and to begin the endless process of conquering the world' stems from the collision of an 'inferiority complex and a complex of superiority towards all the other nations'.* 'In the end,' Erofeyev wrote, 'everything can be explained through impotence. The collapse is inevitable. But against this collapse the entire force of impotence will be set, and our country will battle its way through a bloodbath.'[9]

---

* The Yalta conference in February 1945 was the second of three wartime summits where Stalin and the West split Europe along more or less the lines that would define the Cold War.

In person, Erofeyev paints an even bleaker picture of Putin's goals. 'I think he would like to have these Baltic countries, first of all,' he says.

> He knows that in Riga and Lithuania there are so many Russians that it would be a good pretext for him to take them . . . There are no limits to his imagination. When people say that these places are already Europe, that Estonia is already more European than many other European countries, he doesn't care about that. Everybody will be against a Russian invasion in the Baltic countries, including [the local ethnic] Russians, almost all of them. But he doesn't care. So [an invasion] is a possibility. It's a dangerous possibility. The further we go, the more danger we are going to have around us. It's like an infection. It's like a cancer.

Even the most hawkishly minded western Russia analysts would not put it in quite those terms. Erofeyev has a novelist's licence for broad diagnoses and mild hyperbole. But his view is not so very far out of line with the more sceptical wing of the Russia-watching community. There are many experts who argue that not only Putin but also a large portion of the Moscow establishment regard the Baltic states as annoying lost sheep to be brought home by a second 'gatherer of the lands', much as the tsar Peter I first conquered them at the start of the eighteenth century. Since Putin is himself an enthusiastic amateur historian with an inclination to derive his *casus belli* from the deep past, it is important to try and understand the factors that have shaped Russia's view of the Baltic sea region.

Returning What Is Russia's

Putin's proprietorial interest in the Baltic is partly personal. He grew up in St Petersburg, a former imperial capital that once controlled a significant fraction of the sea's coastline. He and a number of his closest associates have set up a colony of dachas by the shore of lake Komsomol'skoye, barely 40 miles from the Finnish border. His ex-wife Lyudmila Putina was born in Kaliningrad and worked as a flight attendant for the local branch of Aeroflot.[10]

He appears to bear a particular grudge against Estonia. During the Second World War his father, also called Vladimir, was part of an NKVD 'destruction battalion' sent on a 'suicide mission' behind the German lines in the Baltic state. His job was to execute Estonians who collaborated with the Nazi occupation and sabotage any resources or infrastructure he could find. He was wounded but made it through the deployment. Putin Jr's chief of staff, Anton Vaino, is also the grandson of Karl Vaino, the last staunchly pro-Kremlin leader of communist Estonia, who was forced out of office in 1988 by his nationalist rivals. It was no accident that Putin included the Estonians alongside the Ukrainians on a list of 'traitors to the USSR' that was picked up by US intelligence and published in the WikiLeaks cables.[11]

For Putin and other Russian nationalists, though, the country's claim to dominion over the Baltic is primarily a historical birthright. Since the twelfth century, when the principalities of Novgorod and Pskov commanded much of the south-eastern Baltic's river-borne trade and extracted tribute from various Estonian statelets, successive incarnations of the Russian state have treated the region as a source of both power and danger.[12]

The perception of danger is especially pertinent. From the semi-legendary 'battle on the ice' of 1242, when Alexander Nevsky's Novgorodians beat off an invading force of Teutonic knights and their Estonian auxiliaries on the frozen surface of lake Peipus, to Charles XII of Sweden's deep thrust into the Russian empire in 1707 to 1709, the Baltic was once as much of a threat to the Russian lands as vice versa.

In the fourteenth century, Lithuanian armies under the grand duke Algirdas twice attacked the Kremlin itself. During the 'time of troubles' at the turn of the seventeenth century, Muscovy teetered on the brink of becoming a 'Polish province' and the Swedes besieged Novgorod.[13] In 1605 the Poles contrived to install a puppet tsar, known as the 'False Dmitry'. This aroused such intense anger that after the Muscovites overthrew and lynched him the following year, his corpse was dragged around the city by the genitals, chopped up and then burnt, before the ashes were loaded into a cannon and fired off in the direction of Warsaw.

These episodes may have been largely forgotten across much of the West but they are an indelible part of Russian mythology. In 2005 Putin created a new national day to commemorate the final expulsion of the Poles from Muscovy in 1612.[14] It is striking that one of the first structures the Russian occupiers erected in the ruined Ukrainian city of Mariupol was a statue of Nevsky, who appears to be going through a particular vogue at present as a symbol of resistance against hostile incursions from the west.[15]

The unfounded notion that NATO enlargement in the Baltic sea area might be a prelude to an invasion of Russia is only the latest incarnation of a very old pattern. For centuries Russia's leaders have been grabbing territory from their neighbours on the basis that the only truly safe frontier is a frontier with Russian soldiers on either side of it.

Another important historical model for Putin is Peter I, the Russian emperor who defeated Charles XII in Ukraine, founded St Petersburg and permanently established Russia as a Baltic power. In June 2022, four months into the full-scale invasion of Ukraine, Russian state television broadcast a glowing documentary on Peter's western conquests and an exhibition dedicated to the tsar toured the country. 'Peter the Great waged the Great Northern War for twenty-one years,' Putin said afterwards. 'It would seem that he was at war with Sweden, he took something from them. He did not take anything from them, he returned [what was Russia's]. Apparently it is also our lot to return [what is Russia's] and strengthen [the country].'[16]

Mikhail Suslov, an expert on Russian political ideology at Copenhagen university, says Peter I has an 'ambivalent' role in Russia today. He is revered as the leader who restored what is felt to be the country's rightful patrimony to the west. But he is also remembered as a westerniser who opened it up to European influence, borrowing Swedish and German administrative practices and hiring so many Baltic German officers to modernise his armed forces that one frustrated Russian soldier sarcastically asked to be 'promoted to the rank of German'.[17]

There are some obvious points of comparison between Peter I and Putin, in part because Peter set so much of the template for subsequent Russian rulers. Both have strongly concentrated power in their own persons, with only a close inner circle of trusted allies privy to their decision-making. Both have been obsessed with history, particularly as a means of legitimising their actions: it was Peter who had the ancient chronicles of Kyiv and Novgorod moved to Moscow.[18] Both have had a taste for theatrical naval parades on the Baltic. Both have seen conspiracies around every corner and used the full apparatus of state repression, including torture and executions, to squash them. And both have run what would in any democratic society be unsustainably extractive war economies. The American biographer Robert K. Massie calculates that in the first nine years of the Great Northern War Peter I drafted 300,000 soldiers from a total population of 8 million. Scaled up to contemporary Russia, that would be 5.4 million conscripts.[19]

The Falsification of History

From the early 1990s, Russia's official policy towards its western neighbourhood began to harden. Andrey Kozyrev, Yeltsin's moderate foreign minister, heaped pressure on the Baltic states over their treatment of Russian-speaking minorities, supposedly to head off 'neo-imperialists' in Moscow who, he feared, might otherwise lobby for an outright invasion.[20] At one point Kozyrev went so far as to say there might be 'cases where the use of direct military force will be needed to defend our compatriots abroad'.[21] That said, he was also the last representative of the Russian government to acknowledge that the Baltic states had been illegally occupied by the USSR.[22]

These controversies are acutely relevant. In May 2024 Putin tasked an academic called Sergei Karaganov with drawing up techniques to 'deter the West'.[23] Karaganov, an old arch-rival of Kozyrev, is notorious in the Baltic states as the man who formulated the 'Karaganov doctrine', which argued that Russia should aim to keep Russian speakers abroad so that they could serve as 'strings of influence'.[24]

Putin has enthusiastically embraced this doctrine. Under his presidency, the Russian state has repeatedly tried to use 'compatriots' in the Baltic states and other countries as tools of foreign policy. In 2007 Putin created the Russkiy Mir Foundation, which is run by Vyacheslav

Nikonov, a grandson of Molotov and a former senior administrator in the KGB. Agnia Grigas, a Lithuanian-American expert on Russian compatriot policy, likens it to a weaponised version of the British Council or the Goethe Institute, nominally offering Russian language and culture courses but also propagating the Russian regime's views of history, attempting to subvert foreign media narratives and encouraging Russophones to remain loyal to Moscow. For some years Russkiy Mir used to maintain a centre in Latvia, another in Lithuania and two in Estonia, which the local security service said were staffed by 'former Soviet intelligence cadres'.[25]

In the middle of the 2010s Grigas counted a total of 61 organisations associated with the Russian state in Estonia, 81 in Latvia and 97 in Lithuania. Among them are 'antifascist' groups that openly push Russian propaganda lines, such as the notion that the situation in Russophone-majority north-east Estonia is 'the same as south-east Ukraine'. Others have recruited local Russian speakers for paramilitary camps in the 'motherland', which featured training in information warfare tactics.[26]

Many of these groups have since been shut down, or fragmented, and the 'Russian' populations in the Baltic states are in general nothing like the trump card for Putin that they have been made out to be. But he does not necessarily need them to join a Kremlin-sponsored insurrection in any meaningful numbers. All he needs them to do is provide him with an excuse for an intervention.

There are other grounds on which Russia might choose to attack one of its western neighbours. The most obvious is to try and humiliate and weaken NATO by exposing its inability to defend its allies. Then there is the widespread perception in Russia that some of the eastern flank countries pose a danger in their own right. A 2023 poll carried out in five Russian cities for the Estonian foreign ministry asked respondents to rank various European states on a scale from one to sixteen, with one being the most serious threat. They gave Ukraine a median score of one, Poland three, and the Baltic states between four and eight, while Finland was rated between eight and nine.[27]

While it is impossible to imagine any of these countries staging an invasion of Russia, they are certainly regarded by the regime and much of the population as impudent and hostile outposts of NATO. It is also feasible that the very existence of successful, prosperous democratic states just across the frontier is understood as an ideological hazard because of the risk that liberal values might prove contagious.

There is one more potential basis for a Russian assault on Poland or the Baltic states. In a survey, Russians were invited to name the thing that made them most proud of their national history. Eighty-three per cent said it was the 'Great Patriotic War' of 1941 to 1945. The Soviet victory over Nazi Germany on the eastern front has acquired the status of a secular religion. Since the dissolution of the USSR in 1991, the cult has gathered further momentum, in part because it was one of the few national symbols that most Russians could rally behind without reservation.[28]

The Russian regime explicitly regards its version of the war as a matter of national security. Since 2014 its military doctrine has classified 'subversive information activities ... aimed at undermining historical, spiritual and patriotic traditions related to the defence of the Motherland' as a 'main military risk'.[29] Two years later the state archive was placed under the direct control of Putin's office. The Russian armed forces even have a unit tasked with resisting the 'falsification of history'.[30]

For this reason the Baltic states' demolition of Red Army memorials and other challenges to the standard Russian narrative of the 'Great Patriotic War' might conceivably provide Putin with a pretext for a military attack. In this scenario, they would be denounced as Nazis and slotted into the ideology of a battle between the forces of light and darkness in much the same way the Ukrainians have been.

The idea may sound deranged to casual observers in the West, but some of the foundations have already been laid. In February 2024 the Russian interior ministry issued warrants for the arrest of Kaja Kallas, the Estonian prime minister, as well as the Lithuanian culture minister and more than seventy other politicians from the Baltic states. It did not specify what they were accused of but the Kremlin complained they were 'essentially mocking historical memory'. 'They must answer for their crimes against the memory of those who liberated the world from Nazism and fascism! And this is just the beginning,' Maria Zakharova, the chief spokeswoman for the Russian foreign ministry, said at the time.[31]

'One of the reasons Putin started this war was the so-called "denazification" of Ukraine,' says Mikhail Polianskii, a Russia expert at the Peace Research Institute Frankfurt.

And this is one of the goals that he still holds on to despite all of the evidence about the actual situation on the ground in Ukraine. So if you think about the pretext for possible conflict with any of the three Baltic states or Poland in ideological terms, he has one.

Tournament of Shadows

Regardless of whether Moscow will ultimately resort to military force against a NATO ally, it is already exhausting almost the full spectrum of sub-military species of aggression. The terms politicians and the media usually use to describe these activities – 'hybrid warfare' or less frequently the 'Gerasimov doctrine',[32] named after the Russian general Valery Gerasimov who made a speech setting out his predictions for a blurrier future of warfare in 2013 – are liable to elicit an exasperated rolling of the eyes from professional researchers.

They are irritated by the misleading implication that these tactics are something new, rather than continuations of old Russian concepts such as 'special operations', 'active measures' and the 'tournament of shadows', as the German-born Russian foreign minister Karl Nesselrode is said to have called the Great Game against Britain for control of central Asia in the nineteenth century. More significantly, the experts point out that the 'hybrid' term actually denotes the Russian analysis of western methods of political warfare.[33] This is not just academic nitpicking. Getting the theoretical framework right matters a great deal, for two reasons: we need to understand what the Russians think they are doing now, and we need to work out what it is for.

If this story starts anywhere in particular, it starts with Evgeny Messner, another Russian German who came from the Kherson governorate in Ukraine. Messner was an extraordinarily gifted autodidact who stormed upwards through the ranks of the Russian military during the First World War. He was also an arch-conservative and fervent anti-communist who fought against the Bolsheviks with the White Russian army. After his side lost the Russian civil war, Messner moved to Belgrade and ultimately wound up leading the Wehrmacht's Russian-language propaganda department.[34]

Messner's big idea, probably influenced by the total war he had seen on the eastern front, was that the dividing line between the armed forces and the rest of society had vanished: 'All are participating in the war with different and gradual intensity and persistence.'[35] This led him to develop the concept of *myatezhvoina*, which literally means 'insurgency war' but can more accurately be translated as 'subversion war'. In the age of the Cold War, he wrote, it was 'easier to disintegrate the [enemy] state than to conquer it with weapons'. The psychology of the opposing population was a new domain of warfare and grinding it down was a higher objective than anything that guns or bombs could achieve. Messner also thought that there was no longer any clear distinction between peacetime and wartime: 'The line between peace and war has been erased. There is no longer a change between peace, war, peace again. Peace is intertwined with war; strategy with diplomacy.'[36]

Messner's writings were disregarded in the USSR. In the early Putin era, however, he was rediscovered by Russian military theorists, and his doctrines were married together with corresponding elements of the Soviet and post-Soviet philosophies of war. In 2007 Aleksandr Vladimirov, a retired major general who led the Russian International Affairs Council's panel of military experts, wrote that 'modern humanity exists in a state of permanent war . . . with constantly alternating phases of active armed struggle and constant preparation for it.'[37]

The accelerant for this ideology was the Arab spring at the start of the 2010s. The more imaginative commanders in the Russian military joined the dots between the Georgian 'rose' revolution of 2003, the Ukrainian orange revolution of 2004, mass protests against the Belarusian dictator Aleksandr Lukashenko in 2006, and the popular uprisings across the Arab world. This was, they concluded, a pernicious western strategy of interference against Russian interests.

The 'colour revolutions' were, in the opinion of the Russian chief of the general staff Valery Gerasimov, a manifestation of the new

American philosophy of 'hybrid warfare'. In 2013 the Russian military theorists S. G. Chekinov and S. A. Bogdanov published an influential paper arguing that the West would attack its 'victims' with a 'new-generation' war fuelled by modern information technologies, with the goal of achieving a 'distributed attack and strik[ing] damaging point-blows at the country's social system with the purported aims of promoting democracy and respect for human rights'.[38]

In other words, what we in the West tend to describe as hybrid warfare is seen by the Russians as a toolbox that we invented and that can legitimately be used against us in return, not least because we are perceived as the hidden hand guiding Ukraine's campaign of sabotage and strikes on Russian soil. There is clearly an awful lot of projection going on here. It is far from clear that the majority of the Russian defence establishment sincerely saw NATO as a direct threat at the time. Reiner Schwalb, a retired German brigadier general, served as his country's military attaché in Moscow from 2011 to 2018. In the early years, he says, relations were so friendly that Gerasimov thanked him for NATO's campaign in Afghanistan. In Schwalb's experience the atmosphere only began to sour after the Maidan protests and subsequent Russian annexation of Crimea in 2014.

Since then Russia's 'hybrid' measures have exceeded anything that could reasonably be described as self-defence. Messner's two enduring postulates – that war is the fundamental condition of the modern world and that the decisive battleground is the mind of the individual civilian – remain the basis of the campaign against Europe.

Immanuel Kant, Russian Agent

Through the eyes of the Russian regime, then, we are already at 'war', even if the shooting phase has not begun yet and may never begin. 'It's not a question of "Will there be a war?" There is war,' says Krišjānis Kariņš, Latvia's foreign minister and former prime minister.[39] 'It's a question of "Will we do enough to make sure that this war does not spread in Europe?"' The main objective of this phase is 'controlled chaos', a state where our decision-making, both as states and societies, is hampered by doubts and uncertainties. The methods loosely fall into five categories. The first, economic coercion, has already been dealt with at some length in previous chapters.

The second category takes place in the sphere of information. Russia's efforts to sow lies, foment mistrust and suborn the democratic processes across the West have been exhaustively documented, to the point where their reach and efficacy are sometimes overstated. We are more than capable of doing all these things to ourselves. Giving Moscow too much credit for our generally poor standards of informational hygiene not only over-eggs Russia's hold on our populations but also distracts attention from how many of these problems are home-grown.

The countries around the Baltic have had more experience with these techniques than any other part of the West. 'Disinformation is like Covid,' a senior minister from one of the Baltic states says. 'After a while, you build up immunity. You get better at recognising it every time.' But that is not quite the whole truth. While there is some evidence that media literacy is improving in the frontline countries, a significant minority of people are still susceptible to Russian narratives. One analysis found that up to a tenth of Lithuania's population was 'living in a Russian disinformation field'.[40]

Much of Russia's propaganda in the region has until recently been quite a blunt instrument. After the German-led NATO battlegroup was first deployed to Lithuania in 2017, for example, Lithuanian politicians were bombarded with anonymous emails claiming that German-speaking men had raped a five-year-old girl in foster care at a town next to the base. The standard tropes included the ineptitude, corruption and 'fascist' inclinations of the authorities, the abuse of Russian speakers, and fabricated incidents of the sexual abuse of children.[41]

The quality of the disinformation varies a great deal. More than a third of the items detected by a propaganda monitoring project in 2022 concerned the military situation on the ground in Ukraine.[42] About a fifth of the Russian-language messages targeting the Baltic states rehearsed tropes about the Russophobia of their national majorities.[43] There is the usual diet of smears against Ukrainian refugees and conspiracy theories about US-sponsored biological weapons programmes.

Some of the fake news has been simply bizarre. When Evika Siliņa was appointed prime minister of Latvia in 2023, an English-language website called The Baltic Word made up a story that she had a background as an actress in the French adult film industry, using pictures of a porn star who looked nothing like Siliņa. The Baltic Word is an intriguing case study in how Russia's tactics are changing.

Today its 'news' section consists almost entirely of neutrally formulated texts cribbed from public broadcasters and news agencies in the Baltic states. This seems to be intended to lend a sheen of credibility to the 'opinion' pages, which are heavily propagandistic and published under bylines with Lithuanian- and Latvian-sounding names. They take genuine news stories and distort or exaggerate them to paint NATO and the Baltic governments in the worst possible light. Lithuania, one article claims, is out to 'neutralise' Kaliningrad. France and the Baltic states are 'ready to invade Ukraine'. The Baltic states 'use migrants and then eject them'.

Often these messages are amplified by Russia's fellow travellers within Europe. An investigation in the 'shadow war' series by a consortium of Nordic public broadcasters identified at least 152 people in Norway, Sweden, Denmark and Finland who frequently propagated Russian narratives. Among them were Johan Bäckman, a Finn who works for a think-tank subordinate to the Russian presidential administration, and Jesper Larsen, a Danish 'citizen journalist'.*[44] Voice of Europe, a Russian propaganda channel on YouTube, featured at least sixteen MEPs from Germany, Poland, Estonia, Denmark and other countries.[45] According to the Czech authorities, who first exposed the scheme, the outlet paid hundreds of thousands of euros to some of its guests.[46]

The technological sophistication of these campaigns is also increasing. Russia has used artificial intelligence tools to create clones of more than 700 western news websites.[47] It seems to be exploiting AI to solve the problem of generating enough propaganda in tricky languages with comparatively few native speakers, such as Latvian.[48]

---

* Bäckman describes himself as a social critic and human rights activist, while Larsen has denied propagating Russian disinformation.

There is also a good deal of concern about AI-powered 'deepfake' videos and audio clips.

As the Voice of Europe scandal suggests, there is often a fine line between disinformation, corruption and the cultivation of figures who are to some degree in ideological alignment with Russia. Among Germany's elite, for example, Putin has personally nurtured ties not only with paid-up intermediaries such as the former chancellor Gerhard Schröder and Matthias Warnig, the ex-Stasi agent in charge of Nord Stream, but also Schröder's widely revered predecessor Helmut Schmidt, whom the Russian president invited to his dacha in 2013 and who later criticised the EU sanctions against Moscow.[49]

These efforts continued after February 2022. In May 2024 investigative journalists from several Baltic sea countries exposed a plan to fly 105 German researchers and businesspeople on a Gazprom-owned plane to Kaliningrad for a conference marking the 300th birthday of Immanuel Kant, who had spent most of his life in the city when it was Prussian Königsberg. The summit, where the Russian deputy prime minister read out a greeting from Putin himself, was part of the same Baltic Russian influence project described in chapter four.[50]

Russia has paid particularly close attention to the right-wing populist Alternative for Germany (AfD) party. In 2017 a cache of leaked emails from the Russian embassy in Berlin revealed that staff had described Markus Frohnmaier, a future AfD MP, as a politician who 'would be our own, absolutely controlled representative in the Bundestag'.[51] Maximilian Krah and Petr Bystron, the party's top two candidates in the 2024 European parliament election, were accused of taking money that ultimately came from the Russian intelligence services (both have denied these allegations).[52]

But these tendrils of political influence are by no means limited to Germany. In June 2024, a consortium of European media outlets reported on leaked intelligence documents about a Russian state-backed organisation called the Fund for Support and Protection of the Rights of Compatriots Living Abroad (Pravfond), which had apparently been running influence and interference operations in forty-eight countries, including Denmark, Sweden and the Baltic states. Pravfond is alleged to have financed not only various propaganda vehicles but also Vadim Krasikov, a contract killer hired by the FSB security agency to assassinate a former Chechen rebel commander in Berlin.[53] Even in Poland, where the elite consensus has long been far more sceptical of the Kremlin, an alleged Russian intelligence asset identified only as 'Janusz N' has been prosecuted for courting politicians across the spectrum. (At the time of writing, his trial had yet to begin but he had previously pleaded not guilty to a smaller set of similar charges.) In 2016 he supposedly persuaded two unwitting senators from Donald Tusk's centre-right Civic Coalition movement to meet loyalist Russian MPs in the Ukrainian city of Dnipro.[54]

That Buoy Is Mine

The third category of Russian active measures, electronic and cyber interference, will be addressed in the context of war planning in the following chapters. The fourth is border provocations. These range from routine incursions by military units to periods in which the Russian and Belarusian regimes encourage migrants from north Africa, the Middle East and south Asia to fly into their territory and then funnel them towards the borders of the EU.

Russian combat jets and, less frequently, naval vessels have been toying with NATO territory for more than a decade. On average the fighter jets stationed in Estonia, Lithuania and Latvia under the alliance's Baltic air policing programme intercept Russian aircraft every three or four days. Usually they stop short of NATO airspace; occasionally they do not.[55] At one point in June 2022, for example, several Russian warships entered Danish waters.[56] Within a single week in May 2024, two Russian strategic bombers and a fighter escort veered about a mile and a half into Finnish airspace near the coastal city of Loviisa, and the Swedish air force scrambled two Gripen interceptors to chase an Su-24 off the southern tip of Gotland.[57]

The main thing that has changed on this front in recent years is an apparently futile effort to intimidate Finland after it joined NATO. From the end of 2023 Helsinki indefinitely closed all eight crossings on its Russian land border in response to what it called a 'hybrid attack' in the form of directed non-European immigration.[58] Russia has stationed a brigade with nuclear-capable Iskander-M missiles on its side of Karelia, easily with firing distance of the Finnish border.[59] Satellite images suggest it has been concentrating strategic bombers and attack helicopters at the Olenya/Olenegorsk airbase south of Murmansk, which is about a hundred miles from Finnish Lapland.[60] According to the Estonian foreign intelligence service, it is planning to base its new 44th army corps at Petrozavodsk, which is a similar distance away from the Karelian frontier of south-east Finland.[61] Finnish officials are, however, entirely sanguine about these developments.

There has been more consternation at Russia's periodic flirtations with physically tweaking its western frontiers. In May 2024 its defence ministry issued a draft decree that suggested it might unilaterally revise its maritime borders around several tiny islands in the eastern gulf of Finland, and between Kaliningrad and the Lithuanian part of the Curonian spit.[62] The document was swiftly withdrawn without explanation but set nerves jangling as far away as the Åland islands between Finland and Sweden, which had been occupied by Russia during the Napoleonic wars and coveted by the USSR in the 1930s and 1940s.[63]

At about 3 a.m. the next day, Russian officials removed roughly twenty-five of the buoys marking its border with Estonia in the middle of the river Narva. The frontier between the two countries is an exceptionally sensitive issue: while it exists in practice, a treaty pinning it down in legal terms has been in limbo since 2005. Once a year the two sides used to sit down and negotiate how the precise location of each floating marker in the Narva would change to reflect the shifting riverbed, haggling over a few square metres of silt. That system broke down in 2023 and the line could no longer be agreed.[64] So Russia simply stole the buoys it objected to.[65]

Brain-Damaged Dogs

The final genus of 'hybrid' activity is outright violence, against both things and people. The most extreme cases have been murders and assassination plots, including an apparently speculative plan to try and kill Volodymyr Zelensky at Rzeszów-Jasionka airport in Poland,

and a hammer attack on the Russian opposition activist Leonid Volkov in Vilnius.[66] The notable thing about both cases, which came to light in the same week of April 2024, is that Russian and Belarusian operatives allegedly recruited Polish citizens to carry out the dirty work rather than doing it themselves.

In fact this seems to be an increasingly common phenomenon, possibly because Russia's military intelligence networks in many NATO states have been so heavily thinned out by diplomatic expulsions. 'Russia's intelligence capacity has been degraded,' says a senior official from one of the Baltic states. 'The operational environment here was always difficult from a Russian perspective because of the hostility towards them. That doesn't mean that they stop. Russia is always trying to find new avenues of influence. They are constantly trying to find new solutions.'

A *Wall Street Journal* investigation published a few weeks after the attempt on Leonid Volkov's life suggested that the Russians were increasingly hiring marginalised or disgruntled young 'misfits' for a range of low-level tasks such as arson, minor sabotage and spraying inflammatory graffiti.[67] These are not so much carefully calibrated bespoke operations as mass-produced and often outsourced disruption.[68]

Czechia has accused Russia of making 'thousands' of attempts to sabotage Europe's railway infrastructure.[69] There have been similar cases in Sweden.[70] In Germany, two Russian-German dual nationals have been charged with 'systematically' spying on civilian and military infrastructure with the apparent aim of directing bomb attacks on the supply routes for Ukraine.[71] The authorities are also reported to have discovered several plots to sabotage US military bases on German soil.[72] Russia appears to be losing whatever inhibitions it may once have had about acts of sabotage and intimidation on European soil. In the view of Supo, Finland's main domestic security agency, the Russians no longer care about getting caught.[73]

There also appears to be an increasingly military focus to the incidents. 'It is, in a way, an intelligence-gathering exercise because all of this feedback will inform Russian options for when there is finally a conflict with Europe as a whole,' says Keir Giles, a Russia analyst at the Chatham House think-tank in London.

All of this is probing the resilience of European logistics, particularly in Germany and Poland. And it is looking at the vulnerabilities of the systems that would take NATO reinforcements eastwards in the event of a conflict, because that's going to be a prime target for Russia to interdict or destroy.[74]

There is, however, still room for further escalation if Moscow wants to test what it might take NATO's member states to trigger the Article 5 clause. One option is to conduct a large number of small but simultaneous acts of sabotage against a critical infrastructure network such as a railway node or a power grid. The Baltic states are steeling themselves for this kind of eventuality in 2025, when they will disconnect themselves from the electricity grid they have shared with Russia and Belarus since the Soviet era.[75]

Another is a bigger and more focused Nord Stream-style attack. Russia could escalate from assassinating its own citizens in Europe to attempting to kill individual Europeans. In the summer of 2024, CNN disclosed that western counter-intelligence had foiled a plot to kill several defence industry leaders including Armin Papperger, the chief executive of Rheinmetall, Germany's largest arms manufacturer.[76] Equally it could stage some kind of outrage against the Russian-speaking minority in one of the Baltic states, perhaps on the Lithuanian side of the Suwałki gap, in the Latvian region of Latgale or in north-eastern Estonia.[77]

Europe is not powerless in the face of these molestations. The frontline states in particular are getting better at what one Estonian commentator calls 'hybrid defence'.[78] They have stopped issuing visas for Russian tourists, banned Russian state propaganda outlets and fenced off large portions of their frontiers with Russia and Belarus. Their cybersecurity systems have drastically improved since the Estonian 'Bronze' Night of 2007. They have not only expelled dozens of Russian spies working under diplomatic cover but also quite deliberately disrupted and publicised many cases of espionage that they might once have chosen to monitor more quietly.

This is mole-catching season. 'Right now, maybe some of the visible cases are when the European [counter-intelligence] services are simply cutting the activity off,' says Krišjānis Kariņš, the Latvian foreign minister.

[Usually] counter-espionage works on the basis that the spies don't realise they're actually being followed, and by letting them work, you actually see where the roots are. Well, there are times when the counter-espionage services in any of our countries will say things are getting too much now, or now is the time to send a clear signal that we see what's happening.

In the age of social networks, generative AI and declining trust in politicians, public institutions and conventional media outlets, disinformation is harder to stop. The tools available to states are limited. Some are introducing media literacy classes to schools on the Finnish model and most have issued guidelines to the rest of the population. Sweden has re-established its psychological defence agency, which tracks propaganda, funds research and provides training courses for officials and NGOs. 'There's huge interest from other countries in actually learning from our experiences: how are we doing it in Sweden? Is it working? If so, why is it working?' says Magnus Hjort, the agency's director.

One particularly striking grassroots initiative is the North Atlantic Fellas Organisation, or NAFO for short. The online sub-culture of self-proclaimed 'brain-damaged dogs' emerged more or less spontaneously on Twitter/X in the first year of the full-blown war in Ukraine, when Kyiv's supporters started piling on to Russian propaganda with memes and sarcasm, often using personalised images of grinning shiba inus as their mascots.

It works partly through blistering humour and partly through sheer weight of numbers, like bees forming a scrum around wasps that invade their hive. 'It came out of people messing around on the internet and drawing funny pictures,' says Mark Adam Harold, Vilnius-based political advisor on the night-time economy. 'Then it turned into the idea that if you donate to Ukraine's defence you'll get this [shiba inu] picture to signify your membership. But very quickly it just got completely out of hand because there was so much demand.'[79]

Flemming Splidsboel Hansen, an expert on Russian information operations at the Danish Institute of International Studies, says their influence tends to be greatly overrated. 'It's very clear to me, when you look at the writings in Russian academia, for example, that they are not able to achieve the effect that they're looking for,' he says.

> RT is their number one tool and they haven't really cracked the code of how to operate on social media. There are kind of admissions that it doesn't really work the way they would ideally want it to work. They want to unlock the gates to the cognitive domain of British and German voters and so on. But it's difficult.

I was surprised by how many disinformation experts in the eastern flank states said things had been relatively quiet not just since 2022 but for some years before the full-scale invasion of Ukraine, perhaps partly for this reason.

Jānis Sārts, the head of NATO's Centre of Excellence for Strategic Communications in Riga, says the focus of Russia's propagandists has been shifting away from the Baltic states for some years, and towards the Global South and other areas where they seem to feel they can get a better return on their efforts. 'Over the last five, seven years, I'd argue that most of the Russian activity has been focused on other European and transatlantic targets [rather] than the Baltics,' he says. 'It's a false assumption that they do most of it here.'

Our Foreign Country

The biggest question of the lot remains to be answered: will Russia risk a direct war with NATO? Most western analysts suggest that it is in no position to do so, at least for the time being. But its military mobilisation and manufacturing systems are running hot. Putin's decision in May 2024 to appoint as his new defence minister Andrei Belousov, a civilian economist, appears to indicate that he is gearing up for the long haul.[80]

Yet the most optimistic experts on the Russian military believe the balance of power around the Baltic sea has tilted so much in NATO's favour that Moscow has already implicitly conceded it cannot win a war in the region. 'Whatever the scope of the outcome of the war [in

Ukraine], Russia will not be able to rebuild a position of military superiority in the Baltic theatre, or even to set an approximate balance of forces with NATO,' Pavel Baev, of the Peace Research Institute Oslo, has argued.[81]

Reiner Schwalb, the former German military attaché to Moscow, also has doubts about Russia's ability to fight a war against NATO, albeit for slightly different reasons. 'They know they cannot do it,' he says.

> The will has to be backed up by the capabilities. Russia does not have these capabilities. It will not be able to return to a two or three-year military service with two million soldiers and four million reserves unless it is attacked. The Russian population would not approve of it. And that is something that Putin is terrified of . . . Despite all the repression that takes place in this country, there is a panicked fear that a movement [against the regime] could emerge.

Another common argument goes like this: yes, Putin has a profoundly distorted view of the world. He supposedly rises in the early afternoon and starts his day with a breakfast news digest in the form of three leather-bound reports from his intelligence agencies, which do their best to confirm his prejudices about Russia's strength and the weakness of the treacherous West.[82] As a result he disastrously overestimated his army's power to overwhelm Ukraine, much as Yeltsin allowed himself to be persuaded in 1994 that Grozny could be taken 'by a single parachute regiment in two hours' with a 'bloodless blitzkrieg', only for the first Chechen war to drag on for twenty pyrrhic months.[83] But surely, despite his hubristic parallel mental reality, Putin must realise that even if he could seize NATO territory by force the aftermath would be an uncontrollable nightmare with the potential to destroy his hold on power.

Quite apart from the likelihood of a sustained partisan resistance campaign in the mould of the Forest Brothers, the Baltic states have such fiercely cherished national identities and such recent memories of overthrowing Soviet occupation that it is hard to imagine how their incorporation into Russia could be anything other than a disaster, with the potential to fire up separatist sentiment among other nationalities in the federation.

In the Soviet era the Baltic republics were known in Russia as *nasha zagranitsa*, 'our foreign country', a miniature version of the West. They were never treated by Moscow's ideologists as an intrinsically inseparable part of the Russian world in the way that Ukraine has been. 'The three Baltic countries were always difficult for Russia to cope with,' says Reinhard Krumm, the Riga-based director of the Baltic states bureau for the Friedrich Ebert Foundation.

> The Russian empire, the Soviet Union and even the Russian Federation were aiming to 'civilise' other people . . . But with the Balts, the Russian state understood there's nothing to 'cultivate'. Still, Moscow feels that small states in general should not interfere in international affairs, that they should not politically box way above their weight, and ideally they should just shut up and make sure that the Russian minorities are treated well. But all this is not sufficient for Moscow [to justify] any kind of a full-fledged invasion against three NATO member states.[84]

Peter Viggo Jakobsen, an expert on strategy at the Royal Danish Defence College, broadly agrees. 'I don't buy the argument that if Russia "wins" in Ukraine, whatever that means, then they'll go to the Baltics next,' he says. 'My understanding of it . . . is that there hasn't actually been much revisionism regarding the Baltics, because they've essentially given up on that.'

Jakobsen also doubts that Russia will be able to rebuild enough military capacity to invade NATO, especially since it is struggling to find buyers for the natural gas that traditionally propped up its state budget. 'Where will they get their soldiers from?' he says.

> How will they actually equip these new forces with meaningful military equipment? And how can they do more than adopt a defensive position in order to ward off the threat that they see in the armed forces of NATO? I do understand their plans, but I don't

see them as evidence of offensive intent. And I cannot see how they'll find the money, because 70 per cent of their [state] income comes from oil and gas.

René Nyberg, a veteran Finnish diplomat who served as his country's ambassador to Russia from 2000 to 2004, at the start of the Putin era, says:

> The loss of the Baltic states is mentally acceptable [to Russia] because they were so different. They were friends with the German world; a foreign body in the Soviet Union . . . They also feel that Finland was never a real part of imperial Russia. We're [historically] part of the Swedish world, not the Russian world, and they accept that.

Nyberg's expectation is that in any case Putin will not outlast the conflict in Ukraine. 'This war is existential for Ukraine,' he says.

> But it is also existential for Putin. The Ukrainians will never give up, and Putin will not stop . . . How long will the Russian elite and the military want to continue a forever war? And will they still be [the] elite? This is one thing. And the second thing is, and this is a real historical fact: when change occurs in Russia, it will be a surprise, and it will happen very quickly, and you can't predict it. I just don't believe that he will survive.

It is also possible that the Russian regime will not risk a war with NATO simply because it does not feel that it needs to. Fiona Hill, a Russia scholar from Britain who used to work as a US intelligence analyst and as a senior Eurasia advisor to Donald Trump during his presidency, believes a more probable scenario over the next few years is one in which Putin uses the threat of an invasion but stops short of following through on it. 'Putin sees the military as an instrument and as coercive power,' she says.

> So in this sort of timeframe he doesn't have to send the tanks across the bridge at Narva into Estonia, for example, but he can use that menace to back up other kinds of coercive activities, all the so-called

'hybrid' threats . . . What Putin is probing for is weakness, and if he can instrumentalise the military, he will do that. But he doesn't have to do it in a full-scale military assault.

A Game of Numbers

After George W. Bush met Vladimir Putin for the first time in 2001, at a countryside estate in the mountains of northern Slovenia, the US president famously said he had gazed into the eyes of his Russian counterpart and been 'able to get a sense of his soul'. What Bush saw in those eyes was a 'very straightforward and trustworthy . . . man, deeply committed to his country and the best interests of his country'.[85]

When the diplomat Chris Alexander first looked into Putin's eyes in 1995, however, he saw an unreconstructed relic of the old KGB, a vessel for a paranoid and imperialist worldview that most observers in the West believed was dying out with the last vestiges of the Cold War. At the time, Alexander held a relatively junior post in the Canadian embassy in Moscow, and Putin was approaching the end of his stint as deputy mayor of St Petersburg.

From the embassy and from the Russia desk of the Canadian foreign ministry back in Ottawa, Alexander was tasked with observing the Kremlin over the formative decade from 1993 to 2003, as the *siloviki* (people of force/power) networks from the KGB and the Soviet military seized control of the levers of power and installed Putin at the helm. Even in the early 2000s, when Bush and many other western leaders felt the new Russian president was a man they could work with, Alexander was profoundly worried at the way things were heading.

Putin, he says, is driven by a feeling of having been 'bereft and orphaned' since the Soviet system collapsed from the end of the 1980s and he had to burn the files at his KGB station in Dresden so that they would not fall into the wrong hands. 'Putin was a true believer, a true nationalist, and he carried that kind of lumpen, blind belief in Russia's greatness, that Russia can do whatever it wants, that Russia will inevitably have these ever-expanding borders,' Alexander says. 'And I think everything else just slotted into place around that.'

Alexander is exasperated that so many Russia-watchers are still, in his view, failing to recognise the intensity and consistency of the threat NATO is up against. '[Putin and his inner circle] are looking for an opportunity to embarrass NATO, something that would in the past have been considered a case for Article 5 but now they think NATO would not react to it,' he says.

That is most likely to be a little green men-type operation in Latvia or Estonia, when a helicopter crashes or something and suddenly people come out from under their rocks, screaming bloody murder and calling for autonomy with weapons turning up.* That is a real possibility in the next couple of years.

There are plenty of experts who share Alexander's alarm. 'The [revanchist] ambition can be nurtured during extended periods when there's no indication of Russia doing anything about it because it's too weak,' says Keir Giles from the Chatham House think-tank in London.

After all, it wasn't Putin that invented the idea that Russia should be restored to having dominion over its neighbours. That was very much a Yeltsin thing, too. It's just at the time Russia wasn't in a position to do anything about it, so people generally ignored the things that were said about invasions and ambitions.

Giles thinks the West is in danger of making a similar mistake today. 'Russia is so intensely focused on Ukraine, and in particular its military power is so concentrated there, having denuded the rest of the western frontier,' he says.

That doesn't necessarily mean that there wouldn't be the ability to reconstitute the army, as they're working very hard on doing at the moment, and then map it back to where they want it to be faster than even the front-line states, who take this kind of thing quite seriously, are able to rebuild their defences and counter it.

---

* 'Little green men' was the term coined for the Russian soldiers who occupied Crimea in 2014, wearing masks and plain combat uniforms without any insignia.

Depending on what sort of political and military shape NATO is in over the next few years, Russia may not even require an especially sizeable capacity to achieve its primary goal of pinning back the alliance. 'There is no doubt that it's going to be a larger military that Russia has by the end of this process, even with the ridiculous amount of attrition that's going on [in Ukraine],' Giles says.

And then what do you actually need in order to challenge NATO, along with the rest of that western periphery? It doesn't need to be a large force at the moment, if you are counting, as Putin might, on being able to do something swift and then cement it before NATO reacts . . . Then you don't need anything like the quantity of troops that they built up around Ukraine because, relatively speaking, the Baltic states are still a military vacuum.

A high-ranking European intelligence officer broadly agrees with Giles's assessment. 'Russia has demonstrated the ability to make very stupid decisions that only harm itself at the end of the day,' the source says.

From a military-strategic point of view, things have got a bit better since most of the forces [usually stationed] around the Baltic states and Finland are committed in Ukraine and suffering heavy losses. But at the same time, we have to bear in mind that the air force and the navy have not suffered heavy casualties.

In quantitative terms, the source says, Russia can probably regenerate its forces in only a few years. 'The important thing is they will have war veterans and above all they will have human mass,' the official continues. 'From an equipment perspective, the Russian equipment will again be low quality but each T-62 or T-55 tank consumes a Javelin [anti-tank rocket], or maybe two or three. It's all a numbers game.'

Jeffrey Mankoff, a Russia scholar at the US National Defense University, says that while the Kremlin may not be able to keep spending 6 or 7 per cent of its GDP on the military indefinitely, it can sustain the war economy at its current level for some time. He is also concerned that Putin may be led into a catastrophic misjudgement by the jingoistic and wildly over-optimistic assessments fed to him by his spy agencies, much as he was in Ukraine. 'The one we saw at the start of the war in Ukraine was bad enough,' Mankoff says.

> But if you're talking about the potential for a conflict between Russia and a nuclear-armed NATO, then the consequences are potentially much, much worse. And if you couple the information management problems with the fact that Putin has surrounded himself with these hardline advisors who are telling him about Russia's historic mission and about the decadence of the West, I think that creates a pretty dangerous cocktail.

Readers will make up their own minds about this broad range of analyses, and I am sure they will reach quite various conclusions. For what it is worth, since April 2024 the RAND Corporation, a think-tank with strong links to the US government, has been running a straw poll that asks analysts to assign a probability to a Russian invasion of one of the Baltic states before April 2027. After a few months, virtually all of the seventy-nine responses fell below 10 per cent, although it is inevitably hard to know to what extent this really reflects the balance of expert opinion, and the timeline is at the very shortest end of the possibilities.[86]

My own view is that there is enough reason to believe Russia may have both the motivation and the means to gamble on a war with NATO at some point before 2030. We do not need certainty about the future in order to find it prudent to take sufficient precautions. 'The signs do indeed seem to be there that Russia is actually preparing for a possible military conflict against the Baltic states,' says Kristi Raik, head of foreign policy at the International Centre for Defence and Security (ICDS), a well-regarded Estonian think-tank.

> That doesn't mean it will necessarily happen, but the risk is real. It's a difficult issue to deal with in public, because I think it's not healthy for our society to get into some kind of panic mode about a war unavoidably coming at some point. But of course we need to get prepared and take it very seriously.

This is one factor that will have an absolutely central influence on Russia's decision whether or not to attack NATO, and it is to a great extent under our control: our ability to defend ourselves and to persuade Moscow that we are ready to do so. We have to be capable of fighting, sustaining and winning a war. We also have to be capable of projecting a collective determination to do all three. That is the subject of the final chapters in this book.

9

Peace Through Superior Firepower

Europe's Struggle to Defend Itself

> Covenants, without the Sword, are but Words, and of no strength to secure a man at all.
>
> Thomas Hobbes, *Leviathan* (1651)[1]

From a low hill overlooking a sandy Latvian plain mottled with pine forests, a British artillery staff sergeant radios for air support. There is a pause of ten minutes or so, punctuated by the boom of an M777 howitzer somewhere to the north, as a Spanish Eurofighter crew scrambles from the Ämari airbase in Estonia. The aircraft can be heard long before it appears as a faint high-altitude speck, skirting the range of a nearby missile defence battery and scouting the enemy's force disposition.

Without access to the NATO tactical computers that track every feint and gunshot of the battle, it is, frankly, hard to form an accurate impression of how things are going. No commander is going to tell a visiting journalist that their unit is being carved up like a joint of beef. At the British camp in a woodland clearing a couple of miles away to the north-east, though, the mood is fairly exuberant. 'We're sowing the seeds of doubt among the enemy, causing absolute carnage, making them question not only why they're here, but where we are,' says Lance Corporal Conrad Froud of the Royal Yeomanry reserve regiment. 'I think they called us the "British bogeymen" by the end.'

A few days before the start of this wargame in September 2023, a detachment of eighty-seven soldiers from the UK army's Royal Lancers armoured cavalry regiment set out from their base in north-eastern Poland and crossed the Suwałki gap into Lithuania, suffering only a couple of breakdowns en route. Now they are fighting their way through Ādaži, a 28-square-miles training area near Riga, as they simulate an attack on the eleven-nation Canadian-led NATO battlegroup charged with the defence of Latvia, in an exercise known as Titan Shield.

For the past 48 hours they have been harrying a much larger force of about a thousand allied troops, who have dug into defensive positions around a river. Operating by night, in mobile and independent squads of half a dozen soldiers traversing the terrain in Jackal and Panther patrol vehicles and then dismounting to outflank the foe, the Britons have been given the liberty to deploy virtually every ruse and distraction they can think of. I am not permitted to say which country's tactics they are supposed to be emulating, but perhaps the reader can guess.

One patrol circled south behind the enemy lines and called in artillery fire from the rear, uncorking pandemonium among the defenders. Another captured a map detailing the other side's positions. A third approached an Italian dugout and pretended to be Canadian reinforcements. The Italians gave them tea and coffee and posed for pictures on their armoured vehicles before one of the Britons held out a phone and translated the message: 'Sorry, we're the enemy, and you're dead.' It was only on the last night of the battle that a column of Polish PT-91 Twardy tanks turned up to reinforce the NATO lines and the British forces were beaten. 'We could have a disproportionate effect at night, not just because of our equipment, but also because of an offensive spirit and because these guys [the British troops] have been training pretty hard while we've been based down,' says Major Guy Parker, the unit's commanding officer.

> The [NATO] battlegroup here is constantly 'ripping', as we call it in the military . . . It's constantly got a churn from all the different nations coming through. They don't have the same collective understanding of how each other, the left and the right, are going to fight. They've got eleven nations, eleven different languages, and many speaking English as a second or even third language, whereas we've got a very small collective force that's been together for coming up to six months . . . As a result, I think in the battle they probably underestimated our willingness to win.

Europe Will Beg Us Not To Go Further

The dash from Poland to the Baltic states, the assaults on hastily fortified positions, the struggle to form a cogent whole out of a Babel of various nationalities: Titan Shield is a miniature of a war NATO hopes it will never have to fight. It is conducted with great earnestness and the commanders do their best to make it as realistic as it could be. But everyone involved is aware that a geographically limited skirmish on this scale is a primary-school food fight in comparison to the real thing.

There are many different scenarios as to how it could start. Most of them are laden with pessimism. In the early 1990s a British reporter asked a Latvian defence ministry official how long the country's army could hold out against a Russian incursion. The reply was: about 12 minutes.[2] By 2015 the estimate had at least reached 60 hours. The best-known paper-based exercise is a set of wargames carried out by RAND after the first Russian invasion of Ukraine in 2014: Russian units from the western military district launched a primary thrust towards Riga and a secondary axis towards Tallinn through the predominantly Russian-speaking north-east of Estonia. They outnumbered the more lightly armed and less manoeuvrable NATO forces *in situ* by approximately two to one.

'The outcome was, bluntly, a disaster for NATO,' the researchers wrote. In every iteration of the game, the Russian tanks reached the outskirts of the Baltic capitals within one and a half to two and a half days. The ultimate outcomes ranged from a risky and costly NATO counteroffensive to the acceptance of a new border. The worst of them would lead to 'the collapse of NATO itself and the crumbling of the cornerstone of western security for almost seventy years'.[3] Even at the time, other analysts in the West felt this was simplistic doom-mongering. The facts have also changed substantially since then: the NATO battlegroups in the Baltic states and Poland, the accession of Sweden and Finland, the ragged second Russian invasion of Ukraine and the florescence of drone warfare.

But the RAND report left a long shadow. In 2016 Sir Richard Shirreff, a newly retired British general, published a novel called *War*

With Russia, which drew on his three years as the deputy supreme allied commander of NATO's forces in Europe. It starts with Moscow staging the lynching of three ethnic Russian students in Latvia as a pretext for an invasion. 'When NATO fails to react to our seizure of the Baltic states, it will have failed, been defeated and probably collapse,' Putin is told by his fictional chief of staff on the eve of the invasion. 'At that moment it will cease to pose a threat to Russia. Without NATO, Europe will be forced to beg us not to go any further.'[4]

The Russians overwhelm Latvia through airborne landings, bombardments and a crippling cyber-attack before NATO's political governing body can agree on how to respond. The alliance begins to despair of ever recovering the lost territory. In the end it wins only through a kind of military *deus ex machina*, a daring and multi-pronged digital, aerial and special forces offensive that allows its troops to seize control of the nuclear warheads in Kaliningrad and force Putin to back off.

The grimmest thought experiments involve Russia taking advantage of a separate global catastrophe that divides the West's attention and resources, such as another pandemic or a Chinese amphibious attack on Taiwan. In 2021, a few months before the full-scale Russian invasion of Ukraine, the British analyst Julian Lindley-French and the retired US generals John R. Allen and Ben Hodges contemplated both and more.

Their book begins in 2029 with an outbreak of an engineered 'Covid-29' virus that devastates the West. The Chinese air force swoops on a US fleet in the South China sea, sinking an elderly cruiser and prompting Washington to start pulling the bulk of its forces out of Europe in order to shift them to the Asian front. Simultaneously, Russia takes out Britain's flagship aircraft carrier off the coast of northern Norway with a cyber-attack and a swarm of drones. After an intense assault on mainland Europe's infrastructure, Russian marines and special forces grab the Arctic tip of Norway. Two Russian armies then take control of Estonia and the Suwałki gap, forcing the rest of the NATO allies in Europe to sue for peace.[5]

All of these stories were as much admonitory as predictive, even if some of them significantly overestimated what Russia could do. They were meant to shake the West out of its complacency and false sense of security. Their message is not just that if we wish to prevent them from coming true we must take drastic action, and fast. It is that what happens in NATO's frontline countries will affect us all. 'Europe is not safe unless the Baltic region is safe,' Madeleine Albright, the incoming US secretary of state, said in 1997.[6] This is not a truism but an existential truth.

A Human Being Is Nothing

This chapter will examine the starting conditions for a NATO–Russia war centred on the Baltic. The next one will describe how such a war might play out and how the alliance can manage the risk of nuclear conflict.

The analysis needs to begin on a conceptual level. One of my least favourite words is 'deterrence'. Over the two decades after the end of the Second World War, military theorists in the US developed ideas about how to prevent another great-power conflict with the USSR in the age of nuclear weapons, complementary to the concept of mutually assured destruction. It is not that the principles they came up with are useless. As we will see later in this chapter, in many ways the strategists of the Cold War era had a more sophisticated and pragmatic understanding of escalation dynamics than we tend to today, and there is plenty we can learn from them.

But the translation of deterrence theory into practice can be excruciatingly subjective, relying as it does on a mixture of atomic gamesmanship, conventional war-planning, political contingency, messaging and psychology. It is also far from clear that most western leaders have an appetite for the risks it entails. Nor is there any straightforward way to define what having 'enough' deterrence means on the eastern flank in the 2020s. 'There are some military experts who argue that deterrence is somehow not really relevant any more and we should not even be talking about deterrence. We need to talk about defence,' says Kristi Raik of the International Centre for Defence and Security in Tallinn. 'What matters is that there are very concrete defence plans and we know exactly what will happen in the case of an invasion, and what NATO's response could be.'

That is why I have come to the Polish city of Szczecin to meet Lieutenant General Jürgen-Joachim von Sandrart, the commander of NATO's multinational corps north-east. This is the alliance's only sizeable headquarters east of what used to be the Iron Curtain, with responsibility for overseeing the defence of the Baltic. A bluff, likeable soldier whose family has been ordering troops around since the Napoleonic wars, Sandrart is pretty forthright about the challenges NATO faces in the region, and states:

> If we want to prevent Moscow from perceiving an opportunity that they could exploit to their advantage or to achieve their aims, using military means, using war as an instrument – or hybrid, I think you should keep that in mind – then we would be well advised to be ready in advance. That means that in Moscow's perception we must be so prepared for defence that when Moscow assesses its opportunities it cannot come to a positive conclusion. That would be successful deterrence.[7]

Like every other NATO general I have spoken to, Sandrart insists that the alliance is already capable of defending the Baltic sea area if it has to, albeit at considerable cost, and that it is well on its way to building an insurmountable wall of deterrence. 'But if that doesn't work,' he says,

> then we have to be set up in such a way that we can end the war swiftly and victoriously. And this war against Russia cannot lead to a situation like the situation in Ukraine, where Russia succeeds through an initial operation in gaining significant territory that we can then only win back with great effort.

What bothers Sandrart most these days is a thing he calls the 'opportunity gap'. On paper, the allies are superior to Russia in almost every department. They have a total of about 3.5 million military personnel. They have a clear technological edge in most domains. They control a greater portion of the waters, skies and shorelines of the Baltic sea than any power has ever controlled before. Their economic capacity is more than an order of magnitude higher than Russia's.

But clearly not all of these resources can be allocated to securing the eastern flank. A number of indispensable items, such as ammunition and air defence systems, are in desperately short supply. And getting the personnel and materiel that are available into place would take time and an enormous amount of administrative exertion.

Russia, Sandrart says, has five significant advantages over NATO in the Baltic. The first is geography. Moscow has an abundance of possible lines of communication and can cut off the alliance's sole land route into the Baltic states by taking the Suwałki gap. The second is that the Kremlin, as the putative aggressor, would decide 'when, how, where and why' to start a conflict. Given Russia's proficiency at exploiting the blurry boundaries between war and peace, the thirty-two allies may not agree that an invasion has begun which demands a military response until it is too late to salvage the territory that has already been lost.

The third is the Russian disregard for life. The West is acutely sensitive to casualties, especially when civilians die. Outside the main building of Sandrart's base in Szczecin is a prominent memorial that lists the name and rank of every single corps member who has died in action. We should be proud that we care so much. But this care does also result in a certain aversion to risk. Russia, on the other hand, has deliberately killed thousands of Ukrainian non-combatants and proven willing to expend tens of thousands of its own poorly trained and equipped troops on 'meatgrinder' offensives.

The fourth advantage, Sandrart says, is logistics. 'Russia's infrastructure for the rapid deployment of forces over roads, railways and the air from any part of its geography to its borders is ready,' he says. 'We've seen in Ukraine that the deployment to the border can happen swiftly and without delay.'

On the NATO side, things are much trickier. Up to 300,000 soldiers and their equipment must be transferred to the eastern flank by road, rail and sea routes that cross through several countries, each with its own rules and bureaucratic processes. It is still not really clear how this is supposed to work. Some progress has been made on the creation of 'military corridors', cross-border pathways with a simplified and unified set of regulations. But who will drive the trains? Where will the lorries come from? Can German or Polish motorway bridges withstand the weight of a column of American M1 Abrams tanks? And given the shortcomings of the Autobahn network, is there more than a single functional railway route capable of carrying allied heavy weapons from Germany to the Baltic states by way of Poland?[8]

This is related to what Sandrart sees as Russia's fifth and final trump card: unity of command and effort, 'from the foxholes all the way up to the president'. It is a single country whose assets can at least in theory be wholly subordinated to the war effort. Power is hugely centralised under the general staff at its national defence control centre in Moscow, which encompasses forty-nine government agencies, from the police to infrastructure and economic management. There is an established system for requisitioning material from the private sector.[9] 'It is one nation, one regime, one *nomenklatura*, one autocratic leadership system, from politicians to the military, going all the way through horizontally and vertically,' Sandrart says.

These days NATO leaders like to talk about the need for 'whole-of-society' and 'whole-of-government' endeavours. But these have already been entrenched in Russia for years. The corresponding situation in NATO remains a bit of a mess. The member states have different threat perceptions. It is possible that Hungary or another Kremlin-friendly state in the alliance might obstruct the activation of Article 5, the prerequisite for a joint war effort. Once this hurdle has been overcome, there is still potential for considerable tension between NATO's political and military leadership structures over the conduct and objectives of the conflict.

Then there is the issue of 'interoperability', the military jargon for getting various national forces to work together as an effective whole. Usually this discussion focuses on kit. Charles de Gaulle once asked how it was possible to govern a country with 246 varieties of cheese. Much the same question applies to a military alliance with at least fourteen kinds of 155 mm artillery shells.[10]

The disparities in specifications and regulations drive many NATO commanders up the wall. 'We have to improve our nation-based systems, with [their] scarce possibilities to exchange ammunition, for example,' says Alexander Sollfrank, the German lieutenant general in charge of the alliance's Joint Support and Enabling Command (JSEC) in Ulm.

But there are also issues that are much easier to solve: administrative limitations . . . Although it might not be allowed right now, technically there's no problem in many cases. Where's the problem, for example, with a paratrooper from a European nation A using a parachute from a neighbouring nation B after having been trained on this system, or attaching equipment from one nation to the helicopter of another nation?

The problem, though, is not limited to equipment. It affects the soldiers, too. They have their own national languages, cultural codes, training systems and military customs within the umbrella of NATO doctrine. 'These are troops from different countries, who have never or rarely trained together,' the newly appointed chief of the British defence staff rants at his hapless prime minister in Richard Shirreff's thriller.

They fire different-sized ammunition from different weapons systems; they've got radios which may or may not talk to one another, and they speak multiple different languages. None of which is exactly clever when you are trying to call down accurate artillery fire, while enemy rounds are killing the men around you, and one mistranslated number might result in a ton of so-called friendly fucking shells landing on you or your mates.[11]

As I saw in Ādaži, the resulting misalignments can provide the enemy with all sorts of opportunities for mischief. Nowadays senior officers habitually play down the significance of these snags, pointing to a calendar of almost constant multinational exercises where the allies' troops practise side by side in the field. The thriving barter market for ration packs at the Latvia battlegroup base does suggest this has instilled a certain collective esprit de corps (apparently the Canadian poulet and vegetables is the most popular).

Deep Battle

I am not sure quite what I was expecting from the Berlin security conference at the end of 2023, but it was certainly not the impassioned speech that Sönke Neitzel, Germany's preeminent military historian, delivered during a panel discussion on territorial defence. 'Are we quick enough?' Neitzel asked.

> It's really, I think, the crucial question because we can't exclude that ... the Bundeswehr will have to fight. And we are going to stand by the coffins at the graves of the soldiers and we are going to be asked: what have you done? What? What exactly have you done? And we will have to explain to the mothers and the fathers why the soldiers could not fulfil their jobs. At the moment we can only die gallantly if there's war. I mean, it's very clear. The forces are going to fight, but they will die without drones, drone defence, without enough supply.[12]

It was all reminiscent, Neitzel said, of how the Holy Roman Empire, a ragbag conglomerate of German states, had struggled to agree on how to respond to Napoleon's invasion at the dawn of the nineteenth century. 'They were washed away,' he said. 'Historical buildings can be washed away. That's the lesson from history.'[13] The chair of the panel made a valiant attempt to brush the remarks off by suggesting the audience watch Ridley Scott's epic *Napoleon*, which had just hit German cinemas. But the words shook me. Was the situation really as bad as that? The short answer is: possibly, but it does not have to be. The long answer starts with the prospects for a potential land war by the southern shores of the Baltic sea.

At the 2023 NATO summit in Vilnius, the alliance's leaders signed off on three new regional defence plans for the eastern flank. One covers the High North, another the Baltic and its surroundings, and a third south-eastern Europe down to the Mediterranean. They are meant to express an 'iron-clad commitment to defend ... every inch of allied territory at all times'.[14] That is, NATO's forward presence will in theory no longer be a largely symbolic 'tripwire' intended to warn Russia that it cannot attack the frontline states without sucking in the alliance's nuclear powers. It will be expanded and reconfigured with the goal of mounting a credible fightback from the first minutes of any invasion.

The contents of these plans are strictly classified. The impression I get from conversations with sources in a number of European capitals is that they are probably not as detailed as one might think: more general guidelines and aspirations than meticulous stage-by-stage scripts, with many of the specifics left to be hammered out at national level.

In any case, the basic mechanics are already in the public domain. This book's analysis starts with land warfare. At present, the first line of defence is the troops on the ground: the militaries of the frontline states, supported by a total of 15,000 to 20,000 forward-deployed US and NATO multinational personnel. Then comes the Very High Readiness Joint Task Force, about 20,000 strong, with a 'spearhead' brigade of roughly 5,000 soldiers who can theoretically be dispatched within two or three days.

This is followed by two more multinational 'initial follow-on' brigades, or another 10,000 soldiers.[15] Overall, the idea is to have 30 battalions (approximately 30,000 soldiers), 30 air squadrons and 30 warships in the conflict zone within 30 days: the so-called '4x30' principle.[16] Under the new NATO force model, however, the ambition is to have 'well over' 100,000 troops ready to go at ten days' notice, rising to 300,000 at 'high readiness', which seems to mean anything from a fortnight to a couple of months.[17] 'If that is implemented, then I think that we have more than enough conventional capability to convince Russia that they cannot win any fight or take any part of NATO in 72 hours and not face armed resistance,' says Professor Peter Viggo Jakobsen at the Royal Danish Defence College.

How many of them can actually be mustered, adequately equipped and transferred to the battlefield, however, is another question. The armed forces of the larger European NATO states, such as Britain and Germany, are significantly smaller than their target strengths and in some cases shrinking, with no obvious quick fixes for their recruitment shortfalls. Some have discussed reviving mass conscription but there are reservations about whether this would be practical or affordable.

Most of the soldiers must be held back for roles such as homeland defence and other commitments. As modern land warfare becomes increasingly complex and dependent on having the right tools in the right place at the right time, logistics and 'sustainment' alone are estimated to soak up as much as two-thirds of the available personnel.[18]

Their militaries are also constrained by scarcities of equipment and 'cold-start-ready' units that can be deployed at short notice. According to one estimate, produced a few months before the second Russian invasion of Ukraine, Europe's armed forces can only deploy at most 3 per cent of their total strength for fighting at any given point in time. The authors likened them to a '21st-century Maginot line'.[19] One US general has complained that this means only a handful of European countries would be able to field much more than a single full-strength brigade (4,000–5,000 personnel) in practice.[20]

Germany, for example, has promised to make a mechanised division (typically 20,000 infantry or so, with armoured transport and fighting vehicles) available to NATO in 2025, ready to go within thirty days. A second division is supposed to be added from 2027.[21] But a leaked memo from Lieutenant General Alfons Mais, the head of the German army, suggested he expected to miss the 2025 target, believed the 2027 one to be unrealistic and felt that without significant reform the army 'will not be able to hold its own in high-intensity combat'.[22]

It is not really fair to pick on Berlin alone. In Britain, the defence secretary Ben Wallace admitted to a parliamentary inquiry:

> We have not had an armoured division that could really deploy since 1991 . . . If I look on paper at the current armoured division we have, it is lacking in all sorts of areas. It is lacking in deep fires, in medium-range air defence, in its electronic warfare and signals intelligence capability, in its modern digital and sensor-to-shooter capability. On top of that, it is probably lacking in weapons stocks.[23]

France maintains that it can mobilise a division of 19,000 soldiers and 7,000 vehicles within a month but there are similar concerns about the spectrum of its capabilities.[24] There are even some doubts about Poland's ability to staff fully and kit out two new divisions for the defence of its eastern frontier.[25]

These countries also tend to be very short on ammunition. NATO requires its members to store enough to sustain at least a month of high-intensity combat. It is hard to know exactly how much they do have, as this information is jealously guarded. But in most cases it is probably not very much at all. Various estimates suggest Germany may have only a couple of days' worth. On one exercise in Texas, the British army 'ran out of every bit of ammunition . . . in about eight days'.[26] Sir Richard Barrons, a retired general and former head of the UK's Joint Strategic Command, said he suspected that in a conflict comparable to the war in Ukraine, Britain's reserves would not last much longer than a week.[27]

Defence budgets are now beginning to rise across much of the alliance, although its European members still account for only 28 per cent of the total, compared to 65 per cent from the US alone.[28] But procurement is a slow business, typically taking anything between seven and fifteen years for army assets, and is exposed to ruptures in global supply chains.[29]

Much of the public discourse on this subject has concentrated on what are known in the military argot as 'exquisite platforms', expensive and high-tech weapon systems with long development cycles. Yet one of the main lessons from Ukraine, according to Mariusz Błaszczak, a former Polish defence minister, is that these are of little use in an intense land war without the mass to back them up:

> Many self-proclaimed experts argued that modern war would be fought mainly in cyberspace or using light infantry and unmanned systems, and that only good reconnaissance systems were the key to ensuring full security. However, as reality has shown, these were wrong. Of course, we need modern systems . . . but the priority is traditional platforms – tanks, artillery, air defence.

But even the simplest components are hard to come by. Again, ammunition is a particularly glaring example. An artillery shell might sound like an uncomplicated thing to make: a steel body, perhaps 10 kg of high explosives, a fuze, a propellant and a guidance system in fancier models such as the American M982 Excalibur. Russia's factories are now churning out anything from 3 to 5 million shells each year for about $1,000 apiece. The countries of the EU are manufacturing them at about a third of that rate and quadruple the cost.[30] There are only a handful of companies on the continent that can make the explosives, and they in turn are struggling with international shortages of the underlying chemical ingredients, which are sourced from as far away as China.³¹ For more complex items such as cruise missiles, the difficulties are significantly worse.

Then there are the logistical challenges. The soldiers from the US will have to be shipped across the Atlantic to North sea ports in Europe such as Bremerhaven, where they will join their European comrades on trains and in motorway convoys through Germany and Poland. At each stage they can expect to be attacked by the Russians, who will hope not only to disrupt NATO's lines of communication but also to intimidate Germany and other states into backing out of the conflict. This has been part of Moscow's 'deep battle' military theory for the past century.³² 'If we don't think about being contested, shame on us,' says Brigadier General Ronald Ragin, head of the US army's 21st Theater Sustainment Command.

> Why would the enemy allow us to put ten divisions in ten days anywhere and build that type of combat capability against him, which he's going to have to fight? What we believe is that we'll be contested in all domains. There will be hybrid warfare starting in your strategic support areas and your ability to deploy. You'll be contested coming across the Atlantic. You'll be contested in our ports within theater. We as a coalition have to think through: how do we operate in that environment? How do we operate when our convoys are contested? How do we operate when our railways are interdicted?

Then there are the issues with European infrastructure and red tape outlined earlier in this chapter, and particularly the dearth of other options if the main nodes are physically knocked out by the Russians. 'If we have bureaucracy in place that prevents this agile movement, then we have a real problem not to lose the first battle,' Alexander Sollfrank told a conference in 2023. 'The other side knows exactly where our limitations are and where our obstacles are.'³³

Ben Hodges, who is now a senior logistics advisor to NATO, says this is one of the most pivotal elements of deterrence. 'The key is demonstrating to the Russians that we can move forces as fast as or faster than them in peacetime conditions. That's the trick: it's peacetime conditions, because we're talking about deterrence,' Hodges says.

We have to be able to do these things while the Russians are starting to indicate that they're getting ready to do something. Peacetime conditions mean we won't have the primary priority access to Deutsche Bahn cargo, for example, or we're still following EU road regulations, and all the other aspects of normal life are still going on.

A Test of Will

What will they find when they reach their destination? That depends a great deal on the scale, shape, speed and competence of the Russian offensive, as well as the extent to which Moscow can use the element of surprise. What follows is necessarily a little speculative, given the sheer number of imponderables: the condition of NATO's forces, the level of political and civilian will behind them, the extent to which Russia regenerates its military presence around the Baltic, and how well Russia and NATO have each learned the lessons from Ukraine.

In the least bad scenario, NATO will have had enough time to prepare and execute what Russian military theorists refer to as the 'IMVU' (integrated mass air strike), an overpowering preliminary bombardment involving more or less every kind of non-nuclear ground-attack missile at its disposal, launched from the air, the sea and from land, and supplemented by cyberweapons and special forces operations.[34] The Russian armed forces would then run into stiff resistance from the moment they rolled on to NATO territory. The three Baltic states have recently begun building a 'defence line' around their borders with Russia and Belarus, based on similar fortifications laid down by the Ukrainians. It will probably consist of more than a thousand hardened bunkers, each with room for a dozen or so soldiers and access to nearby ammunition stores.

Donatas Palavenis, a Lithuanian army major and researcher at the Baltic Institute of Advanced Technology in Vilnius, says the point is to

> fix, block and canalise incoming military forces into engagement areas, thus making favourable conditions for destroying them with combined arms manoeuvres . . . As the Baltic states have no defence

depth to delay the enemy, the fight would be conducted for each centimetre of territory, thus requiring a set of man-made obstacles and fortifications to minimise their losses.[35]

At least in the Estonian section, there will be various other measures to slow down an invading force, including ditches, concertina wire, 'dragon's teeth' anti-tank obstacles and potentially anti-vehicle mines. 'It includes all necessary means to fight against the enemy,' says Lieutenant Colonel Kaido Tiitus, a senior Estonian reserve force officer and advisor to the defence ministry. 'This is protection, this is positions, this is fire against the enemy. This is counter-mobility against the enemy.'

Poland has also announced that it will spend €2.4 billion on an 'east shield' along similar lines across roughly 430 miles of its frontiers with Belarus and Kaliningrad. Władysław Kosiniak-Kamysz, the defence minister, described the project as 'the largest operation to strengthen the eastern border of Poland, the eastern flank of NATO, since 1945'. He also suggested the country might *in extremis* add anti-personnel mines, which are banned under the 1997 Ottawa convention.[36]

If the Russians can get past these lines, it will by no means be the end of their problems. The Baltic states have comparatively small but exceptionally well-rehearsed professional armed forces: 4,200 full-time active personnel in Estonia, about 6,500 in Latvia and 15,000 in Lithuania, in addition to more than 25,000 conscripts across all three countries.[37] These will be expanded over the coming years and can be supplemented with a total of well over 100,000 high-readiness reservists, as well as at least 160,000 further people with military training, including members of various paramilitary organisations and even hunting societies.

There is currently a multinational NATO battlegroup of between 1,000 and 2,000 soldiers in each of the Baltic states. The German battalion at Rukla in Lithuania is to be enlarged into a 'permanent' mechanised brigade of roughly 4,800 personnel by 2027. Canada aims to turn its battlegroup at Ādaži into a brigade-level force, including 2,200 'persistently deployed' Canadian troops.[38] Britain will continue to maintain only a battalion-sized force at Tapa in Estonia but has promised to hold the 'balance of a brigade' ready in case it is needed.[39]

Māris Andžāns, director of the Riga Centre for Geopolitical Studies, says these numbers are not even close to sufficient. 'These incomplete brigades are still far from [a level] Russia would respect,' he says. They may represent a large number of NATO members, but

> the Russians don't think in terms of flags. They think in terms of manpower and tanks and aircraft. So for them, it's not a big deal, and they can always raise the game to the nuclear level. We would need at least a [NATO] division in each of the Baltic states.

If the war in Ukraine is anything to go by, it is quite likely that these forces would have to fight simultaneously on several fronts, which could include amphibious and airborne infantry assaults. At that point the central factor will be timing: how long the defenders can hold their ground, and which side can get what units where and how fast.

Ben Hodges, the retired US general, has suggested that a frontline state under attack might have to cling on for as long as two weeks before reinforcements arrive in any useful numbers.[40] Other analysts such as Robert Pszczel, a Polish former diplomat and head of NATO's information office in Moscow, say that is too pessimistic.[41]

Even if NATO itself dithers, though, there are other sources of help. For starters, there is the UK-led Joint Expeditionary Force, a sub-NATO 'high-readiness' alliance that includes the Netherlands and the Nordic and Baltic countries. Poland, with about 200,000 active personnel, and Finland, with 24,000 but capacity to call up another 280,000 reservists at speed, are expected to conserve the bulk of their troops for homeland defence but would hardly stand by if the Baltic states were invaded.

Finland in particular might well establish a new line of attack over its land border with Russia. 'It's something that the Russians have to take into consideration: you attack the Baltics and the right flank opens,' says Pekka Toveri, a former director of the Finnish defence command's intelligence division. 'We have a lot of capabilities to influence that right flank without even leaving our own area, because we have the long-range capabilities.'

Plenty of observers are in any case unimpressed by Russia's proficiency in manoeuvre warfare. This is where armed forces try to move around rapidly and gain a positional advantage instead of getting bogged down in an attritional slog as on the battlefields of eastern Ukraine. In this respect, NATO's more devolved and flexible command structures could be a considerable asset, especially if the alliance succeeds in implementing its theory of 'mosaic' warfare: confusing and overwhelming the enemy with attacks from every direction and on every level of the spectrum, from missiles and special forces to drones and cyber.[42] Logistics can also work to the Kremlin's disadvantage on hostile territory. Beyond their country's unusually broad-gauge railway network, the Russian armed forces rely on a very limited fleet of lorries, which in practice makes it hard for them to locate their supply depots much more than 90 miles behind the artillery, which in turn exposes them to getting hit.[43]

'The dilemma begins for the Russians as soon as they must transition into an offensive operation and win territory without recourse to their own infrastructure,' says Lieutenant General Sandrart. This was evident during the early phases of the second Russian invasion of Ukraine, when Russia struggled to maintain food and fuel supplies, concentrated its ammunition stocks in easily identifiable dumps, left forward command posts vulnerable and formed long columns of armour waiting to be picked off by Ukrainian Javelin and N-LAW anti-tank missiles.[44] Keir Giles points out that Moscow has made the same mistakes since the first Chechen war in the 1990s, although he would not count on it making them again.[45]

However, some NATO forces are investing a lot of thought and effort into mobile 'deep reconnaissance strike' teams that can penetrate the enemy's lines and ravage the logistics convoys to their rear. This is one of the concepts that Major Guy Parker and his troops from the British Royal Lancers were testing with impressive results at the Titan Shield exercise I observed in Ādaži.

If the situation does end up degenerating into a war of attrition, the decisive factors will be the NATO states' ability not only to continue mobilising significant resources but to keep on funnelling them to the front lines: enablement and sustainment. 'You can assess very clearly from the war in Ukraine that enablement is one precondition for a successful fight,' says Alexander Sollfrank. 'If you're not capable of sustaining your fighting, you will not win the war. War is a test of will – we can see that – and a test of logistics.'

That in turn means that securing the Suwałki gap will be of paramount importance. In 2016 American war planners estimated that NATO would have no more than 72 hours to set up its defences in the corridor before Russia could close it off with a two-pronged offensive from Kaliningrad and Belarus.[46] The odds may have improved somewhat since then but the urgency of the task remains.

Fortunately, the strip of borderland is quite favourable territory for the defending side. Fairly hilly by the standards of the Baltic littoral, more than half of its surface area is taken up by swamps, dense forests and some 3,000 lakes, which provide cover, obstacles and natural funnels that force the invaders to concentrate their forces. There are few metalled roads that could withstand a squadron of armoured vehicles. In summer the dirt tracks through the woodlands frequently become quagmires. It is not friendly terrain for Russian tanks or artillery. Equally, though, the shortage of reliable lines of communication could be a serious problem for NATO if Russia can cut the main roads and railways.[47]

But the land war would not take place in isolation. Indispensable as infantry, armour and artillery are, the contest will also be decided at sea, in the skies, in space, over the airwaves, through the internet and above all in the political climate and the minds of individual leaders on either side. The final chapter will assess the balance of power across the full breadth of twenty-first-century warfare.

10

The Battle for the Baltic

How to Win a War With Russia

> A new stage in the forms and methods of warfare has begun. We can see how scientific and technological progress has set the wheel of history in motion and brought to the battlefield technologies that . . . will become the basis for global security in the future. It will be up to us to decide whether the democratic world or the world of tyranny will master these technologies faster.
> Valery Zaluzhny, former commander-in-chief,
> Ukrainian armed forces, 2024[1]

The Baltic sea is often triumphantly spoken of as a 'NATO lake'. What started as a semi-ironic internet meme quickly became a commonplace in public discourse. There is an element of truth in it: the strategic situation has changed significantly since February 2022. Now that Sweden and Finland are members, the alliance controls more than 95 per cent of the Baltic's coastline and all of its sizeable islands, as well as the western entrance through the Kattegat and both sides of the Gulf of Finland, Russia's only maritime route to Kaliningrad.

Finland's accession opens up a new sea line for ferrying troops and supplies into the Baltic states, as well as a land route from Norway's North sea coast. There are now two new NATO navies that were built for coastal defence, amphibious landings, submarine warfare and intelligence gathering. A stack of missiles on Gotland could provide a measure of mastery over the central Baltic. Estonia and Finland are melding together and upgrading their anti-ship missile batteries in readiness to 'close' the gulf with a 'NATO barrier' against Russian shipping if they have to, in the words of Estonia's defence minister.[2] There have even been proposals to block Russian ships from entering or leaving the sea altogether.[3]

With the want of good news elsewhere, a bit of self-congratulation is forgivable, right up to the point where it shades into complacency. Russia's Baltic fleet is currently depleted by the war in Ukraine and risks being split in two in its home waters.[4] Nor has the Russian navy acquitted itself with any distinction in the Black sea. The Ukrainians have sunk a third of its warships, which have proven vulnerable to missile and drone strikes. Moscow has been reduced to rigging up netting in its ports to try and shield them.[5] Nor are the Russian 'bubbles' of layered missile systems in the Baltic everything they have been cracked up to be.[6] 'We've learned a great deal from the war in Ukraine about sea warfare,' says Karsten Schneider, president of the German maritime institute and the former chief of staff in Germany's naval command.

> It's a centuries-old insight that Russia is very, very wary at sea. In many wars, the Russian fleets went back into their ports after a short while and were used only to defend the ports. That was the case in the Crimean war. It was the case in the Second World War, and the first. After all, the one time they did it differently, in the Russo-Japanese war [1904–5], it ended in a catastrophe. Now it's the same. They withdrew again, even though they had superiority at sea, because the entire fleet is not set up to fight.

Schneider expects history to repeat itself if there is a conflict in the Baltic, with the Russian navy pinned back in its harbours. 'Everything speaks against [them using] submarines,' he says.

> Surface ships would be suicide. So we can assume their approach will be to shoot outwards in every direction from this area denial bubble they have built up in Kaliningrad and try to prevent the Baltic states from being resupplied by sea. Now this might be easier for the West, because you can also approach from the other side, from Sweden, offering an additional line of communication which will of course also need to be defended.

The retired rear admiral believes Russia will, in effect, be bottled up at sea. 'I was the commander of a fast patrol boat in the Cold War,' Schneider says.

It was our job to close the Baltic sea approaches [to the Soviet navy]. That would be even easier now. The forces of the Baltic fleet would be unable to leave the Baltic sea. It's completely clear. No surface ship can get through and probably no submarine, either. So the question is: what can they do to us in the Baltic sea? That is, to what extent can they prevent us from supplying the Baltic states and Finland? . . . If the Russian navy does make an appearance, they will just fire off their Kalibr [anti-ship] missiles. And [for NATO] it will be a matter of doing the missile defence and above all of attacking their bases: quick, hard, with missiles launched from the air, the ground and the sea.

But there are also those who argue that owning the littoral is not the same as owning the sea. 'You could say: OK, strategically, given the fact that Sweden and Finland are in NATO, the picture is significantly different than it was before,' says Michael Hart, a former air vice-marshal and long-serving intelligence officer in the British Royal Air Force.

But even if strategically that's the case, there's still an awful lot of room for tactical activity. The reality of where Kaliningrad is and the capabilities that the Russian navy and Russia generally has around the Baltic means that you can never call it a NATO lake. It's as complacent as Mussolini calling the Mediterranean an Italian lake.

One potential hitch is that the kind of asymmetric naval warfare we have seen in Ukraine can cut both ways. Russia's room for manoeuvre may be more restricted than it was. Yet its drones, submarines and missile batteries could still do quite serious damage to NATO's ships. The anti-ship missiles that Schneider mentioned are not a negligible danger. The most advanced of them, the Kalibr 3M-54T – codenamed 'Sizzler' in the West – is believed to have a range of up to 400 miles, enough to hit targets in the Öresund and indeed pretty much anywhere else in the Baltic up to the Åland islands with a twisty trajectory that makes it harder to shoot down.[7] Even the most basic export variant in the Kalibr family, with a 130-mile range, can reach as far north as the Latvian port of Liepāja or anything that strays more than 60 miles south of Gotland.[8] It is hard to know how many of them might sneak past NATO's destroyers and onshore missile defences. It is also a fair bet that both sides would deploy an inordinate quantity of sea mines.

'Any future conflict in the Baltic is going to be characterised by the fact that not a lot is going to be left floating after a while. It's a narrow sea. Ships are going to get sunk,' Hart says. That might make the bigger naval players with assets outside the Baltic, notably Britain and Germany, wary of sending in vessels they could easily lose. 'The environment in which the British could sail to Helsinki in the 1850s, bombarding ports along the way, is completely different,' Hart says. 'There's something about the extent to which you want to commit ships that you might need elsewhere, in the North sea or the north Atlantic, to operate in the Baltic.'

Sebastian Bruns, a senior researcher at Kiel university's Institute for Security Policy and an informal advisor to the German navy, is also unpersuaded that NATO can simply shut Russia down at sea by choking off the gulf of Finland. 'I'm not convinced that this is something that NATO would be able to do, because we're talking about hundreds and hundreds of anti-ship missiles,' he says. 'So one way or another they would have to be fortified enough that they survive the Russian onslaught or even a cyberattack.'

Bruns says it is hard to know what to expect from Russia on the water, not least because the West does not yet have a good sense of what unorthodox tactics it might deploy. Judging the strength of a navy, Bruns says, is tough, because alongside the number of ships you have to consider their tonnage, their age and the quality of the weapon systems on board. But in terms of quantity, the Russian Baltic fleet cannot be completely written off. It has, for example, twenty-eight corvettes, smaller and faster warships that carry a range of missiles. That is more than the neighbouring NATO navies put together. 'It's a bit of a game of risk, a toss-up,' Bruns says.

And then of course the interesting question is: how much Black sea is in the Baltic fleet? In other words, they might have all the ships and boats, but if they're not able to fight with co-ordinated maritime systems, they're going to meet the same fate. They're going to sink to the bottom of St Petersburg harbour before they know it.

The Battle in the Skies

If Russia's navy has had a rough war in Ukraine, its air force, the VKS, has not fared much better. Despite having a 13:1 numerical advantage over the enemy, its warplanes have so far failed to achieve air superiority. If only 10 per cent of the fleet has been destroyed, as NATO estimates, that may be precisely because Moscow is wary of losing any more of its warplanes and has used them quite conservatively to deploy glide bombs and long-range air-to-surface missiles.[9] 'Are they hesitant to really get involved?' Scott Kindsvater, a retired US air force general, has asked. 'Or are they preserving certain assets as a strategic reserve for a fight with NATO?'[10]

Before 2022, there were doubts about whether in a war over the Baltic the West could secure the dominion over the skies that it has become accustomed to in every conflict since the Second World War. Spooked by the fairly effective Russian air campaign in Syria and the emergence of the Russian S-400 air defence system, some suggested it could take NATO several weeks to wrest back air superiority from Russia. 'They have closed the gap,' Frank Gorenc, the commander of the US air forces in Europe and Africa, said in 2015. 'They learned a lot along the way, and they made moves to close the asymmetric advantage posed by the quality of our air force. They've done it.'[11]

Now the analytical pendulum is swinging in the other direction. Justin Bronk, a British air power researcher at the Royal United Services Institute (RUSI) think-tank, argues the VKS's training is so abysmal that the force 'lacks the institutional capacity to plan, brief and fly complex air operations at scale'. Its pilots typically get only half as much flight time as their NATO counterparts. They skimp on target practice and flights in challenging conditions. They do not have the advanced simulators required for practising manoeuvres in large formations.[12] Michael Hart claims that 'What we've seen in both

Ukraine and Syria is evidence that Russia . . . doesn't really conceptualise or deploy air power effectively.'

> They tend to use a pair of aircraft to attack a target, followed by another pair, probably against a different target, and so on. So it's a sum of disconnected activity rather than a coherent campaign to achieve control of the air and then integrate offensive air power with surface manoeuvre and fires.*

Russia's air force is also getting old. More than half of its warplanes were made more than thirty years ago.[13] The wear and tear of sorties over Ukraine are taking their toll. Moscow does have newer models. The Sukhoi Su-57, its first more or less fifth-generation fighter, will be familiar to viewers of *Top Gun: Maverick* and is touted by the Russian state as a rival to the American F-35. But its development has been delayed by western sanctions on technology exports and at present only twenty-two of them are thought to be available.[14] At least one of them has already been destroyed by a Ukrainian drone, highlighting their vulnerability.[15] This is one of the domains where NATO appears to have a significant advantage in procurement. The allies already have roughly 800 fifth-generation jets and are manufacturing another hundred or so each year. Russia, by contrast, is believed to produce only twenty units a year of its main warplanes, such as the Su-34.[16]

At the same time, western air defence systems have performed well in Ukraine. The Patriot has proven adaptable enough to knock out Russia's 'hypersonic' Kinzhal ballistic missiles, once billed as a wonder weapon.[17] The German IRIS-T and the American-Norwegian NASAMS, both making their debut on the battlefield, are reported to have had 100 per cent hit rates.[18] Even the Gepard armoured flak cannon, designed in the 1960s and retired by the German military so long ago that it had trouble sourcing extra ammunition for the Ukrainians, has turned out to be a handy asset.[19]

---

* A crude summary: in US military doctrine (and across many NATO allies), surface manoeuvre means land units that move to occupy ground, conduct reconnaissance, disrupt supply lines, pull enemy units out of shape; while fires are any systems used to destroy, degrade or harass targets: traditionally artillery and missiles, but increasingly involving other elements such as cyber and information

On the other side, the Russian S-400, which is the core of Kaliningrad's air defences and once tempted Turkey so much that it jilted the US in order to spend $2.5 billion on the system, has been repeatedly taken out by Ukrainian missiles.[20] An upgraded version, the S-500 Prometheus, was deployed in 2024 but one of the batteries was almost immediately blindsided by a Ukrainian strike on a nearby radar.[21] Given the Russian military industry's chronic troubles with scaling up the production of new weapons, it may also take some years to arrive in the Baltic. 'From what we have seen, the Russians would have their air force cleared from the skies by NATO fixed-wing [warplanes] and anti-air capabilities,' says Phillips O'Brien, professor of strategic studies at the University of St Andrews in Scotland. 'Ukraine has stymied Russia with [Soviet-era] Mig-29s and a small number of western anti-air systems. NATO as a whole would fare much better.'

But there may be a danger of overcorrecting our assessment of Russia's air and missile capabilities in the region. Some of the old concerns are still valid. NATO warplanes will have a hard time over the Baltic states if the alliance cannot first eliminate Russian missile defences, as the Russians themselves have discovered in Ukraine.[22] Matthew Galamison, a US naval aviation commander, and Michael Petersen, a professor at the US Naval War College, have made the case that the balance of power is swinging towards twenty-first-century ground-based systems, which make it 'more difficult than ever to build a sanctuary for aircraft to operate' in.[23]

Jack Watling, an analyst at RUSI, went further in a provocative recent book on the future of warfare, suggesting that in a conflict with a military 'peer' power such as Russia even NATO air forces would be reluctant to risk their expensive jets on providing close air support to land operations. Ultimately, Watling concluded, combat jets were so hobbled by 'rapidly diminishing survivability' and the proliferation of sophisticated and more expendable drones that there might be no point in spending hundreds of billions on developing new ones.[24]

Then there is the question of the air defence systems needed to protect the eastern flank. NATO's own internal modelling suggests the allies can supply only 5 per cent of the air defence systems needed to protect the eastern flank. '[Air defence] is one of the biggest holes we have. There's no denying it,' one official told the *Financial Times*.[25] Germany has set up a procurement coalition, the European Sky Shield Initiative, but the early results have been distinctly modest.

That presents the European states with some invidious dilemmas. 'I think it would be relatively similar to what you see in Ukraine,' says Fabian Hoffmann, an expert on missile technology at Oslo university.

> Ukraine is very effectively able to establish individual air and missile defence bubbles that are really, really difficult to penetrate and overwhelm. But then you also just have vast areas where there is no coverage because they lack the assistance. That is, on a country by country basis, pretty much the case [in the Baltic sea region]. For Germany, it would be pretty much impossible to cover all its critical infrastructure. So it would have to make the same choices as Ukraine is doing right now: if I'm going to protect my critical civilian infrastructure around Berlin, Hamburg and Munich, and that means, for example, that Frankfurt and Hanover are not protected to the same extent.

It is just not possible, Hoffmann says, to create a missile defence shield that covers everything, especially since you need to combine systems with different ranges if you want to build a really safe 'bubble'. The irony is that it would be easier to do this in the Baltic states, on account of their relatively small size, than it would for a larger country such as Poland or Germany. In other words, Tallinn could be saved but it might be at the expense of Dresden or Gdańsk.

But this vulnerability is also on the Russian side. The Ukrainians have used the few hundred Storm Shadow/SCALP cruise missiles they received from Britain and France to surgical effect, striking deep behind enemy lines. The JASSM, a similar weapon made in the US and recently acquired by Finland and Poland, may also be road-tested in Ukraine before long. The German-Swedish Taurus, which has a more robust navigation system and a world-class design for penetrating even the most rugged bunkers, is a formidable prospect. One of the reasons Germany has been so reluctant to hand the missiles over to Kyiv is thought to be that most of its stocks have already been assigned to targets in case of a war on NATO's eastern flank.

The Electronic Battle, Part One

Not long before Christmas 2023, an open-source intelligence analyst who posts on Twitter/X under the pseudonym Markus Jonsson started publishing maps on which most of the southern Baltic was lit up in various shades of red. The airwaves over northern Germany and Poland, the Baltic states and southern Finland were humming with bursts of GPS interference, affecting thousands of aircraft. Markus Jonsson triangulated the source of the disturbance and concluded that the 'Baltic jammer' was located in Kaliningrad.[26]

The jamming continued intermittently for months. In March 2024, an RAF jet carrying Grant Shapps, the UK defence secretary, and an entourage of journalists back from a NATO exercise in north-eastern Poland was subjected to a thirty-minute blast of GPS disruption.[27] By the end of April, the Finnish telecoms agency had logged about 1,200 incidents where planes had suffered some kind of GPS malfunction over the previous four months, compared to 239 over the entirety of 2023 and only eight in 2021.[28] Eventually Finnair felt obliged to suspend flights between Helsinki and the Estonian city of Tartu after two passenger jets were forced to turn back.[29] The foreign ministers of the Baltic states condemned the 'hybrid attack' from Russia and warned that it could lead to a serious air accident.[30]

The Baltic jammer did for electronic interference what the Nord Stream bombings had done for the sabotage of submarine infrastructure eighteen months earlier, abruptly bringing to the world's attention a phenomenon that had been going on at a low level for some years. Pilots in the Baltic sea area have been sporadically reporting the otherwise inexplicable loss of GPS signals since the first Russian invasion of Ukraine in 2014.[31] Russian cyber-attacks, an adjacent category of nuisance, have also been detected in the region since at least as far back as the 2007 Bronze Night in Estonia. These measures have become part of the background noise of life around the Baltic. But in a war they could both be decisive.

Electronic warfare, the use of electromagnetic radiation to block communications (jamming) or distort them (spoofing), has existed since the Second World War. The technology has evolved significantly over the past few decades. It has been especially prominent in the second Russian invasion of Ukraine. Russia's electronic interference systems have turned out to be remarkably effective. High-tech guided munitions supplied by the US, including GPS-directed Excalibur artillery shells and HIMARS rockets, have routinely been drawn away from their intended targets. Ukraine has been losing as many as 2,000 drones a week to electromagnetic disruption. The mobile Russian Shipovnik-Aero jamming array, with a range of more than 10 miles, can not only seize control of drones but also pinpoint the locations of their pilots. There has been speculation that Russia's electronic warfare capabilities may already match or even exceed NATO's.[32]

When I put these suggestions to Jürgen-Joachim von Sandrart, he was fairly dismissive. Other figures in NATO say they are quietly confident it will have an edge in the electromagnetic spectrum. Their organisation may be tight-lipped about what it can do, they say, but this is to be interpreted as a sign of strength rather than weakness. Then again, they would say that for the sake of deterrence.

Russia certainly has some impressive assets. The Murmansk-BN system, usually stationed on the Kola peninsula east of Norway and northern Finland but also deployed to Ukraine, can meddle with radio, TV and mobile phone signals more than 3,000 miles away.[33] Others, such as the Krasukha-4 and the R-330Zh, can shut down radars and even satellite communications at shorter ranges. The RB-341V Leer can hijack mobile phone networks and plant false information on up to 6,000 handsets, albeit with a range of only 4 miles.[34] In 2017 it was used to spam Ukrainian soldiers' phones with messages that read 'Your body will be found when the snow melts' and 'Nobody needs your kids to become orphans'.[35]

I am still more unsettled by a conversation with Thomas Withington, an electronic warfare expert for the RUSI think-tank. 'The Baltic's an interesting one, isn't it?' he says.

If we do see any Russia-NATO confrontation in that part of the world, I expect that it will almost certainly start, very early on in the conflict, with a higher-altitude detonation – almost certainly near space or in space – of a large nuclear weapon.

That would result in a 'massive' electromagnetic pulse (EMP) that fries 'basically anything, any electronics that are unshielded: most of them just stop working.'

Good grief, I reply. What is the potential radius for that sort of bedlam? How do the Russians prevent it from nobbling their own war machines? While that would depend on the altitude and the yield of the warhead, Withington says, he has run a simulation of an EMP blast a hundred miles above Los Angeles. He found the effects would be noticeable in Washington DC, more than 2,000 miles away on the opposite side of the US. The impact does fall off quite sharply the further you get from the epicentre, but even in Texas there would still be quite significant havoc on any devices that are not electromagnetically shielded.

The contest for control of the airwaves has taken on greater importance with the revolution in twenty-first-century sensor technology. Much has been made of the rise in drone warfare. The scale and pace of the developments in this field, spurred on by the application of machine learning and other AI-based approaches, are extraordinary. In Ukraine, drones carry out reconnaissance, drop munitions or become munitions in their own right. They have curtailed the 'kill chain', the time between spotting and eliminating a target, to as little as eighty seconds.[36] In some battles, direct drone attacks are reported to have accounted for up to 90 per cent of the casualties.[37] Ukraine is estimated to be burning through about 10,000 of the devices each month.[38]

But drones are only one element in what Jack Watling calls the 'transparent battlefield'. Satellites with synthetic aperture radar are now sharp enough to identify the denomination of a coin dropped on a pavement. Soldiers carry microphones that can not only detect the sound of an armoured vehicle 6 miles away but determine its model. Vibrometers, which use lasers to measure how an object such as an engine is trembling, are so sensitive they can take a pigeon's pulse at a distance of 19 miles.[39] Large volumes of information are also scraped from the mobile phones of soldiers and non-combatants.

In theory it is almost as though today's commanders are playing an old-fashioned real-time strategy computer game with the fog of war switched off. That is not always how it works in practice: on an electronically contested battlefield the data can be both so overwhelming and so hard to coherently piece together that a UK army commander complained the operation 'ate like an elephant and shat like a mouse' in one large-scale exercise.[40] But machine-learning techniques developed by US defence contractors such as Palantir and Google are increasingly binding the various feeds into what the Pentagon calls a 'single pane of glass'. At a secret location in central Europe known only as the 'Pit', for example, British and American officers are reported to be monitoring the war in Ukraine through one of these systems at a level of detail and precision greater than the Ukrainians themselves can achieve.[41]

The upshot, in Watling's view, is that in the near future it will become almost impossible to move a unit of any useful size without being detected. In other words, the element of surprise is exceedingly difficult to attain. While there is scope for ingenious tactical manoeuvres that exploit the weak points in the enemy's sensor array, the really decisive thing is timing: reading the rhythms of your opponent's decision-making and striking during the few minutes when you suspect they are off balance.[42]

The Electronic Battle, Part Two

For slightly different reasons, it is similarly hard to read how the cyber dimension of a NATO–Russia war might work out. Russia's capabilities are not easy to assess. In 2015 Moscow's hackers wiped out an electricity distribution centre and thirty substations in the Ivano-Frankivsk oblast of western Ukraine, cutting off power to about 230,000 households for several hours.[43] Another, broader attack two years later, aimed at banks, energy firms and various arms of the Ukrainian government, is said to have destroyed data on 10 per cent of the country's computers.[44]

Since 2022, though, the anticipated digital armageddon has failed to materialise, in large part because Kyiv has put a lot of effort into bolstering its defences with western assistance.[45] '[The Russians] actually did some very good attacks,' says Heli Tiirmaa-Klaar, at the Digital Society Institute in Berlin.

> But these were also mitigated very fast by the Ukrainian and western side. Let's not forget the famous Microsoft vulnerability in the early days of the war, when they tried to stop the whole civilian transportation system in Ukraine. It was quite effective but it was also mitigated very quickly by how the cyber vulnerabilities were discovered.

This has left states highly reliant on technology companies to identify threats and come up with solutions. Sometimes this reliance can be quite uncomfortable. On the morning when the Kremlin began its full-scale invasion of Ukraine, hackers from Russia's military intelligence agency knocked out Viasat, the private sector satellite firm that provided the backbone of Kyiv's government and military communications. Only a few days later, Elon Musk said he would supply the Ukrainians with Starlink terminals, which have a high-speed connection to a constellation of more than 6,000 commercial satellites, far more than any Russian electronic warfare system can neutralise. Yet Musk, who had been buttonholed by Russian officials, refused to extend the coverage to Crimea, hamstringing a Ukrainian raid on the naval base at Sevastopol.[46]

The Russian menagerie of cyberwarfare is large and complex. In its lower levels there are gangs that use fairly primitive tools en masse on an opportunistic basis. The more sophisticated of these groups, which have an ambiguous relationship with different arms of the government, can deploy quite advanced malware and tactics. At the top end are in-house units that conduct carefully planned bespoke operations, sometimes to devastating effect.

In May 2023 Russian hackers penetrated the servers of Kyivstar, Ukraine's largest telecoms company. They bided their time for seven months, possibly stealing information such as the contents of text messages and the locations of individual phones. On Christmas Eve they then 'completely destroyed the core' of the firm's IT infrastructure. 'The attack is a big message, a big warning, not only to Ukraine, but for the whole western world to understand that no one is actually untouchable,' Illia Vitiuk, the head of cybersecurity at the Ukrainian security service, said afterwards.[47]

It was not an overstatement. The Baltic region has plenty of experience with this kind of disruption. In 2017 near-simultaneous attacks took down Latvia's emergency services hotline and infected the phones of the US NATO commander in Poland and at least half a dozen of his soldiers, to the point where they were asked to jump into lakes to demonstrate that they did not have any hidden electronic devices on their persons.[48] Recently Russian intelligence seems to have infiltrated IT networks at the top of Supo, Finland's domestic security and counter-espionage agency, including the computer of its director, Antti Pelttari.[49] Shortly before the 2023 NATO summit in Vilnius, a group of hackers thought to be working for Russia's military intelligence agency obtained and leaked a trove of Lithuanian government planning documents, including the security details for a dozen world leaders and the names of the snipers keeping watch over proceedings.[50]

The SVR, Russia's foreign intelligence service, has pulled off a number of highly ambitious cyber-escapades. In 2019 its hackers gained entry to the systems of SolarWinds, a Texan IT company, and used it undetected for more than a year as a platform for a spectacular 'supply chain' attack, the victims of which included the Pentagon, the US Treasury department and Microsoft.[51] They are also suspected of having devised and implanted a back door to the fundamental open-source software that underpins virtually every publicly available server on the planet. The alarm was raised only thanks to a perceptive Microsoft engineer called Andreas Freund, who spotted the warning signs and investigated them in his spare time.[52]

Heli Tiirmaa-Klaar believes Russia may be holding back its 'crown jewels' for a possible war with NATO. 'Once you are already in the real military conflict, then using cyber methods is not a priority any more,' she says.

> If you can destroy targets and run over the territory with tanks, it doesn't really matter if there are cyber-attacks or not. This is not

going to give you a strategic advantage or disadvantage. That's why I think the Russians have not been using their most advanced cyber methods in Ukraine, since they are already in the war and they don't need to create chaos and misunderstanding and this kind of disruption that they could do without actual military involvement. So they certainly have many different capabilities which they probably did not display in Ukraine.

Part of the problem is basic cybersecurity hygiene lapses by western governments. In 2024 a reporter from *Die Zeit* used a loophole in the German authorities' Webex video-conferencing software to gain access to the digital 'meeting rooms' of the chancellor and the finance and business ministers.[53] As the Kyivstar and SolarWinds hacks illustrate, though, a bigger headache is the sheer range of the potential targets: not just ministries and armed forces, but the organisations and private companies on which their critical infrastructure depends.

'NATO is all the member states and all the suppliers and the sum total of NATO's many missions,' says Jiro Minier, another Berlin-based cybersecurity expert. 'NATO is fundamentally meant to be a mechanism that brings together all these disparate national objectives and bureaucracies and points them in one direction. And so, inevitably, the attack surface is absolutely massive. There's no doubt about it.'

The standard way of dealing with this is to be extremely careful about who is responsible for what and which information is kept where, in order to limit the damage that can be done through a single breach in the defences. But it is not the only way. Minier reaches for the metaphor of a medieval castle, with the keep at its heart surrounded by various layers of concentric walls. 'It's not just a question of being on the defensive and thinking about withstanding the siege,' he says.

> Even before the siege begins, you have to be thinking about things such as: can you break it? Can you conduct a foray? Can you conduct reconnaissance? Can you try to change [your opponent's] decision-making calculus about whether to actually put you under siege in the first place? Fine, if you're anticipating a siege: where are your supplies coming from? How prepared are you? Who's going to come to your relief?

How Not to Fight a Nuclear War

During a break in writing this chapter, I took my children to the Berlin aquarium. On the way, we passed the Kaiser Wilhelm memorial church on Breitscheidplatz, which was damaged by an Allied bomb in 1943 and has been left ever since in a state of partial ruination to warn Germany and the world about the tragedy of war. It prompted a lot of questions from my six-year-old son. One of them was: why cannot one side simply drop an atom bomb on the other to win the conflict? Not wanting to frighten him, I gave him the explanation I had grown up with as a child of the 1990s: nobody would use an atom bomb because if they did, the other countries that have them would respond in kind. No one wants a scenario where we end up doing to ourselves what the Chicxulub asteroid did to the last dinosaurs. The main point of atom bombs is to prevent wars between the states that own them.

But it was in fact a perfectly decent question and the real answer is darker and more complicated. Vladimir Putin and other figures in his regime have repeatedly indicated that they might in fact be prepared to use a nuclear weapon, most probably a smallish tactical warhead aimed at a military target in Ukraine. At various times western intelligence services have differed quite considerably in their assessments of how likely this is. The lowest estimates I have heard are well below 5 per cent. The highest, discreetly disseminated by the CIA to its partner agencies in the summer of 2022, is understood to have been 30 per cent. It is impossible to predict what would happen once humanity's most serious taboo has been breached. But we cannot wholly exclude an uncontrollable cycle of escalation that rapidly leads to all-out nuclear war.

This poses NATO governments with a dilemma that resembles Pascal's wager: there might be only a very small chance that God exists and hell is real. But if he does and it is, leading an un-Christian life will land you in an eternity of torment. Pascal thought the only rational response was to behave as though the proposition were true. There are some western states, particularly but not only the US and Germany, that use similar logic and argue for restraint in dealing with Russia.

The trouble with this approach, though, is that it gives Putin 'escalation dominance': he can take ever more provocative steps in the belief that his nuclear threats will keep the most powerful actors in the West from sanctioning a proportional response to his acts of aggression. '[The Russians] have really been developing and updating their deterrence thinking over the past decades and I think here they are really ahead of us, because we have kind of stopped thinking about it [in many western countries],' says Lydia Wachs, a nuclear policy researcher at Stockholm University. Nuclear blackmail is, she says, a 'tool of coercion': 'They are trying to weaken western cohesion. They are trying to exploit our vulnerabilities and public opinion in western countries, and also to weaken our support for Ukraine.'

The implications for the Baltic could scarcely be more serious. If Putin thinks our hands are tied by fear of atomic war, he will be encouraged to keep probing the boundaries of what he can get away with, potentially all the way up to seizing a slice of NATO territory and declaring that it is under the Russian nuclear 'umbrella'. One school of thought suggests that in a war with the alliance he might be tempted to try and 'escalate to de-escalate', using a nuclear weapon at an early stage in the hope of unnerving the Americans and western Europeans. In the Cold War, for example, the Warsaw Pact states drew up a plan to fire about 400 low-yield 'tactical' nuclear warheads at Germany and other central European targets in the first wave of an offensive.[54]

> The scenario that is most alarming is that Putin would invade one or more of the Baltic states with conventional forces, but at the same time he would put both his European and global nuclear forces on full alert and would tell us that if we get involved, if we support the Baltic states, then he is ready to use nuclear force,

says Tomas Ries, a senior lecturer in security and strategy at Sweden's national defence college who has studied and shaped nuclear policy since the end of the 1970s.

> NATO is not ready for that. It's not capable of dealing with a situation like that. I can say that categorically, because I was working

on it for about six years with NATO during the Cold War. I know what it takes to develop a nuclear deterrent, and we don't have any of that now. Zero.

Putin might try to show that he is in earnest, Ries suggests, by detonating one or two of his smaller warheads in the air over the sea 'with zero collateral damage or military effect, but simply as a warning that would really shake European politicians'. He continues:

> When I look back at what we saw in the Soviet times, and what we got out of the [Soviet] archives afterwards, there was a part of the Soviet military establishment that was dead set on using nuclear weapons basically just to blow us to pieces, and then the armoured divisions would roll through the rubble ... So I suspect that in Russia there is still a willingness [to do something similar]. Putin's statements and the people around him, and some of the puppets like Sergey Karaganov, have spread this message to us. It seems like they're trying to prepare us psychologically to be afraid of the Russian nuclear war capability.

At a fundamental level, deterrence on the eastern flank depends on convincing the Russian regime that this kind of approach will not work. That is why many analysts argue that the West needs to improve its collective 'nuclear IQ'. What this tends to mean in practice is a return to the strategies devised for dealing with the problem in the early decades of the Cold War. An especially important one is what Thomas Schelling, the great American game theorist and the godfather of modern thinking about deterrence, called the 'competition in risk-taking'.[55]

'Competitions between nuclear powers take the form of a nuclear crisis. It's not a war; it's a crisis,' says Fabian Hoffmann, the Oslo university missile and nuclear policy expert.

> And in times of crisis there is a rising likelihood that we will see a military confrontation. What nuclear powers learned, and what Russia still does very effectively, is to manipulate that risk to achieve their political objectives. Basically, the states in a nuclear crisis

engage in a reciprocal increase in the risk of direct military confrontation that could end in nuclear war until one side drops out. If you think about the Cuban missile crisis, for example, in this case the Soviet Union dropped out. Of course, it's not entirely black and white. There were concessions on both sides. But one side gives in. The other side gets away with victory.

The argument Hoffmann and other nuclear weapons experts make is that this system is counter-intuitively safer and more stable than the alternative. Russia still thinks in the old patterns of nuclear signalling: from its perspective, it is playing a one-sided game against an opponent who seems deeply uncertain of the rules. The least we can do is show we understand them by taking some 'counter-escalatory' measures of our own. 'If you look back at the Cold War archives, people talked about deploying nuclear weapons all the time: in the Vietnam war, in the Korean war, in the Afghanistan war with the Soviet Union,' Hoffmann says.

> They just never did it. I can understand how for a person who does not deal with these likelihoods on a daily basis it may not be very comfortable to think there is a 0.1 chance that this ends in a nuclear disaster . . . But I honestly believe, by and large, these are calculated risks.

Most of the countries around the Baltic sea grasped this a long time ago because they have been facing down nuclear blackmail for years. In 2015, for example, the Russian ambassador to Copenhagen threatened to use atomic weapons if Denmark joined NATO's missile defence scheme. Later that year Moscow's delegates to a summit of the Elbe group, a back channel between the Russian and American armed forces, are reported to have said the Kremlin would deploy nuclear warheads if NATO sent troops to the Baltic states. In the end, the threats amounted to nothing.[56] Several experts I interviewed said this thinking also remained strong in the parts of the British, French and American establishments that still remember the lessons of the Cold War. There are signs that it is beginning to percolate across the wider West, particularly since early June 2024, when the Germans and Americans relented and gave Ukraine permission to use their weapons to strike military targets on Russian soil.[57]

Yet the situation gets much trickier when there are question marks around the US commitment to Europe. It is hard enough for the Europeans to sustain conventional deterrence on their own. Doing it in the nuclear domain is a big ask. Russia is estimated to have 4,380 serviceable nuclear warheads and another 1,200 older ones that have been 'retired' but could be brought out of storage.[58] Europe's only nuclear powers, Britain and France, are thought to have a little over 500 between them, with serious technical limitations.[59]

The Front Line Is Everywhere

If much of the analysis in this chapter seems frustratingly uncertain, that is because the conditions are themselves frustratingly uncertain. War cannot be forecast like the weather. Even the best-informed experts in February 2022 could not have foreseen the course that the conflict in Ukraine would take. Many did not even see it coming. An irony of the war is that in some ways we now know significantly more about what Russia can do than about what NATO can. Nor is there any reason to assume that the next war would be like the last one.

But it is possible to draw some general conclusions. The first is that the Baltic sea region is not a NATO lake. The local balance of power has certainly tilted in the alliance's favour, and some of its generals may even be sincerely confident that it would hold the upper hand in a war, but Russia has plenty of options at its disposal.

Second, everything depends on what happens in Ukraine. The weaker Russia's position becomes on the ground, the less likely it is to gamble on military adventures elsewhere. The West has an existential interest in enabling the Ukrainians to win their war. Even if Kyiv cannot ultimately reconquer all of the territory Russia has occupied, a strong Ukraine is one of the best deterrents NATO could possibly have.

Third, it is pure magical thinking to imagine that a Russian attack on the Baltic could be limited to the Baltic. I have used the term 'frontline states' throughout this book because I think it expresses something meaningful about how they regard and deal with the threat from Russia. In a direct conflict with NATO, though, each of the allies would to some extent become a frontline state. Moscow would seek to gain the advantage wherever it could, through every tool in its armamentarium. Physical distance is little comfort. Russia may even single out precisely the countries that are further away from the focus of the land war and more susceptible to pressure. Conversely, it is a racing certainty that the war would arrive on Russian soil, too. The prime military targets include Kaliningrad, command centres and logistical hubs in the western military district, the naval bases around St Petersburg, and the railway line between St Petersburg and the Kola peninsula.

Fourth, the best way to prevent a war is to be unmistakably capable of winning one. Deterrence is a compound of conventional and nuclear strength, political resolve, and communication. On all of these fronts the West has a lot of ground to make up. But above all it has to get better at marrying them together in peacetime. The widespread reluctance to compare the current state of affairs to a second Cold War is understandable and in some respects absolutely justified: the analogy is sloppy and leaning too heavily on it could result in grave mistakes. Yet the Cold War-era understanding of deterrence and calculated risk deserves to be dusted off and updated for the twenty-first century.

Fifth, the US is indispensable for deterrence and defence in the Baltic, and the security of the Baltic is indispensable for the US. Without American nuclear missiles and land forces, Europe would struggle to keep Russia at bay on the eastern flank. Even vague intimations that Washington might not be fully committed to NATO risk undermining the entire edifice. Donald Trump's suggestion in February 2024 that he would allow the Russians to 'do whatever the hell they want' to allies that underspend on their militaries prompted consternation across the continent.[60] 'As long as you can take for granted that US military forces will react to a Russian provocation in the Baltics that results in fighting between local Baltic and NATO forces and Russian forces, then I'm not worried,' says Peter Viggo Jakobsen. 'As long as Russia believes that will happen, then there's no problem. But if they start doubting that, it's serious.'

Regardless of who is sitting in the Oval Office, the US is increasingly preoccupied elsewhere. Especially in the Pacific, it has many other demands on its attention and resources. As the former general Ben Hodges points out, though, it needs its European allies. 'We depend on our bases in almost every country in Europe and all around the Mediterranean,' Hodges says.

> They're not here for us to guard the Germans. They're here for us, but also for what we do in Africa and the Middle East. The Ramstein airbase [in south-west Germany], the headquarters of the Africa command [in Stuttgart], all these things are in Europe. So we would be screwing ourselves if we're not in NATO and we're not here, not fully committed to their defence.

Sixth and last, that means the Europeans have to step up, whatever happens in Washington. The situation we face is no less dangerous than it was in the Cold War, when most of the bigger countries spent more than 3 per cent of their GDP on defence. In 2024 the alliance's collective military expenditure was on track to reach 2 per cent, compared to only 1.47 per cent a decade earlier. Twenty-three of the thirty-two allies were expected to meet or surpass the threshold that year.[61] Europe's combined defence budgets hit a total of $380 billion, or roughly the same as Russia's. As the 2023 Vilnius summit officially stated, however, 2 per cent is a minimum, not a ceiling. A number of member states must make up for decades of underinvestment just to deliver the capabilities they have promised on paper, let alone to achieve NATO's goal of increasing its total capacity by a third.[62]

What matters just as much as the money is the underlying mindset. Beyond the frontline states, most European leaders have not yet candidly told their populations how much is at stake and the extent to which ensuring their safety will require sacrifices from all of us. Some of these sacrifices are financial, such as higher taxes, cuts to other areas of public spending or the 'security premium' on the prices for many goods that comes with attempts to reduce dependencies in our supply chains. Others are inconveniences, such as additional bureaucracy or the periodic allocation of civilian transport to military exercises.

Yet the hardest and most fundamental thing we will have to give up is the psychological comfort we have become used to. Security is not a thing to be restored; it is a thing to be created. There is no going back to the innocence of the 1990s. Baltic sea countries such as Finland, Estonia and Sweden have been preparing their publics for every kind of prospective crisis: where to shelter from a rain of missiles, how to cope with sustained power cuts or internet outages, how to survive if you are forced to flee your home and seek refuge in the woods.

It is not pleasant to live in a mental world full of risks and dangers. In many of us there is an innate impulse to switch off the news and turn away, or to assume that these precautions are all very sensible for the Estonians but have nothing to do with us. Humankind, as the bird says in T. S. Eliot's *Four Quartets*, 'cannot bear very much reality'. But the countries of the Baltic have already grasped what the rest of us urgently need to understand: in the end it comes down to a straightforward choice. We can face up to these possible futures and calmly prepare ourselves to make the best of them. Or we can blank them out and then suffer the consequences.

Epilogue

> In my childhood I had a very strong, although nebulous, sense that the world is out of joint, crippled, turned inside out. Later, I began to think, and to this day I still think – that by now we are living after the end of the world, which, however, does not absolve us of responsibility.
>
> Tomas Venclova, letter to Czesław Miłosz in the late 1970s[1]

If you were going to write a single-volume history of Europe, you would be hard pressed to spend much more than ten pages on the Baltic sea. For millennia the centre of the action was elsewhere: the Mediterranean, France, Germany, the Netherlands, Britain, the Russian mainland. The north-east of the continent was treated as a no man's land between empires, distinguished chiefly by extremes of poverty and violence. Its most dramatic events – the northern crusades, the Livonian war, the Great Northern War and even the overthrow of Soviet occupation – remain obscure to most Europeans, let alone to the wider world.

The little intellectual and cultural glamour that it sometimes acquired was mostly borrowed or accrued by association. Immanuel Kant and Hannah Arendt lived for many years in Königsberg; Copernicus made many of his observations from the nearby Polish town of Frombork/Frauenberg; Descartes spent the end of his career in Stockholm; and Richard Wagner the beginning of his in Latvia, where Rothko and Eisenstein were also born. But you would not really think of any of them as Baltic figures.

Even the idea of the Baltic sea as a region is very young and nebulous. Although it was pushed energetically by politicians and academics from the early 1990s and held up for a time as a world-leading model of local cooperation between countries, it tends not to inspire much enthusiasm or affection among the inhabitants of these nations.[2] Germany, Russia and Poland, the biggest of the littoral states, seldom took the alphabet soup of Baltic cross-border networks seriously and their business was largely confined to 'soft' areas of policy such as transport and the environment rather than high politics.[3]

It is understandable, then, that the Baltic is usually thought about in a fairly disjointed way or not at all. Aside from trade, if the region has been brought together and brought to the world's attention by anything in the past, it has been by conflicts between the great Eurasian powers. Today the struggle between Russia and the West is not only knitting the countries of the Baltic into the tightest coherence they have ever experienced; it is also thrusting this traditionally peripheral part of Europe into the middle of events.

One of the two core arguments of this book is that these states have been forced in various ways to develop precisely the kind of broad and deep resilience for which other western countries are currently fumbling. The other is that they are emerging as a new power centre in their own right.

The question is how Europe as a whole can benefit from that power and resilience at a moment when it has lost its bearings and when its perspective on the future has narrowed to a defensive angst, plagued by fears of both relative and absolute decline. Its share of global GDP, adjusted for currency fluctuations, has fallen from 20.2 per cent at the turn of the millennium to 14.3 per cent today. While its productivity has actually held up quite well in comparison to America's, the auspices for the coming years are not good.[4] Europe is a long way behind the US and China on critical technologies such as quantum computing, artificial intelligence and batteries. It is in danger of losing parts of its high-tech industry to rival regions with lower energy prices and more lavish subsidy regimes.[5]

The demographic trends are also alarming. Europe's total population probably started shrinking in 2024. Its workforce certainly did.[6] Many of its governments have tried to plug the gaps by importing labour from the outside world. Combined with the heavy influx of irregular immigration over the past decade, that has resulted in the highest level of population turnover countries such as Germany and Sweden have experienced in centuries. Both factors have produced a politics in which anxieties about change and the loss of control and status predominate. Many European leaders have expressed worries about the health of democracy on the continent.

Most importantly, the arrival of full-scale war on their borders and the possibility of being abandoned by the US have also produced a sense of impotence and learned helplessness. 'Europe,' Emmanuel Macron said in April 2024,

> stands at a point where it could die of itself . . . We are once again in one of those moments when Europe fears its decline, is doubting itself. Once again, our Europe has lost its self-esteem. That is strange when you look at everything it has done and what we owe it, but there it is.[7]

None of the countries around the Baltic sea is immune to these effects. Their politics, too, are influenced by pessimism, wariness of immigration and squabbles over scarce economic resources. They do not have complete answers to any of these problems. But they do provide at least some starting points and countervailing tendencies.

The Unruly and Unreasonable Patient

It might seem odd to call as a witness George Kennan, one of the most influential American diplomats of the Cold War. Kennan began his career with postings in Tallinn and Riga, developing enough sympathy for the Baltic peoples to declare his support for their independence movements in May 1990, more than a year before most western policymakers arrived at the same conclusion. In 1996 Lennart Meri visited his home in Princeton, to award him one of Estonia's highest decorations.[8]

But Kennan saw the region primarily through a Russian lens and in 1997, towards the end of his life, he published a jeremiad against NATO's expansion into central and eastern Europe, which he said would prevent Moscow from becoming a partner of the West and result in 'the most fateful error of American policy in the entire post-Cold War era'.[9] So it is an irony that today his earlier insights are better understood by these newer members of the alliance than by anybody else. In 1946, when he was the deputy ambassador to Moscow, Kennan wrote his famous 'long telegram', which was later expanded into an anonymous essay for *Foreign Affairs* magazine and became the nucleus of the West's strategy for handling the Soviet Union.[10] Much of it applies still, and almost uncannily well.

Kennan's first point was that the West had to contend with a 'political force committed fanatically to the belief that with [the] US there can be no permanent *modus vivendi*'. Moscow was 'inaccessible to considerations of reality in its basic reactions' and, as such, it was the gravest geopolitical challenge the West had ever faced. It should be faced with the same 'thoroughness and care' as a war.

Not all of this is true in the 2020s. Despite its aspirations to dislodge the 'decadence' of western liberal democracies, Putinism is not really an export brand to anything like the extent that Soviet communism used to be. The KGB's successor agencies have mastered a great number of dark arts but they are also capable of egregious blunders and their sway over our societies and political systems is frequently overstated. It is China that now poses the greater challenge over a great many more fronts.

But the frontline states of the Baltic understand that Kennan's basic point still holds: there can be no stable *modus vivendi* with a state that is seeking to re-establish a sphere of influence over our allies and is prepared to use violence to achieve it. That is why their leaders maintain that the only viable strategy against this Russian regime is what Kaja Kallas calls 'smart containment': unwavering support for Ukraine, the long-term maintenance of sanctions, the prosecution of war crimes, and a collective military capacity that could credibly defend NATO territory at its easternmost borders. There is no way back to business as usual or the world we used to think we knew.

Second, Kennan believed that the Soviet Union had to be demystified. The adversary, he wrote, should be studied

> with [the] same courage, detachment, objectivity and [the] same determination not to be emotionally provoked or unseated by it,

with which [the] doctor studies [an] unruly and unreasonable individual ... there is nothing as dangerous or as terrifying as the unknown.

The analogy with a doctor treating a deranged patient is a good one. Time and again, the larger powers of the West have allowed their view of Russia to be clouded by sentimentality, as Kennan himself did in the end. They hoped in the face of all the available clinical evidence that one more 'reset' or concession could restore the patient's sanity, and blamed themselves when it did not. Underpinning all these mistakes was the notion of Russia as a 'special' country governed by special rules, with entitlements and grievances that had to take priority over those of its neighbours.

The Baltic states are hardly dispassionate in this respect. But their understanding of Russia has been proven right enough times to be regarded as realistic. It is not only founded on instinct (or, as some western Europeans suggest, on blind prejudice). Their intelligence agencies have consistently had as good a fix on Russia as any of their peers below the CIA and MI6. Many of their decision-makers speak Russian and have formative memories of Soviet occupation. They have sizeable ethnic Russian populations within their borders. Sheer proximity means they need to know and care more about these matters than most states that are further away.

Yet it is also worth triangulating their perspective with that of Finland, whose long history of delicately calibrated realpolitik towards Moscow has left its contemporary leaders with a great degree of equanimity and inside knowledge. Alexander Stubb, the Finnish president, has warned his peers against using 'belligerent' rhetoric and argued that the West should pay more attention to Russia's fundamentally weak position. In his view, we should fret less and do more. 'What I call on all European states to do is to become more Finnish. In other words, more prepared,' Stubb said shortly after taking office. 'You have to prepare for the worst in order to avoid it.'[11]

Kennan's third insight was that while Moscow was 'impervious to the logic of reason', it was also 'highly sensitive to the logic of force'. Where it encountered real resistance, it would usually back down.

Since the Soviets were significantly weaker than the West as a whole, 'their success will really depend on [the] degree of cohesion, firmness and vigour which [the] western world can muster. And this is [a] factor which it is within our power to influence.' That is truer today than it was eighty years ago. Western unity is not an end in itself. It is the means by which these countries assert themselves and regain the upper hand in this contest without fighting. And this depends not only on strength of arms but on the will to use that strength as leverage.

Always a Developing Region

But Kennan's final and most important argument is often forgotten when people cite the long telegram. 'World communism,' he wrote, 'is like a parasite which feeds only on diseased tissue.' As a result, domestic and foreign policy were deeply interrelated. 'Every courageous and incisive measure to solve internal problems of our own society,' Kennan continued,

> to improve [the] self-confidence, discipline, morale and community spirit of our own people, is a diplomatic victory over Moscow worth a thousand diplomatic notes and joint communiqués. If we cannot abandon fatalism and indifference in [the] face of [the] deficiencies of our own society, Moscow will profit.

We are no longer dealing with a globally infectious strain of Russian Marxism. Insofar as Russia has a foothold in the West, it is by exploiting and exacerbating our doubts and vulnerabilities at home. The words from the exiled Lithuanian poet Tomas Venclova quoted at the start of this chapter have a resonance today: it does often feel as though we are living after the end of the world. But that does not absolve us of our responsibility to take part in building a new one.

So what does the Baltic tell us about how that world should look? I have come to the Öresund strait at the western end of the sea to visit an old friend in the Swedish port of Malmö. Most weekdays, she joins 14,000 other residents on a train that runs 5 miles along a bridge above the water, dips beneath it into a tunnel and emerges in Copenhagen, the Danish capital.[12]

This mundane commute is a remarkable thing from a historical perspective. The Öresund used to be a geopolitical barrier rather than a link. At times the toll that the Danish Crown levied on ships crossing the sound until 1857 was one of its chief sources of revenue.[13] In 1657 a Swedish army marched across the frozen sea and ultimately came within 15 miles of Copenhagen, forcing a peace that gave them lasting control over the previously Danish lands around Malmö. There are still Swedes who recall hearing the gunfire on the other side of the sound during the brief Nazi German invasion of Denmark in 1940, when their own country contrived to preserve an uncomfortable neutrality. Even within my lifetime, the Öresund was an external border of the EU until 1995 and of NATO until 2024.

Now, though, it is the nexus of some of the closest ties between any pair of neighbouring countries on the planet. At the centre of an economic corridor running from Hamburg to Gothenburg, Malmö and Copenhagen are working towards agglutinating into a single metropolitan area that accounts for a quarter of their nations' combined GDP.[14] Danes traverse the bridge for shopping or slightly more affordable housing, Swedes for cheaper alcohol and Copenhagen airport's international connections, and both for work and tourism. The two cities' ports have been merged into a single legal entity under the first arrangement of its kind in the world. 'To forget swearing and cursing,' the Danish poet Benny Andersen wrote in an ode to the bridge when it opened in 2000, 'and drink a toast to each other / so that They and We are becoming Us / that's better than fighting.'[15]

The project is imperfect. City councillors on both sides have grumbled to me that it is running out of momentum. That is symptomatic of a wider phenomenon: seamlessly intertwined as the Nordic states may seem to the outside world, there is friction enough between them that at one EU summit in the late 1990s the Swedish and Finnish prime ministers nearly resorted to fisticuffs in the queue for the toilets until they were pulled apart by Nelson Mandela.[16]

But the underlying achievement stands. This is what Europe is supposed to be good at: wiring together countries in a way that harnesses their different strengths and makes war between them inconceivable, even if there is the occasional dust-up when people are standing in a line for the loo. The strong identities of the states involved are often more of a bug than a feature. They do inevitably make it harder for Europeans to wield the same collective power as a unitary state on the international stage. The patchwork of differing regulations and national protectionisms is a serious nuisance for NATO.

But one of the main things the countries of the Baltic sea region has to offer is a better template for unity in diversity, even when one or two of the states are misaligned with the rest. They have shown over and over again that a shared basis of values and perceptions of danger is enough for a constellation of small nations to move the course of world events. They are a model of what foreign policy analysts call minilateralism: the art of building coalitions sufficiently flexible and coherent to bypass the sclerosis in bigger international institutions.

Benjamin Tallis, a Berlin-based foreign policy analyst, has made a project of tying these various strands into a coherent intellectual framework that he calls neo-idealism. I think of it, a little crudely, as a collage of social liberalism, Nordic economics and Polish-Baltic attitudes towards liberty and its defence around the world.

One of its chief precepts is 'progressive' security.[17] On the one hand, that means a joined-up grand strategy composed of higher defence budgets, more active and coordinated foreign policy, and a hard-nosed approach to the economics of trade and energy, with less dependency on countries with autocratic regimes. The autonomy of 'small' democratic states and above all their freedom to determine their own alignment are to be put at a premium.

On the other, the 'progressive' part of the formula is based on giving the West's populations a sense of heading towards something better and enough hope to warrant short-term sacrifices: 'un-cancelling the future', as Tallis puts it. That entails more state interventions and redistribution in the economy, an 'eco-modernist' pitch of prosperity built on sustainable sources of energy, and an unapologetic advocacy of social and cultural liberalism, including a willingness to celebrate the dynamism that mass immigration can bring in combination with rigorous integration and an insistence that newcomers embrace the host society's core values.[18]

It is a neat way of binding together everything that is most hopeful about the Baltic, even if none of the littoral states is currently anything like as open to migration as the model envisages. Another distinctive strand of Baltic thought was well formulated by Artis Pabriks, the Latvian foreign minister, a decade ago. 'We don't look alike, we don't speak one language, we don't live in one country and we don't have a joint team in [the] world ice hockey championship,' he told the Baltic sea parliamentary conference in 2014. 'But we share the Baltic sea, a common history, values and the spirit of dynamism, skilfulness and creativity. However, what is more important – we share the same dreams about our region's future: to be competitive, stable, advanced and always a developing region.'[19] Those last four words are crucial. We are apt to forget that Europe's boundaries and meaning have always been in flux. At a time when they are more uncertain than they have been in three decades, the future belongs to countries that can seize the initiative because their idea of Europe has not yet ossified and they are more intent on outcomes than processes.

A prime example is the seemingly interminable Franco-German debate on how to reform the EU's governance structures in order to accommodate Ukraine and other candidates for admission without changing the bloc's treaties. Just get on and let the Ukrainians and the Moldovans in, says Gabrielius Landsbergis, the Lithuanian foreign minister, who sees the bickering as wasteful displacement activity. Be grateful that Europe is still attractive and a symbol of hope to most of its eastern neighbours. Sort out the geopolitics and the technicalities will look after themselves. After all, Landsbergis notes, that is what happened after the Baltic states joined in 2004.

A corollary of this attitude is the ability to mobilise national resources for what really matters. The paradigm here is Finland. As we saw in chapter two, it not only plays the game of grand strategy with a clear-eyed view of its objectives and runs a broadly defined system of 'comprehensive security' that is increasingly regarded as a blueprint for the rest of Europe. It can also call on what Alexander Stubb, its president, has described as 'almost North Korean' levels of

EPILOGUE

readiness in the population to defend the country, with more than 80 per cent of Finns willing to take up arms if they have to.[20]

This is the cornerstone of resilience: clear, calm communication of how high the stakes are, combined with the embrace of a liberal nationalism that reinforces other kinds of belonging, such as membership of NATO or the wider West, rather than crowding them out. As Philip Selznick, the American sociologist, once wrote: 'We need a stronger idea of community, one that will justify the commitments and sacrifices we ask of ourselves, and of one another, in the name of a common good.'[21]

Since this book has been larded with quotes from Lennart Meri, it seems appropriate to end with one. In 1992, at the first summit of the Council of the Baltic Sea States in Copenhagen, the Estonian foreign minister stood above a floor depicting a map of the Baltic, which he called the 'axis of our lives'. His colleagues, Meri said, should not be afraid of the word 'identity'. They should be afraid of its disappearance.

'The suppression of identity,' he continued,

> would easily give us a common Baltic sea region, a unified Europe, but it would be a Europe of the barracks. It would be the opposite of the true Europe. Europe's phenomena, its philosophical, intellectual and economic values, are founded on the circumstance that living side by side with big peoples even the smallest peoples can defend their identity. As you know, the Estonians have escaped from the barracks of totalitarianism to join you at this table. You have the prosperity we lack. We have the experiences you don't.[22]

It has become fashionable for western European leaders to say they should have listened to the countries of the Baltic sooner. Yet we are still not listening hard enough. It is no longer just a question of heeding the warnings that were ignored. It is a matter of recognising that they are the West's geopolitical avant-garde. In an increasingly dangerous and unpredictable world, they have not only grasped that everything we have built is at risk unless it can be secured. They have also articulated and realised a positive vision of how to put the West back on the front foot, and a compelling idea of what Europe could be: more hopeful, more assertive in defence of its values and interests, more conscious of solidarity with other liberal democracies, more open to the potential of technology, more confident of its own distinctive strengths, less constrained by fear. In the dark years ahead we will need a future to aspire to. The Baltic is, as Meri said, the factory of that future.

Acknowledgements

This book came into existence primarily thanks to two people. The first is Joseph Zigmond at the publisher John Murray, who not only gave me a firm push over the edge into writing it but has guided it through the long road into print with a good deal of encouragement, wisdom and, on occasion, much-needed bloody-mindedness. I am also grateful to Lauren Howard, Caroline Westmore and the others at John Murray who spent countless hours chewing through the text with both rigour and sensitivity.

The other is Mike Smith, the foreign editor at *The Times*. The project started life as a series of reports for the newspaper from the Baltic world, at a time when few editors in the British press paid so much as a first thought to the subject, let alone a second. Mike was not only immediately alive to its interest and importance but also gave unstinting support to numerous reporting trips around the region and asked all sorts of intelligent questions that opened up new angles of inquiry.

I would like to thank all the other present and former *Times* colleagues who have helped me with patience, good suggestions and better humour since I was a stuttering trainee fresh out of journalism school. In particular: David Aaronovitch, Anne Ashworth, Roger Boyes, Ian Brunskill, Alistair Dawber, Daniel Finkelstein, Gemma Fox, Tony Gallagher, Fiona Hamilton, James Harding, Ben Hoyle, Suzy Jagger, Valentine Low, Jane Macartney, Sam Masters, Jim McLean, Robbie Millen, Tim Montgomerie, David Rose, Fay Schlesinger, Madeleine Spence, Anna Temkin, Emma Tucker, Bruno Waterfield, Roland Watson, Tom Whipple, Giles Whittell and John Witherow.

Sarah Williams, my agent at the Sophie Hicks literary agency, has championed this book tirelessly and deserves a large share of the credit.

ACKNOWLEDGEMENTS

Two institutions in Germany provided invaluable assistance. My friends and colleagues at the Körber-Stiftung in Hamburg – in particular Florian Bigge and Gaby Woidelko – have been a wonderful sounding board and Körber has been one of the few German organisations consistently bringing attention to the Baltic. Much of this book was written during a residency at the WZB social science research centre in Berlin, whose generosity and guidance were much appreciated. Special thanks to Gritje Hartmann, Christian Rauh, Claudia Roth, Kerstin Schneider, Michael Zürn and to the other researchers at the global governance department for their constructive comments on a partial early draft.

A proverb holds that it takes a village to raise a child; to which the instinctive British rejoinder is that it takes a village to raise an idiot. In writing this book I have relied enormously on the expertise of a great number of scholars of the Baltic sea region and related subjects, who were not under any obligation to take the time to explain their life's work in language that a journalist could understand, but did so anyway.

I am especially in debt to the researchers, writers and friends who went far and above the call of politeness and either provided extensive research material and contacts or scoured through drafts of various chapters to weed out the most egregious mistakes. If the results are still idiotic at the end of this process, it is my fault, not theirs. They are: Minna Ålander, Chris Alexander, Daunis Auers, Henrik Berggren, Una Bergmane, Miller Birk, Heiko Borchert, Sebastian Bruns, Aaron Burnett, Marcel Dirsus, Dan Ekholm, Indra Ekmanis, Arndt Freytag von Loringhoven, Lidia Gibadło, Marta Grzechnik, Jörg Hackmann, Michael Hart, Ben Hodges, Fabian Hoffmann, Therese Larsson Hultin, Thom Humphreys, James Jackson, Britta Jacob, Sanita Jemberga, Dariusz Kacprzak, Anders Kasekamp, Mareike Kleine, Jarosław Kuisz, Mart Kuldkepp, Georg Löfflman, Lina Lund, Jiro Minier, Aliide Naylor, Phillips O'Brien, Anu Partanen, Mikhail Polianskii, Sabine Schu, Brendan Simms, Kristina Spohr, Viktorija Starych-Samuolienė, Benjamin Tallis, Jan Tattenberg, Simon Vaut, Karolina Wigura, Maria Wilczek and Alexey Yusupov.

Most of all, I would like to express my love and gratitude to my family, and especially to my parents and grandparents, for everything

ACKNOWLEDGEMENTS

they taught me; to my parents-in-law, for all their kindness; to my wife Pippa, who has been my biggest source of happiness and borne a huge share of the burden involved in this project; and to our sons Walter and Arthur, who I hope will grow up in a safer, more optimistic world where this sort of book is no longer necessary.

Notes

Abbreviations

AP: Associated Press
BNN: Baltic News Network (independent news website)
BNS: Baltic News Service (main news agency)
ERR: Eesti Rahvusringhääling (Estonian Public Broadcasting)
HELCOM: Baltic Marine Environment Protection Commission
LETA: Latvian News Agency
LRT: Lietuvos nacionalinis radijas ir televizija (Lithuanian National Radio and Television)
LSM: Latvijas sabiedriskais medijs (Public Broadcasting of Latvia)
RFE/RL: Radio Free Europe/Radio Liberty
RUSI: Royal United Services Institute
SVT: Sveriges Television (Swedish Television)
TVP: Telewizja Polska (Polish Television)
Yle: Yleisradio Oy (Finnish Broadcasting Company)

Introduction

1. For more on Bergman's connection to Fårö, see Oliver Moody, 'Why Film Buffs Flock to a Lonely Swedish Island', *The Times*, 20 February 2023.
2. BNS, 'Lithuanian Officials Puzzled by Russia's Threat to Deploy Nuclear Weapons in Kaliningrad', LRT, 14 April 2022.
3. See e.g. Florian Hassel, 'Nord-Stream-Anschlag: Verdacht gegen ukrainischen ex-Geheimdienstler', *Süddeutsche Zeitung*, 12 November 2023.

4. Nate Ostiller, 'Russian Missile Ship Set on Fire Near Kaliningrad, Ukraine's Intelligence Claims', *Kyiv Independent*, 8 April 2024; however, Swedish media reports said the attack had taken place about 28 km south of the island of Öland, a considerable distance away from Kaliningrad. See e.g. 'Expert: Ukrainas attack i Östersjön slår mot Rysslands förmåga', *Dagens Nyheter*, 9 April 2024.
5. There is some dispute between experts as to how seriously this demand was meant. Some suggest it was primarily intended to provide Putin with another pretext for the invasion and an opportunity to frame it as the result of NATO's intransigence. See e.g. Steven Pifer, 'Russia's Draft Agreements with NATO and the United States: Intended for Rejection?', Brookings Institution, 21 December 2021; and Wolfgang Richter, 'NATO-Russia Tensions: Putin Orders Invasion of Ukraine', German Institute for International and Security Affairs, 16 March 2022.
6. Gabrielle Tétrault-Farber and Tom Balmforth, 'Russia Demands NATO Roll Back From East Europe and Stay Out of Ukraine', Reuters, 17 December 2021.
7. Keir Giles, *Russia's 'New' Tools for Confronting the West: Continuity and Innovation in Moscow's Exercise of Power*, Chatham House research paper (2016), p. 19.
8. Pekka Hakala, 'Putin uhkaili Euroopan "pikkumaita": Pitäkööt mielessä ennen kuin puhuvat iskuista syvälle Venäjälle', *Helsingin Sanomat*, 28 May 2024.
9. Klaus Wiegrefe, 'Der Tag, an dem der Krieg begann: Wie Merkel den NATO-Beitritt der Ukraine verhinderte', *Der Spiegel*, 15 September 2023.
10. Ed Corcoran, 'Peace from the Baltics', Foreign Policy in Focus, 16 April 2024.
11. See Jonas J. Driedger and Mikhail Polianskii, 'Utility-based Predictions of Military Escalation: Why Experts Forecasted Russia Would Not Invade Ukraine', *Contemporary Security Policy* (vol. 44, no. 4, 2023), pp. 544–60.
12. E.g. Victoria Vladimirova, 'Путин отказался от гонки вооружений', Snob.ru, 20 January 2015. It seems probable that Putin has misattributed this quotation to Bismarck.
13. Estonian foreign intelligence service, *International Security and Estonia 2023*, 8 February 2023, pp. 11–12.
14. See Giles, *Russia's 'New' Tools for Confronting the West*, p. 5.

15. Estonian internal security service, *Annual Review 2023–2024*, 12 April 2024.
16. Lauri Nurmi, 'Pentagon: Suomen ja Baltian varauduttava Venäjän hyökkäykseen – "Uhka, mutta ei välitön"', *Iltalehti*, 17 April 2024.
17. NATO, 'Statement by the North Atlantic Council on Recent Russian Hybrid Activities', 2 May 2024.
18. Mykola Bielieskov, 'The Russian and Ukrainian Spring 2021 War Scare', Center for Strategic and International Studies, 21 September 2021.
19. Reinhard Bingener and Markus Wehner, *Die Moskau-Connection: Das Schröder-Netzwerk und Deutschlands Weg in die Abhängigkeit* (C. H. Beck, 2023), pp. 255–6.
20. Information provided to the author by the Swedish armed forces.
21. 'Ryskt flyg övade anfall mot Sverige', *Svenska Dagbladet*, 22 April 2013.
22. NATO, *Secretary General's Annual Report 2015*, p. 21.
23. Ann-Sofie Dahl, 'Sweden and Finland: Partnership in Lieu of NATO Membership', in Ann-Sofie Dahl (ed.), *Strategic Challenges in the Baltic Sea Region: Russia, Deterrence and Reassurance* (Georgetown University Press, 2018), p. 130.
24. David Cenciotti, 'Russian Tu-22M Backfire Bombers Escorted by Su-27 Flankers Simulate Night Attack on Sweden', *The Aviationist*, 22 April 2013.
25. Oskar Forsberg, 'ÖB: "Sverige kan försvara sig en vecka"', *Aftonbladet*, 3 January 2013.
26. See Oliver Moody, 'How NATO Weapons in the Baltic Are Sinking Russian Ambitions', *The Times*, 16 February 2023.
27. Elisabeth Braw, 'Sweden Shows Us the Way to Defend our Infrastructure', *The Times*, 1 April 2024.
28. Elisabeth Braw (ed.), *Key Issues Report: Revamping Crisis Resilience and Security in the Post-Pandemic World* (Royal United Services Institute, 2020), p. 12.
29. For further sources and a deeper analysis of the difficulties with Sweden's civil defence reforms, see Eric Adamson and Jason Moyer, 'In from the Cold: Rebuilding Sweden's Civil Defense for the NATO Era', *War on the Rocks* blog, 9 April 2024.
30. Suomen Tietotoimisto, 'Kruununprinsessa Victoriasta koulutetaan upseeri', *Helsingin Sanomat*, 25 April 2024.
31. Henry Foy and Richard Milne, 'Sweden Ready to Fortify Crucial Baltic Island, says PM', *Financial Times*, 12 March 2024.

NOTES

32. Tom Dunlop, 'British Forces Defend Sweden During Mock Invasion', *UK Defence Journal*, 14 May 2023. See also 'Så skulle en attack mot Sverige kunna se ut: "Ett väldigt realistiskt scenario"', SVT, 7 May 2023.
33. Annica Ögren, 'Sveriges medlemskap i Nato: "Vi behövde flyga med så hög fart som möjligt"', *Svenska Dagbladet*, 23 April 2024.
34. See e.g. the *Guinness Book of World Records* and the French national geographical institute, both of which locate the heart of the continent at a spot north of Vilnius in Lithuania, based on the geometric centre of gravity of a Europe that stretches from the Atlantic to the Urals and the Caucasus.
35. Carmen Gebhard, *Unravelling the Baltic Sea Conundrum: Regionalism and European Integration Revisited* (Nomos Verlagsgesellschaft, 2009), p. 18.

Chapter 1: Tiger Leap

1. Included in Doris Kareva (ed.), *Six Estonian Poets* (ARC Publications, 2015), p. 14.
2. Information from panels in Vabamu Museum of Occupations and Freedom, Tallinn.
3. A shorter version of my interview with Kaja Kallas was published as 'Russia Could Threaten NATO Within Three Years, Says Estonia', *The Times*, 15 January 2024.
4. World Bank, 'GDP per capita (Current International $) – Estonia', comparison between 1990 and 2023.
5. Organisation for Economic Co-operation and Development, *PISA 2022 Assessment*.
6. See e.g. Rosie Kinchen, 'The Country Where Full-time Childcare Costs £15 a Week', *Sunday Times*, 21 January 2023.
7. UN, *Uncertain Times, Unsettled Lives: Shaping Our Future in a Transforming World, Human Development Report 2021/2022*, p. 284.
8. Transparency International, *Corruption Perceptions Index 2023*, p. 4.
9. Invest in Estonia, *The Full List of Estonian Unicorns* (March 2023).
10. Kiel Institute for the World Economy, *Ukraine Support Tracker* (updated February 2024). See also Estonian ministry of defence, 'Pevkur in Kyiv: Estonia to Send Ukraine Artillery Ammunition and Other Military Aid Worth 20 Million Euros', 21 March 2024.

NOTES

11. 'Von der Leyen to ERR: Member States Can Learn a Lot From Estonia', ERR, 1 May 2024.
12. 'Toomas Ilves, Estonia's American-European', *The Economist*, 29 October 1998.
13. Quoted in Ivan Krastev and Stephen Holmes, *The Light That Failed: A Reckoning* (Allen Lane, 2019), p. 39.
14. Neil Taylor, *Estonia: A Modern History* (Hurst, 2020), p. 93.
15. Toivo U. Raun, *Estonia and the Estonians* (Hoover Institution Press, Studies of Nationalities in the USSR series, 1991), pp. 154–5.
16. Andrejs Plakans, *A Concise History of the Baltic States* (Cambridge University Press, 2011), p. 351.
17. David J. Smith, 'Estonia: Independence and European Integration', in David J. Smith et al., *The Baltic States: Estonia, Latvia and Lithuania* (Routledge, 2017), p. 35.
18. Taylor, *Estonia*, pp. 111–12.
19. From Aliide Naylor, *The Shadow in the East: Vladimir Putin and the New Baltic Front* (I. B. Tauris, 2020), p. 20.
20. Lennart Meri, *Botschaften und Zukunftsvisionen: Reden des estnischen Präsidenten* (Bouvier, 1999, ed. and tr. Henno Rajandi), p. 76.
21. John Hiden and Patrick Salmon, *The Baltic Nations and Europe: Estonia, Latvia and Lithuania in the Twentieth Century* (Longman, 1991), p. 133.
22. Aldis Purs, *Baltic Facades: Estonia, Latvia and Lithuania Since 1945* (Reaktion Books, 2012), p. 95.
23. Peter Kaasik, 'Targeted Migration to Estonia in the Post-Second World War Period', in Meelis Saueauk and Meelis Maripuu (eds), *Propaganda, Immigration and Monuments*, Proceedings of the Estonian Institute of Historical Memory (March 2021), pp. 53–100.
24. Plakans, *Concise History of the Baltic States*, p. 379.
25. Meri, *Botschaften und Zukunftsvisionen* (ed. and tr. Rajandi), p. 76.
26. Purs, *Baltic Facades*, p. 188.
27. Hiden and Salmon, *The Baltic Nations and Europe*, p. 173.
28. Raun, *Estonia and the Estonians*, p. 223.
29. 'A Country Created Through Music', *The Atlantic*, 12 November 2015.
30. For a colourful account of the Baltic Way, see Stefan Hedlund, 'The Mice That Roared', in Charles Clarke (ed.), *Understanding the Baltic States: Estonia, Latvia and Lithuania Since 1991* (Hurst, 2023), p. 85.
31. Hiden and Salmon, *The Baltic Nations and Europe*, pp. 154–5. Other translations suggest Gorbachev said the 'existence' of the Baltic peoples was in danger.

32. Priit Vesilind, and James and Maureen Tusty, *Singing Revolution: How Culture Saved a Nation* (Varrak, 2008), pp. 153–6.
33. Nils R. Muižnieks, 'The Influence of the Baltic Popular Movements on the Process of Soviet Disintegration', *Europe-Asia Studies* (vol. 47, no. 1, 1995), pp. 3–25.
34. Meri, *Botschaften und Zukunftsvisionen* (ed. and tr. Rajandi), p. 92.
35. Daunis Auers, *Comparative Government and Politics of the Baltic States: Estonia, Latvia and Lithuania in the 21st Century* (Palgrave Macmillan, 2015), p. 220.
36. Taylor, *Estonia*, pp. 171 and 181.
37. Roman Frydman, Andrzej Rapacinski and John S. Earle, *The Privatization Process in Russia, Ukraine and the Baltic States* (Central European University Press, 1993), pp. 134ff.
38. Smith, 'Estonia', in *The Baltic States*, p. 132.
39. Anatol Lieven, *The Baltic Revolution: Estonia, Latvia, Lithuania and the Path to Independence* (Yale University Press, 1994), p. 356.
40. Ibid., p. 282.
41. Kaarel Piirimäe, *Contributions of the Baltic Independence Campaigns to Soviet Collapse*, in Clarke (ed.), *Understanding the Baltic States*, p. 104.
42. John Odling-Smee, the British economist in charge of the IMF's programme for the former USSR in the early 1990s, recalls being taken aback by the sheer youth and determination of the officials he met from the Baltic states: 'Their representatives . . . were so different from the Soviet bureaucrats we met in Moscow that it was difficult to believe they were from the same system.' From John Odling-Smee, *Towards Market Economies: The IMF and the Economic Transition in Russia and Other Former Soviet Countries* (Hamilton Books, 2022), p. 20.
43. Meri, *Botschaften und Zukunftsvisionen* (ed. and tr. Rajandi), p. 94.
44. 'Thatcher, Major Influence on 1990s Estonian Economic Policy, Dead at 87', ERR, 8 April 2013.
45. EU, Eurostat, Euro Indicators, 'Government Debt Down to 89.9% of GDP in Euro Area', 22 January 2024.
46. Lieven, *Baltic Revolution*, pp. 287–8. There is another wonderful anecdote about an occasion when Meri visited Bush in the White House. As the small talk turned to fishing, Meri supposedly pulled out a marker pen and drew a cross to mark Kamchatka on the very expensive globe in the Oval Office, to show Bush where the best fish were to be had. See Vesilind, Tusty and Tusty, *Singing Revolution*, p. 163.

47. Meri, *Botschaften und Zukunftsvisionen* (ed. and tr. Rajandi), pp. 198–200.
48. Paul Goble, 'When a Western Leader Spoke the Truth Directly to Putin – and Putin Couldn't Take It', Window on Eurasia blog, 10 July 2017.
49. The Australian prime minister Gough Whitlam abandoned the non-recognition policy in 1974 but the position was reversed a year later.
50. Samuel Petrequin and Lorne Cook, 'EU Leaders Endorse Joint Ammo Purchases for Ukraine', AP, 23 March 2023.
51. See Oliver Moody and Bruno Waterfield, 'Trump-proof? NATO's Eastern Flank Pushes Reluctant Europeans to Spend More on Defence', *The Times*, 3 July 2024.
52. Organisation for Economic Co-operation and Development, *PISA 2022 Results: Factsheets – Estonia*, 6 December 2023.
53. e-Estonia, 'New e-Estonia Factsheet: National AI "Kratt" Strategy', 26 June 2020.
54. See 'Short History of the Estonian Space Industry', Krakul.eu, 19 January 2021, and Naylor, *Shadow in the East*, pp. 142–3.
55. Valimised, 'Statistics about Internet Voting in Estonia'.
56. Anto Veldre, 'Sissejuhatus X-teesse (osa 1)', Republic of Estonia Information System Authority blog, 28 August 2015.
57. The Latvian political scientist Daunis Auers says Latvia had this idea first with a website called Manabalss (MyVoice), launched in 2011.
58. For a more critical analysis of the system, see Külli Taro, 'Democracy Looking for a Way Forward Everywhere in the World', ERR, 16 April 2024.
59. Gudrun Persson, 'Russia and Baltic Sea Security: A Background', in Dahl (ed.), *Strategic Challenges in the Baltic Sea Region: Russia, Deterrence and Reassurance* (Georgetown University Press, 2018), pp. 20–4.
60. Naylor, *Shadow in the East*, p. 34.
61. Damien Sharkov, 'Majority of People Fear War in Russia's Eastern European Neighbours', *Newsweek*, 4 July 2017.
62. Marko Lehti, Matti Jutila and Markku Jokisipilä, 'Never-Ending Second World War: Public Performances of National Dignity and the Drama of the Bronze Soldier', in Jörg Hackmann and Marko Lehti (eds), *Contested and Shared Places of Memory: History and Politics in North Eastern Europe* (Routledge, 2013), p. 35.
63. Agnia Grigas, *Beyond Crimea: The New Russian Empire* (Yale University Press, 2016), p. 164.

64. Christopher Coker, 'The West and Russia: Another Front in the New Cold War', in Dahl (ed.), *Strategic Challenges in the Baltic Sea Region*, p. 58.
65. Lehti, Jutila and Jokisipilä, 'Never-Ending Second World War', in Hackmann and Lehti (eds), *Contested and Shared Places of Memory*, pp. 15–16.
66. 'RIA: Estonia's State Institutions Hit by Largest Cyberattack to Date', ERR, 12 March 2024.
67. 'Ukraine Group Meeting in Ramstein Briefed on Estonian Co-Led IT Coalition', ERR, 20 March 2024; and Sten Hankewitz, 'Estonians Help Moldova Strengthen Cyber Security Capacity', *Estonian World*, 19 March 2024.
68. Ann-Dorit Boy, 'Maulwurf im Hörsaal?', *Der Spiegel*, 18 January 2024.
69. 'National Library of Estonia Advances Media Literacy', RaRa, 31 October 2024.
70. Open Societies Institute Sophia, *The Media Literacy Index 2023: Measuring Vulnerability of Societies to Disinformation* (June 2023).
71. BNS, 'Wartime Composition of Estonian Defense Forces Increased to 43,700 Positions', *Postimees*, 8 May 2023.
72. Lieven, *Baltic Revolution*, p. 312.
73. Tim Kelly, 'Estonia Must Double Defence Spending to Counter Russia, Military Chief Says', Reuters, 28 March 2024.
74. Alexandra Clobes, Oliver Morwinsky, Fausta Šimaitytė, 'Baltic Bastions: New Defence Strategies for Lithuania, Latvia and Estonia', Konrad-Adenauer-Stiftung, country report, 29 January 2024.
75. Taylor, *Estonia*, pp. 192–3.
76. Oliver Moody, 'Estonia "Does Not Want More UK Troops to Bolster Military Presence"', *The Times*, 12 July 2023.
77. 'President: Clear That Defense League Can Deliver Painful Blow to an Opponent', ERR, 28 January 2023.
78. Latvia followed suit in 2024: LETA, 'National Defence Training to be Compulsory in Latvian Schools', BNN, 16 April 2024.
79. Estonian Defence Resources Agency, *Riigikaitse: Õpik gümnaasiumidele ja kutseõppeasutustele* (2024).
80. See Oliver Moody, 'Estonia Learns from Finland's Resistance to Russian Aggression', *The Times*, 22 January 2024.
81. 'Kalle Laanet Resigns as Justice Minister', ERR, 16 March 2024; 'Appellate Court Finds Teder, Korb, Center Party Guilty in Porto Franco Case', ERR, 18 March 2024; 'Mayor of Tallinn Ousted in City

Council Vote', *Postimees*, 26 March 2024; 'Norstat Ratings: Reform Party Support Slump Lowest in Five Years', ERR, 27 March 2024.
82. Tarmo Michelson, 'Mart Laar vassis ja valetas', *Õhtuleht*, 9 February 2001.
83. Kadri Põlendik, 'Cybercriminals Steal Data of Around 700,000 Apotheka Pharmacy Customers', ERR, 4 April 2024.
84. 'State High Schools Exams Halted as IT System Fails to Cope with Workload', ERR, 6 April 2024.
85. Vambola Paavo, 'Estonia Needs a Restart in the Economy', *Postimees*, 19 April 2024.
86. Kaarel Piirimäe, 'Estonia "Has No Time": Existential Politics at the End of Empire', *Connexe 6: Espace baltique: dynamiques identitaires et stratégies politiques en question(s)* (2020), pp. 21–50.
87. Meri, *Botschaften und Zukunftsvisionen* (ed. and tr. Rajandi), p. 77.

Chapter 2: Total Defence

1. Kimmo Rentola, *How Finland Survived Stalin: From Winter War to Cold War, 1939–1950* (Yale University Press, 2024, tr. Richard Robinson), p. 66.
2. *The Kalevala* (Oxford World's Classics, 1989, tr. Keith Bosley), pp. 116–17.
3. That is, 80,000 m³ against Notre-Dame's 84,000 m³. See Teollisuuden Voima Oy, 'Olkiluoto-3: Basic Facts'.
4. 'Finland's Newest Nuclear Plant is Warming the Sea, Harming Wildlife', Yle, 2 June 2023.
5. 'Sauli Niinistö to Write EU Report on Civilian and Defence Preparedness', Yle, 20 March 2024.
6. See John F. Helliwell et al., *World Happiness Report 2024*, University of Oxford Wellbeing Research Centre, p. 15; Ian Shine, 'Finland Is on Track to Meet Some of the World's Most Ambitious Carbon Neutrality Targets. This is How It Has Done It', World Economic Forum, 1 June 2023; Patrick Butler, 'No Grammar Schools and Lots of Play: The Secrets of Europe's Top Education System', *Guardian*, 20 September 2016.
7. Timo Hirvonen, 'From Wood to Nokia: The Impact of the ICT Sector in the Finnish Economy', EU, Economic and Financial Affairs, country focus reports (vol. 1, no. 11), 4 June 2004.

NOTES

8. CEIC Data, Finland GDP per capita.
9. *Assessment of Public Finances 2023: Correcting the Course of the Public Finances Even More Challenging Than Expected*, Bank of Finland Bulletin (vol. 97, no. 5/2023), 9 January 2024.
10. Harri Pietarinen, 'Ekonomisti yllättyi Suomen talouskasvun synkkyydestä – kasvu heikointa sitten sisällissodan', *Helsingin Sanomat*, 22 April 2024.
11. EU, Eurostat, 'Half of EU's Population Older Than 44.4 Years in 2022', 22 February 2023.
12. German federal statistical office, 'Key Table: Fertility Rate, Total', 21 July 2022.
13. Juha Pekka Raeste, 'Hurja lasku', *Helsingin Sanomat*, 25 March 2024.
14. See e.g. Anu Partanen, *The Nordic Theory of Everything* (Duckworth, 2023), pp. 162–3.
15. 'Finland's Shrinking High Schools Are Importing Pupils from Abroad', *The Economist*, 27 June 2024.
16. Partanen, *Nordic Theory of Everything*, p. 319.
17. 'Stubb Thanks Haavisto for Unbelievably "Fair and Honest" Presidential Race', *Helsinki Times*, 12 February 2024.
18. Dan Steinbock, *The Nokia Revolution: The Story of an Extraordinary Company That Transformed an Industry* (Amacom, 2001), p. 34.
19. Ibid., p. i.
20. Jari Ojala and Ilkka Nummela, 'Feeding Economic Growth: Agriculture', in Jari Ojala, Jari Eloranta and Jukka Jalava (eds), *The Road to Prosperity: An Economic History of Finland* (Suomalaisen kirjallisuuden seura, 2006), p. 73.
21. David Kirby, *A Concise History of Finland* (Cambridge Concise Histories, 2006), pp. 48–9.
22. Henrik Meinander, *Mannerheim, Marshal of Finland: A Life in Geopolitics* (Hurst, 2023), p. 3.
23. Partanen, *Nordic Theory of Everything*, p. 16.
24. Steinbock, *Nokia Revolution*, pp. 5–6.
25. Jonathan Clements, *Mannerheim: President, Soldier, Spy* (Haus, 2012), pp. 261–2.
26. Ibid., p. 205.
27. H. M. Tillotson, *Finland at Peace and War 1918–1993* (Michael Russell, 1993), pp. 94–8.
28. 'Finnish MP's Decision to Send Message to Russia via Ukrainian Rocket Sparks Heated Debate', Yle, 9 January 2023.

29. Oliver Warner, *Marshal Mannerheim and the Finns* (Weidenfeld & Nicolson, 1967), p. 146.
30. Ann Marie Dailey, 'Molotov Cocktails in Winter: What 1939 Finland Tells Us About Ukraine Today', Atlantic Council, New Atlanticist blog, 2 March 2022.
31. Tillotson, *Finland at Peace and War*, p. 162.
32. Henrik Meinander, *A History of Finland* (Hurst, 2020), p. 201.
33. Rentola, *How Finland Survived Stalin*, pp. 19ff.
34. Clements, *Mannerheim: President, Soldier, Spy*, pp. 260ff.
35. Väinö Linna, *Unknown Soldiers* (Penguin Modern Classics, 2016), p. 438.
36. Rentola, *How Finland Survived Stalin*, pp. 160–1.
37. Meinander, *Mannerheim, Marshal of Finland*, p. 238.
38. Rentola, *How Finland Survived Stalin*, p. 105.
39. Meinander, *Mannerheim, Marshal of Finland*, pp. 180–1.
40. Kirby, *Concise History of Finland*, pp. 247–72.
41. Martti Haikio, *Nokia: The Inside Story* (Financial Times/Prentice Hall, 2002), pp. 64–71.
42. Sampo Vaarakallio, 'Esko Ahoa esitetään venäläispankin johtopaikalle', Yle, 17 March 2016.
43. 'Ein Finne an Schröders Seite', *Manager Magazin*, 15 August 2008. For an analysis of the payments to Lipponen's consultancy firm, see 'Gazprom Lobbyists Among Finland's High-Ranking Government Officials', Warsaw Institute, *Baltic Monitor*, 29 June 2019.
44. Pekka Vanttinen, 'Calls to Investigate Finnish Politicians with Russia Ties Grow', Euractiv, 11 October 2022.
45. President of Russia's office, 'Joint Press Conference with President of Finland Tarja Halonen Following Russian-Finnish Talks', 23 November 2006.
46. Manfred Ertel and Reinhard Krumm, '"Sensibel für die eigenen Ängste": Staatspräsidentin Tarja Halonen über die Risiken der Nato-Osterweiterung, die Stabilität im Ostseeraum und Europas Verhältnis zu Russland', *Der Spiegel*, 8 April 2001.
47. For her own retrospective assessment of this period, see 'Former Finnish President Halonen Reflects on Russia Relations and NATO Membership', Yle, 23 December 2023.
48. See Oliver Moody, 'The West is Skating on Thin Ice, Warns Finland's Putin-Whisperer', *Sunday Times*, 4 December 2021.

NOTES

49. Vesa Tynkkynen and Petteri Jouko, *Towards East or West? Defence Planning in Finland 1944–1966*, National Defence University Helsinki, Finnish Defence Studies (2017), pp. 11–35.
50. Ibid., pp. 42–57.
51. Arto Nokkala, 'It is About Protection: Defence in Finland's Steps to NATO', in *Studia Europejskie – Studies in European Affairs* (no. 4, 2022), p. 44.
52. Tillotson, *Finland at Peace and War*, pp. 252–66.
53. 'Finland to Raise Wartime Strength to 280,000 Troops', *Helsinki Times*, 17 February 2017.
54. Kai Sauer, 2023 Helsinki Security Forum opening session, 29 September 2023.
55. Michael Jonsson, *Finland's Military Capability 2020*, Swedish Defence Research Agency, Northern European and Transatlantic Security series, p. 4.
56. Finnish defence forces, 'Training 2020 Looks Into the Soldier's Mind, Too', 31 May 2019.
57. Finnish ministry of defence, 'Minister of Defence Jyri Häkämies at CSIS in Washington', 6 September 2007.
58. Tillotson, *Finland at Peace and War*, pp. 256ff.
59. 'Finland and Baltics Employ Different Defence Strategies', Yle, 25 April 2024.
60. Anne Kauranen, 'Finland Counted Its Bomb Shelters and Found 50,500 of Them', Reuters, 29 August 2023.
61. Richard Milne, 'Finland Boosts War Readiness in Face of Russian Aggression', *Financial Times*, 6 May 2024.
62. Joona Aaltonen, 'Suomi selvittää TNT-tehtaan perustamista – Häkkänen: Olemme palaamassa kylmän sodan toimintatapaan', *Helsingin Sanomat*, 5 May 2024.
63. Finnish security committee, 'Concept of Comprehensive Security: Building National Resilience in Finland', 6 July 2022.
64. Jyri Raitasalo, 'Finnish Defense: "Left of Bang"', *Prism* (vol. 10, no. 2, 2023), pp. 83–5.
65. 'Leading Countries Based on Per Capita Electricity Demand in Europe in 2023', Statista, February 2024.
66. International Energy Agency, *Finland 2023: Energy Policy Review*, p. 125, table 6.1; and *Peat Land Atlas 2023* (Heinrich Böll Stiftung, 2023), p. 27.
67. Tere Vadén et al., *Country Report Finland: Energy Without Russia*, Friedrich-Ebert-Stiftung, 2 October 2023, pp. 2–5.

68. Anne Kauranen, 'Finnish Group Ditches Russian-Built Nuclear Plant Plan', Reuters, 2 May 2022.
69. Bert Losse, 'Opec als Vorbild: Entsteht ein neues Rohstoffkartell?', *WirtschaftsWoche*, 30 November 2023.
70. See e.g. Pekka Tuomela, Tuomo Törmänen and Simon Michaux, 'Strategic Roadmap for the Development of Finnish Battery Mineral Resources', Geological Survey of Finland, open file research report, 23 August 2021.
71. Finnish Minerals Group, 'New Minerals Containing Rare Earth Elements Found in Sokli', 30 October 2023.
72. Terrafame, 'Terrafame to Start Uranium Recovery by the Summer of 2024', 21 December 2022.
73. Henri Vanhanen, 'Finland and NATO: When Push Came to Shove', RUSI commentary, 24 May 2022.
74. Charly Salonius-Pasternak, *The Defence of Finland and Sweden: Continuity and Variance in Strategy and Public Opinion*, Finnish Institute of International Affairs briefing paper (no. 240, June 2018), p. 6.
75. Matti Koivisto, 'Ylen kysely: Enemmistö suomalaisista kannattaa Suomen Nato-jäsenyyttä', Yle, 28 February 2022.
76. Finnish ministry of defence, 'Capacity to Produce Heavy Ammunition Will Be Significantly Increased', 12 December 2023.
77. Miranda Bryant, 'Football, Ice Hockey . . . Shooting? Finland Hopes Hobby Will Boost National Defence', *Guardian*, 19 February 2024.
78. See Minna Ålander, 'A Quiet Revolution in the North: Change and Continuity in Finnish and Swedish Security Policies', in Damian Szacawa and Kazimierz Musiał (eds), *The Baltic Sea Region After Russia's Invasion of Ukraine*, Institute of Central Europe policy papers (no. 11/2022), p. 51; and Kaja Kunnas, 'Viron puolustusministeri: Venäjän epärationaalista iskua Natoa vastaan ei voi sulkea pois', *Helsingin Sanomat*, 4 April 2024.
79. Antii Kirkkala, '"Puolustamme arvoja, jotka ovat tehneet Suomesta mallimaan"– näin Alexander Stubb puhui sanasta sanaan', *Verkkouutiset*, 28 October 2023.
80. Lauri Nurmi, 'Viron puolustusministeri Iltalehdelle: Suomen ja Viron ohjuksilla luodaan Suomenlahdelle Nato-sulku', *Iltalehti*, 12 August 2022.
81. For a good analysis of the situation, see Minna Ålander and William Alberque, 'NATO's Nordic Enlargement: Contingency Planning and Learning Lessons', War on the Rocks, 8 December 2022.

NOTES

82. Antti Pihlajamaa and Iro Särkkä, 'Finland and Collective Defence: The Finnish Role in Northern Europe and Beyond', in Matti Pesu (ed.), *NATO's New Northern Direction: The Evolving Role of the Alliance in Europe's North*, Finnish Institute of Foreign Affairs, foreign policy paper, no. 11 (April 2024), pp. 33–4.
83. Oliver Moody, 'Finland's Presidential Rivals Clash Over Hosting NATO Nuclear Weapons', *The Times*, 8 February 2024.
84. From panels in the Northern Ostrobothnia Museum, Oulu.
85. 'Finns Party Fire Local Politician Following Racist Facebook Rant', Yle, 9 October 2023.
86. 'Second Stabbing at Oulu Shopping Centre in a Week, Police Suspect Racist Motive', Yle, 19 June 2024.
87. European Union Agency for Fundamental Rights, *Second European Union Minorities and Discrimination Survey: Being Black in the EU* (23 November 2018), p. 15. In the 2023 edition of the report, 66 per cent of black people in Finland said they had experienced racial discrimination over the previous five years, but the levels were slightly higher in Germany and Austria.
88. Roosa Welling, '"Merkittävin suomenkielisen vihapuheen julkaisualusta" – Tällainen on Suomen vihapuheen ykkösfoorumi', *Helsingin Sanomat*, 29 May 2024.
89. 'Survey: One in Three Won't Vote for Pekka Haavisto Because of His Partner', Yle, 2 February 2024.
90. Häikiö, *Nokia*, p. 69.
91. Natasha Frost, 'How Nokia's Collapse Turned a Sleepy Town in Finland Into an Internet Wonderland', *Quartz*, 29 October 2019.
92. Nokia, 'Nokia's Digitalization of Its 5G Oulu Factory Recognized by the World Economic Forum as an "Advanced 4th Industrial Revolution Lighthouse"', 3 July 2019.
93. University of Oulu, 'Finland Elevates High-Tech Profile with NATO Partnership, Establishing 6G Test Centre in Oulu', 18 March 2024.
94. Rentola, *How Finland Survived Stalin*, pp. 221–2.

Chapter 3: The Witch and the Sage

1. *Latvju modernās dzejas antoloģia* (Grāmatu DrNeaugs, 1930), p. 7, and quoted in Aleksandrs Čaks, *Selected Poems* (Shearsman Books, 2019, ed. and tr. Ieva Lešinska), p. 9.

NOTES

2. See Oliver Moody, 'Russian Minority in Latvia Told to Choose Putin or Democracy', *The Times*, 2 October 2022.
3. Veiko Spolitis, 'Major Cleanup Across Latvia: Cities Remove References to Pushkin and Turgenev', *Postimees*, 29 March 2024.
4. Statistical bureau of Latvia, 'Latvijas 2021. gada tautas un mājokļu skaitīšanas galvenie rezultāti'.
5. 'Russian TV Channels Banned in Latvia But Still Available', LSM, 19 January 2023.
6. 'War Crime Supporters in Latvia to Have Their Citizenship Revoked', BNN Bloomberg, 19 April 2022.
7. Paul Goble, 'Moscow Losing Another Nation's Orthodox Church – This Time Latvia's', *Eurasia Daily Monitor* briefing for the Jamestown Foundation, 13 September 2022.
8. Nicolas Camut, 'UN Experts Slam Latvia for Clamping Down on Russian-Language Minorities', *Politico*, 8 February 2023.
9. Andrius Sytas, 'Russian Citizens Take Language Test to Avoid Expulsion from Latvia', Reuters, 9 May 2023.
10. 'What's Happening With Russian Speakers in Latvia?', Baltic Ways podcast, 10 January 2023.
11. SKDS, 'Less Than Half of Russians in Latvia Condemn Russia's War in Ukraine: Survey', LSM and LSM Rus, 7 July 2022.
12. Indra Ekmanis, 'Why Isn't Latvia the "Next" Crimea? Reconsidering Ethnic Integration', *Orbis* (vol. 64, no. 3, 2020), p. 489.
13. Latvian Embassy, Berlin, open letter to ARTE Deutschland, 16 April 2018.
14. See Anatol Lieven, *The Baltic Revolution: Estonia, Latvia, Lithuania and the Path to Independence* (Yale University Press, 1994), p. 123 for an excursus on how various Latvian painters, engravers and sculptors, including the creators of the revered freedom monument in Riga, found ingenious ways to depict the hero's bear ears without making him look utterly silly. Some hid them under his hair; others detached them and stuck them on his helmet instead; while others still insisted that the ears were simply a metaphor and never actually existed on Lāčplēsis's head.
15. Andrejs Pumpurs, *Lāčplēsis* (2005, tr. Arthur Cropley), in Krista Grendze, *Night Songs: Tellings and Re-tellings of Stories from the Fatherland* (2019), pp. 60–1. Cropley has said that his version in iambic pentameter, the only verse translation of the poem readily available in English, is '90 to 95% true to the original'. Readers will have to judge its quality for themselves.

16. Ibid., p. 294.
17. Andrejs Plakans, *A Concise History of the Baltic States* (Cambridge University Press, 2011), p. 132.
18. See Erwin Rau, 'Russia and the Baltic Sea: 1920–1970', *Naval College War Review* (vol. 23, no. 1, 1970), pp. 23–30.
19. Plakans, *Concise History of the Baltic States*, p. 155.
20. Aigi Rahi-Tamm and Andres Kahar, 'The Deportation Operation "Priboi" in 1949', in Toomas Hiio et al. (eds), *Estonia Since 1944: Report of the Estonian International Commission for the Investigation of Crimes Against Humanity* (2009), pp. 361–84. See also Michael North, *The Baltic: A History* (Harvard University Press, 2016, tr. Kenneth Kronenberg), p. 271.
21. Ieva Lešinska (ed. and tr.), *Six Latvian Poets* (Arc Publications, 2011), p. 10.
22. Beatrise Reidzāne and Sandis Laime, 'Latvian Folklore Studies and Mythology', in *Latvia and Latvians Part 2: Culture in Latvia* (Latvian Academy of Sciences, 2018, ed. Jānis Stradiņš and tr. Eduards Bruno Deksnis), p. 107.
23. Juris Kronbergs, 'A Brief Introduction to Latvian Poetry', in Lešinska (ed. and tr.), *Six Latvian Poets*, p. 25.
24. Plakans, *Concise History of the Baltic States*, p. 163.
25. Artis Pabriks and Aldis Purs, *Latvia: The Challenges of Change* (Routledge, 2002), pp. 32–9.
26. Juris Rozenvalds, 'Die russische Minderheit zwischen Integration und Isolierung', in Erwin Oberländer et al. (eds), *Lettland 1918–2018: Ein Jahrhundert Staatlichkeit* (Ferdinand Schöningh, 2018), p. 155.
27. Dace Dzenovska, 'The Clash of Sovereignties: The Latvian Subject and its Russian Imperialism', *HAU: Journal of Ethnographic Theory* (vol. 12, no. 3, 2022).
28. John Hiden and Patrick Salmon, *The Baltic Nations and Europe: Estonia, Latvia and Lithuania in the Twentieth Century* (Longman, 1994), p. 134.
29. Quoted in Jānis Kudiņš, 'The Rock Opera "Lāčplēsis" ("Bearslayer", 1988): Symbolic Meaning in the Historical Change Process and the Cultural Memory of Latvia', *Lietuvos Muzikologija* (Lithuanian Musicology) (vol. 21, 2020), p. 97.
30. Ibid., pp. 97–100.
31. Aija Veldre Beldavs, 'I Sing Out Nine, You're Working on One: Historical Latvian Ritual Insult Song Warring "Apdziedāšnās"', PhD thesis submitted to Indiana University (April 2001).

NOTES

32. Una Bergmane, 'Von der Perestroika zur Wiederherstellung der Unabhängigkeit', in Oberländer et al. (eds), *Lettland 1918–2018*, p. 129. Peters became a potent force in the Latvian independence movement and was later appointed the country's first ambassador to post-Soviet Russia and director of the Krišjānis Valdemārs Foundation.
33. Lieven, *Baltic Revolution*, p. xxvii.
34. Ivars Ījabs, 'Zwischen Pluralismus und effektiver Regierung: Lettlands Demokratie seit der Wiederherstellung der Unabhängigkeit', in Schrödinger et al. (eds), *Lettland 1918–2018*, p. 140.
35. See e.g. *Amnesty International Report 2009: Latvia*.
36. Niels Muižnieks, 'No One Should Have to be Stateless in Today's Europe', Council of Europe blog, 2008.
37. Rozenvalds, 'Die russische Minderheit zwischen Integration und Isolierung', in Oberländer et al. (eds), *Lettland 1918–2018*, p. 158.
38. Ibid., p. 156.
39. Office of Citizenship and Migration Affairs, *Latvijas iedzīvotāju sadalījums pēc valstiskās piederības*, January 2022.
40. Saiema of the Latvian Republic, 'Saeima Expands the Constitution with a Preamble', 20 June 2014.
41. See De Facto and Ella Semjonova, 'What to Do About Kremlin Supporters in Latvia?', LSM, 25 March 2024, and 'Requirement for More Russians to Pass Language Test Moves Forward', LSM, 2 May 2024.
42. Camut, 'UN Experts Slam Latvia'.
43. 'Latvian Government Backs Move Away From Russian in Schools', LSM, 23 April 2024.
44. 'Ušakovs: Harmony Turns to Constitutional Court About Language Restrictions for Pre-Election Promotion', BNN, 28 March 2024.
45. Pabriks and Purs, *Challenges of Change*, p. 77.
46. Rozenvalds, 'Die russische Minderheit zwischen Integration und Isolierung', in Oberländer et al. (eds), *Lettland 1918–2018*, pp. 163–5.
47. 'SKDS: Krievijas rīcību Ukrainā nosoda 40% krievvalodīgo, no tiem vairums – pret Uzvaras parka pieminekļa nojaukšanu', LSM, 7 July 2022.
48. LETA, 'Aptauja: Krievijas sāktais karš pasliktinājis latviešu attieksmi pret Latvijas krieviem', LSM/RE! *Panorāma*, 13 July 2023.
49. Iveta Kažoka, *Desire for Stability Versus Desire for Change: Polarization of Attitudes During Latvia"s General Elections of 2022* (Friedrich-Ebert-Stiftung, 2022), pp. 17–18.

NOTES

50. Christo Grozev, Michael Weiss and Roman Dobrokhotov, 'Exclusive: Latvian Member of European Parliament is an Agent of Russian Intelligence, Leaked Emails Confirm', *The Insider*, 29 January 2024.
51. European Parliament, Motion for a Resolution, B9-0266/2024, 22 April 2024, p. 3.
52. LSM and Agnija Ladziņa, 'MP Grevcova Under Scrutiny Yet Again For Claims About Occupation of Latvia', LSM, 23 January 2023.
53. De Facto, Matīss Arnicāns and LSM, 'Occupation Museum's Arson May Have Been Orchestrated From Prison', LSM, 29 April 2024.
54. 'Latvian Citizen Charged by US with Supplying Advanced Avionics to Russia', LSM, 29 March 2024.
55. LETA, 'Latvia's Unemployment Level Remains the Highest in Latgale Region', BNN Bloomberg, 9 April 2024.
56. Ekmanis, 'Why Isn't Latvia the "Next" Crimea?', *Orbis* (vol. 64, no. 3, 2020), pp. 496–7.
57. Indra Ekmanis, 'Diversity in Daugavpils: Unpacking Identity and Cultural Engagement Among Minority School Youth in Eastern Latvia', *Europe-Asia Studies* (vol. 71, no. 1, 2019), p. 17.
58. See e.g. Agnia Grigas, *Beyond Crimea: The New Russian Empire* (Yale University Press, 2016), pp. 140–60.
59. See e.g. Claire Bigg, 'Latvia: Ethnic Russians Divided on Moscow's Repatriation Scheme', RFE/RL, 15 August 2006.
60. Andres Kasekamp, 'Are the Baltic States Next?', in Dahl (ed.), *Strategic Challenges in the Baltic Sea Region: Russia, Deterrence and Reassurance* (Georgetown University Press, 2018), pp. 63–4.
61. 'Which TV Programs Make PBK a Propaganda Channel?', Propastop blog, 10 March 2020.
62. Andis Kudors, 'Latvia: Disinformation Resilience Index', Prism UA, 31 July 2018.
63. Valeriya Mechkova et al., 'Measuring Online Political Activity: Introducing the Digital Society Project Dataset', *Journal of Information Technology & Politics* (2024), p. 8.
64. Benjamin Bathke, 'How Russian Journalists in Latvia Navigate Life in Exile', Reuters Institute, University of Oxford, 5 May 2023.
65. 'Russian Independent TV Rain Stripped of Its License in Latvia', LSM, 6 December 2022.
66. Bathke, 'How Russian Journalists in Latvia Navigate Life in Exile'.
67. Eugen Olariu, 'The Impact of Russian Propaganda in Latvia',

European Conservatives and Reformists (a right-wing bloc in the European Parliament), 15 February 2023.
68. 'Media Literacy and Safe Use of Media', European Commission, YouthWiki, Latvia, section 6.8.
69. Dmitri Teperik et al., *Resilience Against Disinformation: A New Baltic Way to Follow?* (ICDC, 2022), p. 15.
70. Olariu, 'Impact of Russian Propaganda in Latvia'.
71. Kudors, 'Latvia: Disinformation Resilience Index'.
72. 'RFE/RL Opens Bureau in Riga With Focus on Russian-Language Content', RFE/RL, 12 January 2023.
73. 'Latvia's Population Dropped by 11,000 Last Year', LSM, 3 June 2024.
74. Dace Dzenovska, 'Existential Sovereignty: Latvian People, Their State, and the Problem of Mobility', in Rebecca Bryant and Madeleine Reeves (eds), *The Everyday Lives of Sovereignty: Political Imagination Beyond the State* (Cornell University Press, 2021), p. 155.
75. Aija Lulle and Iveta Jurkane-Hobein, 'Strangers Within? Russian-Speakers' Migration from Latvia to London: A Study in Power Geometry and Intersectionality', *Journal of Ethnic and Migration Studies* (vol. 43, no. 5, 2017), p. 599.
76. See e.g. UN, *World Happiness Report 2023*, p. 34.
77. *Standard Eurobarometer 92 – Autumn 2019*, EU report (2019), and *Standard Eurobarometer 97 – Summer 2022*, EU report (2022).
78. Olariu, 'Impact of Russian Propaganda in Latvia'.
79. Kažoka, *Desire for Stability Versus Desire for Change*, p. 18.
80. Jeffrey Sommers and Kaspars Briškens, *Three Decades of Transition: Lessons Learned and Prescriptions Offered for Latvia's Economic Development* (Friedrich-Ebert-Stiftung, 2021), p. 9.
81. Richard Milne, 'US Ire Prompts Latvia to Root Out Systematic Banking Failures', *Financial Times*, 2 March 2018.
82. Aldis Purs, *Baltic Facades: Estonia, Latvia and Lithuania Since 1945* (Reaktion Books, 2012), p. 147.
83. EU, Eurostat, 'Living Conditions in Europe – Income Distribution and Income Inequality' (2022), fig. 4: Gini coefficient for equivalised disposable income per inhabitant, 2021.
84. Mindaugas Klusas, '"We Have Never Been So United Again." Latvian Filmmaker Revives January 1991 Events in Vilnius and Riga', LRT, 12 January 2023.
85. Dzenovska, *Existential Sovereignty*, p. 166.
86. Strangely, there are many Latvians who argue that their nation was

once a colonising power. In the seventeenth century the duchy of Courland and Semigallia, whose territory loosely corresponded to the Kurzeme and Zemgale regions of modern Latvia, established short-lived colonies on Tobago and St Andrew's island (Kunta Kinteh) near the mouth of the river Gambia. This is a source of pride to some Latvians, who see it as a sign that their people were once a notable force on the world stage. However, there is no compelling evidence that any ethnic Latvians were involved in the settlements. See Dace Dzenovska, *School of Europeanness: Tolerance and Other Lessons in Political Liberalism in Latvia* (Cornell University Press, 2018), pp. 19–42.

87. John Stuart Mill, 'On Liberty', quoted in Jason Tyndal, 'Culture and Diversity in John Stuart Mill's Civic Nation', *Utilitas* (vol. 25, no. 1, 2013), p. 115.
88. Gotthard Friedrich Stender, *Pasakas un stāsti* (Steffenhagen, 1789), p. 382, quoted in Reidzāne and Laime, 'Latvian Folklore Studies', p. 93.
89. President of the Republic of Latvia's office, 'President Levits' Lāčplēsis Day Congratulations', 10 November 2020.
90. Sergejs Kruks, 'The Latvian Epic Lāčplēsis: Pass-Partout Ideology, Traumatic Imagination of Community', *Journal of Folklore Research* (vol. 41, no. 1, 2004), p. 28.

Chapter 4: Poison Lake

1. Aeschylus, *Agamemnon*, line 958, in Alan H. Sommerstein (ed.), *The Oresteia: Agamemnon, Libation-Bearers, Eumenides* (Loeb Classical Library, 2009, my translation), p. 112.
2. Ulla Rosenquist, *Hafenstädte und Fischerdörfer: Küstenkultur der Insel Bornholm* (Bornholms Turistråd, 1991), pp. 46–8.
3. Jari Tanner, 'Damage to Gas Pipeline, Telecom Cable Connecting Finland and Estonia Caused by "External Activity"', AP, 10 October 2023.
4. Roland Gerth and Bergit Forchhammer, *Immer wieder nach Bornholm* (Harenberg, 1992), pp. 100–1.
5. Volker Thiel, *Leben auf Bornholm: Gespräche mit Einheimischen und Zugezogenen* (Filos-Verlag, 2006), p. 28.
6. Gerth and Forchhammer, *Immer wieder nach Bornholm*, p. 15.
7. For waterspouts, see: 'Niezwykłe zjawisko na Bałtyku. Zdjęcia podbijają sieć', Wprost, 31 May 2023; foul smells: 'Latvian Bog Likely Source of

Sunday's Stench in Helsinki', Yle, 7 April 2024; tree pollen slicks: Harry Baker, 'Mysterious "Sea Swirls" Off Poland's Coast Have a Surprising Explanation', Live Science, 11 May 2023; blue-green algae: 'Summary of the National Blue-Green Algae Monitoring June–August 2023: Varying Blue-Green Algae Summer Both in Lakes and at Sea', Suomen ympäristökeskus, 5 September 2023; fata morgana: 'Baltijos jūroje užfiksuotas retas reiškinys: to kasdien nepamatysite', TV3.lt, 22 May 2023.

8. For 'Moss' globes (actually clumps of algae shaped by the wind), see: Ingrid Raagaard, 'Mysteriöse grüne Kugeln am Strand gespült', *Bild*, 1 February 2024; ice spheres: Katarzyna Grzelak, 'Dziesiątki lodowych kul nad Bałtykiem. To zjawisko pogodowe nieobserwowane od lat', *National Geographic Polska*, 8 February 2021; giant lumps of amber: Tomasz Turczyn, 'Bałtyk. Duża bryła bursztynu wyrzucona na plażę w Darłowie. Fart spacerowiczów. Zdjęcia', *Sławno Nasze Miasto*, 13 April 2024.
9. H. E. Markus Meier et al., 'Overview: The Baltic Earth Assessment Reports (BEAR)', in *Earth System Dynamics* (vol. 14, no. 2, 2023), p. 521.
10. For a more detailed but fairly readable summary, see Minna Pyhälä, Vivi Fleming-Lehtinen and Maria Laamanen (eds), 'Eutrophication Status of the Baltic Sea 2007–2011: A Concise Thematic Assessment', HELCOM, *Baltic Sea Environmental Proceedings* (no. 143, 2014), pp. 5–6 and 32–6.
11. 'Baltijos jūroje aptiko "mirties zoną": plotas – didesnis už Lietuvą', Delfi, 16 June 2023.
12. Agata Pavlinec, 'Niebezpieczne materiały na dnie Bałtyku – czy jest się czego obawiać?', Onet, 1 May 2024.
13. Marcus Reckermann et al., 'Human Impacts and Their Interactions in the Baltic Sea Region', *Earth System Dynamics* (vol. 13, no. 1, 2022), pp. 41–2.
14. Katja Lamminen, 'Itämereen upotetut sotakemikaalit kulkeutuvat kaloihin, entä ihmisiin? Rahaa vaaditaan myrkkyjen tutkimiseen ja poistamiseen', *Maaseudun Tulevaisuus*, 3 October 2023.
15. Hans Sanderson et al., 'Environmental Impact of the Explosion of the Nord Stream Pipelines', *Scientific Reports* (vol. 13, 2023), pp. 1–3.
16. 'Human Activity Is Causing Toxic Thallium to Enter the Baltic Sea, According to New Study', Woods Hole Oceanographic Institution, 2 May 2024.
17. Meier et al., 'Overview', p. 521.
18. Markus Ahola et al., 'Climate Change in the Baltic Sea: 2021 Fact Sheet' (HELCOM and Baltic.Earth, 2021), p. 23.

NOTES

19. German federal maritime and hydrographic agency, 'Nordsee und Ostsee waren im Winter 2022/23 bis zu 1,5 Grad wärmer als im langjährigen Mittel', 17 March 2023.
20. Reckermann et al., 'Human Impacts', p. 23.
21. *The Baltic Sea – Our Common Treasure: Economics of Saving the Sea* (BalticSTERN, 2013), p. 17.
22. Cornelia Jaspers et al., 'Invasion Genomics Uncover Contrasting Scenarios of Genetic Diversity in a Widespread Marine Invader', *Proceedings of the National Academy of Sciences* (vol. 118, no. 51, 2021), pp. 1–8.
23. Craig Baker-Austin et al., 'Emerging Vibrio Risk at High Latitudes in Response to Ocean Warming', *Nature Climate Change* (vol. 3, 2013), pp. 73–7.
24. Markku Viitasalo and Erik Bonsdorff, 'Global Climate Change and the Baltic Sea Ecosystem: Direct and Indirect Effects on Species, Communities and Ecosystem Functioning', *Earth System Dynamics* (vol. 13, no. 2, 2022), p. 711.
25. Heikki Peltonen, Riku Varjopuro and Markku Viitasalo, 'Climate Change Impacts on the Baltic Sea Fish Stocks and Fisheries: Review with a Focus on Central Baltic Herring, Sprat and Cod', *Coastline Reports* (vol. 21, 2013), pp. 37–9.
26. 'Larmet: Hundratals tumlare fastnar i fiskenät i Öresund och Kattegatt', SVT, 5 April 2024.
27. Jan Henricson, 'På vakt för att rädda Östersjöns ejdrar', *Svensk Jakt*, 12 May 2023.
28. 'Red List of Marine and Coastal Biotopes and Biotope Complexes of the Baltic Sea, Belt Sea and Kattegat', HELCOM, *Baltic Sea Environment Proceedings* (no. 75, 1998), p. 47.
29. 'State of the Baltic Sea 2023: Third HELCOM Holistic Assessment 2016–2021', HELCOM, *Baltic Sea Environment Proceedings* (no. 194, 2023), p. 13.
30. See Oliver Moody, 'Scavengers Welcome on Bornholm, the Danish Island Aiming for Zero Waste', *The Times*, 20 March 2023.
31. Dieter Gantenbein et al., 'EcoGrid EU: An Efficient ICT Approach for a Sustainable Power System', paper presented at the 2012 IEEE Sustainable Internet and ICT for Sustainability conference, p. 1.
32. Adrijana Buljan, 'Denmark and Germany to Build Bornholm Energy Island Together', offshoreWIND.biz, 29 August 2022.
33. Sophie Eastaugh, 'Bornholm: The Danish Island Aiming for Zero Waste', BBC, 26 October 2023.

34. European Commission Directorate-General for Maritime Affairs and Fisheries, 'When Artificial is Beneficial', 1 June 2023.
35. Bernd Radowitz, '"Fish Hotels": OX2 and Vattenfall Want Cod and Mussels to Make Offshore Wind Farm Home', Recharge, 16 March 2023; and 'Ostsee: Windparks als Algenzuchtstationen?', Natur.de, 15 March 2023.
36. Moomin Characters Limited, '#OURSEA Campaign Spawned More Than 1 Million Euros to Save the Baltic Sea', 9 August 2021.
37. 'Denmark Ranks Highest on the Climate Change Performance Index', State of Green, 12 December 2023.
38. Amanda Flyvbjerg, 'Landmænd skal frivilligt droppe marker og rejse ny skov: "Vil give en kæmpe ændring i landskabet"', Danmarks Radio, 25 June 2024.
39. Pyhälä, Fleming-Lehtinen and Laamanen (eds), 'Eutrophication Status of the Baltic Sea 2007–2011', p. 5.
40. One Danish marine ecology professor estimates that at the current rate it could be 400 years before the sea is clear of nutrient pollution: 'Forsker: Det vil tage 400 år at genoprette havmiljø i Østersøen', Danmarks Radio, 10 May 2024.
41. Council of Europe, committee on the environment, agriculture and local and regional affairs, Martti Tiuri, 'State of the Environment of the Baltic Sea' (2002).
42. Lars M. Svendsen et al., 'Updated Fifth Baltic Sea Pollution Load Compilation: PLC-5.5', HELCOM, *Baltic Sea Environment Proceedings* (no. 145, 2015), p. 8.
43. Tiuri, 'State of the Environment of the Baltic Sea'; and International Union for Conservation of Nature, James Workman, *Plasticus Mare Balticum: A Synthesized Collection of Five Independent Research Reports on Plastic Pollution in the Baltic Sea* (2020), p. 5.
44. UN Environment Programme speech, Laura Piriz, 'Success Story: Baltic', 16 August 2017, and Ross Davies, 'The Remarkable Decline of Oil Spills in the Baltic Sea – Lessons Learnt?', *Offshore Technology*, 12 October 2014.
45. Jan Thulin and Andris Andrushaitis, 'The Baltic Sea: Its Past, Present and Future', *Proceedings of the Religion, Science and the Environment Symposium V on the Baltic Sea* (2003), p. 5.
46. Birgitte Skovlund Asmussen, 'Danmark forbyder skibe at udlede miljøskadeligt vand', Danmarks Radio, 11 April 2024.
47. Camila Ekblad, 'The Return of the White-Tailed Eagle: Ecology of

NOTES

Predator-Prey Relationships in the Baltic Sea and Arctic Inland', *Annales Universitatis Turkuensis* (2022), p. 4.
48. Piia Elonen, 'Kala joka katosi', *Helsingin Sanomat*, 4 June 2023.
49. The Baltic Sea Energy Summit, The Marienborg Declaration, 30 August 2022.
50. 'Klartecken för stor vindkraftspark i havet utanför Gotland', SVT, 3 April 2024.
51. Amalie Thorlund Jepsen, 'Seks gigantiske havvindmølleparker sat i udbud', Danmarks Radio, 22 April 2024.
52. Christian Geinitz, 'Baltischer Ökostrom für Deutschland', *Frankfurter Allgemeine Zeitung*, 8 May 2023.
53. See e.g. Barney Jopson, 'The Problem with Europe's Ageing Wind Farms', *Financial Times*, 22 February 2024, and Daniel Wetzel, 'Die nächste Windkraft-Niederlage', *Welt*, 19 April 2024.
54. See e.g. Dorte Holden Langemark, Marie-Louise Rafn and Maya Søgård Volff, 'Dansk Folkeparti forlader forliget bag Energiø Bornholm', Danmarks Radio, 23 May 2024.
55. Lukas Trakimavičius, 'A Sea of Change: Energy Security in the Baltic Region', Euractiv, 23 March 2023.
56. See e.g. Toomas Pott, 'Riigikogu Starts to Discuss Power Plant Construction Plans', ERR, 18 April 2024.
57. Bernd Henningsen, Tobias Etzold and Krister Hanne (eds), *The Baltic Sea Region: A Comprehensive Guide – History, Politics, Culture and Economy of a European Role Model* (Berliner Wissenschafts-Verlag, 2017), p. 280.
58. For a fair-minded analysis, see Nina Tynkynnen, 'The "Russian Issue" in Transnational Governance of the Baltic Sea Environment: Analysis of Drivers and Constraints of Russia's Participation', *Marine Policy* (vol. 98, 2018), pp. 220–6.
59. Workman, *Plasticus Mare Balticum*, pp. 32–3.
60. Bryon McKinney, 'Russia's Shadow Fleet: Understanding its Size, Activity and Relationships', S&P Global blog, 17 March 2023.
61. Patrick Wintour, '"Russia Doesn't Care": Sweden Sounds Alarm Over Unsafe Oil Fleet', *Guardian*, 18 April 2024.
62. Pekka Vänttinen, 'Hundreds of "Ghost Tankers" in Gulf of Finland Pose Risk for Maritime Safety', Euractiv, 20 March 2023.
63. 'Russian Oil Restrictions Could Be Threat to Environment in Gulf of Finland', ERR, 4 February 2023.
64. See e.g. 'Marinchefen: Vi misstänker att ryska skuggflottan spionerar', SVT, 22 April 2024.

65. Michael Weiss and Holger Roonemaa, 'Exclusive: Inside Russia's Environmental Influence Operation Targeting the Baltic Sea', Yahoo! News, 26 April 2023.
66. Michael Weiss and Holger Roonemaa, 'How "Putin's Chef" Prigozhin is Now Targeting Europe', *Daily Beast*, 2 March 2021.
67. 'Baltijos šalys "Inter RAO" skolingos beveik 13 mln. Eur', *Verslo Žinios*, 22 May 2023.
68. European Commission Directorate-General for Energy, 'Estonia, Latvia & Lithuania Agree to Synchronise Their Electricity Grids With the European Grid by Early 2025', 3 August 2023.
69. 'How Heavily Does Germany Rely on Russian Energy?', *The Economist*, 4 May 2022.
70. 'BASF verkauft alle deutschen Gasspeicher an Gazprom', *Welt*, 4 September 2015.
71. 'Bundeskartellamt erlaubt Rosneft Kauf großer Anteile an deutscher Raffinerie', *Der Spiegel*, 24 February 2022.
72. Henryk Hielscher and Florian Güßgen, 'Wie der Kernkraftentsorger seinen russischen Eigner loswerden will', *WirtschaftsWoche*, 4 April 2024.
73. 'So viel verdient Altkanzler Schröder', RedaktionsNetzwerk Deutschland, 2 March 2022.
74. 'Gerhard Schröder erhält mehr als halbe Million Euro für Altkanzler-Büro', *Der Spiegel*, 29 September 2017.
75. Marcin Miodek and Bernhard Hartmann, '"Das ist ein neuer Ribbentrop-Molotov-Pakt!": Eine historische Analogie in der polnischen Energiedebatte', *Osteuropa* (vol. 59, no. 7/8, 2009), pp. 295–305.
76. Sarah Marsh and Madeline Chambers, 'Germany Freezes Nord Stream 2 Gas Project as Ukraine Crisis Deepens', Reuters, 22 February 2022.
77. America Hernandez and Zosia Wanat, 'Russia Halts Gas Shipments to Poland and Bulgaria', *Politico*, 26 April 2022.
78. Terje Solsvik, 'Russia Stops Gas Flows to Finland Over Payments Dispute', Reuters, 21 May 2022.
79. Anna Pruchnicka and Essi Lehto, 'Russia's Inter RAO to Halt Power Exports to Finland Due Lack of Payment', Reuters, 13 May 2022.
80. Jan M. Olsen, 'Russia Cuts Off Natural Gas Supply to Denmark, Company Says', AP, 1 June 2022.
81. 'Russia Indefinitely Suspends Europe's Gas Flow', Deutsche Welle, 2 September 2022.
82. Ting Lan, Galen Sher and Jing Zhou, 'The Economic Impacts on

Germany of a Potential Russian Gas Shutoff', IMF working paper (no. 144, July 2022), p. 5.
83. See Helen Thompson, 'Geopolitics Lurks Behind Europe's Gas Storage Success', *Financial Times*, 8 April 2024.
84. Filip Rudnik, 'Gazprom in 2023: Financial Losses Hit Record High', OSW Centre for Eastern Studies, 14 June 2024.
85. 'Down the Pipe: Russia's Gas Business Will Never Recover from the War in Ukraine', *The Economist*, 2 May 2024.
86. Kostas Poursanidis, Jumana Sharanik and Constantinos Hadjistassou, 'World's Largest Natural Gas Leak From Nord Stream Pipeline Estimated at 478,000 Tonnes', *iScience* (vol. 27, no. 1, 2024), p. 5.
87. Jörg Diehl, Roman Höfner, Martin Knobbe et al., 'Wie die Ermittler dem mutmaßlichen Nord-Stream-Taucher auf die Spur kamen', *Der Spiegel*, 14 August 2024; Mattias Carlsson, 'Ukrainske dykaren Volodymyr Zhuravlov, 44, efterlyst för sprängningen av Nord stream', *Expressen*, 14 August 2024.
88. Niklas Pollard and Anne Kauranen, 'Sweden Says Telecoms Cable With Estonia Damaged but Operating', Reuters, 17 October 2023.
89. Tuomas Rimpiläinen, 'Kiinalaisaluksesta otetut kuvat vahvistavat ankkuriteoriaa kaasuputkitutkinnassa', Yle, 24 October 2023.
90. Finbarr Bermingham, 'Beijing Admits Hong Kong-Flagged Ship Destroyed Key Baltic Gas Pipeline "By Accident"', *South China Morning Post*, 12 August 2024.
91. Victor Abramowicz, 'Moscow's Other Navy', Lowy Institute blog, 21 June 2018.
92. Sidarth Kaushal, 'Stalking the Seabed: How Russia Targets Critical Undersea Infrastructure', RUSI blog, 25 May 2023.
93. 'Big Tech and Geopolitics Are Reshaping the Internet's Plumbing', *The Economist*, 20 December 2023.
94. Helene Fouquet, 'China's 7,500-Mile Undersea Cable to Europe Fuels Internet Feud', Bloomberg, 5 March 2021.
95. Elisabeth Braw, 'Balts Say Russian Navy Bullying Undersea Cable Crews', RFE/RL, 5 May 2015.
96. Oliver Alexander, a Danish open source intelligence analyst, posts regular Twitter/X updates on their movements: @OAlexanderDK
97. Jens Stoltenberg, NATO pre-ministerial press conference, 11 October 2022.
98. 'Attacks Against NATO Allies Critical Infrastructure to Be Met With Determined Response – NATO Chief', Reuters, 29 September 2022.

NOTES

99. Bruno Waterfield and Oliver Moody, 'Nord Stream: Russia Has Mined European Undersea Pipelines and Cables, NATO Fears', *The Times*, 3 May 2023.
100. Letter from the German federal ministry of the interior in response to a written enquiry from the CDU MP Knut Abraham, 14 October 2022.
101. See e.g. Andrius Balčiūnas, 'Can Damaged Cables Lead to War? NATO's Preparations to Defend Critical Infrastructure', LRT, 5 December 2023. These broad-brush regional defence plans are supposed to be fleshed out at national level.
102. Sean Monaghan et al., 'NATO's Role in Protecting Critical Undersea Infrastructure', Center for Strategic and International Studies brief (2023), p. 2.
103. 'Poland to Boost Military Protection of Baltic Energy Infrastructure', Reuters, 4 May 2023.

Chapter 5: To Europe, Yes, But With Our Dead

1. Czesław Miłosz, *Beginning With My Streets: Essays and Recollections* (Farrar, Straus and Giroux, 2010, tr. Madeline G. Levine), p. 280.
2. 'Ukrainian No-Fly Zone Would End War Quicker, Says Polish Ambassador', Reuters, 10 March 2022; 'Top Polish Politician Calls For Peacekeeping Mission in Ukraine', Reuters, 15 March 2022; and Aleksandra Krzyszkoszek, 'Zelenskyy Rejects Poland's Proposal of Peacekeeping Mission', Euractiv, 29 March 2022.
3. See e.g. 'Beefing Up Poland's Armed Forces', *The Economist*, 2 November 2023; and Matthew Karnitschnig and Wojciech Kość, 'Meet Europe's Coming Military Superpower: Poland', *Politico*, 21 November 2022. However, Tomasz Siemoniak, who was defence minister from 2011 to 2015, has expressed doubts that a population of 36.8 million can durably sustain a total military strength much greater than 200,000 personnel: 'Polish Population Not Big Enough for 300,000-strong Army, Says Ex-Defence Minister', Polish Press Agency, 20 October 2023.
4. Katarzyna Broda, 'Wiceszef MON: W tym roku powstanie ustawa o obronie cywilnej', *Dziennik Gazeta Prawna*, 31 January 2024.
5. See e.g. Thomas Obst and Samina Sultan, 'Polen vor der Wahl – Wirtschaftsmodell im Wandel', German Economic Institute report (no. 51), 13 October 2023; and Mikołaj Kunica, 'Nasz

NOTES

gospodarczy złoty wiek cały czas trwa – przekonuje waszyngtoński ekonomista, ale ostrzega przed ryzykiem', Business Insider Polska, 4 June 2023.
6. Adriana Sas, 'Gross Domestic Expenditure on Research and Development (GERD) as a Percentage of GDP in Poland from 2000 to 2022', Statista, 4 January 2024.
7. Thomas Obst and Samina Sultan, 'Polen vor der Wahl', pp. 19–20.
8. Aleksandra Krzysztoszek, 'Tusk Promises Poles Will Soon Be Richer Than Brits', Euractiv, 2 May 2024. The original source of this claim appears to be John Burn-Murdoch, 'Britain and the US Are Poor Societies With Some Very Rich People', *Financial Times*, 16 September 2022. It was also repeated at the time by Keir Starmer, who was then the leader of the opposition in Britain. For expert objections, see e.g. Christopher Breen, 'Claims that Poland Will Be Richer Than the UK This Decade Are Overambitious But Only Just', Cebr blog, 13 May 2024.
9. Vanessa Gera and Monika Skislowska, 'Poland Lays Claim to a Leadership Role in Europe as Russia's War Threatens Stability', AP, 25 April 2024.
10. Chancellery of the Prime Minister of Poland, 'Polska i Finlandia gotowe do współpracy na rzecz bezpieczeństwa', 16 February 2024. The trip to Tallinn was cancelled at short notice because Kaja Kallas, the Estonian prime minister, caught Covid.
11. Jędrzej Bielecki, 'Rewolucja dyplomatyczna rządu Donalda Tuska dotarła do Skandynawii', *Rzeczpospolita*, 20 February 2024.
12. Gerhard Gnauck, *Polen verstehen: Geschichte, Politik, Gesellschaft* (Klett-Cotta, 2018), p. 261.
13. Kai-Olaf Lang, 'Polens Außen- und Sicherheitspolitik im Angesicht des Krieges im Osten Europas', *Jahrbuch Polen 2023* (Deutsches Polen-Institut and Harrassowitz Verlag, 2023), p. 28.
14. Jarosław Kuisz, *The New Politics of Poland: A Case of Post-Traumatic Sovereignty* (Manchester University Press, 2023), p. 233.
15. Jędrzej Bielecki, 'Jacek Czaputowicz: Czy ktoś za granicą lubi polski rząd? Nikt nie przychodzi mi do głowy', *Rzeczpospolita*, 18 October 2021.
16. Claudia Chiappa, 'Unlikely Allies Viktor Orbán and Donald Tusk Rail Against EU Migration Deal', *Politico*, 11 April 2023.
17. 'EU Envoys Strike New Deal on Ukraine Food Imports', Reuters, 27 March 2024.

18. See e.g. Jan Puhl and Dariusz Kalan, 'Die Deutschen haben ein löchriges Gedächtnis', *Der Spiegel*, 9 February 2024.
19. Daniel Tilles, 'Proportion of Catholics in Poland Falls to 71%, New Census Data Show', Notes from Poland, 29 September 2023.
20. Daniel Tilles, 'Half of Public Support Tusk's Aim to Introduce Abortion on Demand in Poland, Find Polls', Notes from Poland, 2 February 2024.
21. Karen Hargrave and Sarian Jarosz, 'Is Anti-Migrant Rhetoric Still a Vote-Winner? Unpacking Narratives in Poland's Election', Overseas Development Institute, 19 October 2023.
22. '"Tak" dla związków partnerskich i małżeństw osób tej samej płci', TVP Info, 25 April 2024.
23. Gilles Ivaldi, 'Populist Radical Right Attitudes and Voting in Germany, France, Italy and Poland: A Brief Overview Ahead of the 2024 EP Elections', SciencesPo, *Le Baromètre de la confiance politique* (no. 15, March 2024), pp. 3–5.
24. See e.g. Ben Stanley, 'Nie ufamy wyborcom PiS-u tak samo, jak nie ufamy PiS-owi. To problem dla naszej demokracji', *Kultura Liberalna*, 19 March 2024.
25. 'Sondaż: 40,4 proc. Polaków uważa, że Polska nie jest dziś państwem prawa', *Rzeczpospolita*, 4 June 2023.
26. It is worth consulting Jarosław Kuisz and Karolina Wigura, *Posttraumatische Souveränität: Ein Essay* (Suhrkamp, 2023) for an account of how this concept exerts an equally powerful influence over Finland, the Baltic states and other countries that came under the Soviet Union's sway after the Second World War.
27. Peter Oliver Loew, *Danzig: Biographie einer Stadt* (C. H. Beck, 2011), p. 232.
28. Thomas Urban, *Von Krakau bis Danzig: Eine Reise durch die deutsch-polnische Geschichte* (C. H. Beck, 2000), p. 286.
29. Małgorzata Omilanowska, 'Gdańsk: Specificity of Its Architecture in the Modern Era. The Question of National and Regional Identity', in Alexander Drost and Anna Mazurkiewicz (eds), *Baltic Borderlands: Gdańsk – Danzig – Gduńsk and the Impact of Exchange* (Gdańsk University Press, *Studia Historica Gedanensia*, vol. 13, 2022), p. 194.
30. 'Wojna Gdańska z Polską', *Sieci*, 4 July 2019.
31. For the case that it did, see Tomasz Nyczka, 'Paweł Adamowicz nie żyje. "Paweł mocno przeżywał hejt" – mówi prezydent Poznania Jacek Jaśkowiak', *Gazeta Wyborcza*, 14 January 2019.

32. Paweł Machcewicz, 'Poland Besieged: Law and Justice and Its Politics of History', from the script of a lecture delivered online at a Ghent University conference, 'Populist Historicities', 3 September 2021.
33. 'Alfabet Buntu: Paweł Machcewicz', Archiwum Osiatyńskiego, 19 September 2018.
34. For a good discussion of this school of thought, see Stefan Auer, *Liberal Nationalism in Central Europe* (Routledge, 2006), pp. 60ff.
35. Adam Zamoyski, *Poland: A History* (HarperCollins, 2009), p. 286.
36. Auer, *Liberal Nationalism in Central Europe*, p. 62.
37. Norman Davies, *God's Playground: A History of Poland*, vol. II, *1795 to the Present* (Columbia University Press, 1983), pp. 52–3.
38. Joshua D. Zimmerman, *Jozef Pilsudski: Founding Father of Modern Poland* (Harvard University Press, 2022), p. 372.
39. Ibid., p. 136.
40. Ibid., pp. 410–11.
41. Robert Frost, 'Imagining the Past and Remembering the Future', in Stanley Bill and Simon Lewis (eds), *Multicultural Commonwealth: Poland–Lithuania and Its Afterlives* (University of Pittsburgh Press, 2023), p. 192.
42. Auer, *Liberal Nationalism in Central Europe*, p. 65.
43. Adam Michnik, interviewed by myself and my *Times* colleague Paulina Olszanka. Part of the interview, translated by Paulina Olszanka, was published as Oliver Moody and Paulina Olszanka, 'The Former Solidarity Comrades Who Are Now Election Rivals in Poland', *Sunday Times*, 14 October 2023.
44. Kuisz, *New Politics of Poland*, p. 203.
45. 'Premier Tusk o krytykach integracji europejskiej. "Dziś stoją i stroją durne miny . . ."', TVP Info, 1 May 2024.
46. Dębski was eventually levered out of office by the Tusk government in 2024.
47. Nicolas Camut, 'Commission to Unblock Over €100B in EU Funds For Poland', *Politico*, 23 February 2024.
48. The exception is Andrzej Duda, who appears to be one of the few European leaders to have built up a genuine rapport with Donald Trump. My colleagues in Washington reported that Duda had been instrumental in persuading Trump to push Europe's NATO members to increase their defence budgets to 3 per cent of GDP: David Charter and Alistair Dawber, 'Donald Trump "Would Force NATO Members to Spend 3% on Defence"', *The Times*, 4 May 2024.

NOTES

49. See Oliver Moody, 'Why Poland's New Foreign Minister Reminds People of Boris Johnson', *The Times*, 1 January 2024.
50. Radosław Ditrich, 'Marynarka Wojenna urośnie w siłę. Na razie nie wygląda to dobrze', Forsal.pl, 29 January 2024; and Dominik Kimla, '2023 BaltExpo Preview: The Beginning of Poland's Naval Renaissance', Defense-Aerospace.com, 9 October 2023.
51. Grzegorz Sobczak, 'Polish Navy Charts a Better Course', *European Security & Defence*, 18 April 2023.
52. Tomasz Kwasek and Marcin Strembski, 'Położono stępkę pod przyszły ORP Wicher', Onet, 31 January 2024.
53. Marta Grzechnik, 'Gdynia 1920–1939: Poland's Gateway to the World', in Alexander Drost and Anna Mazurkiewicz (eds), *Baltic Borderlands*, pp. 208–13.
54. Marta Grzechnik, 'Love of Wide Open Waters: The Polish Maritime Programme According to the Baltic and Western Institutes in the Aftermath of the Second World War', *Acta Poloniae Historica* (vol. 117, 2018), p. 210.
55. Agata Kowalska-Szubert, 'Dutch Loanwords in Contemporary Polish' (Wrocław University PhD thesis, 2021), pp. 146–54.
56. Dragana Nikše, 'MOL and Gaz-System Shake Hands on Deal for Poland's First FSRU', Offshore Energy, 7 May 2024.
57. Adam Michnik, *Letters from Prison and Other Essays* (University of California Press, 1987), pp. 188–9 and 214.
58. Dominika Kozłowska, 'Solidarnosc, eine friedliche Revolution und ihre Bedeutung heute', in Katarzyna Domagała-Pereira, Bartosz Dudek and Basil Kerski (eds), *Solidarność: Die unvollendete Geschichte der europäischen Freiheit* (Herder, 2023), p. 220.
59. Kuisz, *New Politics of Poland*, p. 30.
60. Bartosz Dudek and Elżbieta Stasik, '"Die Sprache der Freiheit ist Polnisch": Gespräch mit Joachim Gauck', in Domagała-Pereira, Dudek and Kerski (eds), *Solidarność*, pp. 154–67.

Chapter 6: Turning Time

1. '"Neues Deutschland-Tempo": Olaf Scholz weiht LNG-Terminal in Lubmin ein', Euronews, 14 January 2023.
2. German federal government, 'Regierungserklärung von Bundeskanzler Olaf Scholz am 27. Februar 2022'.

3. In 2023 the volume of Germany's combined exports and imports from and to Poland, Sweden, Denmark, Finland, Lithuania, Latvia and Estonia was €297.8 billion, compared to €254.5 billion of trade with China and €252.6 billion with the US: German federal statistical office, 'Außenhandel: Rangfolge der Handelspartner im Außenhandel der Bundesrepublik Deutschland (vorläufige Ergebnisse) – 2023', 18 June 2024.
4. German federal ministry of digital and transport affairs, 'Innovationsclub: Wissing und Baltische Staaten präsentieren Reformvorschläge für Digitalpolitik der EU', 24 November 2023.
5. See e.g. 'SPD-Chefs fordern weniger Rüstungsexporte', *Der Spiegel*, 7 January 2020.
6. See e.g. German federal ministry of defence, 'Verteidigungsminister: "Wir müssen kriegstüchtig werden!"', 10 November 2023; and Lars Klingbeil, 'Zeitenwende: Der Beginn einer neuen Ära', speech delivered at the Friedrich-Ebert-Stiftung, 5 September 2022.
7. Olaf Scholz, 'The Global Zeitenwende: How to Avoid a New Cold War in a Multipolar Era', *Foreign Affairs*, 5 December 2022.
8. 'US-Mittelstreckenwaffen in Deutschland', Bundeswehr, 27 July 2024.
9. Thomas Block and Nils Heisterhagen, 'INSA-Umfrage: Wähler wollen, dass DIESE Probleme jetzt angepackt werden', Bild, 16 June 2024.
10. 'Mehrheit der Deutschen befürwortet höhere Verteidigungsausgaben', Zeit Online, 29 April 2024; and 'Ukraine-Krieg Bewertung der Ukraine-Politik von Deutschland im Januar 2024', Statista, 5 January 2024.
11. Peter Tiede, '"Mit Schaum vorm Mund . . .": Scholz legt sich mit Boris Johnson und Hillary Clinton an', Bild, 19 May 2024.
12. See e.g. Jonas Schaible and Steffen Winter, 'Unterstützung für Kiew: Der Ukrainekrieg wird für die CDU zum Wahlkampfproblem', Spiegel, 16 June 2024.
13. 'Russland und Mecklenburg-Vorpommern: Chronologie der Landespolitik', Norddeutscher Rundfunk, 19 May 2022.
14. 'Schwesig und die Klimastiftung: Eine Frage der Glaubwürdigkeit', Tagesschau, 6 March 2023.
15. Its lead was, however, winnowed away to a certain extent over the first half of 2024. See e.g. 'Umfrage sieht AfD in MV weiterhin vor SPD und CDU', *Nordkurier*, 6 June 2024.
16. West Pomerania-Greifswald district administration, 'Wahl der Kreistage der Landkreise sowie der Stadtvertretung Schwerin und der

Bürgerschaft Rostock in Mecklenburg-Vorpommern am 9. Juni 2024: Endgültiges Ergebnis', 13 June 2024.
17. University and Hanseatic city of Greifswald, 'Europawahl und Kommunalwahlen 2024: Wahlenübersicht', 12 June 2024.
18. German federal electoral administrator, 'Bundestagswahl 2021 – Strukturdaten: 015 Vorpommern-Rügen – Vorpommern-Greifswald I.' Unemployment data are from 2021 and compared against numbers from the Federal Agency for Labour in the same year. GDP per capita figures are from 2018 (€25,124) and set against the national figure for the same year from the Federal Statistical Agency (€40,594).
19. See e.g. 'Umfrage: USA-Skepsis vermehrt in Ostdeutschland', RedaktionsNetzwerk Deutschland, 7 February 2023.
20. Frank Biess, *Republik der Angst: Eine andere Geschichte der Bundesrepublik* (Rowohlt, 2019).
21. '"Die Ängste der Deutschen" im Langzeitvergleich', R+V-Studie, 12 October 2023.
22. Sebastian Schug, 'Dudenhöffer-Studie: "Der Verbrenner ist für die nächsten hundert Jahre gesichert"', *WirtschaftsWoche*, 27 March 2024.
23. 'Abkehr vom Blick Richtung Zukunft: Viele junge Menschen würden lieber in der Vergangenheit leben', *Der Spiegel*, 23 April 2022.
24. Thomas Petersen, *Glück in schwierigen Zeiten* (Institut für Demoskopie Allensbach, 2023), p. 27.
25. Ismene Poulakos and Sonja Kittel, 'Deutschland auf der Flucht vor der Wirklichkeit', Rheingold Institut, 27 July 2023.
26. See Oliver Moody, 'NATO Should "Prepare for Russian Missile Strikes in Europe"', *The Times*, 28 January 2024.
27. Federal Association of Energy and Water Businesses, 'Entwicklung der Heizungsstruktur des Wohnbestandes in Deutschland', 22 April 2024, and German federal statistical office, 'Stromerzeugung 2021: Anteil konventioneller Energieträger deutlich gestiegen', 17 March 2022.
28. Daniel Brössler, *Ein deutscher Kanzler: Olaf Scholz, der Krieg und der Angst* (Propyläen, 2024), pp. 132–3.
29. See Oliver Moody, 'Germany Steals a March in New Dash for Gas', *The Times*, 22 July 2023.
30. 'Turkey's First FSRU Inaugurated', Offshore Energy, 23 December 2016.
31. 'Deutsche ReGas schließt FEED-Phase des H2-Hub Lubmin ab', Deutsche ReGas, 12 September 2024.

32. Martin Grieve et al., 'So entging Deutschland knapp einem Blackout', Handelsblatt, 9 December 2023.
33. 'Rosneft Deutschland bleibt unter Treuhandverwaltung', RBB24 (Rundfunk Berlin-Brandenburg), 8 March 2024.
34. German federal government, 'So läuft der Ausbau der Erneuerbaren Energien in Deutschland', 9 April 2024.
35. 'Erneuerbare Energien: Windkraft löst Kohle ab', Norddeutscher Rundfunk, 7 March 2024.
36. Federal Association of Energy and Water Businesses, 'Windenergie in Deutschland – Zahlen und Fakten', 16 January 2024; and German federal office for the environment, *Erneuerbare Energien in Deutschland: Daten zur Entwicklung im Jahr 2023* (March 2023), p. 10.
37. Calculation based on German federal statistical office, 'Stromerzeugung 2022: Ein Drittel aus Kohle, ein Viertel aus Windkraft', 9 March 2023, and 'Stromerzeugung 2023: 56% aus erneuerbaren Energieträgern', 7 March 2024.
38. German federal government, 'Fragen und Antworten zu den Energiepreisbremsen', 1 January 2024.
39. German federal statistical office, 'Bedeutung der energieintensiven Industriezweige in Deutschland' (2024).
40. Peter Sonnenberg, 'BASF sucht Schulterschluss mit China', Tagesschau, 24 February 2023; and Hartmut Reitz, 'BASF will in Ludwigshafen mehr Stellen abbauen', SWR, 23 February 2024.
41. 'Deindustrialisierung: Zwei Drittel der Unternehmen haben Teile ihrer Wertschöpfung bereits verlagert', Deloitte, 14 November 2023.
42. Federal Association of Energy and Water Businesses, 'BDEW-Strompreisanalyse Februar 2024', 23 February 2024, p. 26; and David Böcking, 'Selbst die Ölpreiskrise war im Vergleich harmlos!', *Der Spiegel*, 13 April 2024.
43. Alfons Mais, LinkedIn post, 24 February 2022.
44. Tobias Heimbach, 'Munition für maximal zwei Tage Krieg: Bundeswehr muss ihre Arsenale auffüllen – doch bislang bestellt sie nur wenig', Business Insider, 10 October 2022.
45. Florian Dorn, Niklas Potrafke and Marcel Schlepper, *European Defence Spending in 2024 and Beyond: How to Provide Security in an Economically Challenging Environment*, CESifo *EconPol* policy report (vol. 8, no. 45, 4 January 2024), pp. 9–10.
46. See e.g. Bundestag, 'Wehrbeauftragte: Bundeswehr benötigt 300 Milliarden Euro', 14 March 2023; and Matthias Gebauer and Marina

Kormbaki, 'Vier Milliarden für Eurofighter sind eine gute Investition', *Der Spiegel*, 19 April 2024.
47. Bundestag, *Jahresbericht 2022 der Wehrbeauftragten*, 28 February 2023, pp. 18 and 37–40.
48. Bundestag, *Unterrichtung durch die Wehrbeauftragte: Jahresbericht 2023*, 12 March 2024, pp. 9, 38 and 151.
49. German federal government, 'Regierungserklärung von Bundeskanzler Olaf Scholz am 27. Februar 2022'; and 'Deutschland hat bald größte konventionelle NATO-Armee in Europa', *Der Spiegel*, 31 May 2022.
50. German federal ministry of defence, *Verteidigungspolitische Richtlinien 2023*, pp. 7–8, 14, 24, 29 and 31.
51. Ibid., p. 10.
52. Frank Specht, '80 Prozent des Sondervermögens sind laut Pistorius bereits gebunden', Handelsblatt, 20 March 2024.
53. Hauke Friedrichs, 'Bundeswehr-Sondervermögen: Was für die Bundeswehr bestellt wurde – und was ihr noch fehlt', Zeit Online, 4 June 2024.
54. 'Verteidigungsministerium schöpft Budget für Munition nicht aus', *Der Spiegel*, 19 January 2024. German officials give two explanations for the delay: ammunition production capacity is scarce across Europe, and orders are typically made through very large 'framework agreements' that take time to negotiate and finance.
55. Rheinmetall, 'Größter Auftrag der Firmengeschichte: Rheinmetall erhält Rahmenvertrag über 155mm-Artilleriemunition für die Bundeswehr von bis zu 8,5 MrdEUR brutto', 20 June 2024.
56. Carlo Masala, *Bedingt abwehrbereit: Deutschlands Schwäche in der Zeitenwende* (C. H. Beck, 2023), p. 57.
57. German federal ministry of defence, 'Bericht zur materiellen Einsatzbereitschaft der Hauptwaffensysteme der Bundeswehr II/2021', 15 December 2021, pp. 4–17.
58. Masala, *Bedingt abwehrbereit*, pp. 16 and 51.
59. Hans-Peter Bartels, 'Warten auf den "Operationsplan Deutschland"', *Cicero*, 15 February 2024.
60. Thorsten Jungholt, 'Operation "Total Defence"', *Welt am Sonntag*, 3 January 2024.
61. Michael Schöllhorn, 'Industriepolitische Perspektive', in Norbert Lammert and Wolfgang Koch (eds), *Bundeswehr der Zukunft: Verantwortung und künstliche Intelligenz*, Konrad-Adenauer-Stiftung, 17 January 2023, p. 362.

62. Bundestag, *Unterrichtung durch die Wehrbeauftragte: Jahresbericht 2023*, p. 6.
63. Ibid., pp. 20, 29, 131–2 and 136.
64. Ibid., pp. 6 and 33.
65. Max Biederbeck and Christian Ramthun, 'Der Truppe gehen die Gewehre aus', *WirtschaftsWoche*, 28 June 2024.
66. Bundestag, *Unterrichtung durch die Wehrbeauftragte: Jahresbericht 2023*, p. 7.
67. Matthias Gebauer and Marina Kormbaki, 'Scholz, Pistorius und die Wehrpflicht: Der eine denkt vom Frieden her, der andere vom Krieg', *Der Spiegel*, 7 June 2024.
68. UN, Operational Data Portal: Ukraine Refugee Situation, as of 31 March 2024.
69. See e.g. 'Scholz fordert EU-Partner zu mehr Militärhilfe für Kiew auf', *Welt*, 17 April 2024.
70. German federal government, *Agreement on Security Co-operation and Long-Term Support Between the Federal Republic of Germany and Ukraine*, 16 February 2024, pp. 1–2.
71. Stefanie Babst, *Sehenden Auges: Mut zum strategischen Kurswechsel* (dtv, 2023), pp. 209–10.
72. Brössler, *Ein deutscher Kanzler*, p. 241.
73. 'Scholz richtet Worte an "Jungs und Mädels": "Weil ich nicht tue, was ihr wollt, deshalb führe ich"', RedaktionsNetzwerk Deutschland, 15 April 2022.
74. German federal statistical office, 'China Still Germany's Most Important Trading Partner in 2023, But By a Narrow Margin', 14 February 2024.
75. Jürgen Matthes and Christian Rusche, 'Scholz-Besuch in China: Fünf Indikatoren, die zeigen, wie abhängig Deutschland von China ist', German Economic Institute, 3 November 2022.
76. Ole Döring, 'Der Kanzler wahrt Deutschlands Gesicht', *Cicero*, 18 April 2024.
77. Georg Fahrion and Martin Knobbe, 'Immerhin bei den Äpfeln gibt es einen Durchbruch', *Der Spiegel*, 16 April 2024.
78. German federal government, *Strategy on China*, 13 July 2023, p. 10.
79. Matthias Wachter et al., *Analyse bestehender Abhängigkeiten und Handlungsempfehlungen* (Bundesverband der deutschen Industrie/Federation of German Industries, 2022), pp. 1–16.
80. Jürgen Matthes, *Wie ist der starke Importanstieg aus China im Jahr 2022 zu erklären und wie haben sich die Importabhängigkeiten entwickelt?*, German Economic Institute report (no. 34, 2023).

81. Bundestag, 'Parlamentarisches Kontrollgremium: Nachrichtendienste warnen vor Gefahren durch Russland und China', 17 October 2022.
82. *The Berlin Pulse: Of Paradigms and Power Shifts*, Körber-Stiftung, 27 November 2023, pp. 17, 23 and 31.
83. Jürgen Matthes, *Deutsche Direktinvestitionen nach China und Hongkong auf neuem Höchststand – von Diversifizierung kaum eine Spur*, German Economic Institute, report in brief (no. 7), 16 February 2024.
84. Julian Olk and Mathias Peer, 'Siemens-CEO Busch: "Ohne China ist Diversifizierung nicht möglich"', Handelsblatt, 14 November 2022.
85. Table Briefings, 'Friedrich Merz: Schärfere China Ton-Lage als Scholz und Merkel', Table.Media, 18 September 2024.
86. Deutsche Presse Agentur, 'Friedrich Merz hält China für Bedrohung der deutschen Sicherheit', Zeit online, 21 April 2024.
87. Ralph Bollmann, *Angela Merkel: Die Kanzler und ihre Zeit* (C. H. Beck, 2021), pp. 305–7; Erik Brattberg, 'Merkel's Mixed Legacy on China', Carnegie Endowment for International Peace, 30 September 2021.
88. Marcel Fratzscher, *Geld oder Leben: Wie unser irrationales Verhältnis zum Geld die Gesellschaft spaltet* (Berlin Verlag, 2022), p. 111.
89. For a helpful discussion of the verdict's implications, see Clemens Fuest et al., 'Die deutsche Schuldenbremse: Stabilitätsanker oder Investitionsblocker?', ifo Schnelldienst, January 2024.
90. Jan Techau, 'EU, Germany: Compromise on Contested 2025 Budget Will Not Emerge Until Late Fall', Eurasia Group analysis note, 26 April 2024.
91. Mark Copelovitch and Daniel Ziblatt, 'Why the Debt Brake is a Threat to Democracy in Germany', WZB-Mitteilungen, 27 March 2024.
92. On the German tax burden in 2023: German federal statistical office, Pascal Schmidt, 'Fachgespräch zum Bruttoinlandsprodukt 2023: Staatsfinanzen 2023', 15 January 2024, p. 15; the EU comparison based on 2022 figures: EU, Eurostat, 'Tax Revenue Statistics', 26 October 2023, fig. 1; the German debt-to-GDP ratio in 2023: Deutsche Bundesbank Eurosystem, 'Die deutschen Staatsschulden steigen 2023 um 62 Milliarden Euro auf 2,62 Billionen Euro, Schuldenquote sinkt von 66,1 auf 63,7 Prozent', 28 March 2024; and the EU comparison, also based on 2023 figures: EU, Eurostat, 'Third Quarter of 2023: Government Debt Down to 89.9% of GDP in Euro Area', 22 January 2024, p. 2.

93. Marco Stamegna et al., *The Economic Impact of Arms Spending in Germany, Italy, and Spain* (Munich Personal RePEc Archive, 2024), p. 11. See also Moritz Schularick, 'Arming for Growth', Kiel Institute for the World Economy policy article, April 2024 (originally published in *Der Spiegel*, 27 March 2024).
94. Norbert Röttgen, *Nie wieder hilflos!: Ein Manifest in Zeiten des Krieges* (dtv, 2022) and *Demokratie und Krieg: Deutsche Politik und deutsche Identität in Zeiten globaler Gefahr* (dtv, 2024).
95. 'Umfrage: Die 80er sind das Lieblingsjahrzehnt der Deutschen', *Der Tagesspiegel*, 28 December 2015.
96. New Social Free Market Initiative, 'Analyse zur deutschen Bürokratiebelastung: Wie kann ein spürbarer Bürokratieabbau erreicht werden?', 15 November 2023.
97. 'Free Exchange: Working From Home and the US–Europe Divide', *The Economist*, 1 May 2024.
98. Veronika Grimm et al., *Wachstumsschwäche überwinden – in die Zukunft investieren*, Expert Council for the Assessment of Macroeconomic Development, 2023 annual report, p. 6.
99. See e.g. 'Sieben von zehn Bundesbürgern sagen: Ich bin stolz, deutsch zu sein', Idea.de, 24 September 2020; and 'Studie: Worauf sind Deutsche stolz? Grundgesetz, Kultur und Sozialstaat', Deutschlandfunk Kultur, 19 February 2019.
100. Bettina Stangneth, *Überforderung: Putin und die Deutschen* (Rowohlt, 2023), pp. 15–16 and 135.

Chapter 7: The Hobbits

1. Quoted in Lennart Meri, *Botschaften und Zukunftsvisionen: Reden des estnischen Präsidenten* (Bouvier, 1999, ed. and tr. Henno Rajandi), p. 200.
2. Krėvė-Mickevičius's extensive recollections of the meeting were published in the third interim report of the US House of Representatives' select committee on communist aggression: *Report of the Select Committee to Investigate Communist Aggression and the Forced Incorporation of the Baltic States into the USSR* (83rd Congress, second session, 1954), pp. 341–4.
3. David Kirby, *The Baltic World 1772–1993: Europe's Northern Periphery in an Age of Change* (Routledge, 1995), p. 356.

NOTES

4. Artillery: Alexandra Brzozowski, 'Denmark Will Send Its "Entire Artillery" to Ukraine', Euractiv, 19 February 2024; F-16 coalition: Danish ministry of defence, 'Denmark Will Take on Co-Lead Role in International Air Force Coalition to Support Ukraine', 11 October 2023; cyber defence: Andreas Nygaard Just, 'EU skal have en cyberbrigade som modsvar til russisk "troldehær"', Danmarks Radio, 27 May 2024.
5. Oliver Moody, 'Swedes Axe China-Backed Confucius School Scheme as Relations Sour', *The Times*, 21 April 2020.
6. Ammunition procurement: Government of the Republic of Estonia, 'Prime Minister Kallas: Ammunition Procurement for Ukraine Shows That Estonia's Voice Is Being Heard', 24 March 2023; troops on the ground: Lee Ferran, 'Estonia "Seriously" Discussing Sending Troops to "Rear" Jobs in Ukraine: Official', Breaking Defense, 13 May 2024.
7. Trade statistics: Central Statistical Bureau of Latvia, 'Main Import/Export Partners in 2021'; embargo debate: 'Stopping Trade with Russia Debated in Latvia', LSM, 26 March 2024.
8. Richard Milne and Ben Hall, 'Baltic Leaders Urge NATO Members to Bring Back Conscription', *Financial Times*, 24 March 2024.
9. 'Blinken: Baltic States Are "Leading the Way in NATO"', LSM, 25 March 2024.
10. See e.g. 'Baltic Parliamentarians Visit US to Urge Aid for Ukraine', LSM, 19 April 2024.
11. Czechia is part of the Baltic sea's catchment area, mainly by way of the river Oder. Czechs also launched a satirical campaign to reclaim Kaliningrad, which had originally been named Královec in honour of the Bohemian king Ottakar II. Even the interior ministry and weather forecasters on national television took part. See 'Královec. How the Czech Republic Retakes the City of Kaliningrad', Ukraïner.net, 17 November 2022.
12. Veronika Melkozerova, 'Czechs Raise Funds to Buy 800,000 Artillery Shells for Ukraine', *Politico*, 7 March 2024.
13. Daniel Goffart, Max Haerder and Sonja Álvarez, 'Die Lücken, die der Kanzler lässt', *WirtschaftsWoche*, 21 March 2024.
14. Stuart Lau and Rym Momtaz, 'China Downgrades Lithuania's Diplomatic Status Over Taiwan Row', *Politico*, 21 November 2021.
15. 'Lithuania Closes Embassy in China After Last Diplomats Leave Amid Taiwan Spat', AP, 16 December 2021.

16. For a detailed account of the trade war, see Wendy Cutler and Shay Wester, *Resilience & Resolve: Lessons from Lithuania's Experience with Chinese Economic Coercion*, Asia Society Policy Institute report, April 2024, pp. 7–17.
17. Joe Miller, Guy Chazan and Andy Bounds, 'German Business Hits Out at China After Lithuania Trade Row Snares Exports', *Financial Times*, 17 December 2021.
18. Stuart Lau, 'Slovenia to Bolster Trade Ties With Taiwan, Wading Into Row With China', *Politico*, 18 January 2022; and Priyanka Shankar, 'Why Are Baltics Skeptical of China Relations?', *Deutsche Welle*, 22 August 2022.
19. Cutler and Wester, *Resilience & Resolve*, pp. 11–12.
20. The very modest amount of Chinese investment in Lithuania also made this decision much easier for Vilnius than it would have been for some other European states such as Germany, which have a great deal more riding on their relations with Beijing
21. 'Lithuanian President Holds Private Meeting With Dalai Lama', 15min.lt, 9 November 2013. In the spring of 2024 Grybauskaitė made a trip of her own to Taiwan, where she met President Lai and said the two territories had an instinctive mutual understanding because of their similar geopolitical situations: 'Former Lithuanian President Dalia Grybauskaitė Visits Taiwan', Delfi, 23 May 2024.
22. Saulius Jakučionis (BNS), 'Police Investigate Vandalised Hong Kong Messages on Lithuania's Hill of Crosses', LRT, 31 December 2019.
23. Cutler and Wester, *Resilience & Resolve*, pp. 7–8.
24. Airport scanners: BNS, 'Lithuania Blocks Chinese Tech at Airports Over Security Concerns', LRT, 17 February 2021; drones: Karolis Broga, 'Drone Producers Will Phase Out Chinese Components This Summer – DefMin', Delfi, 24 May 2024.
25. Sabine Siebold, 'Lithuania Says EU Must Prepare for Risk of "De-coupling" From China', Reuters, 12 May 2023.
26. Republic of Lithuania's ministry of foreign affairs, *For a Secure, Resilient and Prosperous Future: Lithuania's Indo-Pacific Strategy* (July 2023), pp. 5–7.
27. Remarks by Jose W. Fernandez, US undersecretary of state for economic growth, energy and the environment, during a press conference at the Building Resilient Economy and Resisting Economic Coercion summit in Vilnius, 6 May 2024.

28. Ausra Park, 'Lithuania and Russia's Kaliningrad: Analysing the Most Recent "Crisis" That Shook the EU', Australian Institute of International Affairs, 11 August 2022.
29. 'Kaliningrad: Russia Warns Lithuania of Consequences Over Rail Transit Sanctions', BBC, 21 June 2022.
30. Tim Lister and Rob Picheta, 'Why Kaliningrad, Russia's Toehold in Europe, Could Be the Next Flashpoint in Its War Against Ukraine', CNN, 22 June 2022.
31. Quoted in Vaidotas Beniusis, Philipp Fritz and Pavel Lokshin, 'Deutsche Soldaten sind nicht hier, um die Kartoffelernte zu bewundern', *Welt*, 11 July 2022.
32. Quoted in ibid.
33. For an analysis that suggests the guidance was probably correct in a strictly legal sense, see Finn-Ole Albers, *The European Commission's Guidelines Regarding Transit Through Lithuania*, Warsaw Institute, 8 November 2022.
34. This account is drawn from Wolfgang Görtschacher and Laima Sruoginis, *Raw Amber – An Anthology of Contemporary Lithuanian Poetry* (Poetry Salzburg, 2002), pp. 14–18.
35. See e.g. Anatol Lieven, *The Baltic Revolution: Estonia, Latvia, Lithuania and the Path to Independence* (Yale University Press, 1994), p. 28.
36. Thomas Lane, 'Lithuania: Stepping Westward', in Thomas Lane et al., *The Baltic States: Estonia, Latvia and Lithuania* (Routledge, 2017), pp. xxiv–xxxi; and Andrejs Plakans, *A Concise History of the Baltic States* (Cambridge University Press, 2011), pp. 199–204.
37. Lane, 'Lithuania', p. xxx.
38. V. Stanley Vardys and Judith Sedaitis, *Lithuania: Rebel Nation* (Routledge, 2011), pp. 29–30.
39. John Hiden and Patrick Salmon, *The Baltic Nations and Europe: Estonia, Latvia and Lithuania in the Twentieth Century* (Longman, 1994), pp. 104–5.
40. Lithuania was originally assigned to the German sphere of influence but transferred to the Soviets through an amendment added to the non-aggression treaty a month later.
41. Neil Taylor, *Estonia: A Modern History* (Hurst, 2020), p. 80.
42. Yad Vashem, 'The Jews of Vilna Between the Two World Wars'.
43. Lane, 'Lithuania', p. 55.
44. Ibid., p. 154.
45. Quoted in Tomas Venclova, 'A Fifth Year of Independence: Lithuania, 1922 and 1994', in *East European Politics and Societies* (vol. 9, no. 2, 1995), p. 365.

46. Landsbergis was expected to leave office at the end of 2024 after his Homeland Union party had lost a parliamentary election that October.
47. Lane, 'Lithuania', pp. 64–7; and Dan Kaszeta, *The Forest Brotherhood: Baltic Resistance Against the Nazis and Soviets* (Hurst, 2023), pp. 131–3.
48. Nijolė Gaškaitė-Žemaitienė, 'The Partisan War in Lithuania from 1944 to 1953', in Arvydas Anušauskas (ed.), *The Anti-Soviet Resistance in the Baltic States* (Genocide and Resistance Research Centre of Lithuania, 2006), pp. 26–41.
49. Kaszeta, *Forest Brotherhood*, pp. 187–99. Dan Kaszeta notes that the scheme appears to have been the basis for another Le Carré novel, *The Secret Pilgrim*.
50. Dalia Kuodytė, 'The Contacts Between the Lithuanian Resistance and the West', in Anušauskas (ed.), *Anti-Soviet Resistance in the Baltic States*, pp. 82–3.
51. Vardys and Sedaitis, *Lithuania*, p. 73.
52. BNS, 'Lithuania Marks 81st Anniversary of Soviet Deportations', LRT, 14 June 2022.
53. V. Stanley Vardys, 'Soviet Social Engineering in Lithuania: An Appraisal', in V. Stanley Vardys (ed.), *Lithuania Under the Soviets: Portrait of a Nation 1940–65* (Frederick A. Praeger, 1965), p. 248.
54. Lane, 'Lithuania', pp. 71–3.
55. Vardys, *Soviet Social Engineering in Lithuania*, p. 251.
56. Purs, *Baltic Facades*, p. 80.
57. Lane, 'Lithuania', p. 91.
58. Görtschacher and Sruoginis, *Raw Amber*, pp. 73–85.
59. Vardys and Sedaitis, *Lithuania*, p. 140.
60. Ibid., pp. 104–5.
61. David Lidington, 'The Contemporary Political Dimension', in Charles Clarke (ed.), *Understanding the Baltic States: Estonia, Latvia and Lithuania Since 1991* (Hurst, 2023), pp. 214–15.
62. Document 68, 'Aufzeichnung des Vortragenden Legationsrats Stüdemann', 12 March 1990, in *Akten zur Außenpolitik der Bundesrepublik Deutschland: 1990, 1. Januar bis 30. Juni* (De Gruyter, 2021), pp. 280–4.
63. Vardys and Sedaitis, *Lithuania*, pp. 170–1.
64. Document 113, 'Gesandter Heinichen, Paris, an das Auswärtige Amt, 26.4.1990', in *Akten zur Außenpolitik der Bundesrepublik Deutschland: 1990, 1. Januar bis 30. Juni*, pp. 476–7.
65. Document 115, 'Gespräch des Bundesministers Genscher mit dem sowjetischen stellvertretenden Außenminister Karpow', 30 April 1991,

in *Akten zur Außenpolitik der Bundesrepublik Deutschland: 1991, 1. Januar bis 30. Juni* (De Gruyter, 2022), pp. 481–6.
66. Document 134, 'Gespräch des Bundesministers Genscher mit der litauischen Ministerpräsidentin Prunskiene', 11 June 1990, in *Akten zur Außenpolitik der Bundesrepublik Deutschland: 1990, 1. Januar bis 30. Juni*, pp. 577–81.
67. Document 372, 'Gespräch des Bundeskanzlers Kohl mit dem sowjetischen Präsidenten Gorbatschow', 9 November 1990, in *Akten zur Außenpolitik der Bundesrepublik Deutschland: 1990, 1. Juli bis 31. Dezember* (De Gruyter, 2021), pp. 1546–59.
68. Vardys and Sedaitis, *Lithuania*, p. 172.
69. Lieven, *Baltic Revolution*, pp. 246–53.
70. This view was privately expressed not only by the US, Britain and Germany but also by Algirdas Saugardas, the Lithuanian foreign minister. See Document 125, 'Vermerk des Vortragenden Legationsrats Adam', 11 April 1991, in *Akten zur Außenpolitik der Bundesrepublik Deutschland: 1991, 1. Januar bis 30. Juni*, pp. 501–5.
71. Document 57, 'Gespräch des Bundeskanzlers Kohl mit dem französischen Staatspräsidenten Mitterrand in Paris', 15 February 1991, in ibid., pp. 213–18.
72. Jelena Ćirić, 'Lithuanians Send Iceland 30 Thank Yous on 30th Anniversary of Independence Recognition', *Iceland Review*, 11 February 2021.
73. Hiden and Salmon, *The Baltic Nations and Europe*, p. 208.
74. The obvious counter-argument here (and one frequently made at the time) is to contend that the states trapped between Nazi Germany and the USSR would have been indefensible anyway. I am not sure that this is true. As John Hiden and Patrick Salmon (*The Baltic Nations and Europe*, pp. 64–5) have pointed out, a Baltic defensive alliance could have called on up to 500,000 men under arms, many of them with recent combat experience. Poland had beaten back the Red Army in 1920 and even in the late 1930s was in a position to seriously contemplate undertaking a pre-emptive attack on Nazi Germany in concert with France. Collectively, these countries could have mustered a very credible level of deterrence with or without western military support. The diplomatic obstacles to building such an alliance – not least the Vilnius question and the reconciliation of Poland and Lithuania – were certainly formidable. But if Britain and France had really put some imaginative effort into banging heads together, it is conceivable that the French vision of an 'eastern

NOTES

Locarno' constellation could have been realised. The question is at any rate one of the most interesting 'what ifs' of interwar Europe.
75. Meri, *Botschaften und Zukunftsvisionen* (ed. and tr. Rajandi), p. 235.
76. Christopher Coker, 'The West and Russia: Another Front in the New Cold War?', in Dahl (ed.), *Strategic Challenges in the Baltic Sea Region: Russia, Deterrence and Reassurance* (Georgetown University Press, 2018), pp. 53–4.
77. See e.g. Emmanuel Macron and Olaf Scholz, 'Macron and Scholz: We Must Strengthen European Sovereignty', *Financial Times*, 27 May 2024.
78. For a pithy analysis, see e.g. 'Charlemagne: Ukraine's European Allies Are Either Broke, Small or Irresolute', *The Economist*, 21 March 2024.
79. World Bank, 'GDP per capita (Current US$) – Latvia', comparison between 2003 and 2022.
80. Élysée, 'Closing Speech by the President of the French Republic', GLOBSEC summit in Bratislava, 31 May 2023. The 'missed opportunities' line was an allusion to Macron's predecessor Jacques Chirac, who had twenty years previously told the same countries they had 'missed an opportunity to keep your mouths shut' over the US-led invasion of Iraq.
81. Victor Goury-Laffont, 'Hawkish Macron Refuses to Back Down on Possibility of Western Troops in Ukraine', *Politico*, 14 March 2024.
82. Élysée, 'Europe Speech', delivered at the Sorbonne in Paris, 25 April 2024.
83. €2.69 billion from France, €2.74 billion from Sweden, €4.78 billion from Denmark: Kiel Institute for the World Economy, 'Ukraine Support Tracker', data from 29 February 2024.
84. Vivienne Machi, 'Macron Sends $438 Billion Military Budget Plan to French Parliament', *Defense News*, 4 April 2023; and Laura Kayali, 'France Will Reach NATO Defense Spending Target in 2024', *Politico*, 15 February 2024.
85. Vardys and Sedaitis, *Lithuania*, p. 50.

Chapter 8: Imperium of Hopelessness

1. Viktor Jerofejew (Victor Erofeyev), *Der große Gopnik* (Matthes & Seitz, 2023), p. 595.
2. See e.g. Alex Ward, 'NATO Troops Say Russia Is Hacking Their

Smartphones', Vox, 4 October 2017; and Charlie Parker, 'Russia Targets British Soldiers' Mobile Phones', *The Times*, 12 May 2024.
3. Eva Mathews, 'China Suspected in Hack of Journalists at News Corp', Reuters, 5 February 2022.
4. See Mikhail Polianskii, 'Russian Foreign Policy Research and War in Ukraine: Old Answers to New Questions?', *Communist and Post-Communist Studies* (vol. 57, no. 2, 2024), pp. 156–72.
5. Mark Galeotti, *Putin's Wars: From Chechnya to Ukraine* (Osprey, 2024), p. 107.
6. See Oliver Moody, 'I Didn't Leave Russia – It Left Me, Says Dissident in Berlin', *The Times*, 29 March 2024.
7. It is well worth reading my colleague Guy Chazan's interview with Ulitskaya about her own experience of exile in Berlin: 'Writer Ludmila Ulitskaya: "In 50 Years, Every Town in Russia Will Have a Navalny Square"', *Financial Times*, 20 February 2024.
8. See Oliver Moody, 'I Didn't Leave Russia – It Left Me, Says Dissident in Berlin', *The Times*, 29 March 2024.
9. Jerofejew (Erofeyev), *Der große Gopnik*, pp. 256 and 286.
10. Catherine Belton, *Putin's People: How the KGB Took Back Russia and Then Took on the West* (William Collins, 2020), pp. 108–9 and 256.
11. See Fiona Hill and Clifford G. Gaddy, *Mr Putin: Operative in the Kremlin* (Brookings Institution Press, 2015), pp. 76–7 and 367.
12. Eric Christiansen, *The Northern Crusades* (Penguin, 1997), p. 35.
13. Jonathan L'Hommedieu, 'History', in Bernd Henningsen, Tobias Etzold and Krister Hanne (eds), *The Baltic Sea Region: A Comprehensive Guide – History, Politics, Culture and Economy of a European Role Model* (Berliner Wissenschafts-Verlag, 2017), p. 63; and David Kirby, *Northern Europe in the Early Modern Period: The Baltic World 1492–1772* (Longman, 1993), p. 119.
14. Adam Zamoyski, *Poland: A History* (HarperPress, 2009), pp. 122 and 403.
15. Anya Free and Julia Khrebtan-Hörhager, 'Alexander Nevsky of Russia, Reanimated and Repurposed', Woodrow Wilson International Center for Scholars, Kennan Institute Russia File blog, 27 October 2022.
16. Andrew Roth, 'Putin Compares Himself to Peter the Great in Quest to Take Back Russian Lands', *Guardian*, 10 June 2022.
17. Robert K. Massie, *Peter the Great: His Life and World* (Cardinal, 1990), p. 303.

18. Ibid., p. 391.
19. Ibid., p. 389.
20. He comes pretty close to blaming the West, too: 'If Europe ignored Russia's concerns about Russian minority populations outside of our borders, then the Russian neo-imperialists and anti-western hardliners would gain increasing political support at home for unilateral actions against our new neighbours under the pretext of defending our compatriots.' From Andrei Kozyrev, *The Firebird: The Elusive Fate of Russian Democracy* (University of Pittsburgh Press, 2020), p. 128.
21. Daunis Auers, *Comparative Politics and Government of the Baltic States: Estonia, Latvia and Lithuania in the 21st Century* (Palgrave Macmillan, 2015), p. 199.
22. Agnia Grigas, *Beyond Crimea: The New Russian Empire* (Yale University Press, 2016), p. 163.
23. George Grylls, 'Russian Academic Who Called for Nuclear Strike on EU Hired by Putin', *The Times*, 5 May 2024.
24. Grigas, *Beyond Crimea*, p. 76. Kozyrev was so alarmed by the support Karaganov's revanchist arguments were gaining in the Russian elite that he decided to expose them to the West through a bizarre piece of theatre. In December 1992 he used a speech at a diplomatic summit in Stockholm to pass off Karaganov's ideas as official Russian policy. Kozyrev described the former Soviet republics as a 'post-imperial space, in which Russia has to defend its interests using all available means, including military and economic ones'. The Germans, the Ukrainians and the Baltic states lodged furious protests and Russia's ambassador to Sweden resigned on the spot. Kozyrev then made a second speech where he explained that these were merely the views of his influential enemies in Moscow, and a 'pale simulacrum of the U-turn in strategy that the real opposition would make if it seized power'. This proved to be all too accurate. See Andrei Kozyrev, *The Firebird*, pp. 174–8.
25. Grigas, *Beyond Crimea*, pp. 31–2 and 148–9.
26. Ibid., pp. 154–5.
27. 'Levada Poll: Russians Consider Baltic Countries a Threat', ERR, 25 January 2023.
28. Marko Lehti, Matti Jutila and Markku Jokisipilä, 'Never-Ending Second World War: Public Performances of National Dignity and the Drama of the Bronze Soldier', in Jörg Hackmann and Marko Lehti (eds), *Contested and Shared Places of Memory: History and Politics in North Eastern Europe* (Routledge, 2009), pp. 25–6.

29. Keir Giles, *Moscow Rules: What Drives Russia to Confront the West?* (Brookings Institution Press, 2019), pp. 120–1.
30. Gudrun Persson, 'Russia and Baltic Sea Security: A Background', in Dahl (ed.), *Strategic Challenges in the Baltic Sea Region: Russia, Deterrence and Reassurance* (Georgetown University Press, 2018), p. 23.
31. Max Seddon and Richard Milne, 'Russia Puts Estonia's Prime Minister on Wanted List', *Financial Times*, 13 February 2024.
32. The phrase was coined by the British researcher Mark Galeotti, who later complained that it had taken on a 'destructive life of its own'.
33. See e.g. Ofer Fridman, *Russian 'Hybrid Warfare' – Resurgence and Politicisation* (Hurst, 2022), p. 7.
34. Ibid., pp. 49–52.
35. Ibid., p. 58.
36. Oscar Jonsson, *The Russian Understanding of War: Blurring the Lines Between War and Peace* (Georgetown University Press, 2019), p. 40.
37. Ibid., p. 59.
38. Jonsson, *The Russian Understanding of War*, pp. 73–5.
39. A few days after our interview, Kariņš was obliged to resign after an investigation concluded that his chancellery had spent too much money on unnecessary private jet flights while he was prime minister.
40. Jurga Bakaitė and Vilius Narkūnas, 'Up to 300,000 Lithuanian Citizens May Live in Russian Disinformation Field – Study', LRT, 23 January 2024.
41. Aliide Naylor, *The Shadow in the East: Vladimir Putin and the New Baltic Front* (I. B. Tauris, 2020), pp. 52–3.
42. Ukraine War Disinformation Working Group interim report, 'Over a Third of Kremlin War Propaganda Has Centred on Battlefield Developments', Debunk.org, 16 December 2022.
43. Ukraine War Disinformation Working Group, 'How Kremlin Propagandists Have Used Soviet Monument Demolitions to Spin Claims of Russophobia', Debunk.org, 19 January 2023.
44. Lisbeth Quass, Frederik Hugo Ledegaard Thim and Niels Fastrup, 'Stort netværk i Norden spreder disinformation: Rusland kører propaganda ud 'med stor kraft', Danmarks Radio, 17 May 2024.
45. Eddy Wax, Elisa Braun and Clothilde Goujard, '"I Hope Ukraine Will Lose": What MEPs Told Russian Propaganda Channel', *Politico*, 11 April 2024.
46. Maik Baumgärtner et al., 'Verdächtiges Internetportal "Voice of

Europe"': Europäische Politiker sollen Hunderttausende Euro aus Russland bekommen haben', *Der Spiegel*, 27 March 2024.
47. 'Stor ökning av AI-nyhetssajter – så används de för att sprida rysk desinformation', SVT, 5 April 2024.
48. Inga Spriņģe and Re:Baltica, 'Pro-Kremlin "Bots" Are Starting to Speak Latvian', LSM, 12 March 2024.
49. Fiona Hill and Clifford G. Gaddy, *Mr Putin: Operative in the Kremlin* (Brookings Institution Press, 2015), pp. 281–2; and Reinhard Bingener and Markus Wehner, *Die Moskau-Connection: Das Schröder-Netzwerk und Deutschlands Weg in die Abhängigkeit* (C. H. Beck, 2023), p. 187.
50. Michael Weiss and Holger Roonemaa, 'The Kremlin's Latest Bait in the Baltics: Immanuel Kant', *The Insider*, 6 April 2024. It seems, however, that only a handful of the Germans on the invitation list actually attended the conference: see Mindaugas Aušra, Indrė Makaraitytė and Jurga Tvaskienė, 'Western Scholars Play Kremlin's Game at Immanuel Kant Congress – LRT Investigation', LRT, 8 May 2024.
51. Franca König and Sandra Lukosek, 'Putins langer Arm: russische Einflussnahme über rechtsextreme Netzwerke in Deutschland und Europa', in Felix Neumann (ed.), *Russlands Einflussnahme auf die deutsche innere Sicherheit*, Konrad-Adenauer-Stiftung, 6 February 2024, p. 71.
52. See e.g. Christian Fuchs et al., 'AfD und Russland: 20.000 Euro, Übergabe in Prag', *Die Zeit*, 4 April 2024; and 'Germany: AfD's Krah Faces Probe on Russia, China "Payments"', Deutsche Welle, 24 April 2024.
53. Lisbeth Quass and Niels Fastrup, 'Hemmelig operation afsløret: Russisk spionfond har betalt millionbeløb for kampagner i Danmark og EU', Danmarks Radio, 2 June 2024; see also Andrew Roth, 'Revealed: Russian Legal Foundation Linked to Kremlin Activities in Europe', *Guardian*, 2 June 2024.
54. 'Rosyjski szpieg wśród polskich polityków. Rusza proces', TVP Info, 11 May 2024.
55. See 'French Fighter Jets Join the Baltic Mission', *The Economist*, 3 December 2023.
56. Basil Germond, 'The Maritime Geopolitics of the Baltic Sea', in Charles Clarke (ed.), *Understanding the Baltic States: Estonia, Latvia and Lithuania Since 1991* (Hurst, 2023), p. 298.
57. Loviisa: Finland: 'Four Russian Jets Violated Airspace, Not One', Yle,

15 June 2024; Gotland: Ossi Carp, 'Ryskt stridsflygplan kränkte svenskt luftrum', *Dagens Nyheter*, 15 June 2024.

58. Essi Lehto, 'Finland Extends Russia Border Closure Indefinitely', Reuters, 4 April 2024.

59. 'Russia Sets Up Missile Brigade in Karelia in "Adequate Response" to Finland Joining NATO', Yle, 22 April 2024.

60. Jarmo Huhtanen, 'Huipputarkka satelliittikuva näyttää, miten Venäjä keskittää strategisia pommittajia Suomen rajan tuntumaan', *Helsingin Sanomat*, 31 March 2024.

61. Estonian foreign intelligence service, *International Security and Estonia 2024*, 14 February 2024, p. 17.

62. Anastazja Mogilewiec, 'Rosja marzy o kontrolowaniu Gotlandii. To wyspa na Morzu Bałtyckim blisko Polski. "Oczy Putina są na nią skierowane"', Onet, 27 May 2024.

63. 'Ålänningarna delade om ryska utspelet: "Är faktiskt jätterädd"', *Dagens Nyheter*, 24 May 2024.

64. 'Russian Border Guards Remove Markers From Estonian Waters in Narva River', ERR, 23 May 2024.

65. For an analysis of the episode in a broader context, see Elisabeth Braw, 'Missing Baltic Buoys Mark Out Maritime Border Faultlines', *Financial Times*, 26 May 2024.

66. Zelensky: Daria Tarasova Markina et al., 'Polish Man Charged in Connection With Alleged Russian Plot to Kill Ukraine Leader Zelensky', CNN, 19 April 2024; Volkov: 'Two Held in Poland Over March Attack on Navalny Aide Volkov', Reuters, 19 April 2024.

67. Karolina Jeznach, Thomas Grove and Bojan Pancevski, 'The Misfits Russia Is Recruiting to Spy on the West', *Wall Street Journal*, 15 May 2024. See also 'Podpalenia na zlecenie rosyjskich służb. Zarzuty działania na rzecz obcego wywiadu', TVP, 29 May 2024.

68. Vilnius and Warsaw: Jurga Bakaitė and Evelina Knutovič, 'Who Is Behind "Sabotages and Diversions" in Lithuania and Poland?', LRT, 23 May 2024; Estonia: 'ISS: Russian Special Services Behind Attack on Estonian Minister's Car', ERR, 20 February 2024.

69. Alice Hancock, 'Russia Is Trying to Sabotage European Railways, Warns Prague', *Financial Times*, 5 April 2024.

70. Sam Jones, John Rathbone and Richard Milne, 'Russia Plotting Sabotage Across Europe, Intelligence Agencies Warn', *Financial Times*, 5 April 2024.

71. Michael Götschenberg and Holger Schmidt, 'Zwei Deutschrussen

festgenommen: Ermittlungen zu Sabotageplänen in Deutschland', *Tagesschau*, 18 April 2024.
72. John Paul Rathbone, Henry Foy and Raphael Minder, 'West Grapples With Response to Russian Sabotage Attempts', *Financial Times*, 4 June 2024.
73. Samuli Niinivuo, 'Suojelupoliisi: Sabotaasin uhka on tiedossa, eikä Venäjä välitä tekojensa seurauksista', *Helsingin Sanomat*, 5 May 2024.
74. See Tom Ball et al., 'Killing, Coups and Chaos: Inside Putin's Secret Spy War on Europe', *The Times*, 28 June 2024.
75. LETA, 'BRELL Disconnection: Baltic States Prepare for Russian Provocations', Baltic News Network, 27 May 2024.
76. Katie Bo Lillis, Natasha Bertrand and Frederik Pleitgen, 'Exclusive: US and Germany Foiled Russian Plot to Assassinate CEO of Arms Manufacturer Sending Weapons to Ukraine', CNN, 11 July 2024.
77. The German military is reported to have simulated a scenario along these lines with Kaliningrad as its focus: Julian Röpcke and Georgios Xanthopoulos, 'Bundeswehr bereitet sich auf Putin-Angriff vor', *Bild*, 16 January 2024.
78. Meelis Oidsalu, 'Estonia Excels in Waging Hybrid Warfare Against Russia', *Postimees*, 21 May 2024.
79. See Oliver Moody, 'Nafo, Not Nato, Take the Fight to Russia's Internet Trolls', *The Times*, 17 July 2023.
80. See Max Seddon, Polina Ivanova and Henry Foy, 'Vladimir Putin Revamps Russia's Creaking War Machine', *Financial Times*, 14 May 2024.
81. Pavel Baev, *Russia's New Challenges in the Baltic/Northern European Theater*, Institut français des relations internationales, *Russia.Eurasie. Visions* (no. 130, November 2023), p. 3.
82. Mark Galeotti, *We Need to Talk About Putin: How the West Gets Him Wrong* (Ebury, 2019), p. 38.
83. Galeotti, *Putin's Wars*, pp. 52–6.
84. Interestingly, this analysis was shared by Oleg Gordievsky, the Cold War-era KGB colonel who famously defected to MI6 in 1974. In the 1990s Gordievsky said: 'From a psychological view, the Baltic states are regarded as the former Soviet Union. The fact that they have turned so completely away from Russia and exercised fully independent policies clearly provokes Moscow's anger . . . For Russian chauvinists, [the possibility of the Baltic states' NATO accession] is a blow below

the belt.' See Daunis Auers, *Comparative Politics and Government of the Baltic States*, p. 74.
85. Ron Fournier, 'Why Putin Plays Our Presidents for Fools', *The Atlantic*, 2 March 2014.
86. INFER Public, 'Will Russia Invade Estonia, Latvia, and/or Lithuania Before 1 April 2027?' (accessed 20 June 2024).

Chapter 9: Peace Through Superior Firepower

1. Thomas Hobbes, *Leviathan or The Matter, Forme and Power of a Commonwealth Ecclesiasticall and Civil* (1651), ch. 17.2.
2. Anatol Lieven, *The Baltic Revolution: Estonia, Latvia, Lithuania and the Path to Independence* (Yale University Press, 1994), p. 320.
3. David A. Shaplak and Michael W. Johnson, *Reinforcing Deterrence on NATO's Eastern Flank: Wargaming the Defence of the Baltics* (RAND Corporation, 2015), pp. 4–8.
4. General Sir Richard Shirreff, *War With Russia* (Quercus, 2016), p. 113.
5. John R. Allen, Frederick Ben Hodges and Julian Lindley-French, *Future War and the Defence of Europe* (Oxford University Press, 2021), pp. 1–20.
6. Joakim Ekman and Mai-Brith Schartau, 'Politics', in Bernd Henningsen, Tobias Etzold and Krister Hanne (eds), *The Baltic Sea Region: A Comprehensive Guide – History, Politics, Culture and Economy of a European Role Model* (Berliner Wissenschafts-Verlag, 2017), p. 159.
7. See Oliver Moody, 'NATO Prepares for Putin Blitzkrieg in the Baltics', *The Times*, 19 January 2024.
8. For a map of the main transport nodes in and out of Germany, see Jannik Hartmann, *Military Mobility: Getting Germany's Transportation Infrastructure Up to Speed* (German Council on Foreign Relations, 2024), p. 3.
9. Keir Giles, *Russia's 'New' Tools for Confronting the West: Continuity and Innovation in Moscow's Exercise of Power*, Chatham House research paper (2016), pp. 25–6.
10. Sabine Siebold, 'NATO Urges Common Standards and Curbs on Protectionism to Boost Artillery Output', Reuters, 24 November 2023.
11. Shirreff, *War With Russia*, pp. 287–8.

NOTES

12. Territorial defence panel at the Berlin security conference, 29 November 2023.
13. See Oliver Moody, 'Europe's Muddled Armed Forces "Could Be Washed Away by Russia"', *The Times*, 30 November 2023.
14. NATO, *Vilnius Summit Communiqué*, 11 July 2023, item one.
15. NATO, *NATO Response Force*, 27 July 2023.
16. NATO, *NATO Readiness Initiative*, 7 June 2018.
17. See e.g. NATO, *New NATO Force Model*, 22 June 2022.
18. Jack Watling, *The Arms of the Future: Technology and Close Combat in the Twenty-First Century* (Bloomsbury Academic, 2023), p. 161.
19. Allen, Hodges and Lindley-French, *Future War*, pp. 195 and 204–5.
20. 'Present at the Destruction: Can Europe Defend Itself Without America?', *The Economist*, 18 February 2024.
21. Matthias Gebauer and Konstantin von Hammerstein, 'Zeitenwende bei der Bundeswehr: Heerjemine – wie schlimm es um die Truppe wirklich steht', *Der Spiegel*, 13 January 2023.
22. Karina Mössbauer, 'Brandbrief zum Zustand der Armee: Das nächste Bundeswehr-Debakel', Bild, 11 April 2023.
23. UK Parliament, Ben Wallace, giving evidence to the House of Lords international relations and defence committee inquiry 'Defence Concepts and Capabilities: From Aspiration to Reality', 1 November 2022.
24. See e.g. Michaela Wiegel, 'Macron und die Armee: Ist Frankreich bereit für den Krieg?', *Frankfurter Allgemeine Zeitung*, 20 March 2024.
25. See e.g. Marek Kutarba, 'Ile dywizji Polska wystawiłaby dziś na wojnę z Rosją', *Rzeczpospolita*, 30 May 2024.
26. John Spellar, MP and former defence minister, speaking in a House of Commons debate on defence: UK Parliament, *Hansard* (vol. 749), 7 May 2024.
27. House of Commons defence committee, *Ready for War? First Report of Session 2023–2024*, 30 January 2024, p. 28.
28. Stockholm International Peace Research Institute, 'Global Military Spending Surges Amid War, Rising Tensions and Insecurity', 22 April 2024.
29. Watling, *Arms of the Future*, p. 8.
30. The figures were estimated by the management consultancy Bain & Company: Deborah Haynes, 'Russia Is Producing Artillery Shells Around Three Times Faster Than Ukraine's Western Allies and For About a Quarter of the Cost', Sky News, 26 May 2024.

31. See e.g. 'Military-Industrial Bottlenecks: There Is an Explosive Flaw in the Plan to Rearm Ukraine', *The Economist*, 26 May 2024.
32. Mark Galeotti, *Putin's Wars: From Chechnya to Ukraine* (Osprey, 2024), p. 260.
33. Territorial defence panel at the Berlin security conference, 29 November 2023.
34. Michael Kofman et al., *Russian Military Strategy: Core Tenets and Operational Concepts* (Center for Naval Analyses, 2021), pp. 54–61.
35. See Oliver Moody, 'NATO's Frontline Nations Are Digging 1,000 Bunkers. Will It Deter Putin?', *The Times*, 14 February 2024.
36. Daniel Tilles, 'Poland Unveils Details of €2.4bn Fortification of Eastern Borders', Notes from Poland, 27 May 2024.
37. Alexandra Clobes, Oliver Morwinsky and Fausta Šimaitytė, *Länderbericht: Baltische Bastionen: Neue Verteidigungsstrategien für Litauen, Lettland und Estland*, Konrad-Adenauer-Stiftung (2024), pp. 3-4; supplemented with Republic of Estonia Defence Forces, 'Estonian Defence Forces' and with NATO, SHAPE, 'Lithuania'.
38. Government of Canada, 'Roadmap – Scaling the EFP Latvia Battle Group to Brigade', 10 July 2023.
39. UK ministry of defence, 'Joint Statement Between the UK MOD and the Estonian MOD', 8 November 2022.
40. Radu Tudor, 'Generalul Hodges: Cred că singura cale de a face față Rusiei este forța. Ideea de a negocia cu ei este ridicolă', CNN Romania, 27 May 2024.
41. Maciej Kałach, 'Polska zostanie kompletnie sama na dwa tygodnie? Jakie wsparcie dostaniemy od NATO w razie ataku', Onet, 29 May 2024.
42. See e.g. Benjamin Jensen and John Paschkewitz, 'Mosaic Warfare: Small and Scalable are Beautiful', War on the Rocks blog, 23 December 2019.
43. Alex Vershinin, 'Feeding the Bear: A Closer Look at Russian Army Logistics and the Fait Accompli', War on the Rocks blog, 23 November 2021.
44. For a detailed analysis, see Roger Näbig, *Logistik: Russlands militärische Achillesferse in der Ukraine*, Konflikte & Sicherheit blog, 6 October 2023.
45. Keir Giles, *Russia's War on Everybody and What it Means for You* (Bloomsbury Academic, 2023), pp. 122–4.
46. Julian E. Barnes, 'Closing the Gap: NATO Moves to Protect

Weak Link in Defenses Against Russia', *Wall Street Journal*, 17 June 2016.

47. For a handy overview of the geography and its tactical implications, see Leszek Elak and Zdzisław Śliwa, 'The Suwalki Gap – NATO's Fragile Hotspot', *Zeszyty Naukowe AON* (vol. 103, no. 2, 2016), pp. 30–5.

Chapter 10: The Battle for the Baltic

1. Speech at the RUSI land warfare conference in London. Published as 'Russo-Ukrainian War as a War of Transition', Ukrainska Pravda, 22 July 2024.
2. Lauri Nurmi, 'Viron puolustusministeri Iltalehdelle: Suomen ja Viron ohjuksilla luodaan Suomenlahdelle Nato-sulku', *Iltalehti*, 12 August 2022. See also Robin Häggblom, 'Finnish-Estonian Cooperation Turning Baltic Sea into a NATO-Lake', Naval News, 25 August 2022.
3. See e.g. 'President: Baltic Sea Should Be Closed If Russia Is Behind Balticconnector Case', LSM, 20 October 2023.
4. For a lucid analysis of its capabilities, see Basil Germond, 'The Maritime Geopolitics of the Baltic Sea', in Charles Clarke (ed.), *Understanding the Baltic States: Estonia, Latvia and Lithuania Since 1991* (Hurst, 2023), pp. 298–9.
5. Sam Joiner et al., 'How Ukraine Broke Russia's Grip in the Black Sea', *Financial Times*, 2 May 2024.
6. See e.g. Robert Dalsjö, Christofer Berglund and Michael Jonsson, *Bursting the Bubble? Russian A2/AD in the Baltic Sea Region: Capabilities, Countermeasures, and Implications* (Swedish defence research agency, 2019).
7. US government, TRADOC, Operational Environment Data Integration Network, '3M54T (SS-N-27 Sizzler) Russian Medium-Range Anti-Ship Cruise Missile'.
8. Center for Strategic and International Studies Missile Threat project, '3M-54 Kalibr/Club (SS-N-27)'.
9. Fleet losses: Chris Gordon, 'Russian Air Force Has Only Lost 10 Percent of Fleet in Ukraine, US Officials Say', *Air & Space Forces* magazine, 10 April 2024; tactics: Douglas Barrie and Giorgio di Mizio, 'Moscow's Aerospace Forces: No Air of Superiority', International Institute for Strategic Studies Military Balance blog, 7 February 2024.

10. Scott Kindsvater, 'Russian Air Force Report Card: Dismal, Could Do Better', Centre for European Policy Analysis, 6 March 2024.
11. Keir Giles, *Russia's 'New' Tools for Confronting the West: Continuity and Innovation in Moscow's Exercise of Power*, Chatham House research paper (2016), p. 56.
12. Justin Bronk, 'Is the Russian Air Force Actually Incapable of Complex Air Operations?', RUSI blog, 4 March 2022.
13. Michael Bohnert, 'The Russian Air Force Is Hollowing Itself Out. Air Defenses for Ukraine Would Speed That Up', RAND Corporation commentary.
14. Ryan Bauer, 'Russia's Su-57 Heavy Fighter Bomber: Is It Really a Fifth-Generation Aircraft?', RAND Corporation analysis.
15. Justin Bronk, 'Damaged Su-57 Emphasises the Vulnerability of Russian Airbases Near Ukraine', RUSI blog, 10 June 2024.
16. Bohnert, 'The Russian Air Force Is Hollowing Itself Out'.
17. Alexander H. Montgomery and Amy J. Nelson, 'Ukraine and the Kinzhal: Don't Believe the Hypersonic Hype', Brookings Institution, 23 May 2023.
18. IRIS-T: Diehl Defence, 'Second IRIS-T SLM Fire Unit Delivered to Ukraine', 25 May 2023; NASAMS: Brian Everstine, 'How Raytheon Rapidly Surged Air Defenses to Ukraine', Aviation Week, 16 November 2023.
19. David Axe, 'Ukraine's Nearly 50-Year-Old Gepards Are Still the Best Air-Defense Guns in the World', Forbes, 8 September 2023.
20. Sofiia Syngaivska, 'The UK Defense Intelligence: Russia May Need to Shift Air Defenses to Maintain Coverage Over Ukraine', Defense Express, 9 November 2023.
21. Stefan Korshak, 'ATACMS Comes Out on Top Versus Russia's S-500 Anti-Missile System', *Kyiv Post*, 24 June 2024; and see Maya Carlin, 'S-500: Russia's New Air Defense That Could Win a War Against NATO?', *National Interest*, 21 May 2024.
22. See e.g. Justin Bronk, *Russian and Chinese Combat Air Trends: Current Capabilities and Future Threat Outlook*, RUSI, Whitehall Report (no. 3-20, 2020), p. 59.
23. Matthew S. Galamison and Michael B. Petersen, 'Airpower Lessons for NATO from Ukraine: Failures of the Russian Aerospace Forces in Ukraine', *Air & Space Operations Review* (vol. 2, no. 3, 2023), p. 19.
24. Jack Watling, *The Arms of the Future: Technology and Close Combat in the*

Twenty-First Century (Bloomsbury Academic, 2023), pp. 180–3 and 204–5.
25. Henry Foy and John Paul Rathbone, 'NATO Has Just 5% of Air Defences Needed to Protect Eastern Flank', *Financial Times*, 29 May 2024.
26. @auonsson, post on X/Twitter, 30 March 2024, 8.35 p.m., https://twitter.com/auonsson/status/1774173721185382667
27. Larisa Brown, 'Russia "Jams Signals" on RAF Plane Carrying Grant Shapps', *The Times*, 14 March 2024.
28. Rasmus Ekström and Eetu Halonen, 'Suomessa ilmoitettujen ilmailun gps-häiriöiden määrä räjähtänyt', *Helsingin Sanomat*, 10 May 2024.
29. Tommaso Lecca, 'Estonia Blames Russia for GPS Interference That Forces Finnair to Suspend Flights', *Politico*, 29 April 2024.
30. Richard Milne, 'Russian GPS Jamming Threatens Air Disaster, Warn Baltic Ministers', *Financial Times*, 28 April 2024.
31. 'Gps-bortfall i luften: En ny vardag för Europas piloter', SVT, 4 May 2024.
32. 'Russia Is Starting to Make Its Superiority in Electronic Warfare Count', *The Economist*, 23 November 2023.
33. Keir Giles, *Russia's War on Everybody and What it Means for You* (Bloomsbury Academic, 2023), p. 85.
34. Bryan Clark, 'The Fall and Rise of Russian Electronic Warfare', *IEEE Spectrum*, 30 July 2022.
35. Mark Galeotti, *Putin's Wars: From Chechnya to Ukraine* (Osprey, 2024), p. 197.
36. David Axe, '80 Seconds From Detection To Destruction: In Krynky, Russian Troops Have Just One Minute of Safety From Ukraine's Drones', Forbes, 29 November 2023.
37. Francis Farrell, 'Battle of Chasiv Yar Begins: On the Ground With Ukrainian Forces Defending City Key to Russia's Plans', *Kyiv Independent*, 3 May 2024.
38. 'Russia and Ukraine Are Filling the Sky With Drones', RUSI, 30 August 2023.
39. Watling, *Arms of the Future*, p. 20.
40. Ibid., p. 74.
41. David E. Sanger, *New Cold Wars: China's Rise, Russia's Invasion, and America's Struggle to Defend the West* (Crown, 2024), pp. 385–405.
42. Watling, *Arms of the Future*, pp. 24–7.
43. Christina Miller, 'Throwback Attack: BlackEnergy Attacks the

Ukrainian Power Grid', Industrial Cybersecurity Pulse, 11 November 2021.
44. 'The Cyberwar in Ukraine Is as Crucial as the Battle in the Trenches', *The Economist*, 20 March 2024.
45. See e.g. Allison Pytlak, 'False Alarms: Reflecting on the Role of Cyber Operations in the Russia–Ukraine War', Stimson Center, 22 February 2024.
46. Brad Dress, 'Musk Acknowledges He Turned Off Starlink Internet Access Last Year During Ukraine Attack on Russia Military', The Hill, 8 September 2023.
47. Tom Balforth, 'Exclusive: Russian Hackers Were Inside Ukraine Telecoms Giant for Months', Reuters, 5 January 2024.
48. Aliide Naylor, *The Shadow in the East: Vladimir Putin and the New Baltic Front* (I. B. Tauris, 2020), p. 49.
49. Jarno Liski, 'IL paljastaa: Supon tiedustelusta rikostutkinta – Venäjän operaatio iski Suomen vastavakoiluun', *Iltalehti*, 7 May 2024.
50. Oliver Moody, 'Russia "Very Likely" to Be Behind Hack of NATO Documents', *The Times*, 7 March 2024.
51. Kim Zetter, 'The Untold Story of the Boldest Supply-Chain Hack Ever', Wired, 2 May 2023.
52. 'A Stealth Attack Came Close to Compromising the World's Computers', *The Economist*, 2 April 2024.
53. Eva Wolfangel, 'Bundeswehr: Jeder konnte sie finden', Zeit Online, 4 May 2024.
54. Carlo Masala, *Bedingt abwehrbereit: Deutschlands Schwäche in der Zeitenwende* (C. H. Beck, 2023), p. 19.
55. Gregory Weaver, 'The Urgent Imperative to Maintain NATO's Nuclear Deterrence', *NATO Review*, 29 September 2023.
56. Gudrun Persson, 'Russia and Baltic Sea Security: A Background', in Dahl (ed.), *Strategic Challenges in the Baltic Sea Region: Russia, Deterrence and Reassurance* (Georgetown University Press, 2018), p. 25.
57. See Gideon Rachman, 'Russia's Nuclear Threats Are Losing Their Power', *Financial Times*, 3 May 2024.
58. Hans M. Kristensen et al., 'Russian Nuclear Weapons, 2024', *Bulletin of the Atomic Scientists*, 7 March 2024.
59. Arms Control Association, '2023 Estimated Global Warhead Inventories'. Britain's nuclear deterrent can only be launched from its Trident submarines, only one of which is usually at sea. Since the first launch would risk giving away the submarine's location and exposing

it to a missile or torpedo strike, some analysts worry that in the worst-case scenario the UK might have only a single roll of the dice. France, by contrast, has both submarine and air-launched nuclear systems but possesses no lower-yield 'tactical' warheads, meaning that its only option is to deploy a larger 'strategic' one, which could be a prohibitively escalatory step. Paris also retains national control over its nuclear deterrent, leaving a question mark over whether it would necessarily use it to defend an ally.

60. Guy Chazan, John Paul Rathbone and Sam Jones, 'Russian Victories Shake Global Leaders' Faith in Ukraine War Prospects', *Financial Times*, 18 February 2024.
61. NATO, 'Defence Expenditures and NATO's 2% Guideline', 18 June 2024.
62. 'Present at the Destruction: Can Europe Defend Itself Without America?', *The Economist*, 18 February 2024.

Epilogue

1. Czesław Miłosz, *Beginning with My Streets: Essays and Recollections* (Farrar, Straus and Giroux, 2010, tr. Madeline G. Levine), p. 39.
2. See Bernd Henningsen, Tobias Etzold and Krister Hanne (eds), *The Baltic Sea Region: A Comprehensive Guide – History, Politics, Culture and Economy of a European Role Model* (Berliner Wissenschafts-Verlag, 2017), pp. 43 and 301.
3. Kazimierz Musiał and Damian Szacawa, 'Changing the Regional Identity of the Baltic Sea Region', in Damian Szacawa and Kazimierz Musiał (eds), *The Baltic Sea Region After Russia's Invasion of Ukraine*, Lubin Institute of Central Europe, policy papers (2022), pp. 22–3.
4. Zsolt Darvas, 'The European Union's Remarkable Growth Performance Relative to the United States', Bruegel, 26 October 2023.
5. See e.g. Antonia Zimmermann, 'Industry Bosses to EU: Help Us Level Up in the Global Green Tech Race', *Politico*, 22 April 2024; and Thomas Moller-Nielsen, 'The Elusive Question of What Can Save Europe From Deindustrialisation', Euractiv, 22 March 2024.
6. Valentina Romei and Arjun Neil Alim, 'Has Europe Already Reached Its Demographic Tipping Point?', *Financial Times*, 24 May 2024.
7. Élysée, 'Europe Speech', delivered at the Sorbonne in Paris, 25 April 2024.

8. Kaarel Piirimäe, '"Geopolitics of Sympathy": George F. Kennan and NATO Enlargement', *Diplomacy & Statecraft* (vol. 35, no. 1), pp. 190–3.
9. George F Kennan, 'A Fateful Error', *New York Times*, 5 February 1997.
10. 'X' (George F. Kennan), 'The Sources of Soviet Conduct', *Foreign Affairs*, 1 July 1947.
11. Richard Milne and Henry Foy, 'Europe Should Talk Less and Prepare More Against Russian Threat, Says Finnish President', *Financial Times*, 11 April 2024. See also Hilla Körkkö and Helmi Muhonen, '"Valmistaudu sotaan, sillä silloin sitä ei tapahdu" – Presidentti Stubb rauhoitteli ruotsalaisia', *Helsingin Sanomat*, 17 April 2024.
12. The 14,000 figure comes from Michael North, *The Baltic: A History* (Harvard University Press, 2015, tr. Kenneth Kronenberg), p. 300.
13. Ibid., p. 67.
14. Øresundsbro Konsortiet, *The Øresund Bridge and its Region: 18 Years* (2018), p. 5.
15. David Margolick, 'Crossing the Oresund', *New York Times* magazine, 10 September 2000.
16. David Arter, *Scandinavian Politics Today* (Manchester University Press, 2015), p. 309.
17. Benjamin Tallis, 'The New Idealism', in Benjamin Tallis, *To Ukraine With Love: Essays on Russia's War and Europe's Future* (self-published, 2022), p. 147.
18. Benjamin Tallis, 'Neo-Idealism: Grand Strategy for the Transatlantic Community', Macdonald-Laurier Institute, 18 July 2024.
19. Ministry of foreign affairs of the Republic of Latvia, 'Intervention by His Excellency Mr Artis Pabriks, Latvian Foreign Minister and the CBSS Chairman at the 16th Baltic Sea Parliamentary Conference', 2 December 2014.
20. Speech at Hertie School in Berlin, 8 May 2024. Survey data from 'Poll: Citizens' Willingness to Defend Finland, Support for NATO Hit All Time High', Yle, 3 December 2022.
21. Quoted in Jan Zielonka, *Counter-Revolution: Liberal Europe in Retreat* (Oxford University Press, 2018), p. 35.
22. Lennart Meri, *Botschaften und Zukunftsvisionen: Reden des estnischen Präsidenten* (Bouvier, 1999, ed. and tr. Henno Rajandi), p. 82.

Index

Adamowicz, Paweł, 136
Adamsson, Jimmie, 123
Ādaži, Latvia, 237–8, 245, 252, 254
Adomėnas, Mantas, 193, 198, 199
aerial warfare, 260–3
Afghanistan, 195, 219, 274
Aho, Esko, 60
Ahonen, Anneli, 65
ÄIO, 36
Åland Islands, 105, 110, 224, 258
Ålander, Minna, 60, 68, 73
Albright, Madeleine, 241
Alexander I, Emperor of Russia, 53
Alexander, Chris, 232–3
algae, 107, 108, 110, 113
Alikhanov, Anton, 187
Allen, John, 240
Alternative für Deutschland (AfD), 153, 155, 178, 222
ammonia, 162
ammunition, 16, 41, 163–4, 182–3, 243, 245, 248–9
Andersen, Benny, 285
Andreasen, Magnus Heide, 113
Andžāns, Māris, 253
'Angels and Maggots' (Michnik), 146–7
antisemitism, 82, 138–9, 140, 191
Arājs, Viktors, 82
ARTE, 77
artificial intelligence (AI), 32, 35, 40, 221–2, 227, 266, 267, 280
asylum seekers, 5, 68, 71–2, 223

Babst, Stefanie, 169–70
Bäckman, Johan, 221
Baerbock, Annalena, 187
Baev, Pavel, 229

Baltic Germans, 79, 103, 189, 213
Baltic Institute of Advanced Technology, 251
'Baltic jammer', 264
Baltic Pipe, 145
Baltic sea, 105–25, 144–6, 256, 275, 279
  algae, 107, 108, 110, 113
  climate change and, 106, 109–11
  conflict zone in, 106, 117
  dead zones, 108
  fauna, 110–11, 113, 115
  fisheries, 105–6, 107, 109, 110
  gas pipelines, 2, 60, 106, 109, 119–25
  halocline, 108, 110
  pollution, 106, 107, 108–9, 114–17
  salinity levels, 108
  telecoms cables, 106, 121
Baltic Way demonstration (1989), 23
Baltic Word, The, 221
Balticconnector, 106, 121
Bank of Finland, 48, 53, 55
Baranowski, Michał, 131, 141
bark-bread, 51
Barrons, Richard, 249
BASF, 118, 162, 172
Battle of Westerplatte (1939), 135, 145
Belarus, 5, 144, 147, 182, 185
  asylum seeker crisis (2021), 5
  German occupation (1941–4), 82
  protests (2006), 218
  Soviet Socialist Republic (1920–91), 24, 83
Belousov, Andrei, 228
Bergmane, Una, 88
Berklavs, Eduards, 86
Berlin, Germany, 271

INDEX

Berlin security conference (2023), 245–6
Bērziņa-Čerenkova, Una-Aleksandra, 201
Biden, Joseph, 171, 186, 202
Biess, Frank, 157
Billström, Tobias, 129
biobanks, 35
Birk, Marie Helene, 105, 107, 113
Bismarck, Otto von, 4, 170
Bittium, 72–3
Błaszczak, Mariusz, 249
Blinken, Antony, 182, 184
Bložė, Vytautas, 195
BND, 22, 159
Bogdanov, S. A., 219
Bolshevik Revolution (1917), 53, 80, 81, 190, 218
Borchert, Heiko, 124
border provocations, 5, 68, 71–2, 223–4
Borisevičius, Vincentas, 194
Bornholm, Denmark, 2, 10, 105–7, 110
    Nord Stream sabotage (2022), 2, 106, 109, 121–5, 145
    smart grid, 111
    wind farms, 111–12, 115
    zero-waste concept, 111–13
Bornholms Affaldsbehandling (Bofa), 111–13
BRELL, 118
British Broadcasting Corporation (BBC), 77, 96
Bronk, Justin, 260
Bronze Night (2007), 38–40, 226, 264
Bruns, Sebastian, 259
BSW, 155
Büchel airbase, Germany, 153
Bulgaria, 100, 120
Bundeswehr university, 165
Bürokratt, 32
Busch, Roland, 173
Bush, George H. W., 23, 28, 197
Bush, George W., 232
Bydén, Micael, 7
Bystron, Petr, 222

Cajander, Aimo, 53
Čaks, Aleksandrs, 84

Canada, 16, 42, 232, 238, 245, 252
Carr, Harry, 193–4
Castle of Light, 86
Catholicism, 133, 138, 194
Chamberlain, Neville, 74, 198
Charles XII, King of Sweden, 212, 213
Chatham House, 225, 233
Chechnya, 223, 229, 254
Chekinov, S. G., 219
chemical weapons, 108, 119
childcare, 16, 36
China
    People's Republic (1949–present), *see* People's Republic of China
    Republic of China (1912–present), 183–6, 192, 240
Chongqing, China, 172
Christ of Nations, 138, 189
Christian Democratic Union (CDU), 154, 174
Christianity, 76, 79, 133, 138
Churchill, Winston, 55, 56, 57
Citizens' Initiative, 34–5
Civic Platform party (Poland), 132, 223
climate change, 113–14, 155
    Baltic sea and, 106, 109–11
    net zero goals, 48, 65
CNN, 226
Coker, Christopher, 201
Cold War (1947–91), 3, 6, 130, 146, 200, 218, 276, 281
    Cuban Missile Crisis (1962), 208, 274
    Finland and, 59, 62–3, 199
    nuclear weapons, 272–4
colour revolutions, 218–19
Communist Party of Finland, 57, 58
comprehensive security, 9, 47, 152, 287
Cooperative Cyber Defence Centre, 39
Copenhagen, Denmark, 285
corruption, 26, 44, 100
Council of the Baltic Sea States, 288
Covid-19 pandemic (2019–23), 220, 240
Crimea, 4, 69, 117, 118, 119, 219, 233, 268
Crimean War (1853–6), 71, 257

INDEX

Cripps, Stafford, 191
Cuban Missile Crisis (1962), 208
cyberwarfare, 39–40, 207–8, 226, 264–5, 267–70
Czaputowicz, Jacek, 132
Czechia, 5, 183, 225

Danish Institute of International Studies, 228
Danzig (1920–39), 135, 144, 152
data cables, 122
data embassies, 40
Daugava river, 75, 85, 104
Daugavpils, Latvia, 77, 95, 96
Davies, Norman, 139
Dębski, Sławomir, 141
decolonisation, 101
defence line, 251
Denmark, 2, 8, 9, 17, 105–8, 113–16
  border provocation (2022), 223
  disinformation in, 221
  energy sector, 111–12, 115, 120
  environmental policy, 113–16
  fisheries, 105–6, 107
  influence campaigns in, 222
  Lithuania, relations with, 196
  media literacy in, 40
  NATO, role in, 274
  Nord Stream sabotage (2022), 2, 106, 109, 121–5, 145
  Sweden, relations with, 284–5
  Ukraine, relations with, 182
deportations
  Estonia, 15–16, 18–19, 30, 43
  Latvia, 83, 85, 86
  Lithuania, 194
deterrence, 37, 165, 241–2, 250, 265, 272–3, 275, 276
Deutsche ReGas, 160
Dienu Virpuļi, 85
Digital Society Institute, 39, 268
disinformation, 40, 64, 65, 98, 219–22, 227–8
Dmowski, Roman, 138–40
Do Europy (Janion), 137
Donbas War (2014–present), 119, 157, 239
Dresden, Germany, 232, 263
drones, 266
Duda, Wojciech, 137

Dukhanov, Mikhail, 53–4
Dzenovska, Dace, 99, 100

East Germany (*formerly* German Democratic Republic, 1949–90), 59, 148, 155, 156, 157, 168
Easter attack (2013), 6–8
eider ducks, 110
Eiseln, Aleksander, 42
Ekmanis, Indra, 96
Elbe group, 274
electromagnetic pulse (EMP), 266
electronic warfare, 264–70
Eliot, T. S., 278
elves unit, 98
Endecja, 138
energy, 2, 65–6, 111–12, 115–25, 178
  gas, see gas industry
  nuclear power, 46, 49, 66, 67, 116
  oil, 114, 116–17, 118
  renewables, 66, 111–12, 115–16, 160, 161
Ennuste, Jaak, 35
Ernesaks, Gustav, 21
Erofeyev, Victor, 207, 209–11
Estonia
  Danish Estonia (1219–1346), 17
  Declaration of Independence (1918), 18, 20
  Declaration of Independence (1991), 24
  German occupation (1941–4), 17, 18, 212
  language, 15, 19, 21
  Republic, First (1918–40), 15, 18, 20, 39, 181
  Republic, Second (1991–), see Republic of Estonia, Second
  Russian Estonia (1710–1917), 17
  Soviet occupation, First (1940–1), 29
  Soviet occupation, Second (1944–91), see Estonian SSR, Second
  Swedish Estonia (1561–1710), 17, 19
  War of Independence (1918–20), 18
Estonian Heritage Society, 22
Estonian SSR, First (1940–1), 15–16, 18, 29
Estonian SSR, Second (1944–91), 15–16, 18–27

357

INDEX

Estonian SSR, Second (1944–91) (*cont.*)
  Baltic Way demonstration (1989), 23
  demographics, 19–20
  deportations, 15–16, 18–19, 30, 43
  Forest Brothers insurgency (1944–53), 20, 229
  migration to, 19
  phosphorite mine protests (1987), 21
  resistance in, 20–1
  Russification, 19, 21
  Singing Revolution (1987–91), 21–4
  technology sector, 32
Eurajoki, Finland, 49
European Commission, 47–8, 187
European Sky Shield Initiative, 263
European Solidarity Centre, 149
European Union (EU), 8, 16, 17, 181, 202
  China, relations with, 185
  Finland and, 59
  fisheries policies, 110
  Germany and, 131, 151, 169, 287
  green energy policies, 115
  Kaliningrad and, 187
  Latvia and, 17, 29, 89
  Lithuania and, 187, 188
  Poland and, 131, 134, 141, 148
  Russo-Ukrainian War sanctions, 186, 222
  Ukrainian accession prospects, 29, 169, 287
exquisite platforms, 249

F-16 aircraft, 121, 182
F-35 aircraft, 61, 153, 164, 261
famines, 51
Fårö, Sweden, 1–2
Federal Republic of Germany (1990–present), 5, 8, 22, 150–79, 201
  armed forces, 152–4, 163–7, 176, 246, 248–9
  Bundestag election (2021), 156
  Bundestag election (2025), 11, 142
  China, relations with, 171–4, 184
  debt brake, 175
  diplomacy, 167–74
  disinformation in, 221
  economy, 175–6, 178
  energy sector, 5, 49, 116, 118, 119–21, 150, 155, 159–62, 174, 178
  EU, role in, 131, 151, 169, 287
  France, relations with, 142
  immigration, 281
  influence campaigns in, 222
  Lithuanian battlegroup, 42, 163, 166, 220, 252
  Meri's speech (1995), 28
  NATO, role in, 42, 151–4, 163–6, 169, 174, 244, 252
  nuclear threats and, 274–5
  Poland, relations with, 141
  technology sector, 152, 155
  Ukraine, relations with, 123, 151–4, 157–9, 163, 166, 168–71, 174, 177–8
  unemployment in, 156
  Vergangenheitsaufarbeitung, 192
  Webex hack (2024), 270
  Zeitenwende (2022), 10, 68, 151, 152–4, 156, 159–79
Federation of German Industries, 173
Fernandez, Jose, 186
Financial Times, 263
Finland, 3, 5, 9, 21, 26, 46–74, 231, 283
  armed forces, 41–2, 62–3, 253
  asylum seeker crisis (2023–4), 68–9
  border provocations (2023–4), 223–4
  Cold War (1947–91), 59, 62–3, 199
  Communist Party, 57, 58
  Continuation War (1941–4), 52, 55–6
  democracy in, 50, 71–2
  demographics, 48
  disinformation in, 221
  economy, 48
  education in, 30, 48, 65
  energy sector, 46, 49–50, 65–6, 67, 116
  Estonia, relations with, 26, 27, 30, 33, 34, 45, 69, 78
  EU accession (1995), 59, 69
  famines in, 51
  grooming scandal (2018), 71
  happiness in, 48
  media literacy in, 40, 64, 65
  mineral industry, 66–7
  Moscow Armistice (1944), 56–7
  NATO accession (2023), 5, 47, 59, 67–70, 120, 223–4, 256

Nazi Germany, alliance with (1941–4), 52, 55–6
net zero goal, 48, 65, 66
nuclear power in, 46, 49–50, 67, 116
oil slicks in, 114
pessimism in, 49
racism in, 71–2
red carpet, 62
resilience culture in, 47–8, 51, 63–7
Russia, relations with, 52–70
Russian Grand Duchy (1809–1917), 53, 71, 231
sabotage in, 225
security strategy for society (2017), 64
Supo, 225, 269
technology sector, 33, 34, 48, 51–2, 58, 72
Ukraine, relations with, 55, 60, 66, 67
Winter War (1939–40), 53–5, 57, 69, 73
'Finlandisation', 59, 62, 199
Finnair, 264
Finns party, 50, 71
First World War (1914–18), 3, 48, 55, 80, 144, 181, 190
fisheries, 105–6, 107, 109, 110
Forest Brothers
  Estonia, 20, 229
  Lithuania, 192–3, 195, 202, 229
France, 16, 190, 199, 201, 202–3
  armed forces, 248
  Germany, relations with, 142
  Lithuania, relations with, 197
  nuclear threats and, 274, 275
  Poland, relations with, 132, 141
Fratzscher, Marcel, 175
Freund, Andreas, 269
Friedrich, Caspar David, 155
Friedrich Ebert Foundation, 230
Frohnmaier, Markus, 222
frontline states, 275–6
Froud, Conrad, 237
Frykvall, Magnus, 7, 8
FSB, 95
Fulda, Andreas, 173

Galamison, Matthew, 262
gas industry, 5, 117–25, 159–62

Baltic Pipe, 145
Balticconnector, 106, 121
FSRUs, 160
see also Nord Stream
Gauck, Joachim, 148
Gaulle, Charles de, 244
Gazeta Wyborcza, 140, 142
Gazprom, 118, 121, 155, 159, 161, 222
Gdańsk, Poland, 135–7, 144, 149, 152, 263
Gdynia, Poland, 144, 145
genomic screening, 35
Genscher, Hans-Dietrich, 197
Georgia, 77, 218
Gepard flak cannons, 261
Gerasimov, Valery, 217
German Democratic Republic (1949–90), see East Germany
German Economic Institute, 173
German Institute for Economic Research, 175
Germany, 150–79
  East Germany (1949–90), 59, 148, 155, 156, 157, 168
  Federal Republic (1990–present), see Federal Republic of Germany
  Nazi period (1933–45), see Nazi Germany
  Russian Civil War (1917–23), 80
  Weimar Republic (1918–33), 81
  West Germany (1949–90), 22, 130, 167, 197
Giles, Keir, 225, 233, 234, 254
golden visas, 100
Gorbachev, Mikhail, 21, 22, 23, 72, 86, 87, 196–9
Gorenc, Frank, 260
Göring, Hermann, 18, 56
Gotkowska, Justyna, 144
Gotland, Sweden, 1–2, 6–8, 108, 110, 115, 117, 146, 223, 256
GPS, 264
Grand Duchy of Finland (1809–1917), 53, 71, 231
Great Game (*c.*1830–1907), 217
Great Northern War (1700–21), 212, 213, 214, 279
Great Patriotic War (1941–5), 30, 216
  see also Second World War
green energy, 66, 111–12, 115, 160, 161

Green party (Germany), 161
Greene, Sam, 3
Greifswald, Germany, 154–7
Grevcova, Glorija, 95
Grigas, Agnia, 215
Gripen aircraft, 7, 223
Große Gopnik, Der (Erofeyev), 207, 209
Grünewald, Stephan, 158
Grzechnik, Marta, 145
GScan, 36
GUGI, 122, 123
gulags, 82, 83, 85

Haavisto, Pekka, 68, 70, 72
Habeck, Robert, 161
Häkämies, Jyri, 63
Haldenwang, Thomas, 173
halocline, 108, 110
Halonen, Tarja, 60
Hanhikivi, Finland, 66
Hanseatic League (*c.*1159–1862), 135, 155
Hansen, Flemming Splidsboel, 228
Hart, Michael, 258, 260–1
Häyhä, Simo, 55
Hektor, Andi, 36
HELCOM, 110–11
Helsingin Sanomat, 73
Helsinki, Finland, 264
Herem, Martin, 41
Hill, Fiona, 231
HIMARS, 41, 265
Hitler, Adolf, 18, 56, 81, 191, 200
Hjort, Magnus, 227
Hobbes, Thomas, 237
Hodges, Ben, 240, 250–1, 253, 277
Hoffmann, Fabian, 263, 273–4
Högl, Eva, 166
Holocaust (1941–5), 82, 137, 191–2
Holy Roman Empire (800–1806), 246
Homeland Union party (Lithuania), 192
homosexuality, 101, 133
Hong Kong, 185
Huhn, Antonia, 157
Hull, East Yorkshire, 15
Hungary, 20, 23, 133, 244
hybrid war, 5, 10, 43, 207–8, 217–32
    border provocations, 5, 68, 71–2, 223–4
    disinformation, 40, 64, 65, 98, 219–22, 227
    influence campaigns, 222–3
    sabotage, 207–8, 225–6
    violence, 207–8, 224–5

Iceland, 199
Idestam, Fredrik, 52
Ijabs, Ivars, 88
Ilves, Toomas Hendrik, 17, 22, 28, 33
immigration, *see* migration
IMVU (integrated mass air strike), 251
influence campaigns, 222–3
Institute for International and Security Affairs, 125
Inter RAO, 118
Interfront, 86, 93
International Centre for Defence and Security (ICDS), 235, 241
International Monetary Fund (IMF), 100
interoperability, 244–5
IRIS-T, 169, 261
Iskander-M missiles, 224
Istanbul Convention (2011), 101
Ivandet, 105, 113
Ivano-Frankivsk, Ukraine, 267

Jakobsen, Peter Viggo, 230, 247, 276
Jälkisuomettumisen ruumiinavaus (Virkki), 59
Janion, Maria, 137
Jansson, Tove, 113
January events (1991), 198, 201, 203
Japan, 186, 257
JAS-39 Gripen aircraft, 7, 223
JASSM missiles, 63, 263
Javelin anti-tank missiles, 17, 234, 254
Jewish people, 82, 138–9, 140, 191
Johansen, Brian, 111–13
John Paul II, Pope, 202
Joint Expeditionary Force (JEF), 124
Jonsson, Markus, 263
Jurasz, Witold, 4, 143

Kaasik, Peeter, 19
Kaczyński, Jarosław, 132, 136, 137, 141
Kaczyński, Lech, 136
Kahl, Bruno, 173

INDEX

Kairamo, Kari, 50–1
Kairišs, Viesturs, 100
Kaiser Wilhelm memorial church, Berlin, 271
Kaitseliit, 20, 42, 43
Kalevala, 46, 79
Kalevipoeg, 79
Kalibr missiles, 258–9
Kaliningrad, Russia, 2, 6, 116, 144, 146, 152, 193, 211, 221, 276
   aerial warfare and, 262
   electronic warfare, 264
   German delegation plan (2024), 222
   sea warfare and, 256, 257
   Ukraine War and, 186–7
Kaljulaid, Kersti, 22, 27, 28, 37
Kallas, Kaja, 15–16, 24, 28, 29, 37, 44, 216, 282
Kallas, Kristina, 30
Kannik, Indrek, 117
Kant, Immanuel, 222, 279
Kaprāns, Mārtiņš, 76, 98
Karaganov, Sergei, 214, 273
Karelia, 54, 56, 57, 224
Kariņš, Krišjānis, 219, 226
Karis, Alar, 42
Kasekamp, Andres, 38, 96–7
Kassautzki, Anna, 156
Kaszeta, Dan, 192
Kattegat, 110, 115, 256
Kaunas, Lithuania, 139
Kekkonen, Urho, 63
Keldysh, Mstislav, 76
Kemi, Finland, 109
Kennan, George, 281–4
Kennedy, John Fitzgerald, 202
Kenya, 122
Kerski, Basil, 149
Kesäranta, Finland, 60–1
KGB, 58, 59, 215, 232, 282
Khrushchev, Nikita, 20, 195, 208
Kiel university, 259
Ķikuts, Pēteris, 75
Kindsvater, Scott, 260
Kinzhal ballistic missiles, 261
Kirill, Patriarch of Moscow, 76
Klaipėda, Lithuania, 118, 190
Knabe, Stephan, 150, 160
Kohl, Helmut, 23, 171, 177, 197, 199
Koidula, Lydia, 21

Koivisto, Mauno, 59
Kola peninsula, Russia, 69, 122, 265, 276
Königsberg, Prussia, 152, 186, 279
Kopečný, Tomáš, 183
Kosiniak-Kamysz, Władysław, 252
Kozłowska, Dominika, 148
Kozyrev, Andrey, 214
Krah, Maximilian, 222
Krasikov, Vadim, 223
Krasukha-4 system, 265
kratt, 32
Krėvė-Mickevičius, Vincas, 180–1
Kriegers Flak II, 115
Kristersson, Ulf, 7
Kruks, Sergejs, 104
Krumm, Reinhard, 230
Kudors, Andis, 97
Kuisz, Jarosław, 134
Kundera, Milan, 17
Kwiatkowski, Eugeniusz, 144
Kyivstar, 268, 270

Laar, Mart, 20, 21, 26, 27, 44
Lāčplēsis (Pumpurs), 79–80, 85–6, 100, 103–4
Lāčplēsis Day, 103
land warfare, 247–55
Landsbergis, Gabrielius, 185–6, 188, 192, 196, 203, 287
Landsbergis, Vytautas, 196–9, 200
Lapland, 67, 224
Larsen, Jesper, 221
Latgale, Latvia, 96, 226
Latvia
   German occupation (1941–4), 82–3
   language, 76, 77–8, 84–5, 86, 88, 89–90, 101–2
   Republic, First (1918–40), 80–1, 83, 87, 181
   Republic, Second (1991–present), *see* Republic of Latvia, Second
   Russian Latvia (1710–1918), 79
   Soviet occupation, First (1940–1), 29, 81–2, 85, 86
   Soviet occupation, Second (1944–91), *see* Latvian SSR, Second
Latvian Russian Union (LKS), 93, 95
Latvian SSR, First (1940–1), 29, 81–2, 85, 86, 104

INDEX

Latvian SSR, Second (1944–91), 23, 24, 75–8, 83–7
  Baltic Way demonstration (1989), 23
  Barricades (1991), 87, 100
  Declaration of Independence (1990), 77, 87
  deportations (1949), 83
  hydroelectric projects, 85, 86
  language in, 84–5, 86
  migration to, 76, 83, 87–8
  poetry in, 83–4
  Russian community, 86–7, 93
  Russification, 84, 86
  Singing Revolution (1987–91), 78, 86
Lauristin, Marju, 22
Law and Justice, 132, 133–4, 137, 140, 143, 148
Lenin, Vladimir, 21, 25, 27
Leningrad, siege of (1941–4), 56
Leopard 2 battle tanks, 7, 165
Leponiemi, Jussi, 72
Letter Concerning Toleration (Locke), 102
Leviathan (Hobbes), 237
Levits, Egils, 92, 101–2, 103
liberalism, 286
  in Latvia, 91–2, 94, 100–3
  in Lithuania, 192
  in Poland, 133, 148
Lidington, David, 196–7
Liepiņš, Zigmars, 85
Lindley-French, Julian, 240
Linna, Väinö, 56
Lipponen, Paavo, 60
Lithuania
  Grand Duchy (1236–1795), 212
  language, 190, 195
  Polish–Lithuanian Commonwealth (1569–1795), 8, 132, 138, 189
  Polish–Soviet War (1919–21), 139, 190
  Republic, First (1918–40), 139, 180–1, 190–1
  Republic, Second (1991–present), *see* Republic of Lithuania, Second
  Russian Lithuania (1795–1915), 189–90, 196
  Soviet occupation, First (1940–1), 29, 180–1, 193, 194
  Soviet occupation, Second (1944–91), *see* Lithuanian SSR, Second
Lithuanian SSR, First (1940–1), 29, 180–1, 193, 194
Lithuanian SSR, Second (1944–91), 23, 24, 188–9, 192–9
  Baltic Way demonstration (1989), 23
  Declaration of Independence (1990), 196–9
  Forest Brothers insurgency (1944–53), 192–3, 195, 202, 229
  January events (1991), 198, 201, 203
  migration to, 195
  Operation Blunderhead (c.1949), 193–4
  Sąjūdis (1988–91), 24, 188, 192, 196
'little green men', 233
Little Ice Age (c.1300–1850), 51
LKS, 93, 95
LNNK, 86–7, 88
Locke, John, 102
logistics, 243–4, 250–1, 254
Long Telegram (Kennan), 282–4
Loviisa, Finland, 49, 109, 223
Lubmin, Germany, 119, 150, 154, 156, 160
Lührmann, Anna, 168, 169
Lukashenko, Aleksandr, 218
Lützerath, Germany, 161
Luxembourg, 40

Määttänen, Niku, 64
Machcewicz, Paweł, 137, 147
McKibbin, Sandy, 193–4
Macron, Emmanuel, 132, 142, 202–3, 281
Maidan uprising (2013–14), 219
Mais, Alfons, 163, 248
Makarov pistols, 41
Malmi, Karoliina, 73
Malmö, Sweden, 284–5
Mankoff, Jeffrey, 3, 234
Mannerheim, Carl Gustaf, 53–4, 55, 56
Männiku, Tallinn, 43
manoeuvre warfare, 253–4
Marijampolė, Lithuania, 192–3
Marin, Sanna, 50, 60–1, 66, 71, 154
Mariupol, Ukraine, 213
Marseilles, France, 122

Martinaitis, Marcelijus, 188–9
Masala, Carlo, 165
Massie, Robert, 214
Mecklenburg-West Pomerania, 155
media literacy, 40, 64, 65, 98, 220, 227
Medvedev, Dmitry, 4, 120
Meinander, Henrik, 54, 57
Meri, Lennart, 24–5, 28, 33, 45, 200, 281, 288–9
Merilo, Andrus, 42
Merilo, Jaanika, 33, 35
Merkel, Angela, 119, 155, 156, 170
Merz, Friedrich, 174, 175
Messner, Evgeny, 217–18
Metsavennad, 20
MI6, 193–4
Michnik, Adam, 140, 146–7, 148
Mickiewicz, Adam, 138, 139, 189
Microsoft, 269
Mig-29 aircraft, 262
migration, 5, 68, 71–2, 133, 280–1
Mill, John Stuart, 102
Miłosz, Czesław, 129, 279
minerals, 66–7
Minier, Jiro, 270
miracle on the Vistula (1920), 130
Mitrofanov, Miroslav, 93
Mitterrand, François, 197, 199
Moldova, 24, 40, 70
Molotov, Vyacheslav, 180–1
Molotov–Ribbentrop Pact (1939), 18, 23, 28, 30, 86, 134, 180–1, 191
Mombasa, Kenya, 122
Moskva, 187
multiculturalism, 101
Munich Agreement (1938), 198
Murmansk, Russia, 69
Murmansk-BN system, 265
Muscovy (1282–1547), 212, 213
Musk, Elon, 268
mustard gas, 108
Mutual Assistance Treaties (1939), 81
'My Fatherland is My Love' (Koidula), 21
myatezhvoina, 218
Mykkänen, Kai, 66, 67

Naiskodukaitse, 40
Napoleon I, Emperor of the French, 116

Napoleonic Wars (1803–15), 224, 242, 246
Narva, Estonia, 19, 37, 44, 96, 224, 231
Narva river, 224
NASAMS, 261
Nashi, 39
National Alliance party (Latvia), 87
National Coalition party (Finland), 62
National Defence Council (Finland), 64
National Defence University (Finland), 65
National Defense University (US), 3, 234
National Democratic movement (Poland), 138, 140
Nausėda, Gitanas, 181, 183
naval warfare, 256–9
Nazi Germany (1933–45), 17, 18, 28, 30, 39, 52, 55, 56, 75, 167
  Anglo-German Naval Agreement (1935), 81
  Denmark, invasion of (1940), 285
  Estonia occupation (1941–4), 17, 18, 212
  Finland, alliance with (1941–4), 52, 55–6
  Holocaust (1941–5), 82, 137, 191–2
  Latvia occupation (1941–4), 82
  Lithuania occupation (1941–4), 191–2
  Molotov–Ribbentrop Pact (1939), 18, 23, 28, 30, 86, 134, 181, 191
  Munich Agreement (1938), 198
  Operation Barbarossa (1941), 30, 56, 82, 168
  Poland, invasion of (1939), 134, 135–6
Neitzel, Sönke, 246
Neptune, 150, 160
Neringa, Lithuania, 190, 195
Nesselrode, Karl, 217
net zero goals, 48, 65
Netherlands, 182, 253
Nevsky, Alexander, 212, 213
Newnew Polar Bear, 121–2, 123
Niinistö, Sauli, 47–8, 61, 62
Nikonov, Vyacheslav, 214–15
NKVD, 82, 212

Nokia, 33, 48, 50, 52, 58, 63, 72
Nord Stream, 60, 119–25, 155, 156, 222
  Germany and, 150, 155, 156
  sabotage of (2022), 2, 106, 109, 121–5, 145
NordBalt disruption (2015), 122
Noreika, Jonas, 191–2
North Atlantic Fellas Organisation (NAFO), 227
North Atlantic Treaty Organisation (NATO), 2–5, 8, 9, 16, 25, 37–8, 58, 141, 181–2, 202, 210, 215
  aerial warfare, 260–3
  Afghanistan War (2001–21), 219
  Article 5 clause, 5, 44, 123, 209, 226, 233, 244
  Centre of Excellence for Strategic Communications, 228
  Cooperative Cyber Defence Centre, 39
  cyberwarfare, 39, 267–70
  Czechia and, 183
  Denmark and, 274
  DIANA, 72
  electronic warfare, 264–70
  Estonia and, 28, 29, 42
  expansion, 2–3, 200, 281–2
  Finland and, 5, 47, 59, 67–70, 120, 223–4, 256
  Gerasimov and, 219
  Germany and, 42, 151–4, 163–6, 169, 174, 244, 252
  interoperability, 244–5
  Joint Support and Enabling Command (JSEC), 158, 244
  land warfare, 247–55
  Latvia and, 29, 77, 89
  Lithuania and, 42, 163, 166, 188
  logistics, 243–4, 250–1, 254
  Maritime Command base, 124
  naval warfare, 256–9
  Nord Stream sabotage (2022), 124
  nuclear weapons and, 271–5
  Poland and, 134, 141, 148, 183
  Russian War prospects, 229–36, 237–55, 256–78
  spending targets, 29, 37–8, 41, 174, 203
  Sweden and, 256
  threat perceptions, 244
  Titan Shield exercise (2023), 237–8, 245
  Ukrainian accession prospects, 169
  Very High Readiness Joint Task Force, 247
  Vilnius summit (2023), 169, 246, 269, 277
  wargames, 6, 237–9, 245
North Korea, 287–8
North sea, 107, 115, 256
Northern Crusades (1198–1290), 79, 100, 279
Norway, 62, 69, 121, 131, 133, 160, 240
  influence campaigns in, 221
  media literacy in, 40
  nuclear power, 46, 49, 66, 67, 116, 161
  nuclear weapons, 2, 6–7, 9, 32, 153, 169, 183, 187, 271–5, 276
  Easter attack (2013), 6–8
  Ukraine War and, 183, 187, 271–5
Nurmi, Sami, 52
Nyberg, René, 231

O'Brien, Phillips, 262
oil industry, 114, 116–17, 118
Olenya/Olenegorsk base, Russia, 224
Olkiluoto Nuclear Power Plant, 46, 49–50
OMON, 87
Onkalo spent nuclear fuel repository, 49–50
Open Society Institute, Sofia, 40
Operation Bagration (1944), 82–3
Operation Barbarossa (1941), 30, 56, 82, 168
Operation Blunderhead (c.1949), 193–4
Operation Priboi (1949), 15–16, 85
Orange Revolution (2004), 200, 218
Orbán, Viktor, 133
Öresund, 110, 258, 284–5
Orpo, Petteri, 131
OSCE, 89
Oslo university, 263
Oulu, Finland, 53, 70–4
Ozolas, Romualdas, 203

Paasikivi, Juho Kusti, 57, 74
Paat, Jürgen, 43
Pabriks, Artis, 90–2, 102, 287

Palavenis, Donatas, 251
Palme, Olof, 1
Pan Tadeusz (Mickiewicz), 189
Papperger, Armin, 226
Parker, Guy, 238, 254
Partanen, Anu, 49, 51
Patriot missile system, 261
Pavilionis, Žygimantas, 189, 201–2
PCK, 118, 161
PEACE cable, 122
Peace Research Institute
  Frankfurt, 217
  Oslo, 229
Pelttari, Antti, 269
People's Republic of China, 70, 115
  energy sector, 121, 162
  Germany, relations with, 167, 168, 171–4
  Hong Kong protests (2019–20), 185
  Lithuania, relations with, 183–6
  minerals sector, 52, 66
  News Corp hacking (2022), 207
  PEACE cable, 122
  Sweden, relations with, 171, 182
  Taiwan, relations with, 183–6, 192, 193, 240
  Tiananmen Square protests (1989), 23
People's Republic of Poland (1947–89), 134, 136, 140, 146–9, 195
pesticides, 109, 114
Peter I, Emperor of Russia, 116, 211, 213–14
Peters, Jānis, 86
Petersen, Michael, 262
Petrozavodsk, Russia, 224
pettuleipä, 51
Piirimäe, Kaarel, 45
Piłsudski, Józef, 139–40, 142, 144, 147
PiS, 132, 133–4, 137, 140, 143, 148
Pistorius, Boris, 159, 164
plastics, 112
Pļaviņas, Latvia, 85
poetry, 83–4, 138, 139, 189, 195
Pół-Polacy, 140
Poland, 8
  Baltic sea and, 144–6
  'Christ of Nations' complex, 138, 189
  Germans, expulsion of (1945), 137

Kingdom of Poland (1025–1795), 212
  Molotov–Ribbentrop Pact (1939), 18, 134
  Partitions (1772–95), 134, 138
  People's Republic (1947–89), 134, 136, 140, 146–9, 195
  Piast dynasty (*c*.960–92), 135
  Polish–Lithuanian Commonwealth (1569–1795), 8, 132, 138, 189
  Republic, Third (1989–present), *see* Republic of Poland, Third
  Russian occupation (1815–1915), 3, 8, 134, 138–9
  Second World War (1939–45), 18, 134, 135, 137–8, 140
  Soviet War (1919–21), 130, 139, 190
Polianskii, Mikhail, 217
Polish Institute of International Affairs, 141
Polttoainehankinta, 62
Popular Front
  Estonia, 22
  Latvia, 87, 94
populism, 26, 35, 50, 95, 133, 148, 153, 156, 176
porpoises, 110
Pravfond, 222–3
Prigozhin, Yevgeny, 117
Programme for International Student Assessment (PISA), 31, 48
Prunskienė, Kazimira, 197–8
Prussia (1701–1918), 134, 190
Przegląd Polityczny, 137
PT-91 Twardy tanks, 238
Pumpurs, Andrejs, 79–80, 85
Purs, Aldis, 19
Putin, Vladimir, 4, 5, 9, 59, 93, 116, 122, 149, 208–17, 232, 282
  Alexander's views on, 232
  Georgian War (2008), 77
  Hamburg dinner (1994), 28
  Helsinki summit (2018), 61
  history and, 212–17
  intelligence assessments, 229, 235
  irredentism, 208–14
  NATO, views on, 2–3
  nuclear threats, 183, 187, 271–5
  Soviet collapse and, 232
  strategy, lack of, 4
  Ukraine War and, 231

INDEX

Putina, Lyudmila, 211
Pyplys, Kazimieras, 193

R-330Zh system, 265
R+V, 157
Raal, Carmen, 32, 34
Radio Free Europe, 22, 98
Radio Liberty, 98
Rahvaalgatus, 34–5
Raik, Kristi, 241
railways, 225, 254, 276
Raitasalo, Jyri, 65
RAND Corporation, 235, 239
rare-earth minerals, 66–7
RB-341V Leer, 265
Reagan, Ronald, 58
Reform party (Estonia), 44
regime shifts, 110
Reinys, Mečislovas, 194
Republic of China (1912–present), 183–6, 192
Republic of Estonia, First (1918–40), 15, 18, 39, 181
Republic of Estonia, Second (1991–present), 4, 9, 15–17, 24–45
  armed forces, 41, 252
  average incomes, 26–7
  Bronze Night (2007), 38–40, 226, 264
  childcare, 16, 36
  China, relations with, 184
  corruption in, 26, 44
  cybersecurity in, 39–40, 226
  data embassy, 40
  debt-to-GDP ratio, 27
  disinformation in, 221
  Drang nach Westen, 28
  education in, 16, 30–1, 40, 48
  energy sector, 116
  EU accession (2004), 17, 28, 29
  Finland, relations with, 26, 27, 30, 33, 34, 45, 69, 78
  fiscal puritanism, 27
  GDP per capita, 16
  inflation surge (2022), 45
  kroon, 27
  life expectancy in, 26–7
  media literacy in, 40
  NATO accession (2004), 28, 29
  resilience culture in, 40, 47
  Russia, relations with, 37–44, 182
  Russian community, 39, 44, 96–7, 226
  technology sector, 16, 31–6, 45
  Ukraine, relations with, 17, 38, 41, 42
  unemployment in, 25
  voting in, 16, 34
Republic of Latvia, First (1918–40), 80–1, 83, 87, 88, 104
Republic of Latvia, Second (1991–present), 9, 75–8, 88–104
  armed forces, 42, 252
  asylum seeker crisis (2021), 5
  China, relations with, 184
  corruption in, 100
  cyberattacks (2017), 269
  disinformation in, 98, 221
  economy, 99–100
  EU accession (2004), 17, 29, 89
  golden visas, 100
  happiness in, 99
  language in, 76, 77–8, 88, 89–90, 101–2
  Latvianisation, 76, 77–8, 88, 89–90, 99, 101–2
  media in, 97–8
  media literacy in, 98
  Museum of Occupation arson (2024), 95
  NATO accession (2004), 29, 77, 89
  NATO, role in, 237, 245
  non-citizens, 88, 89, 90
  parliamentary election (2022), 94
  Russia, relations with, 88, 90, 91, 93–8, 182
  Russian community, 76–8, 87–99, 101–4, 226
  Soviet memorials, removal of (2022), 75–6, 92
  Sweden, relations with, 78
  Titan Shield exercise (2023), 237, 245
  Ukraine, relations with, 76, 77, 90, 91, 93, 97
  unemployment in, 92, 96, 99
Republic of Lithuania, First (1918–40), 139, 180–1, 190–1
Republic of Lithuania, Second (1991–present), 8, 10, 183–8, 199–203

INDEX

armed forces, 42, 252
asylum seeker crisis (2021), 5
China, relations with, 171, 183–6
Denmark, relations with, 196
disinformation in, 220
energy sector, 116, 118
EU accession (2004), 17, 29
EU, role in, 187, 188
GDP per capita, 201
Kaliningrad, relations with, 186–7, 193
NATO accession (2004), 29
NATO, role in, 42, 163, 166, 188, 220, 237
NordBalt incident (2015), 122
Poland, relations with, 78
Russia, relations with, 182, 183, 186–8
Russian community, 226
Taiwan, relations with, 183–6, 192, 193
Titan Shield exercise (2023), 237
Ukraine, relations with, 183, 192, 200
Republic of Poland, Third, 5, 10, 16, 23, 129–49
  armed forces, 130–1, 143–4, 248, 253
  asylum seeker crisis (2021), 5
  Catholicism in, 133, 138
  cyberattacks (2017), 269
  disinformation in, 221
  east shield, 252
  education in, 131
  energy sector, 116, 120, 144, 145–6
  EU accession (2004), 134
  EU, role in, 131–2, 141, 142, 148
  France, relations with, 132, 141
  Germany, relations with, 141
  immigration, views on, 133
  liberalism in, 133, 148
  Lithuania, relations with, 78
  NATO accession (1999), 134
  NATO, role in, 141, 148, 183, 237
  parliamentary election (1989), 23
  parliamentary election (2015), 132
  parliamentary election (2023), 132–3
  Titan Shield exercise (2023), 237
  Ukraine, relations with, 29, 129–30, 142, 143, 169

resilience, 9, 40
  in Estonia, 40, 47
  in Finland, 47–8, 51
Rheingold Institute, 158
Rheinmetall, 226
Ries, Tomas, 272–3
Riga, Latvia, 75, 152
Riga castle, Latvia, 103
Riga Centre for Geopolitical Studies, 253
Rinkēvičs, Edgars, 93
Rogozin, Dmitry, 4
Rønne, Bornholm, 111
Rooste, Jürgen, 15
Rosatom, 66
Rosenberg, Alfred, 18
Rosneft, 118, 119, 161
Röttgen, Norbert, 177
round gobies, 110
Royal Danish Defence College, 230, 247
Royal United Services Institute (RUSI), 260, 262, 265
RT, 97, 228
Rukla, Lithuania, 252
rule of law, 86, 101–2
Rusi, Alpo, 59
Russian Baltic fleet, 2, 69, 146, 257–60
Russian Black sea fleet, 187, 257
Russian Civil War (1917–23), 53, 80, 190, 218
Russian Empire (1721–1917), 3, 8, 17, 79
  Crimean War (1853–6), 71, 257
  Estonia (1710–1917), 17
  Finland (1809–1917), 53, 71
  Great Game (c.1830–1907), 217
  Japanese War (1904–5), 257
  Latvia (1710–1917), 79
  Lithuania (1795–1915), 189–90, 196
  Poland (1815–1915), 3, 8, 134, 138–9
Russian Federation (1991–present), 2, 37
  Baltic coastline, 116–17
  Baltic fleet, 2, 69, 146, 257–60
  Black sea fleet, 187, 257
  casualties, attitude towards, 243
  Chechen War, First (1994–6), 229, 254

INDEX

Russian Federation (1991–present) (*cont.*)
  Crimea annexation (2014), 69, 117, 118, 119, 219, 233
  cyberwarfare, 39–40, 207–8, 226, 264–5, 267–70
  energy sector, 2, 65–6, 116–25, 155, 156, 159, 174
  Estonia, relations with, 37–44, 182
  Finland, relations with, 52, 59–70
  Georgian War (2008), 77
  Gerasimov doctrine, 217, 218–19
  Helsinki summit (2018), 61
  history in, 212–17
  hybrid war, 5, 10, 43, 207–8, 217–32
  Karaganov doctrine, 214
  Latvia, relations with, 88, 90, 91, 93–8, 182
  Lithuania, relations with, 182, 183, 186–8
  logistics, 243, 254
  national security strategy (2015), 37
  NordBalt incident (2015), 122
  nuclear weapons, 183, 187, 271–5
  Russkiy Mir concept, 96
  Sweden, relations with, 6–8, 223
  Syrian War (2015–present), 260, 261
  Ukraine War (2014–present), *see* Russo-Ukrainian War
  VKS, 260–3
Russian International Affairs Council, 218
Russian Orthodox Church, 76
Russian Revolution (1917), 53, 80
Russian Tsardom (1547–1721), 212, 213–14
Russkiy Mir Foundation, 214–15
Russo-Japanese War (1904–5), 257
Russo-Ukrainian War (2014–present), 2, 3, 5, 9, 11, 231
  aerial warfare, 260–3
  attrition, 234, 254
  Bucha massacre (2022), 91
  casualties, 243
  Crimea annexation (2014), 69, 117, 118, 119, 219, 233
  cyberwarfare, 267–8, 270
  'denazification' narrative, 217
  Denmark and, 182, 203
  dissidents and, 210
  Donbas annexations (2022), 119
  Donbas invasion (2014), 157, 239
  electronic warfare, 265, 266
  energy and, 117, 118, 119–25, 159–62, 174
  Estonia and, 17, 38, 41, 42
  exquisite platforms and, 249
  Finland and, 55, 60, 66, 67
  France and, 202–3
  Germany and, 123, 151–4, 157–9, 163, 166, 168–71, 174, 177–8
  Kaliningrad and, 186–7
  Latvia and, 76, 77, 90, 91, 93, 97
  Lithuania and, 183, 192, 200
  Moskva sinking (2022), 187
  naval warfare, 257, 258
  Nord Stream sabotage (2022), 2, 106, 109, 121–5, 145
  Poland and, 129–30, 142, 143, 169
  Serphukov fire (2024), 2, 106
  Sweden and, 203
  United States and, 123, 171, 202
Ryti, Risto, 55

S-400 air defence system, 260, 262
S-500 Prometheus, 262
sabotage, 225–6
Saeima, 76, 81
Sahra Wagenknecht Alliance (BSW), 153
Sąjūdis, 24, 188, 192, 196
Salm, Kusti, 38, 41
Sandrart, Jürgen-Joachim von, 242–3, 254, 265
Sārts, Jānis, 228
Sarvanto, Jorma, 55
Saskaņa, 94, 95
satellites, 32, 265, 268
Sauer, Kai, 69
Savisaar, Edgar, 22
SCALP missiles, 263
Schelling, Thomas, 273
Schmidt, Helmut, 222
Schneider, Karsten, 257–8
Schnitzer, Monika, 162, 178
Schöllhorn, Michael, 166
Scholz, Olaf, 152, 153, 177
  China, relations with, 172
  economic policies, 175, 177
  energy policies, 150, 159
  France, relations with, 142

INDEX

Lithuania, relations with, 187
rearmament (2022–present), 152–3, 163–4, 174
Ukraine, relations with, 119, 152–3, 154, 169–71
Zeitenwende speech (2022), 68, 151, 152, 174
Schröder, Gerhard, 119, 222
Schwalb, Reiner, 219
Schwedt, Germany, 118, 161
Schwesig, Manuela, 155
scrubber water, 115
Sczczecin, Poland, 207, 242, 243
Second World War (1939–45), 17, 18, 30, 39, 52, 53–7, 82, 93
   Baltic sea weapons dumping, 108–9, 119
   Battle of Westerplatte (1939), 135, 145
   Continuation War (1941–4), 52, 55–6
   Denmark invasion (1940), 285
   Holocaust (1941–5), 82, 137, 191–2
   memorials, 38–40, 75–6, 92
   Molotov–Ribbentrop Pact (1939), 18, 23, 28, 30, 86, 119, 134, 180–1, 191
   Moscow Armistice (1944), 56–7
   Operation Bagration (1944), 82–3
   Operation Barbarossa (1941), 30, 56, 82, 168
   Tehran conference (1943), 82
   Winter War (1939–40), 53–5, 57, 69, 73
   Yalta conference (1945), 210
Selznick, Philip, 288
Senkùtė, Anelė, 192–3
Serphukov, 2, 106
Šešelgytė, Margarita, 185
17+1 format, 185
Shipovnik-Aero, 265
Shirreff, Richard, 239–40, 245
shock therapy, 99–100
Sikorski, Radosław, 119, 129–30, 131–2
Siliņa, Evika, 77, 95, 221
Sillamäe, Estonia, 19, 44
Singing Revolution (1987–91), 21–4, 78, 86
sisu, 51
Skype, 16, 35

Småland, Sweden, 6–7
smart containment, 282
Sniečkus, Antanas, 195
Social Democratic party of Germany, 119, 153, 155–6, 159
social media, 34, 95, 98, 228
Soglasie, 24
SolarWinds hack, 269
Soldier's Mind programme, 63
Solidarność, 136, 146–9, 195
Sollfrank, Alexander, 158, 244, 250, 254–5
Solzhenitsyn, Aleksandr, 58
song festivals, 21
South China sea, 167, 240
South Korea, 131, 186
Soviet Russia/Union (1917–91), 3, 6
   Afghanistan War (1979–89), 195, 274
   atheism, 194
   Chernobyl disaster (1986), 109
   Continuation War (1941–4), 52, 55–6
   coup attempt (1991), 23, 198
   Cuban Missile Crisis (1962), 208, 274
   dissolution (1991), 59, 87, 116, 198–9
   East Prussia annexation (1945), 186
   Estonia, *see* Estonian SSR
   Finland, relations with, 51, 53–9
   history textbooks, 30
   Hungarian uprising (1956), 20
   Khrushchev thaw (1953), 20
   Latvia, *see* Latvian SSR
   Lithuania, *see* Lithuanian SSR
   Molotov–Ribbentrop Pact (1939), 18, 23, 28, 30, 86, 119, 134, 180–1, 191
   nasha zagranitsa, 230
   nuclear weapons, 272–4
   Operation Priboi (1949), 15–16, 85
   perestroika (1986–91), 21, 196–9
   Polish War (1919–21), 130, 139, 190
   Prague Spring (1968), 20
   Second World War (1941–5), *see* Second World War
   Winter War (1939–40), 53–5, 57, 69, 73
   Yalta conference (1945), 210

INDEX

St Petersburg, Russia, 53, 69, 146, 211, 276
Stabilitātei, 95
Stalin, Joseph, 29, 46, 54, 84, 134, 186, 192, 193, 200
  death (1953), 20
  deportations, *see* deportations
  East Prussia annexation (1945), 186
  Molotov–Ribbentrop Pact (1939), 18, 191
  'nationalist in form, socialist in content', 21
  Tehran conference (1943), 82
  'war against God', 194
  Winter War (1939–40), 53, 56
  Yalta conference (1945), 210
Stangneth, Bettina, 178–9
Starlink, 268
Starship, 36
Stockholm University, 272
Stoltenberg, Jens, 123
Storm Shadow missiles, 263
Stubb, Alexander, 50, 67, 283, 287–8
Sukhoi Su-57, 261
Supo, 225, 269
Suslov, Mikhail, 194, 195
Suwałki gap, 226, 237, 240, 243, 255
SVR, 269
Sweden, 1–2, 6–8, 17
  border provocation (2024), 223
  China, relations with, 171, 182
  Denmark, relations with, 284–5
  disinformation in, 221, 227
  Easter attack (2013), 6–8
  Empire of Sweden (1611–1721), 212, 213
  Estonia, rule of (1561–1710), 17, 19
  Finland, rule of (1150s–1809), 53
  Great Northern War (1700–21), 212, 213, 214, 279
  immigration in, 281
  influence campaigns in, 222
  Latvia, relations with, 78
  NATO accession (2024), 256
  NordBalt incident (2015), 122
  nuclear power in, 116
  Ukraine, relations with, 203
  wind farms, 115
Świnoujście, Poland, 146
Swistek, Göran, 124

Syria, 260, 261
Szczecin, Poland, 146, 242
Szydło, Beata, 143

T-10 parachutes, 163
Taagepera, Rein, 19
Taiwan, 183–6, 192, 193, 240
Tallinn, Estonia, 18, 19, 152, 263
Tallinn University of Technology, 32, 35
Tallis, Benjamin, 286
Tapa, Estonia, 42, 252
Tartu, Estonia, 25, 264
Taurus, 263
Taylor, Charles, 100
TBT, 109
technology sector, 280
  Estonia, 16, 31–6, 45
  Finland, 33, 34, 48, 51–2, 58, 72
Tehran conference (1943), 82
Tejn, Bornholm, 105, 107
telecoms cables, 106, 121
Teutonic Order, 135, 212
thallium, 109
Thatcher, Margaret, 23, 27
Tiigrihüpe, 33
Tiirmaa-Klaar, Heli, 39, 268, 269
Tiitus, Kaido, 252
TikTok, 95, 98
Times, The, 207
Titan Shield exercise (2023), 237–8, 245, 254
Tomahawk cruise missiles, 153
Tough Mobile, 72–3
Toveri, Pekka, 62, 253
transparent battlefield, 266
Trump, Donald, 37, 61, 231, 276
Tsilevitch, Boris, 94
TTF, 120
Tusk, Donald, 131, 132–3, 136, 137, 140–3, 146, 148, 223
TV Dozhd, 97

Ujazdowskie avenue, Warsaw, 140
Ukraine
  cyberwarfare in, 40, 267–8, 270
  Denmark, relations with, 182
  Estonia, relations with, 17, 38, 41, 42
  EU accession prospects, 29, 169, 287

Finland, relations with, 55, 60, 66, 67
France, relations with, 202–3
Germany, relations with, 123, 151–4, 157–9, 163, 166, 168–71, 174, 177–8
Latvia, relations with, 76, 77, 90, 91, 93, 97
Lithuania, relations with, 183, 192, 200
Maidan uprising (2013–14), 219
NATO accession prospects, 169
Orange Revolution (2004), 200, 218
Poland, relations with, 29, 129–30, 142, 143, 169
Russian War (2014–present), *see* Russo-Ukrainian War
Soviet Socialist Republic (1919–91), 24, 83, 109
Sweden, relations with, 203
United States, relations with, 123, 171, 202
X-Road in, 34
Ulm, Germany, 158, 244
Ulmanis, Kārlis, 81–2
unemployment, 25, 92, 96, 99, 156
unicorns, 16
United Kingdom, 5, 196–7
armed forces, 237–8, 249, 254
Brexit (2016–20), 162
Estonian battlegroup, 42, 252
Finnish War (1941–4), 56
German Naval Agreement (1935), 81
GPS jamming incident (2024), 264
Great Game (c.1830–1907), 217
Lithuania, relations with, 196–7, 200
Molotov–Ribbentrop Pact (1939), 191
NATO, role in, 42, 237–8, 249, 252, 254
nuclear threats and, 274, 275
Operation Blunderhead (c.1949), 193–4
Russian Civil War (1917–23), 80
Titan Shield exercise (2023), 237–8, 254
United Nations, 16, 76

United States, 10, 168–9, 182
China, relations with, 184, 185
Cuban Missile Crisis (1962), 208, 274
Helsinki summit (2018), 61
Long Telegram (1946), 282–4
Marshall Plan (1948), 58
NATO, role in, 249, 250, 255
nuclear power in, 49
nuclear threats and, 274, 275
presidential election (2024), 11
SolarWinds attack (2019–20), 269
Ukraine, relations with, 123, 171, 202
University of St Andrews, 262
Unknown Soldiers (Linna), 56
uranium, 22, 32, 46, 65, 67
Urbšys, Juozas, 180
US Naval War College, 262
Ušakovs, Nils, 94

Vähi, Tiit, 34
Vaino, Anton, 212
Vaino, Karl, 212
Valk, Heinz, 22
Valtonen, Elina, 47
Vardys, V. Stanley, 190
Velliste, Trivimi, 22
Venclova, Tomas, 279, 284
Viasat, 268
vibriosis, 110
vibrometers, 266–7
Victoria, Crown Princess of Sweden, 7
Viipuri, Finland, 54
Vilnius, Lithuania, 129, 139, 169, 246
conference on economic coercion (2024), 186
NATO summit (2023), 169, 246, 269, 277
Vilnius University, 190
Virkki, Pekka, 59
Vitiuk, Illia, 269
VKS, 260–3
Vladimirov, Aleksandr, 218
Voice of Europe, 221
von der Leyen, Ursula, 17
Vyborg, Russia, 54, 119

Wachs, Lydia, 272
Wagner, Ingo, 160

INDEX

Wall Street Journal, 225
Wallace, Ben, 248
Wandel durch Handel, 168
War College, Helsinki, 64
War With Russia (Shirreff), 239–40, 245
wargames, 237–9, 245
Warsaw Centre for Eastern Studies, 144
Warsaw Pact, 8, 272
Watling, Jack, 262, 266, 267
Webex, 270
West Germany (1949–90), 22, 130, 167, 197
Westerlund, Björn, 58
Westerplatte, battle of (1939), 135, 145
White civil guard, 57
White Russians, 80, 218
Wicher, 144
Wieliński, Bartosz, 142
wind farms, 111–12, 115, 161
Wissing, Volker, 152
Withington, Thomas, 265

World Economic Forum, 72
World Trade Organisation (WTO), 27, 184
World War Three (2016 documentary), 77, 96
Wyszyński, Łukasz, 145

X-Road, 34

Yantar, 122
Yeltsin, Boris, 89, 214, 229, 233
Ylilauta, 71
Yucca mountain, Nevada, 49

Zakharova, Maria, 216
Zālīte, Māra, 85
Zaluzhny, Valery, 256
Ždanoka, Tatjana, 86, 93, 95
Zeit, Die, 270
Zeitenwende (2022), 10, 68, 151, 152–4, 156, 159–79
Zelensky, Volodymyr, 224
zero-waste concept, 111–13
Zhuravlov, Volodymyr, 121